London in the 1690s
A Social Atlas

Frontispiece: The Four Shillings in the Pound Aid assessment for the parish of St Marylebone, 2 March 1694

Source: Corporation of London Records Office, Assessment Box 42/16.

London in the 1690s
A Social Atlas

Craig Spence

Centre for Metropolitan History

Institute of Historical Research
University of London

2000

To my parents
Joan and George

First published in the United Kingdom in 2000 by

Centre for Metropolitan History
Institute of Historical Research   School of Advanced Study   University of London
Senate House   Malet Street   London WC1E 7HU

ISBN 1 871348 57 9

Printed in Great Britain by Quorn Litho, Loughborough LE11 1HH

Contents

Preface and Acknowledgements

This book is the product of more than three years' research at the Centre for Metropolitan History (CMH) and it is to the members of that establishment that the primary acknowledgements must belong. My co-researcher on the 'Metropolitan London in the 1690s' project was Janet Barnes; her endurance in the face of the many tens of thousands of assessment entries requiring deciphering, transcription and analysis was truly remarkable. It is also important that her contribution in unravelling the detail of the parliamentary statute that enacted the Four Shillings in the Pound Aid should be recognised. The project, developed initially with James Alexander, was funded by the UK Economic and Social Research Council (Award No. R000232527).

With regard to the production of the atlas, Derek Keene, acting as editor, is to be thanked for the assiduous nature with which he read my various drafts. Thanks are also gratefully extended to Heather Creaton whose highly professional reading of the final draft helped resolve a number of textual problems. The atlas was produced within the CMH as camera-ready copy, without the assistance of Olwen Myhill in that process it is certain that publication would not have been possible — an invaluable member of staff if ever there was one.

Others have contributed in various ways to the production of this book. In particular Peter Earle, the project's joint supervisor, was instrumental in directing the 1690s project to this conclusion. James Alexander generously allowed his 1692 Poll Tax database to be utilised by the project, though the interpretation of it presented here is that of the author alone. Humphrey Southall offered much helpful advice of a geographical nature, and has been a persistent supporter of the work in its latter stages. Naomi Crowley supplied useful information regarding the building material of late-seventeenth century London. Bill Campbell of University College London, and Encompass Systems Ltd, gave much help and assistance with the establishment of the computer-based mapping system. My thanks are extended to them all.

Most obviously the study could not have been undertaken without the professional help of those who maintain the archives within which the source material was to be found. The assistance provided by the staff of the British Library, Guildhall Library, the London Metropolitan Archives (formerly the Greater London Record Office), the City of Westminster Archives Department, the Museum of London and, most especially, the Corporation of London Records Office is gratefully acknowledged.

In a broader context my, and Janet Barnes', thanks are extended to our colleagues at the CMH who supplied many valuable opportunities for discussion: Michael Berlin, Iain Black, Justin Champion, Jim Galloway, Robert Iliffe, David Mitchell, Margaret Murphy and Tony Trowles. The members of the Economic and Social History of Pre-Industrial England seminar at the Institute of Historical Research also earn deserved thanks for the criticism and encouragement that they readily offered when aspects of this study were first presented to them.

Finally I give my unreserved thanks to Zoë, who has, for the most part, cheerfully endured my sporadic submersion into the 1690s during the last nine years and to Georgia who has done the same for the last six — her first.

This study has used computer-based technology throughout for data capture, analysis, the production of text, maps, figures and the final camera-ready copy. It is an information technology axiom that it is the operator not the computer that makes mistakes, therefore — and despite the strong temptation to lay blame for any errors or omissions upon the computer — I have no hesitation in crediting any faults the reader may find to the human operator and not the machine.

Craig Spence
London
August 2000

READERS PLEASE NOTE:

The term 'City', with an initial capital letter, denotes the area subject to the jurisdiction of the Corporation of London.

All property values (rent and stock) are expressed as actual values multiplied up from the tax assessments (for the rates, see p. 10).

List of Figures

List of Tables

1. Introduction

The artists of this age have already made the City of London the metropolis of Europe, and if it be compared for the number of good houses, for its many and large piazzas, for its richness of inhabitants it must be allowed the largest, best built, and richest city in the world.[1]

[London] is generally believed not only to be one of the most Ancient, but most Spacious, Populous, Rich, Beautiful, Renowned and Noble Citys that we know of this day in the world: 'tis the seat of the British Empire, the Exchange of Great Britain and Ireland, the compendium of the kingdom, the Vitals of the Commonwealth, the Principal Town of Traffic that I can find accounted for by any of our Geographers.[2]

The city is the centre of its commerce and wealth. The Court of its gallantry and splendour. The out-parts of its numbers and mechanics; and in all these, no city in the world can equal it. Between the Court and the city, there is a constant communication of business to that degree that nothing in the world can come up to it.[3]

Now from all parts the swelling kennels flow,
And bear their trophies with them as they go:
Filth of all hues and odours seem to tell
What streets they sailed from, by the sight and smell.
They, as each torrent drives, with rapid force
From Smithfield or St. Peulchre's shape their course,
And in huge confluent join at Snow Hill ridge,
Fall from the Conduit prone to Holborn Bridge.
Sweepings from butcher's stalls, dung, guts, and blood,
Drowned puppies, stinking sprats, all drenched in mud,
Dead cats and turnip-tops come tumbling down the flood.[4]

Despite its still modest standing on the world stage, late seventeenth-century London struck many contemporaries as the most forceful and dynamic city of Christian Europe. According to a Tuscan visitor in 1669, it was the first city in Europe for its size, for the abundance of its traffic, and for the number of its inhabitants.[5] A decade earlier a lover of London had marvelled at the 'stupendous' qualities of the 'fresh great mercantile town of Amsterdam', which he nevertheless reckoned to be inferior to London in wealth and population.[6] In the 1690s, with more than half a million inhabitants, London had recently overtaken Paris, its only rival in size, and was more than twice as large as Amsterdam. The Dutch city, however, still reigned as the great entrepôt for news, commerce and finance, while as a royal capital Paris undoubtedly had a more splendid face than London's. But London's domination of Britain was extraordinary: as the capital, in the modern sense of that term, since the thirteenth century or earlier, and now as the imperial metropolis of two kingdoms.

One in ten English people lived in the capital, and perhaps one in six resided there at some time during their lives, while the inhabitants of London may have constituted more than 60 per cent of all town dwellers in England.[7] A large proportion of the value of the kingdom was concentrated in London. In the 1680s London, Middlesex, and Surrey contained 18 per cent of the taxable hearths in England and Wales. According to estimates made in the 1690s, the houses within the more restricted area on both sides of the river covered by the London bills of mortality numbered 8 per cent of the national stock, but were worth 46 per cent of the rental value of all houses in the realm. By contrast, the houses in all other towns were reckoned to number no more than 15 per cent of the total and were worth no more than 17 per cent.[8] Overall, in the late 1680s, London contributed more than 40 per cent of the 'ordinary revenue' of the state,[9] and so in this as in many other ways was self-evidently 'the vitals of the commonwealth'. Neither in France nor in the United Provinces were the resources of the country so overwhelmingly concentrated in a single city.

For centuries London's influence had permeated the realm. Its demands for basic supplies, its distributive trade, and the credit and the entrepreneurship of its citizens influenced agrarian production, commerce and manufactures in the regions. It was a powerful magnet to migrants, the chief gateway for trade overseas, and the seat of government, power, and assembly. All these manifestations of London's force became more distinct over the two centuries from 1500 onwards, when its share of the English population increased five-fold. London's growth rate was highest during the fifty years up to 1600, but a century later the high level of mortality was such that migration was probably the most significant contributor to metropolitan expansion. Around 1690 perhaps 10,000 migrants a year came to London, and by comparison with the kingdom as a whole a strikingly high proportion of the metropolitan population was of working age.[10] London's dynamic impact at this time was thus unusually strong, as rich and poor, landed and landless, apprentices and servants, flooded to the capital in pursuit of power, social standing, trade, employment, and stimulation of the intellectual, aesthetic, and bodily kinds.[11] Many of those migrants came from counties close to London, but there is little reason to believe that the capital's migration field was any less extensive than it had been in earlier times.[12] London was also a powerful draw for merchants, craftsmen and religious refugees from across the sea.[13]

Contemporaries knew that the root of London's power lay in its commerce, and foreigners were struck as much by the mercantile as by the courtly culture of the capital. England's commercial growth over the seventeenth century was overwhelmingly concentrated in London. At the end of the century, the share of trade handled by provincial ports was increasing slowly, but in the three years from 1699 to 1701 London handled 80 per cent of England's imports, with a mean annual value of some £4,667,000, 65 per cent of exports, with a mean annual value of some £2,477,00, and 85 per cent of re-exports, with a mean annual value of £1,677,000.[14] London's share of imports demonstrates its significance as a centre both of conspicuous consumption and for internal distributive trade. The share of re-exports, already

substantial by the mid seventeenth century, indicates the city's strategic position within the growing network of transatlantic trade, and the way in which it was able to exploit its long-established links with Continental markets. Manufactured goods, particularly those with a high 'added value' content, had become increasingly important among England's exports — an economic development towards which London's merchants and artisans made substantial innovative contributions. The city had always contained the largest English concentration of manufactures, but by the late seventeenth century products made or finished in London were beginning to capture international markets in a way that had never been the case before. Such activity stood in sharp contrast to the dependency on imports as the prime source for high-quality goods that had prevailed a century before.

The interests of aristocracy, gentry and merchants intermingled in the generation of a culture which was as concentrated upon the metropolis as other aspects of English life. Theatre, public concerts, bookshops, artists, lectures, debates and societies proliferated as never before. In these as in other ways the reputation of London was enhanced. In commerce and manufactures the city came more nearly to rival Amsterdam and other towns of the United Provinces and their hinterland. That rivalry had recently been expressed in naval warfare, for England lay athwart the Dutch seaways to the Atlantic. While Amsterdam demonstrated the most intensive and sophisticated market for commodities

and paper interests during the 1690s, London was not far behind in the development of new financial, banking, commercial and insurance services.[15] Rivalry with France was also important for London, for that too had a commercial basis. The growth of French capacity to harass English sea-borne trade and the strategic shift consequent upon the change of monarchs in 1688–9 resulted in London becoming a significant focus for naval and military stores and production, as well as generating much of the finance that William III needed for the prosecution of his wars.

Such commercial and state rivalries did much to construct the identity of London. Contemporaries rightly sought to understand London by comparing it with Amsterdam and Paris, each of which provided different models of order and magnificence. Despite the efforts of the early Stuart monarchs, London remained in many respects a wretched place, with narrow, twisting streets, and irregular buildings which were widely perceived as old-fashioned in both materials and design. Civil war and the Interregnum had brought earlier projects to a halt and whatever influence Inigo Jones's palladianism may once have had, the dominant models in later seventeenth-century London were Dutch classicism and the great works of Louis XIV's Paris.[16] London's prevailing characteristic was its low-density sprawl, a product of rapid growth. Such low, single-family, houses were often contrasted with those of Paris. Yet in the business heart of London population densities were among the highest ever recorded in an urban context, and even outside the walls where more spacious,

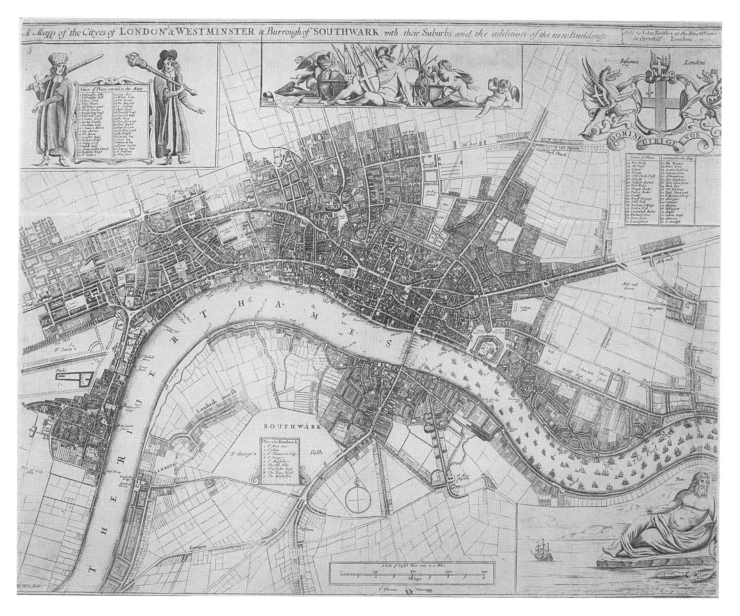

FIG. 1.1 John Oliver's *Map of the City of London, City of Westminster, River Thames, Lambeth, Southwark and Surrounding Areas, c.*1723 (engraved by Oliver pre-1701)
Source: Guildhall Library.

though not necessarily more salubrious, conditions prevailed, there were enclaves where the poor were huddled together in shanty-town conditions. Such disagreeable environments stood in sharp contrast to the fine new streets and squares of houses to be found in some outlying parts of the built-up area, especially toward the court end of town. Social conditions and their physical setting presented a complex and bewildering variety across the capital. In a real sense London was a muddle, whose physical form was matched by the complexity of its administrative arrangements. Nevertheless, this apparent confusion embodied networks of movement, social credit, ideas and information which made an essential contribution to London's success.

One great event bestowed on London a new face which matched its underlying dynamism. The Great Fire of 1666 destroyed the centre of the metropolis, representing a third of the built-up area at that time. Comprehensive plans to reorder the City were quickly dropped, for they suited neither its needs as a commercial organism nor those of the state for a restoration of the revenue flow. The rebuilt City, however, forcefully expressed ideas current among the 'mechanical philosophers' of the day concerning the nature of the universe as a machine. A host of minor adjustments to streets and gradients improved circulation. New houses were to be of uniform appearance, were to use specified materials, and were to conform to a range of standard types. As early as 1669 an Italian visitor noted the symmetry of the new houses, contrasting it with the former style of building.[17] Moreover, many new, and more or less

FIG. 1.2 View of houses in Wych Street, Westminster (Henry Dixon, 1876)
Source: Guildhall Library.

impressive, public buildings were built: the Royal Exchange, the Custom House, parish churches, and St Paul's Cathedral which by the 1690s was nearing completion. Thus London displayed itself not only as one of the largest European cities, but also as one of the most conspicuously modern.

In the mid sixteenth century London's extents were hardly bigger than they had been during its medieval peak, with perhaps 90 per cent of its inhabitants dwelling within the walls and in the suburbs immediately beyond — the ancient jurisdiction of the City of London. But the limits of London were even at that date beginning to expand. Southwark was a substantial bridgehead settlement on the south bank of the Thames, while north of the river lines of housing stretched along the approach roads of the City well beyond its boundaries. The largest extramural settlement lay to the west, and a continuous ribbon of buildings extended the two miles to Westminster. By the early seventeenth century more than half the inhabitants of the metropolis lived outside the City, and by the 1690s more than three-quarters of them did so. The term metropolis was, by the mid sixteenth century, commonly used to indicate London's status as a capital city. In the present study the word is employed to denote the whole conurbation of London, both north and south of the river and extending from Westminster to Limehouse.

The proliferation of new buildings in the outlying parts of London took place within the existing framework of roads and field boundaries, a pattern most noticeable to the west of the City. Here the influence of the court, government, parliament, law courts, and the legal quarter focusing on Chancery Lane and the Inns of Court, was most apparent in both spatial organisation and social composition. On the other sides of the City and on the south bank the new areas were more industrial and commercial in character, but by no means exclusively so. London's overseas and coastal trade focused on the Pool, just below London Bridge. The port, however, influenced the character of London well downsteam to Limehouse and beyond, encouraging the development of specialised complexes and employments on the south bank and to the east of the Tower. The associated settlements in those areas consequently exhibited a distinctively maritime character. Worried by the implications of such vigorous expansion Charles II, soon after his restoration and following the example of his predecessors, attempted to restrict the growth of London through proclamation, but the attempt was quickly abandoned.[18]

The geography of the metropolis was thus shaped by the activities and cultures of three spatially-distinct, yet interdependent, clusters of institutions represented by the court, the law and the mercantile City. Their characteristic material needs and the different labour markets which sustained them generated the particular mosaic of metropolitan neighbourhoods that formed the metropolitan whole — a mosaic that was also influenced by the lie of the land and by drainage patterns, which in newly-built areas could significantly affect the quality of housing and the health of the district. Yet while the broad social and physical characteristics of those neighbourhoods have quickly become an established element of metropolitan discourse and analysis, their complexity, their uncertain boundaries, the intermixture of rich and poor which continued to be an inherent feature of many parts of the city, and simply the processes of change have combined to make their definition and explanation an exceptionally difficult task. From the 1690s there survive a set of sources which for the first time make possible an exploration of the social, economic, and physical geography of London across the greater extents of its area. The aim of the research out of which this atlas has arisen was to assemble the information that would enable such an exploration to take place, and to present in the atlas itself an overview of that material. The atlas thus focuses on the people, houses and neighbourhoods of London at one of the turning points of its history, in a dynamic phase when it dominated the life of the nation as never before or since, and when it was poised to assume its successive roles as the European and then the world's metropolis.

APPROACHES TO THE SOCIAL GEOGRAPHY OF SEVENTEENTH-CENTURY LONDON

In the 1690s an inquiry into the social and economic character of London would not have seemed novel or inappropriate. Following John Graunt's systematic observations on the demography of the city in the early 1660s, informed debate about the size, function, and national impact of the metropolis had become common.[19] Graunt's work focused on the application of political arithmetic — a phrase coined by the economist Sir William Petty — to the size and wealth of London.[20] It grew out of a long-standing concern over the rapid growth of the metropolis, new interests in the measurement and description of the world and attempts to estimate the resources of the nation. Such ideas were also associated with the vibrant commercial culture of the city and the needs of its trade. Political arithmetic opened the door to the statistical analysis of London, but it was not until the twentieth century that further systematic explorations of its seventeenth-century population and social topography were undertaken.

Among the general studies of this theme that of N. Brett-James, *The Growth of Stuart London*, stands out as a comprehensive and methodical account of the physical expansion of London. The work also made effective use of illustrative maps.[21] Many detailed studies followed, but few of them have taken a London-wide perspective. In particular they have addressed three major themes: demography and migration, occupational structure, and the illustration of social conditions through measures of wealth or poverty.

Modern computations of the population of late seventeenth-century London begin with that of P.E. Jones and A.V. Judges.[22] Drawing upon the returns of the 1695 Marriage Duty for the City, they compared Gregory King's contemporary estimate with their own figures.[23] Later the marriage duty returns were re-assessed by D.V. Glass.[24] Shortly afterwards E.A.

Wrigley's important 'simple model' paper took a wider view of the capital's demographic regime, stressing its impact on the country as a whole.[25] This work developed ideas propounded by F. Fisher and others concerning the widespread economic effects of metropolitan growth.[26] A specific account of London's contribution to the population history of the nation was incorporated within Wrigley and Schofield's *Population History of England*.[27] Subsequent studies of London's demography have attempted to measure change over longer time-spans. Finlay and Shearer, for example, presented data for the overall growth of the metropolis between 1550 and 1700, but the uncertain geographical parameters of their work and the small sample of burial registers upon which it was based render their conclusions questionable.[28] In the present work population estimates extrapolated from the Bills of Mortality are considered in conjunction with the distribution of taxpaying households across the metropolis as a whole.[29] Hand-in-hand with the study of early modern demography is the analysis of migration patterns. In the case of London valuable studies of the geographic origins of Londoners and the relationship between migration, assimilation, and neighbourhood settlement patterns have been undertaken.[30]

A variety of approaches have been employed in the study of the working lives of Londoners during the later seventeenth century, ranging from simple occupational categorisations to considerations of particular social groups. Glass, as an element of his analysis of the 1695 Marriage Duty, listed the stated occupations of taxpayers according to their relative

wealth.[31] T.R. Forbes provided a somewhat more structured review of recorded occupations in the parish of St Giles without Cripplegate during the late seventeenth and early eighteenth centuries.[32] A.L. Beier conducted a similar analysis of information from fifteen sample parishes and demonstrated the significant role played by manufacturing activity within the early modern metropolis.[33] J. Alexander continued to exploit the vein of economic classification employing data on stated occupations from the poll tax returns of the 1690s, material which has been incorporated within this present study. These data, though very valuable, survive only for the City of London, and hence reflect the wealthiest sector of London's working population. Moreover, the returns do not include occupational information for all City parishes.[34] In a significant series of publications P. Earle provides an overview of occupational activity in Augustan London, a more detailed study of the economic pursuits of the middling ranks and one of the few systematic studies of the pattern of female employment.[35] Detailed studies of work in particular neighbourhoods include those covering Southwark, the eastern riverside parishes, and eighteenth-century Westminster.[36] These and other studies note the limitations of the occupations stated in tax or other returns as an indicator of the variety of activities by which individuals earned their livelihood. Unfortunately, no other source of information can provide a satisfactory overview.

A number of scholars have used measures of wealth to delineate the metropolitan environment. Glass established measures of household and family size and structure from the 1695 Marriage Duty assessments. Using fiscal information presented within the assessments Glass was able to map the relative wealth of City parishes according to their numbers of 'substantial households'.[37] A similar 'ecological approach' was employed by Jones using the 1638 house valuations for City parishes.[38] Other more localised studies have produced valuable results. Stone used a qualitative approach to outline the development of the West End, emphasising London's unique structure as a European metropolis.[39] Boulton's study of Southwark used a wide range of environmental, social, and economic indicators, but did not attempt comprehensively to map the information.[40] Parliamentary surveys, hearth tax returns and the Bills of Mortality enabled Power to define some of the principal differences in built environment and social character between the eastern and western districts of London, based upon a sample of fourteen parishes.[41]

Power's subsequent work included a more significant cartographic element. His study of mid seventeenth-century Shadwell mapped housing information on to a street plan derived from Ogilby and Morgan's map of 1682.[42] In a further study, which focused on the City of London on the eve of the Great Fire, he was able to plot variations between parishes in dwelling size (indicated by the mean number of hearths per house) and in the occupations of householders. Despite their undoubted value, however, the hearth tax returns provide only a crude indication of the economic status of householders. As Power puts it,

'an even more crucial determinant of (occupational) location, and one which the hearth tax gives no guide to, is rent'.[43] Alexander addressed this problem in his use of the poll tax returns from the 1690s, and by linking them to the assessments of rent and stock in the records of the aids collected in 1693–4. That exercise allowed the patterns of residence for occupational groups in the City of London to be mapped by reference to their wealth. But the value of his conclusions on the distribution of rental values is limited since they rest only on the 63 per cent of poll tax payers who could be identified in the aid assessments.[44] More recently an innovative attempt has been made to associate living conditions in London with the course of the plague epidemic of 1665. J.A.I. Champion builds on Slack's earlier work through an analysis and mapping of the deaths recorded in the Bills of Mortality in relation to the evidence of the contemporary hearth tax, supported by a more detailed investigation of the environmental character of ten sample parishes.[45]

Many of these studies have tended to have limitations in geographic scope, often focusing upon the City, frequently in consequence of the sheer wealth of source material available. Regardless of the significance of such individual studies they do not provide a truly comprehensive overview of the metropolis. Jones's 'ecological' approach, however, was more comprehensive, and also adopted a somewhat more theoretical approach. Rejecting simple pre-industrial models, he identified the features which had been characteristic of London and other cities since the middle ages: a close

spatial proximity of rich and poor but at the same time clear distinctions in the social composition of different geographical areas. By defining foci of communication he argued that core and peripheral neighbourhoods could be identified. Despite the undoubted strength of this thesis, the text took the matter little further while the supporting map decidedly lacked detail.[46]

This atlas adopts an explicitly metropolitan approach in attempting a systematic overview of the social and economic geography of London in the 1690s (so far as the sources allow). The research project upon which it is based was conceived to overcome some of the limitations in scope that occur with neighbourhood studies, and also to provide a solid foundation for future enquiry. The maps and commentaries in the atlas provide an introduction to the more detailed results of that research and so provide a background against which it will be possible critically to assess several models of the social and economic structure of London. It is also hoped that the following pages will suggest areas of future research and study which might usefully contribute to our growing understanding of early modern metropolitan society.

THE EVIDENCE

An overview

An Act of Parliament made in the fifth year of their majesties reign entitled an act for granting an aid of 4s. in the pound for one year for carrying on a vigorous war against France.[47]

In May 1689 England declared war on France, a country giving active and generous support to James II in his campaign to regain the English throne. The initial threat to England was from the west and for two years Ireland was the focus of English military operations. Following the Treaty of Limerick in 1691 England became committed to fight alongside the Dutch, Austrians, and Spanish against France in Germany and the Spanish Netherlands. That war — variously known as the Nine Years War, the War of the Grand Alliance, the War of the League of Augsburg or, more simply, King William's War — developed into a long campaign of attrition in which the outcome of battles was decided more by wealth, numbers and resources than by military skill. Continental warfare was highly expensive and required a continuous flow of money to sustain it.[48] It was underwritten by heavy and repeated taxation at home. This took the form primarily of aids and polls (poll taxes). Aids were used to collect either a fixed sum of money from the nation as a whole or an unspecified sum levied at a standard rate on property and income. Polls were levied on individuals according to their status. In the first regnal year of William & Mary alone Parliament enacted four aids and two polls, behaviour which was repeated to the extent that, by 1691, such methods of revenue generation became virtually annual impositions.[49] The Marriage Duty Act of 1694, incorporating levies which resembled those of the polls, represented a yet further experiment in raising revenue.[50]

In the City of London the tradition of systematically assessing householders for tax contributions,

sometimes on the basis of the rental value of their property, extended back at least 600 years. Many of the returns which survive are partial or concerned only a minority of householders, although the valuation for tithe undertaken in 1638 was comprehensive in its coverage of the City.[51] The hearth tax returns of the 1660s are equally comprehensive, and in addition cover those parts of London which lay outside the City, but they have a limited value as a measure of wealth. The state's fiscal onslaught in the 1690s, however, generated for the first time a comprehensive record of wealth across the metropolis as a whole. The measurement of wealth was a matter of pressing concern, and during the 1690s its taxation contributed about 47 per cent of all tax revenue, by comparison with 9 per cent in 1685.[52] The taxpaying population was interrogated with a new and more exacting vigour. The surviving records of the polls and of the marriage duty assessments provide information which is in some ways comparable to later census material, particularly with regard to household composition. The returns for the aids, the ancestors of the land tax, provide valuations of rent and personal means which seem to be consistent and are certainly comprehensive.[53]

This atlas is based primarily on the detailed assessments for the aids of 1693 and 1694 covering Middlesex and the cities of London and Westminster, which survive in the Corporation of London Records Office. Their survival presumably reflects the responsibility of the City Chamberlain for collecting the tax in those areas. No returns

survive for south of the Thames, and those for a few assessment districts to the north of the river have also been lost. There is, and was, no satisfactory definition of metropolitan London; indeed it has been said that 'Stuart Londoners lacked a firm, clear and generally acceptable term to describe the built-up area of London'.[54] For the purposes of this study, the area covered by the Bills of Mortality by the 1690s has been deemed to represent a common perception of the metropolis which also supplies clear geographical boundaries.[55] The districts north of the river selected for analysis on that basis included the continuous built-up area of London and Westminster, adjacent villages to the north such as Islington and Hackney, and the more scattered settlement along the river to the east of the city. The river Lea marked the eastern limit of the area (Fig. 1.3). The bulk of the assessments used were for the second quarter of 1694, and when no suitable 1694 assessment survived, one from 1693 was used.[56] Where assessments for both years have survived, comparison indicates that differences in total value and in the number of householders were relatively small.

The other major textual sources used for systematic analysis are the returns for the poll taxes, which survive only for the City of London. For most wards and precincts it has been possible to use returns from 1692, but in some cases it has been necessary to use returns from 1694 and 1698.[57] Many (63 per cent) of the householders named in the poll tax returns can be identified in the aid assessments of 1693 and 1694.

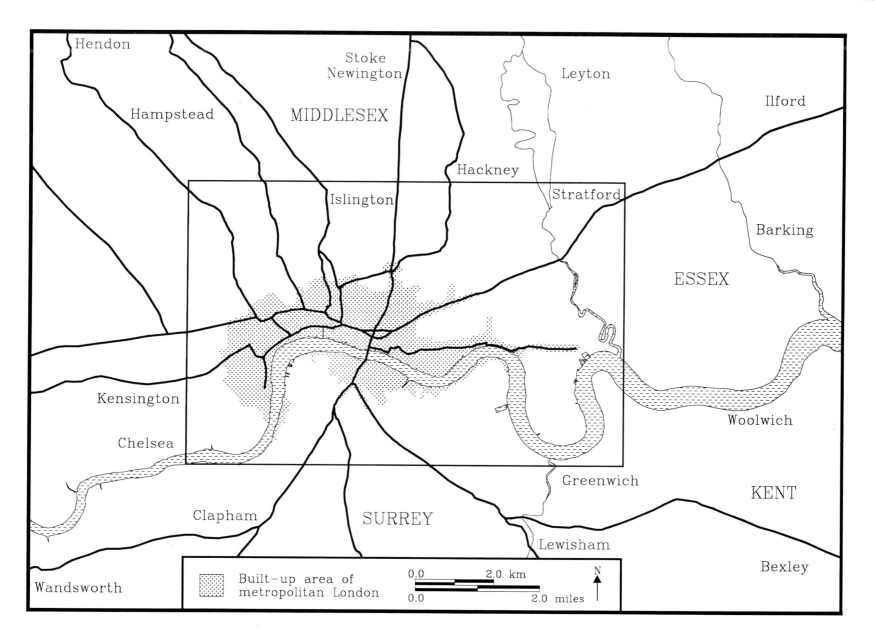

Hendon

Stoke
Newington

Leyton

Ilford

Hampstead

MIDDLESEX

Hackney

Stratford

Barking

Islington

ESSEX

Kensington

Chelsea

Woolwich

Clapham

SURREY

Greenwich

KENT

Lewisham

Bexley

Wandsworth

Built-up area of
metropolitan London

0.0   2.0 km

0.0   2.0 miles

N

FIG. 1.3 Outline of the study area

The third major body of information for the atlas has been drawn from contemporary maps and topographical descriptions.[58] Three major sets of maps were used: Morgan's map of the City and Westminster dated 1682; the parish maps in Strype's edition of Stow's *Survey of the Cities of London and Westminster* published in 1720 (surveyed probably between 1708 and 1720); and Rocque's map of London in 1747. These sources were employed to plot, so far as possible, the street pattern and the extent of the built-up area in the 1690s, and also to define the boundaries of the tax assessment districts. This information was then employed in the spatial analysis of the tax data.

The four shillings in the pound aids of 1693 and 1694

The Acts of 1692 and 1693, under which the quarterly records of 1693 and 1694 were made, were the first to set a rate of assessment at four shillings in the pound.[59] The former was sometimes retrospectively referred to as 'the first Land Tax'. The two acts were virtually identical and were concerned to tax both personal estate and real property. In the category of personal estate, two sources of actual or potential income were taxed. Firstly, the sum of four shillings in the pound was to be levied upon the yearly profits accruing to any such estate held in the form of ready moneys, debts owing, goods, wares, merchandises, other chattels or personalty belonging to or held in trust 'within this realm or without'. Excepted from this were any outstanding *bona fide* debts either owed by or owing to the taxpayer and

judged 'desperate', any stock upon lands, or household goods. Those profits were calculated as 6 per cent (the then statutory maximum rate of interest) of the capital value of the assets, for it was stated that twenty-four shillings were to be levied on every £100 worth of assessed personalty (Paragraph I). This element of the levy was sometimes described as the 'stock tax'. Secondly, those in public service were to pay four shillings on every twenty shillings earned as an official salary. Officers in muster, or paid by the army or navy, were exempted from the tax, but only in respect of salaries earned exclusively from military activities. Governors of garrisons, forts and castles, and their deputies, on the other hand, paid the tax on those portions of their income derived from such posts.[60] Workers in the royal ordnance whose salaries did not exceed £100 a year were completely exempted (II). The taxation of real property was concerned with rental value, and was levied at a rate of four shillings in the pound on 'all and every person and persons bodies politick and corporate guilds mysteries fraternities and brotherhoods whether corporate or not' according to the assessed rack-rent value of all 'lands tenements and hereditaments with as much equality and indifference as is possible' (III). Poor persons whose real property was worth less than twenty shillings a year were exempt. Rectors or vicars in residence were also exempt, unless their property had an assessed value of more than £30 a year or they had 'more than one rectory or vicarage' (LXXVIII).

Residence was an important factor as the tax was assessed and collected locally. Householders were

taxed where they lived, while those known to be abroad were deemed resident at their last known English address (XXX). Subject to a fine of £20, householders were also required to supply the assessors with a true record of all lodgers in their homes, while anyone trying to defraud the Exchequer by moving house was to be charged double tax (XXXII, XXXIII). Rent and stock tax elements were charged at the taxpayer's home, but official salaries were taxed at the place where the duties were performed (XXX). This meant that some taxpayers were assessed in more than one location. Richard Hampden, for example, was assessed to pay £20 rent tax (on an annual rack-rent value of £100) and stock tax of £6 (on £500 worth of personal estate) at Gardners Lane in the parish of St Margaret Westminster, while as Chancellor of the Exchequer his salary of £400 made him liable to pay £80 tax at the government's offices at Whitehall.[61]

In general, tenants paid the assessed tax directly and then deducted the appropriate amounts from their rent payments, but if tenants were foreign ambassadors or ministers their landlords were expected to pay the tax (XIII). Nevertheless, such occupiers frequently found their way into the assessment books. The envoy of the Emperor, for example, was entered in the assessment for St James Westminster as occupying property in Parke Place with a rent tax value of £10. Where rents were paid to charitable bodies, tenants were taxed on the amount by which the true market value of the property they occupied exceeded the rent actually paid (XIX, XX).[62] That situation was noted within the assessments by such comments as 'besides hospital rent'. Sir Basil Firebrass, one of the aid commissioners appointed for the City of London, paid £8 such tax on vaults he rented in the Mincing Lane precinct of Tower Ward.[63]

All Roman Catholics, and indeed any others who refused to swear the oaths of allegiance and supremacy drawn-up at the beginning of William and Mary's reign were required to pay tax at double the standard rate (XLIV). The assessments indicate that there were 232 known, or reputed, Roman Catholics heading households in London and Westminster during 1693–4. The assessors noted them as 'Roman Catholic', 'papist' or 'reputed papist'. Others, who refused to swear the oath of allegiance on the grounds that James II still lived, were recorded as 'Non-jurors'. The assessments note sixty-four such individuals. To circumvent a double tax charge it was permissible to swear the oaths within ten days of the first local commissioners' meeting; only Quakers who had made a declaration of fidelity were able to gain legal exemption from that requirement (XLV).[64] The assessments do not state whether any of the taxpayers had taken either course of action.

The management of the 1690s aids was undertaken by two categories of government official, thus separating the administration of the revenue from its practical collection. The commissioners and assessors were not paid, while the collectors, receivers, and commissioners' clerks were permitted fees calculated as poundage on the sums collected. All those concerned with the administration or collection of the tax were expected to perform their duties diligently and were subject to penalties for negligence (X).

The tax was administered locally by commissioners, men of standing, chosen apparently for their business acumen or, sometimes, legal or political expertise. The Act of 1693 re-appointed the commissioners named in 1692 (V). The men appointed for the City of London included the Lord Mayor, Aldermen and Sheriffs, while among the many appointed for the City and Liberties of Westminster were members of the Privy Council such as Richard Hampden (Chancellor of the Exchequer), Sir Edward Seymour, and Sir John Lowther. It was possible to serve on more than one panel of commissioners. Hampden, for example, was appointed for the counties of Middlesex and Buckinghamshire as well as for Westminster. Other commissioners for Middlesex included: Sir John Trevor, Speaker of the House of Commons (also a commissioner for Berkshire); Edward and James Russell, sons of the Duke of Bedford; Sir John Holt, Lord Chief Justice in the court of King's Bench; and Sir Robert Atkins, Speaker of the House of Lords and Chief Baron of the Exchequer.[65] Those who had not paid as much as twenty shillings a quarter under the poll tax of 1692 were not permitted to serve as commissioners,[66] and if any person were to officiate as a commissioner before being sworn in, they would be liable to a fine of £500 (LV, LXI). The commissioners implemented the requirements of the Act at the local level, which included swearing in any new commissioners and assessors, adjudicating appeals, authorising certificates and warrants, and examining and punishing negligent tax officers, and any taxpayers who attempted avoidance.

Commissioners selected the numbers of assessors they thought appropriate for each taxation district: across the metropolitan area more than 500 individuals were chosen to implement the aid.[67] Assessors included local officials such as vestry men, constables, and bailiffs, who were familiar with and well-known within their localities (VIII). Two of the assessors for the precinct of St Bartholomew by the Exchange in Broad Street Ward, for example, were Samuel Clarke, an auditor of the parish accounts for 1693–4, and Colonel Humphrey Willett, churchwarden in 1695.[68] Once sworn in, assessors received warrants to use all lawful means to construct a valid assessment return. Assessors nominated two trustworthy people to act as collectors of the tax within each district. In the First Precinct of Bishopsgate Ward Without the four assessors nominated as collectors Thomas Kendall, a barber-surgeon, and Thomas Richards, a hat-haberdasher.[69]

The Acts instructed collectors to gather the money according to the certified assessments and pay it to the head-collectors in four quarterly instalments beginning on 15 March and, then, on 2 June, 4 September and 3 December (or within twenty days of those dates allowing time for appeals). Head-collectors were to pass the first amount of accumulated funds to the appropriate receiver-general on 20 March with following payments to be made on 9 June, 12 September, and finally on 17 December.[70] The receivers-general, in turn, were to submit the collected money to the Exchequer on or before 26 March, 20 June, 29 September and 25 December, respectively. This was a remarkably tight schedule given that the 1693 Act had only received the Royal Assent on 25 January 1694 (modern style), with the first commissioners' meeting set for 20 February. The cash book for London's contribution to the 1694 Aid shows that, in practice, money was paid into the Exchequer via the City Chamberlain's office continuously throughout the year from 30 March 1694 until 4 May 1695.[71]

The commissioners' clerks were required to prepare fair copies of the returns, several of which were then signed and sealed for delivery to collectors, head-collectors, and the receivers-general. The paper assessments signed and sealed at the local level, and then presumably deposited in the City Chamberlain's office, were those used to prepare the aid database used in this atlas. One set of the returns was to be signed and sealed by the commissioners and sent to the Exchequer by 20 March (or within thirty days allowing time for appeals). There the King's Remembrancer made a legible fair copy in a book of parchment which was to be forwarded within three months to the Auditor of the Receipt of the Exchequer.

Maladministration was not tolerated. Commissioners were empowered to impose fines on assessors, collectors, or indeed their fellow commissioners, for any refusal to perform their duties or any other manner of negligence (VIII, XV). Negligent receivers were both fined and disqualified from further royal service. Those responsible for the actual collection of money, if suspected of misappropriating revenue, were to be imprisoned until the shortfall had been realised from the sale of their property (XVI). No instances of such actions are recorded for 1693 and 1694, but William Jarman, a collector for the 1694 Aid in Dolphin precinct of Tower Ward, fell foul of the City's tax authorities some seven years later. At a commissioners' meeting convened at the Guildhall on 3 April 1701 goods to the value of £413, belonging to Jarman, were sold in order to offset the sum which he was accused of having collected but not passed on to the receiver-general.[72]

Aggrieved taxpayers could appeal to the commissioners against their assessment. Most appeals on record concern the tax on stocks, which clearly proved difficult to value accurately. Charles Davenant argued that one of the shortcomings of the tax was the way in which it ignored 'how little scruple men make of swearing not to have £100 who are generally thought to be worth £20,000'.[73] In London, sums abated ranged from 1s. 6d. upwards and were usually granted upon the taxpayer's personal oath. An exception was the abatement, by the relatively large sum of £7 12s., for Mr Honour, of Dolphin Court in the parish of St Bride, on account of a 'mistake in the clerks transcribing the book'.[74]

Those who defaulted on their tax payments were to have their goods distrained for four days. If they still refused to pay, the collectors could, with the 'appraisal' of two or three other inhabitants, sell off the goods to raise the amount owed, any surplus being returned to the former owner. To this end it was quite lawful for the collectors, in the hours of daylight and with the appropriate warrants, to break open whatever was required to gain access to such goods. While some householders made legitimate appeals against their level of assessment, others refused to pay or claimed exemption. Their status as employees of the Navy presumably explains the following refusals entered in the book of estreats for the 1694 Aid, under the heading of the Navy Office:

Samuel Hill refuses to pay	2:00:0
Edward Whiston the same	1:10:0
John Waterhouse the same	2:10:0
William James the same	2:00:0
Thomas Hunter the same	2:00:0
Dr Littleton the same	0:13:6
Edward Whitacre	5:00:0
	£15:13:6

Dr Fisher Littleton was the advocate to the Navy and Edward Whittaker its solicitor.[75] Others escaped payment in a more final fashion: John Wilkinson, a goldsmith of Long Ditch in the parish of St Margaret Westminster, was unable to pay a sum of nine shillings on his personal estate because he had 'since [been] hanged for clipping'.[76] If assessed tax was not paid within fifteen days, the commissioners were instructed to sign and issue warrants for the collector or constable enabling them to seize and sell as much as was necessary to pay it, restoring any surplus to the owner (XXVII). In the case of defaulting minors, guardians became liable for the payment, with the usual penalties for refusal.

The assessments themselves vary slightly from district to district, either in the style of presentation adopted by the assessor or in the quality of information recorded. They provide lists of named householders, and some landlords, together with the annual rack-rent (maximum rental) value of their real property and the assessed value of the annual income deemed to have been derived from personal property or stock. They also show, where applicable: the names and worth of lodgers or other family members who held personal property in their own right; buildings which were empty or not used as dwellings; and the special characteristics of some taxpayers, such as Roman Catholics. The following extract from the assessment for the City ward of Lime Street shows how the information was structured:

	Rent £ s. d.	Stock £ s. d.
William Packer	9:00:0	1:04:0
James Read and partner	9:00:0	1:16:0
Charles Chamberlain Esq. Comm[issioner]	18:00:0	7:04:0
Bartholomew Piggott : Beadle	5:12:0	
Robert Woodney : Lodger		0:06:0
Widow Lawrence	4:08:0	

There was no requirement for the assessor to note the composition of the household. Assessors commented rarely on the size or other characteristics of buildings. Where shops, stables, warehouses or other structures are mentioned they were likely to have been separate from the owner's place of residence. This was certainly the case for Thomas Firmin of the precinct of St Edmund Lombard Street, who was assessed for £20 rent tax and £3 12s. stock tax, presumably at his residence, and was charged an additional £3 rent tax for a warehouse five entries further on in the list.[77] Thus, many warehouses and other specialised structures which were within the curtilage of the dwelling were not enumerated. The Acts stated that where householders living in one parish or ward had stock in another parish or ward of the same city they were to pay the tax on both at the place where they lived (XXI). It has therefore been assumed that when individuals were cited as responsible for more than one property or dwelling, their main residence was that at which they were assessed for stock tax. Empty properties were also routinely noted. Owners were to pay tax as if they were resident householders. When the owner of an empty house could not be found and the tax remained uncollected, the commissioners certified returns to that effect (XXV). Assessors occasionally commented on the reasons for vacancy, noting, for example, five houses 'down' in Portugal Street, St James Westminster, and two 'abuilding' in White Horse Yard off Drury Lane. Assessors noted few occupational descriptions, and when they did so tended to note official rather than economic functions. In Westminster, for example, twenty-one Members of Parliament were so described, all of them lodgers. Officers and servants in establishments such as the Excise Office or the Court of Chancery, who were taxed on their salaries, were recorded with some accuracy.

Most of the assessment lists do not define the address or location of taxpayers with any precision. The lists for the wards of the City of London, for example, are usually subdivided according to the ward precincts (administrative divisions corresponding to parishes or parts thereof) but provide no other information, although the order of the lists presumably reflects the route by which assessors perambulated the precinct. On the periphery of the City, however, and in some of the parishes in the western part of the metropolitan area, street names were also included. In several of those districts it is possible, from the names of streets, lanes, alleys, and courtyards, to reconstruct the assessor's route in detail and so to pin down the location of households with some degree of accuracy. In the western ward of the parish of St Paul Covent Garden, for example (Fig. 1.4), the assessors began with the south side of Henrietta Street, walked along its north side, and turned into Bedford Street where they dealt first with its northern end. Assessing the west side of Bedford Street, they turned into Bedford Court and then came out again to complete the southern half of the street. They then covered the north and south sides of Maiden Lane in succession, and then the south and north sides of that part of Shandois (Chandos) Street which lay within the parish. They then shifted north to deal with Rose Street, out of which they turned along the north side of King Street, followed by the south. Finally they

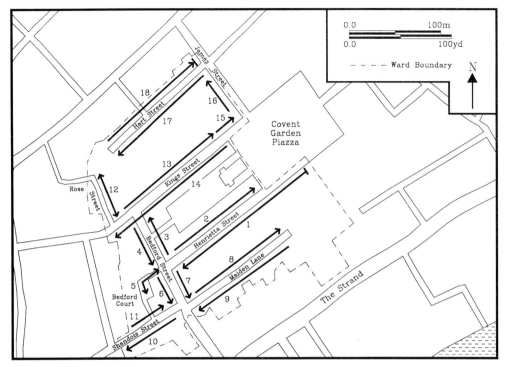

FIG. 1.4 Covent Garden assessor's walk
Source: 1693–4 Aid database.

assessed the householders in the north-west corner of the Piazza, turned north to deal with the west side of James Street, and then into Hart Street, dealing first with the south side and then with the north.[78]

The aid assessments testify to the strength of the government's attempt to value the wealth of the nation. The surviving records, however, present a few problems for assessing the wealth of London. Some people escaped payment, and for some areas the returns are missing. Moreover, the surviving returns cover different seasons and the value of stock present in London would have fluctuated throughout the year. Nevertheless, the local assessments and the Chamberlain's cash book[79] provide figures from which it is possible to calculate both the total tax charge and the sum eventually received. The City of London, Westminster, and the built-up part of Middlesex, comprising the area defined in this atlas as 'metropolitan London north of the Thames', was assessed for total tax of £260,666 6s. 8d., representing a real annual value of £4,155,919 in rent, imputed income from stocks, and official salaries. Of that annual value at least £995,230 (24

per cent) was represented by rents and at least £3,034,669 (73 per cent) was represented by the income from stocks.[80] Rural Middlesex, outside the metropolis, had a value of £604,834 12s. in rents, imputed income from stocks, and salaries, the last associated with the royal palace at Hampton Court. The total assessment for London, Westminster, and the county of Middlesex was £300,734 4s. 4d., representing a real annual value of £4,760,753, of which the metropolitan area represents 87 per cent.

The Chamberlain's cash book also records the revenue actually collected, which at £296,160 8s. 11d. was only marginally less than the sum due, indicating a collection rate of 98.5 per cent. Before paying the funds into the Exchequer, however, poundage paid to officials to the value of £3,737 12s. (1.3 per cent of the cash received) was deducted. In addition to the directly collected tax, Londoners also raised an advance loan of £409,590 for the period 1693–4 on the promise of repayment from future aids with interest at a rate of 7 per cent.

The poll tax

The poll taxes were assessed and collected with equal administrative vigour. In some respects they present less complex problems of interpretation than the aids. The three poll taxes for which the returns have been used (1692, 1694, and 1698) followed almost identical principles in identifying the individuals and items to be taxed and in setting the rates.[81] All adults and children (under 16 years of age) were to be taxed at a basic rate of one shilling, though there was also a variety of surtaxes charged on those described as tradesmen or shopkeepers and merchants or gentlemen, among others. There were, however, exemptions for those in certain groups of the poor, such as those in receipt of alms or poor-relief, or the children of day-labourers. The lists reflect household and family groups, although it is not always straightforward to identify them.[82] They name householders, for whom an occupation is often given, wives, children, servants, apprentices, and lodgers, and indicate marital status. There was also an additional tax levied on those who owned or operated coaches. The returns for the City are arranged by ward and precinct, of which there were over 200.

THE DATA AND METHODS OF ANALYSIS

The collection and organisation of the principal documentary source material for this atlas was undertaken with the central objective of computer-based analysis. Assessments were entered into a computer database system that allowed a wide variety of interrogations, comparisons, and analyses to be performed. Cartographic information was also incorporated within the system, thus allowing social and economic attributes to be mapped.[83]

The 1690s database

The structure of the 1693–4 Aid database was designed to resemble the organisation of the seventy-one original manuscript assessments as closely as possible. Those documents, corresponding to local units of assessment, were relatively consistent in form, but ranged in size from a single sheet containing some twenty names to a ninety-eight page book containing more than 3,000. Locational information — the names of streets, precincts, wards, or parishes — was broken down into a four-part code, which in most cases allowed the identification of individual households. Names of householders, the assessed taxation values, references to landlords, and differing property types were all entered, as were the rarely occurring occupational descriptions.[84] Following an initial examination of the information collected some supplementary data-fields were added, covering, for example, the number of households that each record referred to or the gender of named taxpayers. For the purposes of analysis a subsidiary database was constructed comprising an expanded form of all assessment entries that referred to specific types of property, including brewhouses, coach-houses, markets, schools, shops, stables, warehouses, and wharves. This subsidiary database also covered all properties said to be waste or vacant land, empty houses, or houses in the course of construction or demolition. In total 61,588 assessment entries were collected and entered into the primary database. The assessments provide 53,250 entries for named payers of rent tax and 20,643 entries for named stock tax payers. Of the latter, 3,789 appeared from the context of the return to have been lodgers. For certain types of analysis, concerning the rental value of dwellings, it was possible to exclude some properties such as company halls, the Royal Exchange, and non-residential structures such as warehouses. As has been explained above, some individuals were taxed in more than one place within the metropolis. Given the difficulties of identifying individuals from names alone, it has been impossible to allow for such multiple occurrences, which are likely to have been few within the overall context of the returns.

Useful additional information concerning household structure and occupational attributions in the City of London was obtained from the returns for the 1692 and other poll taxes.[85] These returns form a smaller dataset than that compiled from the aids of 1693–4. The 1693–4 Aid assessments for the City of London list 21,997 households, while in the poll tax records for the same area only 17,565 households have been identified. The identification of households is sometimes problematic, but it seems that the poll tax records only about four-fifths of the total of households listed in the aid assessments. The correlation between the two sets of data is marginally better in the case of those who were assessed for stock tax, with the poll tax including about 85 per cent of those noted in the 1693–4 assessments. The comprehensive nature of the aid returns was further verified by means of a comparison with the 1695 Marriage Duty and other records.[86]

Analysing the data

Four themes were central to the analytical process: formulation of patterns of distribution, economic quantification, measures which illuminate social structure, and, where appropriate, measures derived from cartographic sources. Distribution patterns were established for a range of property types — coach-houses, stables, empty property, warehouses and the like — and also for proportions of householders within certain occupational sectors. Other measures were established, such as household density in relation to the built-up area as identified from contemporary maps. A wide range of economic measures was calculated directly from the aid database, including metropolis-wide rental values (in terms of averages and ranges), value of stock, distribution of stockholders, and more complex measures, such as land values and patterns of wealth. Social structure was analysed at a simple level by establishing patterns of coach ownership or the gender of householders, but also by linking household structure, occupation, and wealth, and by reviewing patterns of multiple-occupancy and property ownership in selected districts. Cartographic sources were used to plot the distribution of infrastructure and patterns of land use.

Throughout the atlas spatial analysis has been a primary concern. Thus a standard range of values was calculated for each City ward or other unit outside the City. (A summary version of those findings is presented in Appendix III.) Rent and stock values were analysed by calculating both metropolitan and district means, and further analysed and mapped by grouping them in the larger aggregated areas discussed below. In order to establish a particular framework for the analysis of rental values, taxpayers were ranked so as to calculate inter-decile groups (Table 1.1).

TABLE 1.1

Inter-decile groups employed in the analysis of rent distribution within the 1693–4 Aid database

Group	Inter-decile range	Mean	Number	%
A	£1 – £3 15s.	£2 10s.	6,211	11.1
B	£4 – £5	£4 10s.	6,733	12.1
C	£5 5s. – £6 15s.	£6	4,204	7.5
D	£7 – £8	£7 12s.	5,822	10.4
E	£8 8s. – £10 17s.	£9 14s.	5,252	9.4
F	£11 – £14	£12 12s.	5,875	10.5
G	£14 7s. – £19 12s.	£16 11s.	4,974	8.9
H	£20 – £25 10s.	£21 15s.	5,508	9.9
I	£26 – £39 4s.	£30 13s.	5,397	9.8
J	£40 – £350	£63 11s.	5,792	10.4
Total	£1 to £350[1]	£17 10s.	55,768	100.0

Note: [1] The highest individual tax assessment was £1,458. This, however, represented a rent generated by part of the Royal Exchange. The value shown above of £350 was considered the highest that could be positively associated with the more representative pattern of individual metropolitan rents. Thus some assessments higher than £350, but derived from poorly defined collections of buildings and/or tracts of open land, have been excluded from the calculation of inter-decile groups.

Mapping the data

As to the buttings and boundings ... [87]

Computer-based mapping was selected as the most appropriate method of cartographic analysis for such a mass of information. As the data were collected by parishes, wards and other units, it was proposed that the first stage in the geographic analysis would be the preparation of a set of maps showing the boundaries of those various taxation districts.

The contemporary surveys showing boundaries and other information vary considerably in quality and detail, and none meet modern trigonometric standards. Boundary features, therefore, were plotted onto outline maps derived from the Ordnance Survey maps of the 1860s, the first survey of the metropolis to meet modern standards. Those Ordnance Survey maps pre-date the extensive rebuilding of the late nineteenth century and incorporate many ancient boundaries. They are well-suited for use in plotting the administrative boundaries and the street pattern of late seventeenth-century London (see Fig. 1.5).[88]

Any spatial analysis of seventeenth-century London that employs parishes and wards as units of analysis has to resolve the problem of the great variation in population totals. An ancient parish or precinct in the City of London might contain no more than twenty households, while a parish in Middlesex could hold 3,000. Though such anomalies can be resolved by statistical methods it was decided that for the purpose of understanding the social topography of the metropolis from a functional point of view 'natural' area units should be formulated. By using the detailed locational information found in many of the tax assessments it was possible to construct a new set of boundaries. The resulting 'natural' areas reflect both topographic and economic elements of the metropolitan structure.[89] Where possible, given the limits of the information available, they respect barriers to movement such as rivers and the City walls, and centre upon market, transport or cultural

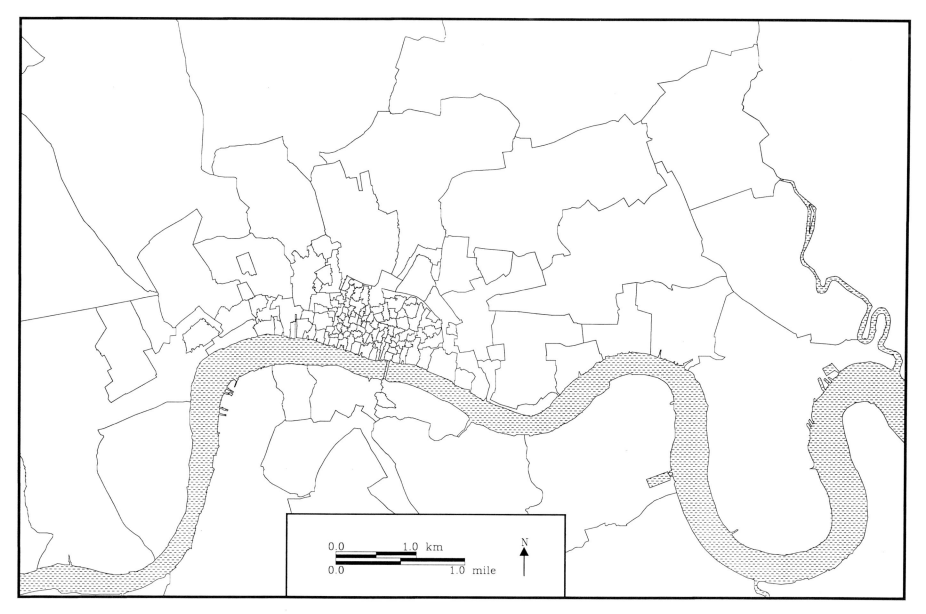

FIG. 1.5 The parish boundaries of London, *c*.1700

Source: Boundary data gathered from sources given in Appendix II. Principal survey base taken from Ordnance Survey maps of the 1860s.

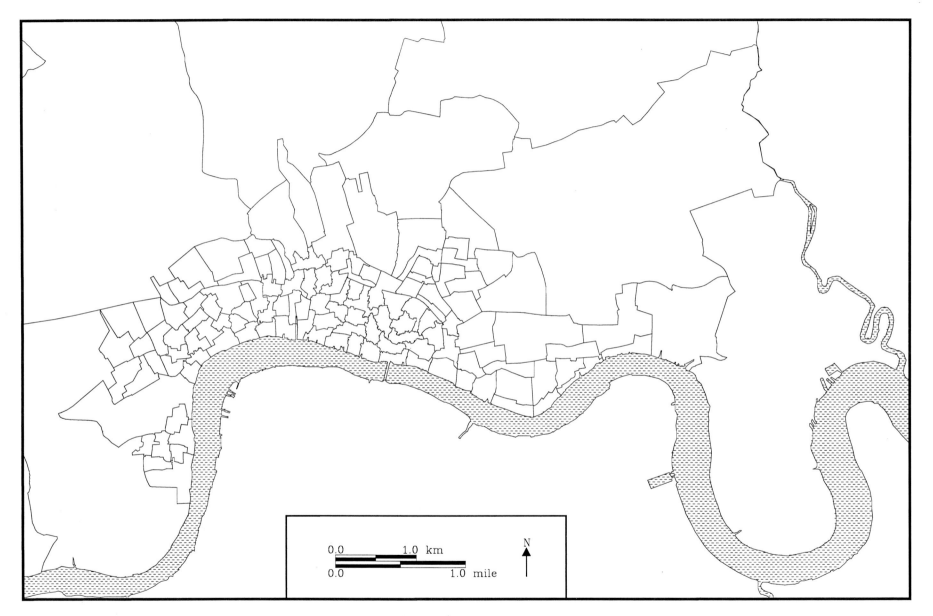

FIG. 1.6 The boundaries of the 450-household analytical areas
Source: 1693–4 Aid database. See also Appendix II.

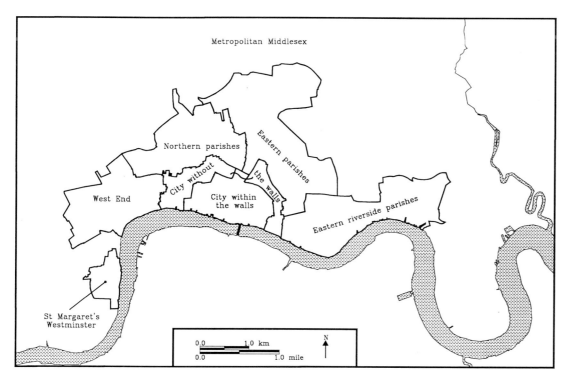

FIG. 1.7 The boundaries of the eight aggregated analytical areas
Source: 1693–4 Aid database. See also Appendix II.

This atlas has been designed to present both the immediate results of the analysis of the 1690s taxation data and the background against which that material will be most usefully understood. The computer-generated maps presented in the atlas are only a small proportion of the many that were produced in the course of the research. The production of maps, all set within a rigorously constructed topographic framework, was part of the investigative and explanatory process. Those published were selected because they convey new and original information or, in the case of secondary material, information not previously presented in this form. Each map is accompanied by text in the form of an expanded commentary and discussion, supported by relevant examples and descriptions. To allow a degree of cross-referencing of data between the mapped areas and the contemporary administrative areas a comprehensive statistical supplement, based on City wards and Westminster and Middlesex parishes, is presented in Appendix III.

The maps take two basic forms: point or symbol, and choropleth. Data concerning specific property types, or secondary information, are most often presented using the technique of point mapping. Quantitative data, usually abstracted from the 1693–4 Aid database, are generally shown in the form of choropleth maps. Colour has been applied to the maps when and where its presence helps to delineate further the mapped data. The maps are not generally

foci (see Fig. 1.6). In this way it was possible to construct 125 analytical areas, each with a population of about 450 households.[90]

While these analytical areas were very useful in producing choropleth maps with a degree of analytical detail that allowed pertinent topographic information to be used in the process of explanation, they were too numerous for clear presentation of the overall pattern.[91] The analytical areas were thus aggregated into eight larger

groups (Fig. 1.7), so as to simplify presentation in figures and tables. The aggregated units use the boundaries of contemporary administrative areas as much as possible and thus provide values that are comparable with data from other sources. While attempts were made to ensure that the numbers of rent tax payers were reasonably distributed between the areas, greater emphasis was placed on the need to respect boundaries and topography than on achieving equality of numbers.

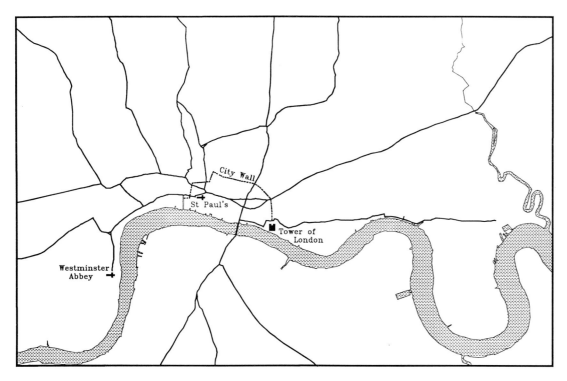

FIG. 1.8 Orientation Map
Source: Centre for Metropolitan History

reproduced at a uniform scale as the limited geographical extent of some data would be lost on a map of the entire metropolitan area. Accurate scales (kilometres and miles, or metres and yards) are provided, however. In order to help the reader locate the data presented in the maps five orientation keys are incorporated: Westminster Abbey, St Paul's Cathedral, the Tower of London, the City wall shown as a broken line, and the major or 'Old Post' roads (see Fig. 1.8). A map showing taxation districts is given in Appendix IV.

The themes present in the atlas are to some extent free-standing. Nevertheless, the text and maps have been ordered in a way which will enable the reader to progress from chapter to chapter and so to build a picture of the social and economic structure of the metropolis as a whole. Thus Chapter Two begins with a description of London's infrastructure starting with the ground upon which the city stood and the water sources that supplied it. Transport systems are dealt with in some detail as the spatial structure of the metropolis was heavily influenced

by the time and cost of travel within it. Chapter Three reviews the character and function of the built environment. Sections cover the nature of metropolitan land use and late seventeenth-century building characteristics. Data from the aids of 1693–4 are employed in a discussion of household densities and land values. Chapters Four and Five present the bulk of the analytical results. Social structure is considered in Chapter Four, where population distribution, household rental values, social configurations, gender patterns, household structure, and patterns of multiple-occupation and property ownership are all discussed. The chapter also reviews information on wealthy and poor districts. Chapter Five uses the values assessed for commercial property to provide a picture of the city's economic environment. The 1692 Poll Tax returns provide a view of the occupational profile of a substantial proportion of householders in the City of London. Information on stockholding in the 1693–4 Aids indicates the value and distribution of the overall wealth of London's inhabitants. Finally, Chapter Six identifies topics for further research and reviews some of the overall conclusions that can be drawn from the study.

Notes:

1. Barbon (1689), 2.
2. Hatton (1708), i.
3. Defoe (1724–6), 306.
4. Swift (1710).
5. Crinò (1968), 206.
6. Howell (1657), 389.

7. Schwarz (1992), 2; Wrigley (1967).
8. Chandaman (1975), 89; Thirsk and Cooper (1972), 771, 792–3. For the value of London in relation to that of the realm, see also below, pp. 48–9.
9. Proportions derived from Chandaman (1975), 107–8, 361.
10. Harding (1990b), 120–3; Beier and Finlay (1986), 9–10; Glass and Eversley (1965), 212; Wrigley and Schofield (1981), 218.
11. Stone (1980), 173–86.
12. Earle (1989a), 86–7; Kitch (1986).
13. Statt (1990); also see numerous works related to the Protestant Huguenot settlement in London, particularly publications of the Huguenot Society, and articles in Scouloudi (1985).
14. French (1992), Table I.
15. Developments vividly summarised in Roseveare (1991).
16. For an important assessment, see Louw (1981).
17. Crinò (1968), 206.
18. Steele (1910), 399–400.
19. Graunt (1662).
20. See Laslett (1992) for an introduction to the work of Graunt and Gregory King; Petty (1662).
21. Brett-James (1935).
22. Jones and Judges (1935–6).
23. King (1696).
24. Glass (1965) and (1966).
25. Wrigley (1967).
26. Fisher (1961).
27. Wrigley and Schofield (1981).
28. Finlay and Shearer (1986); Harding (1990b).
29. Harding (1990b); See below, pp. 63–6.
30. Kitch (1986); Boulton (1987b); Clark (1987); Statt (1990).
31. Glass (1969).
32. Forbes (1980).
33. Beier (1986).
34. Alexander (1989a and b) and (1992). See below, pp. 128–31, for a discussion of this occupational information.
35. Earle (1989a and b) and (1994).
36. Boulton (1987a), 60–98; Power (1978a), (1990); Green (1990).
37. Glass (1966), xxiii.
38. Jones (1980).
39. Stone (1980).
40. Boulton (1987a).

41. Power (1978b).
42. Power (1978a), 31, 37.
43. Power (1986), 212.
44. Alexander (1989a and b) and (1992).
45. Champion (1995); Slack (1985).
46. Jones (1980).
47. Part of the preamble from the assessment for Bridge Ward Within, 1694 (CLRO, Assessment. Box 38, no. 2) referring to the statute 5 & 6 William & Mary c. 1.
48. Childs (1987), 153.
49. The acts concerning aids before the formal institution of the land tax were: 1 William & Mary Session 1 c. 3 (fixed sum), c. 20 (12d. in the pound); 1 William & Mary Session 2 c. 1 (2s. in the pound), c. 5 (12d. in the pound); 3 William & Mary c. 5 (fixed sum); 4 William & Mary c. 1, 5 William & Mary c. 1, 6 William III c. 3, 7 William III c. 5 (all 4s. in the pound). For the acts granting poll taxes, see Arkell (1992), 142–80.
50. Arkell (1992), Glass (1966).
51. Dale (1931).
52. O'Brien (1988), 8–10.
53. Alexander (1992), 185–9; Turner and Mills (1986), *passim*; Ward (1953), 39–41.
54. Glanville (1980), 81–2.
55. Copies of the London Bills of Mortality for the 1690s are held by the Wellcome Library for the History and Understanding of Medicine (msl/coll/Lon); see also Brett James (1935), 248–67. They covered 113 parishes within the City of London, 7 parishes in the City and Liberties of Westminster, and 14 'Out-Parishes in Middlesex and Surrey', of which 9 were south of the river (Christ Church Surrey, St George in Southwark, St Mary at Lambeth, St Mary Magdalen Bermondsey, St Mary Newington, St Mary Rotherhithe, St Olave in Southwark, St Saviour in Southwark and St Thomas in Southwark). On 17 April 1694 the parish of St Mary Whitechapel was divided, with the southern division known as 'Wapping Whitechapel' becoming the separate parish of St John Wapping. Consequently from that date there were 15 'Out-parishes', although the area encompassed by the Bills was unchanged.
56. See Appendix I for a full list of the aid assessments used, which also serves to define the administrative areas. Within the metropolitan area covered by the atlas, assessments are

missing for: the hamlet of Mile End New Town; two divisions of St Giles without Cripplegate (Golden Lane and Glasshouse Yard, and Old Street); the Artillery Ground division of Tower Liberty; Whitehall; The Temple; and Lincoln's Inn.
57. For the returns used, see Appendix I.
58. Listed in Appendix II.
59. 4 William & Mary c. 1; 5 William & Mary c. 1.
60. Thus, Lord Lucas, the Governor of the Tower of London, was assessed to pay £140 a year on his combined salary and rent (valued at £700 a year); his deputy, Colonel Farwell, was similarly assessed at £60 (on a yearly value of £300).
61. 1693–4 Aid database.
62. Paragraph XIX sets out a full list of the exemptions from the tax, which includes any colleges in either university; the colleges at Windsor, Eton, Winchester and Westminster; the college of Bromley, Christ's Hospital, St Bartholomew's Hospital, Bridewell, St Thomas' and Bethlehem Hospital; and charities for the widows and orphans of poor clergymen.
63. Sir Basil Firebrass (Firebrace), a wine merchant free of the Vintners' Company, was Alderman of Billingsgate Ward between 1687–8, during which period he was also Sheriff of London and Colonel of the Orange Regiment, he became Member of Parliament for Chippenham in 1690, 1691, and 1692, being unseated each time. He was later a member of the Committee of the East India Company from 1694 to 1695. A widower by 1695, he lived with his three children Hester, Charles and George. Glass (1966), 106; Woodhead (1965), 69.
64. 1 William & Mary Session 1 c. 18.
65. For Hampden see *DNB*, VIII, 1150–1; for Seymour see *DNB*, XVII, 1250–3; for Lowther see *DNB*, XII, 220–2; for Trevor see *DNB*, XIX, 1149–50; for Holt see *DNB*, IX, 1096–9; for Atkins (Atkyns) see *DNB*, I, 702–4.
66. For the social categories thereby included, see Arkell (1992), Table 1.
67. 1693–4 Aid database.
68. Samuel Clarke was noted as a merchant by the 1692 Poll Tax returns, his rent was £50 per annum. Colonel Willett dwelt with his wife, Mary, seven children (Mary, Sarah, Susan, Francis, Humphrey, Edward and William), three female servants, a male servant and an apprentice, in a property valued at £60 per annum. 1693–4 Aid database; 1692 Poll Tax database; Freshfield (1895), 229, 231; Glass (1966), 320.

69. Thomas Kendall paid £10 rent per annum for a property on Bishopsgate Street, where he lived with his wife and a single apprentice. Kendall's immediate neighbour was his fellow assessor Thomas Richards (Rickards). Richards occupied an apparently larger property, valued at £26, with his wife, child, female servant and apprentice. 1693–4 Aid database; 1692 Poll Tax database.

70. The Receiver General for London and Westminster was Sir Leonard Robinson, Chamberlain of the Corporation of London. The Corporation's Town Clerk, John Goodfellow, acted as the Commissioners' clerk for the City of London. CLRO, Assessment Box 111, no. 9.

71. CLRO, Assessment Box 40, no. 61.

72. CLRO Chamber Accounts 40/207.

73. Davenant (1695), 104.

74. CLRO Assessment Box 27.C.

75. Sainty (1975), 79, 98, 137, 157; CLRO Chamber Accounts 40/113 (1694–5).

76. CLRO, Chamber Accounts 40/113 (1694–5). The clipping of coin was regarded as so serious a problem during the 1680s and 1690s that it became a treasonable offence.

77. Firmin was Common Councillor for Langborn Ward in 1674 and 1680, he was also a commissioner for the 1693–4 Aids for the City of London. A member of the Girdlers' Company he was a successful mercer and merchant during the 1660s and 1670s. Firmin was a noted philanthropist and was closely linked to the early establishment of workhouses for the poor, prison reform, and was a founder member of the Society for the Reformation of Manners. He was also an elected governor of both Christ's Hospital and St Thomas's Hospital. His household comprised his wife, Margaret, two male and three female servants. 1692 Poll Tax database; *DNB* VII, 46–9; Glass (1966), 106; Hitchcock (1992), 148; Woodhead (1965), 69.

78. 1693–4 Aid database.

79. 1693–4 Aid database. CLRO, Assessment Box 40 no. 61.

80. For these values, see below, pp. 48–51, 149–51 and Table 5.10.

81. 3 & 4 William & Mary c. 6; 5 & 6 William & Mary c. 14; 9 William III c. 38. For the principles, see Arkell (1992), Table 1.

82. See below, pp. 89–91.

83. For a more detailed discussion of the computing methods used, see Spence (1994).

84. A copy of the 1693–4 Aid database, as transcribed, is held by the History Data Service in the Data Archive at the University of Essex <http://hds.essex.ac.uk>, study no. 3497 and is also available for consultation at the Centre for Metropolitan History.

85. The Poll Tax database was compiled by James Alexander. It is available for consultation at the Centre for Metropolitan History and also as a printed copy at the Corporation of London Records Office.

86. See below, pp. 63–6, for a description of the verification method.

87. Parish Clerks (1732), *passim*.

88. A digital copy of the base map showing parochial boundaries is held by the Great Britain Historical GIS Project, Department of Geography, University of Portsmouth <http://www.geog.port.ac.uk/hgis>.

89. For a basic definition of 'natural' areas, see Unwin (1981), 114–15.

90. The majority of the areas held household numbers in the range of 350 to 650. However, the following analytical areas in particular deviated from this norm: St Sepulchre Middlesex, 263 households; St Giles Without Cripplegate, both extant liberties, 782 households; St Marylebone and St Pancras, 227 households; St Katherine by the Tower, 839 households; part of St Botolph Aldgate and Wapping Whitechapel, 729 households; Tower Liberty (Intra), 2 households. These extreme values were the result of non-divisible administrative boundaries and/or limitations in geographical extent. After the removal of these six areas from consideration, a mean of 449.94 households was calculated for the remaining 119 areas.

91. Of those areas delineated in Fig. 1.6 three were districts peripheral to the main study area north of the river Thames and eight were areas with no extant 1693–4 Aid data. This resulted in a total of 125 analytically active areas.

2. Metropolitan Infrastructure

London lies near the centre of the Thames Basin, a broad irregular valley formed by glacial activity during the Pleistocene period and subsequently by the erosive powers of the river Thames. In the seventeenth century the extent of the City of London broadly corresponded to the area once occupied by the Roman city of Londinium, its legal boundary having changed little since the twelfth century. Westminster focused upon the abbey and on Whitehall, and included much of the growing suburb that lay to the west of the City.[1]

In 1600 the built-up area did not differ radically in extent, shape or relief from what it had been in earlier centuries. But, as it expanded onto previously unsettled land, it is clear that the underlying physical topography was highly influential in defining the urban pattern. Surface contours, geology, pedology, the availability of water, and even meteorological conditions, all played a part in decisions made concerning the choice of location and land use. Contemporary writers, although often commenting favourably upon London's topographic situation, were less forthcoming in describing the more negative aspects of life in an urban environment. At the end of the sixteenth century Stow enthused that:

> Neither could London be pitched so commodiously upon any other part of the … Thames as where it now standeth. For if it were removed more to the west, it should lose the benefit of the ebbing and flowing: and if it were seated more towards the east it should be … further both from the good air and, from doing good to the inner parts of the realm; neither may I omit that none other place is so plentifully watered with springs as London is.[2]

On the other hand, Evelyn, some sixty years later, described the Thames and London's environment in a less than enthusiastic manner:

> This continual smoke … is manifest … not only upon the earth, but upon the water also, where it leaves a thin web, or pellicule of dust, dancing upon the surface of it; as those who go to bathe in the Thames do easily discern and bring home upon their bodies.[3]

Whatever the opinion of contemporaries, London's geographical position was undoubtedly advantageous for a variety of factors, some natural and others artificially enhanced. One factor which had a clear influence on London's form was that of elevation or relief.

London's contour pattern (Fig. 2.1) was established primarily as a result of the scouring action of the Thames and its various tributaries.[4] The erosive processes of the meandering Thames resulted in the land to the north of the river being generally higher than areas to the south which were more uniformly low-lying. The City lay on a plateau of artificially accumulated deposits that helped to raise it even further above the river, while the neighbourhood around the Strand in Westminster occupied a natural curving bluff some five to ten metres (fifteen to thirty feet) above the surface of the Thames at high-tide.

In terms of geology the low-lying areas near the Thames were characterised by the extensive deposits of the Alluvial Flood Plain which, while providing land useful for horticultural purposes or grazing, were prone to inundation. These alluvial areas were found mainly to the south of the Thames, but also to some extent both east and west of the built-up area north of the river (Fig. 2.1).

To the north of London lay ground composed of the Flood Plain terrace and the Taplow terrace, material geologically earlier than the alluvial deposits. The sands, gravels and brickearth of the terraces were notable for providing a relatively flat and stable construction surface across which the limit of the built-up area progressed northwards to engulf areas such as Shoreditch and Finsbury. The well-drained nature of these deposits ensured that their agricultural function, at least in the immediate vicinity of London, was predominantly that of meadow or pasture.[5] Further toward the north-west of the study area, around Islington and Camden, lay the important Claygate Beds and the Boyn Hill terrace: these deposits of London Clay and brickearth were consequently the focus of much local brick-making activity.[6]

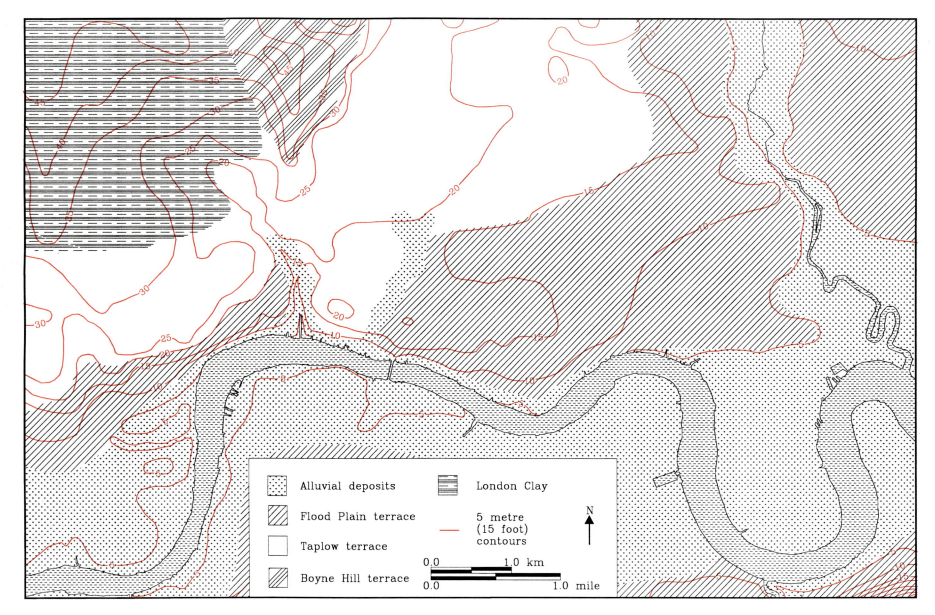

FIG. 2.1 Geomorphology of the metropolitan area, with contour information
Sources: Gibbard (1985), Mylne (1856). Contours derived from nineteenth-century Ordnance Survey maps.

The Thames and its tributaries

The river Thames was central to London's topography. Its east-west alignment was mirrored by the city's linear expansion along its northern shore. On the south bank the suburb of Southwark focused upon the bridgehead and the roads converging upon it. Here the low-lying, marshy, land constrained the lateral expansion of settlement. The parts of the river Thames above and below London Bridge each had a distinctive character. The river upstream was a milieu of myriad small vessels: wherries, ferries, barges and smaller sailing craft. This stretch of the river linked the rapidly-expanding areas of Westminster with the City to the east and Lambeth to the south, and was the terminus for a substantial trade from the upper reaches of the Thames bringing essential supplies to London. The downriver area was known as the Port or Pool of London. The Port began just east of London Bridge where numerous commercial wharves and docks served a multitude of sea-going vessels and attendant lighters. Beyond the Tower of London with its military wharves, the commercial riverside extended haphazardly for a further three kilometres (two miles) downriver to Limehouse. Beyond Limehouse and close to the mouth of the river Lea was the site of the East India Company's Blackwall Yard. This shipbuilding and repair facility took advantage of both a sheltering bend of the river and the marshy landscape of the Isle of Dogs.

The Lea was one of a number of Thames tributaries that since the Middle Ages had provided a valuable inland waterway system for the metropolitan region, although it was the only one which was effectively navigable. Further east lay Barking Creek which linked the river Roding, in Essex, to the Thames. On the south side of the river, near to Greenwich, was Deptford Creek which was fed by the Ravensbourne and was the location of a number of watermills and of shipbuilding activity.

Two rivers of note joined the Thames upriver from London Bridge: the Fleet and the Wandle. The Fleet occupied a valley that lay between the City to the east and Westminster to the west. During the 1670s it was canalised as far north as Holborn Bridge as part of the rebuilding after the Great Fire. The banks were reconstructed with timber and stone, and the channel itself dredged clear of mud and debris.[7] The Fleet canal provided a new means of access to the western parts of the city for barges. It was difficult to maintain, however, and by the 1730s had fallen into disuse. Soon after, it was covered over.[8]

The river Wandle, to the south-west of London, was the location of much industrial activity. The river fell thirty-eight metres (125 feet) from its source to the Thames in a distance of less than fifteen kilometres (nine miles), making it an excellent power source. Petitions by local inhabitants against a proposed waterworks scheme in 1610 put the number of mills, mainly associated with grain processing, at twenty-four and indicate that some 130 people found direct employment there.[9]

The central London stretch of the Thames lay close to the tidal limit of the river, the effects of which were accentuated by the barrier of the closely-arched London Bridge which resembled a dam or weir. As a result the river upstream became very slow moving, particularly during high tides, while downstream of the bridge it had a relatively large tidal regime. In this context it should be noted that the source point for most of the Thames tributaries near the metropolis was the interface of the London Clay deposits and the sands and gravel of the Taplow terrace — the impermeable nature of the clay resulting in a somewhat erratic water-flow. This characteristic resulted from the replenishment of the primary aquifer for the London Basin being dependent upon rainfall over the Chiltern Hills and the North Downs. Consequently, during periods of low rainfall water levels in the tributaries tended to be relatively low, while high rainfall often produced sudden flood conditions.[10]

WATER SUPPLY

In the 1690s London's water supply took three main forms: water drawn directly from rivers, water obtained by sinking wells or building conduits, and piped water supplied by a variety of waterworks undertakings. Water drawn from both the Thames and its tributaries was often potable if taken far enough upstream from the built-up areas. Tributaries that passed through heavily populated areas of the metropolis often became little more than open sewers by the time they discharged into the Thames. Nevertheless, water drawn from such

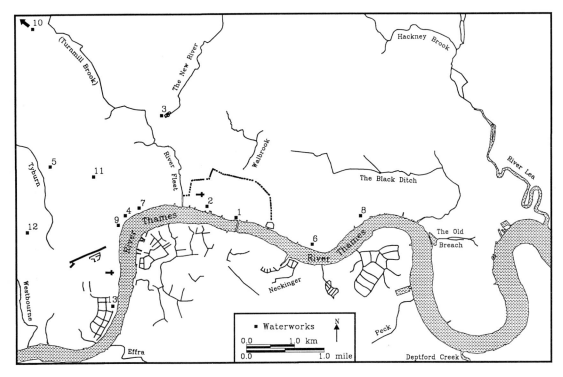

FIG. 2.2 Water-courses and drainage pattern for the metropolitan area, also showing waterworks operating during the late seventeenth century

Sources: Dickinson (1954), Ogilby and Morgan (1676), Rocque (1747), Strype (1720). The numbers relate to Table 2.1 (*q.v.*)

streams still supplied many of the domestic and industrial requirements of the city. In earlier times commercial water-carriers had commonly transported Thames water, and later water from the public conduits, to domestic and other users. By the late seventeenth century, however, that practice had become rare and, if employed at all, the carriers were mainly concerned with the re-distribution of water from the decayed public conduits.[11]

Water supply was one of the major factors influencing the location of the villages within the London area. They were generally sited on areas of exposed gravel known to geologists as dry points. Here the ground conditions provided well-drained soils, a solid constructional surface and, most importantly, springs, or at least the convenience of shallow wells. A similar situation existed in parts of the City, where wells could be conveniently sunk in yards and gardens to produce modest

volumes of water for private, and primarily domestic, consumption.[12]

Conduits were found in both private and public situations across London. By the end of the seventeenth century several such public water supplies already had well-established histories, some of them from as early as the thirteenth century. Stow listed seventeen conduits within the City in 1598, although there were probably other semi-public wells or spring-fed fountains.[13] The conduits, such as the Great Conduit in Cheapside, provided water in the form of public fountains, channelled and piped from springs or streams to the west of the City. While this water was free to domestic users, the greater quantities taken by commercial operators such as brewers, fishmongers and cooks had to be paid for.[14]

The conduits provided a public source of water but many now desired the greater convenience of private piped water supplies, and water companies came to meet this demand. Chief amongst these were the New River Company and the London Bridge Waterworks. The New River Company, a speculative undertaking founded under the direction of Sir Hugh Myddleton, began to supply the city in 1613 — the water being drawn from a source at Ware in Hertfordshire and directed to London by means of a canal, the New River.[15] The London Bridge Waterworks developed as a major supplier from 1701 when it was purchased for £38,000 by the goldsmith Richard Soame. The price included not only the watermills within the northern arches of London Bridge but also the horse-mills at Broken Wharf. Soame was able to form a

TABLE 2.1
Waterworks undertakings operating in London during the late seventeenth century

Number on Fig. 2.2	Waterworks	Year of establishment	Type	Annual value (1693–4 Aid)
1	London Bridge	1581	watermills	£1,500
2	Broken Wharf	1594	horsemills	£600
3	New River[1]	1613	gravitational	£14,500
4	Durham Yard[2]	1650s	–	–
5	Marylebone Fields[2]	1650s	–	£100
6	Wapping Wall[2]	1650s	–	–
7	Somerset House	1660s	horsemill	–
8	Shadwell	1669	horsemills	£387 10s.
9	York Buildings	1675	tide/horsemill[3]	£600
10	Hampstead	1692	–	–
11	Marchant's	1694/5	watermill	–
12	Hyde Park	1690s[?]	–	£300
13	Millbank	1690s[?]	–	£187 10s.

Notes:

[1] Taken over by the London Bridge Waterworks in 1703.

[2] All three were acquired by the New River Company in 1667 for £6,100.

[3] In 1712 the York Buildings Waterworks was one of the earliest industrial undertakings to employ steam power for pumping.

company with a capital of £150,000 by selling 300 shares at £500 each. With the money raised he undertook reconstruction of the London Bridge plant, employing an accomplished engineer named Sorocold to build new pumping engines.[16] By 1702 the company had thirteen engines, occupying four arches of the bridge which, allowing for slack water, raised some eleven million litres (2.5 million gallons) of water a day.[17]

The water companies used two main sources of supply: Thames water and spring or stream water. The pattern shown in Fig. 2.2 clearly demonstrates this basic differentiation. Water was supplied to individual houses in pipes of lead or bored elm, a variety of mechanisms being used to ensure that the companies' reservoirs were kept full. In the 1690s there were at least thirteen waterworks in the metropolitan area. Around the beginning of the eighteenth century, however, commercial pressures brought a number of these, for example the London Bridge Waterworks, under the ownership of single proprietors thus raising fears of a private water monopoly and a marked decline in the condition and availability of public supply.

A list of the waterworks operating in the late seventeenth century is given in Table 2.1 and their locations indicated in Fig. 2.2. The values in the table derive from the Posting Book of the Chamberlain of London which recorded the revenues, based on profits, assessed as a special element of the four shilling aid.[18] The figures indicate the relative values of the undertakings. The property assessments for the four shilling aid itself mention only two water-houses explicitly. One, in Islington, was valued at £10 per annum rent and was probably that of the New River Company, while the other, in Marylebone, was valued at £20 per annum rent and probably belonged to the Marylebone Fields Waterworks.

The householder in both the City and Westminster could take advantage of a number of waterworks to gain a piped supply of wholesome water. Disputes between companies and the problem of illegal tapping of supplies resulted in legislative action both to control and assist the suppliers' activities. Certain geographical limits were designated for each company in the acts that brought them into being, while rights of entry and inspection gave the companies what were in effect statutory powers. The price of water to the domestic consumer was in the region of twenty to twenty-five shillings per year, usually paid quarterly, although this, as contemporary observers noted, would not guarantee a regular supply.[19]

Waste management and pollution

By the 1690s metropolitan London had an estimated population of more than half a million and the refuse, effluent and pollution produced by such a mass of humanity provided a continuing challenge to the civic authorities of the day. A number of solutions, of varying efficacy, were found for some of the more obvious problems, but the more invidious forms of pollution went mostly unchecked.

It had long been the practice for each ward or parish within London to appoint people to supervise street cleansing and repair. The scavengers and rakers operated with the direct assistance of householders to ensure that the streets remained clean and that domestic refuse was removed to, in the case of the City, one of four laystalls. In 1654 the Common Council enacted what amounted to a privatisation of these services when it handed the contract for refuse disposal and street cleansing to one John Lanyon, relieving some 400 ward appointees of the task. After the Great Fire the City-wide system broke down, mainly as a result of inertia on the part of the inhabitants. Contracts continued to be used, however, and were organised on a ward by ward basis.[20]

Drainage and sewerage matters were the preserve of the Commissioners of Sewers who were first appointed in the sixteenth century and undertook a number of drainage-related improvements. In the early seventeenth century they effected the draining of the area around Moorfields and constructed the large Common Sewer, in part by vaulting over the Walbrook. In 1662 the commissioners were further empowered to repair, pave and cleanse highways by supervising the activities of the scavengers and

rakers; they were also given powers to widen streets. The jurisdiction of the London commissioners included the cities of London and Westminster, and also Poplar and other metropolitan districts in Middlesex, Surrey and Kent. After the Great Fire the City established its own commission, while the control of street cleansing in Westminster was conferred upon the Middlesex Justices of the Peace and the parish vestries.[21]

Despite innovative construction projects such as the Common Sewer, most of the population relied on cesspits for the bulk of their waste disposal needs. This was a relatively primitive means of effluent and refuse removal, providing clear archaeological and documentary evidence that the close juxtaposition of cesspits and wells may have resulted in cross-contamination of water supplies.[22] While domestic effluent was relatively little controlled, with an emphasis being placed on a failure to pay rates rather than on pollution *per se*, much effort went into the restraint of water pollution by manufacturing and industrial undertakings. Tanners, brewers and dyers were in many instances located away from the central densely-populated areas and tended to occupy water-courses in the southern and eastern suburbs. The presence of a number of dyers and brewers within the City can be explained by the need for each to be in close proximity to their customers both for logistical and commercial reasons.[23]

Meteorological conditions in London were at this time only just beginning to be influenced by the

urban character of the region. The prevailing winds were from the west with temperatures generally typical of a temperate climate, despite the occasional severe winter, such as that which froze the Thames in 1683–4. The built-up nature of the urban core probably helped to maintain temperatures one or two degrees higher than the surrounding countryside, especially at night. Streets lined with high-fronted buildings may well have contributed to gusty and windy conditions in the city's thoroughfares and open spaces.[24] The position of Blackwall Yard, the Admiralty Yard at Deptford and the newly constructed Howland Great Wet Dock on the partially sheltered western bank of the Thames gives some indication of an awareness of the dangers the prevailing winds might pose to shipping.

The prevailing winds combined with the extensive use of coal as a fuel gave seventeenth-century London a distinctive pattern of atmospheric pollution. John Evelyn, in his pamphlet *Fumifugium or The Inconvenience of the Aer and the Smoak of London Dissipated* (1661), laid the cause of this problem squarely on the use of coal and the location of brewers, dyers, lime burners and soap boilers within the built-up area. He described the damage caused to both buildings and health by the emissions, but his solution was both uneconomic and unrealistic. He suggested that wood, a more expensive fuel commodity, should replace coal and that the offending industries should be re-located some five or six miles downriver, and so downwind, of the metropolis.[25] A more practical solution to the problem was for those who could afford it to move to the West End, which was as William Petty noted, 'So much the more free from the fumes, steams and stinks of the whole easterly pile'.[26]

The effect of the London smoke on health was less well defined, although John Graunt in 1662 linked the poor quality of the London air with increased mortality.[27] More recent analysis has shown that death rates from respiratory diseases, such as *tisick* or asthma, were significantly higher during the 'great stinking fogs' noted in John Gadbury's weather diary than at other times.[28] King William's choice of Hampton Court as a residence, some distance to the west of London and so upwind of the noxious smoke, becomes more understandable when one appreciates that he himself was an asthmatic.[29]

TRANSPORT

Despite its unprecedented size, London in the 1690s was contained within a relatively small compass. A person setting out from the Westminster landing stage of the Horseferry, a point at the western extremity of the urban sprawl would, with a healthy stride through unencumbered streets, have reached the easternmost parts of urban Middlesex, around Limehouse, in less than two hours. At no point in London's warren of streets and alleys would that same person have been more than a half hour stroll from the Thames.[30] Of course, both these measures take little account of the trouble to be had negotiating the crowded and busy thoroughfares of the metropolis. People, horses, carts, coaches and livestock all competed for road space. Such roads were sporadically maintained, poorly lit at night, and often encroached upon by the goods and structures of commerce during the working day. With the seventeenth-century boom in London's population, it is not surprising to find that government, both local and national, began to take an active interest in the structure, regulation and revenue-generating potential of metropolitan transport.

Although the reasons underlying the patterns of movement within a city the size of London were manifold, a general characterisation can be given. For most Londoners during the seventeenth century the closely juxtaposed nature of home and workplace resulted in relatively few regular 'journeys to work'. By the 1690s, however, some members of the commercial and professional ranks had begun to develop a residential pattern that separated their domestic environment from their place of employment, thus initiating some form, even if intermittent, of 'journey to work'. Aside from travelling to the workplace most of the regular transport activity of the metropolis focused upon the carriage of goods from the river or markets to shops, warehouses and workshops.[31]

The most likely occasion for movement by individual Londoners around the city would have been associated with economic or cultural necessity. Food and goods had to be obtained from markets and shops, and churches or meeting-houses were frequented. Business or pleasure would account for other journeys, such as attending the Exchange and coffee houses or going to the theatre. No doubt during the summer months many would eagerly take the opportunity to promenade along the tree-lined walks of Moorfields, Lincoln's Inn and St James's Park or take the relatively short walk, or ride, into the surrounding fields as a simpler recreation, just as they had in Stow's day.[32] Walking, therefore, would have undoubtedly provided the predominant means of internal movement, a point emphasised by the large number of perambulating traders who circulated the city streets crying their wares.[33]

For individual journeys of a greater distance, or for the sake of speed, those with money to spend might privately hire a Hackney coach or waterman's wherry. At the same time, as a result of population and commercial pressures, London's structured transport system continued to grow. By 1700, for example, a number of coaching enterprises had begun to provide regular daily services to the towns and villages on the outskirts of the metropolis.[34]

The road network

The City was the focal point of both the local and the national road network. Contemporary directories and guides, for example, published transport distances measured from the Standard in Cornhill.[35] By the late seventeenth century the primary routes out of London were recognised as having special status being known as the 'Old Post Roads', the major routes along which the official post or mail was carried. The gates in the City wall

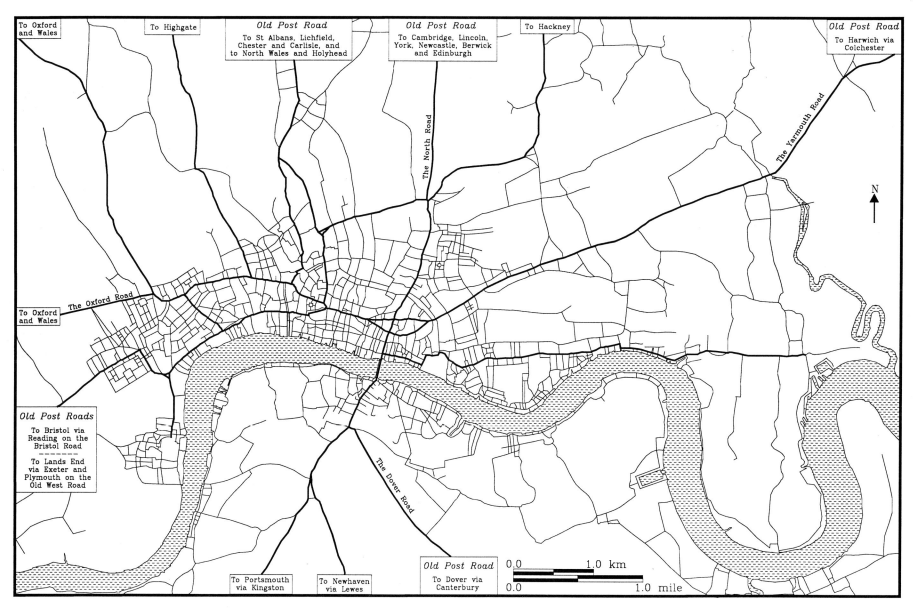

To Oxford and Wales

To Highgate

Old Post Road
To St Albans, Lichfield, Chester and Carlisle, and to North Wales and Holyhead

Old Post Road
To Cambridge, Lincoln, York, Newcastle, Berwick and Edinburgh

To Hackney

Old Post Road
To Harwich via Colchester

The North Road

The Yarmouth Road

N

The Oxford Road

To Oxford and Wales

Old Post Roads
To Bristol via Reading on the Bristol Road
———————
To Lands End via Exeter and Plymouth on the Old West Road

The Dover Road

To Portsmouth via Kingston

To Newhaven via Lewes

Old Post Road
To Dover via Canterbury

0.0   1.0 km

0.0   1.0 mile

FIG. 2.3 The metropolitan road network, showing destinations of 'Old Post Roads', *c.*1700

Sources: Morgan (1682), Ogilby and Morgan (1676), Rocque (1747), Strype (1720).

were nodal points where external and internal roads converged, thus becoming the sites of greatest congestion. Analysis of the City of London's streets, however, has shown the network as a whole to have been characterised by a high degree of integration, facilitating the circulation of people, goods and information.[36] In mapping London's road network (Fig. 2.3) three categories of metropolitan streets have been defined. These were: the major thoroughfares, including the Old Post Roads; the secondary streets that fed the main thoroughfares and provided links between them; and innumerable alleys and yards which branched off the larger streets.[37] In terms of circulation those in the last category were of minor significance, often being dead-ends; in terms of number, however, they formed the greatest element within the City's structural network.[38]

The City's markets present a good example of external routes of communication engaging with internal circulation. Providing the consumer needs of the city was a fundamental urban transaction. A wide variety of transport groups used the market places and through them supplied the manufacturers, retailers and exporters. This led to great congestion at the market foci. The area around St John Street and Smithfield, for example, was the main destination for drovers with their cattle and sheep, but also for pack-horse teams and for many of the wagons, carts and coaches of the carrying trade. Combined with the regular throng of Londoners intent on purchasing the available goods, the markets could easily become overcrowded

obstructions within the general pattern of metropolitan circulation. This problem was to some extent resolved by market relocation undertaken after the Great Fire. Despite initial suggestions that the markets of the City should be moved to more peripheral locations, to the advantage of the carriers if not the inhabitants, the reconstructed markets were to remain fixed in their neighbourhoods. However, by relocating a number away from the main axial routes, some of the obstruction they had caused was alleviated. A good example of the new market design was Newgate Market, moved from Newgate Street into purpose-built accommodation to the south of that important thoroughfare.[39]

The rebuilding that followed the Great Fire provided the opportunity for an extensive reorganisation of the City's streets but, apart from a small number of significant actions taken around the gates and Thames waterfront, few new thoroughfares were constructed. At Ludgate the street was widened and the incline to the river Fleet was reduced, mainly to aid vehicles travelling to and from Westminster. Similar actions were taken on many of the lanes running north from Thames Street. Together with general widening measures this would undoubtedly have led to improvements in access, particular for the carmen. The only major new thoroughfare inserted into the network was that of King and Queen Streets, the impetus for this being associated with the provision of a ceremonial way from the Guildhall to the river rather than for any traffic alleviation purposes.[40]

It is probable that the major roads within the immediate London area were relatively well maintained. The commercial primacy of roads in the metropolitan region is indicated by the fact that half of the turnpike trusts established before 1730 were within thirty miles of London, but only two of these eighty-eight early turnpikes were established on roads that actually entered the built-up core of the metropolis. Given the volume of traffic into and out of London, the apparent delay in turnpiking these particular roads would suggest that the city's road system was in generally good condition.[41]

Local carrying services

London's transport industry comprised a number of sectors, but by far the most active were those concerned with the movement of goods. It was the external carrying services that supplied many of the food requirements of the metropolis. Other, internal, transport specialists moved liquids, fuel and miscellaneous goods. All these transport groups, bar the porters, employed horse-drawn wagons or carts to take their diverse loads from the site of production, or landing, to that of the consumer. These vehicles often damaged roads and buildings, and caused accidents and congestion — problems generally exacerbated by the narrow streets.[42] Such issues resulted in frequent attempts to limit the number of transport operators allowed within the confines of the City walls and to restrict their patterns of movement.

Drays, flat-bed two-wheeled carts, were the chosen vehicle of the brewing trade, a rapidly growing sector of the economy that already had the air of an industrial undertaking by the 1690s. The draymen were mainly employed by the larger common brewers; other brewers tending to carry out all operations, including sales, at a single premises had little use for such services. There were at least 194 London-based common brewers by 1699, who may have been served by 300–500 drays.[43]

Two other important groups of carriers were the woodmongers and the carmen. Woodmongers chiefly carried fuel in the form of firewood or coals, while the carmen provided a more diverse service, transferring loads from the quaysides and markets to individual establishments within the metropolis. The two groups were in continual conflict and in 1694 the City authorities intervened to set the number of licensed woodmongers' carts at 120 while restricting them to the transport of fuel and coals only. The authorities allowed a further 420 carts to be operated by carmen as long as they desisted from the practice of carrying fuel. The trade was a valuable source of income and, according to a contemporary report, a cart and licence known as a 'carroom' had a sale value of £130.[44] Carters, and others, who broke licencing or loading regulations were liable to fines or confiscation of their vehicle. Impounded carts were held in the City's Green Yard which, during the 1690s, was located just north of the City wall in the ward of Cripplegate Without.[45]

The movement of carts was also controlled. Since the early seventeenth century the movement of vehicles around the busy quayside area of Thames Street had

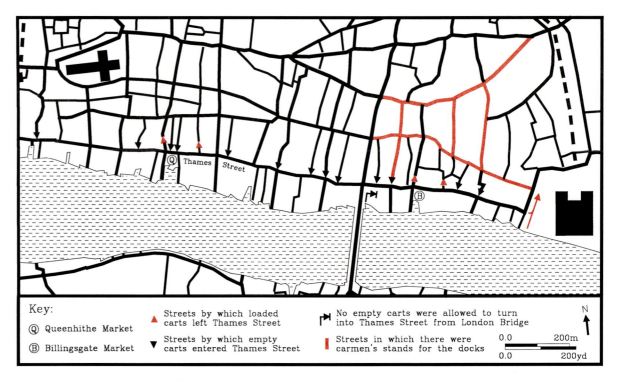

FIG. 2.4 Common Council regulations for the movement of carts into and out of Thames Street, 1617
Source: Stern (1960)

been strictly regulated. According to the regulations of 1617, empty carts were required to stand for hire at specified locations. Carts, once hired, could only enter Thames Street from the north along certain streets, while laden carts could only exit by means of five streets adjacent to Tower Wharf and the two riverside markets of Billingsgate and Queenhithe. Empty carts approaching from Southwark were prevented, by means of a post or bar, from entering Thames Street eastwards from London Bridge. This one-way system suggests that careful thought had

been given to the pattern of circulation and to the needs of the inhabitants of narrower streets which were closed to commercial traffic (Fig. 2.4).[46]

Thames Street and the other waterfront areas were the main focus of the London porters. These manual labourers undertook the loading and unloading of a wide variety of cargoes from vessels in the port. There were four categories of porters: tacklehouse porters who acted as contractors primarily on behalf of the City livery companies; ticket porters who

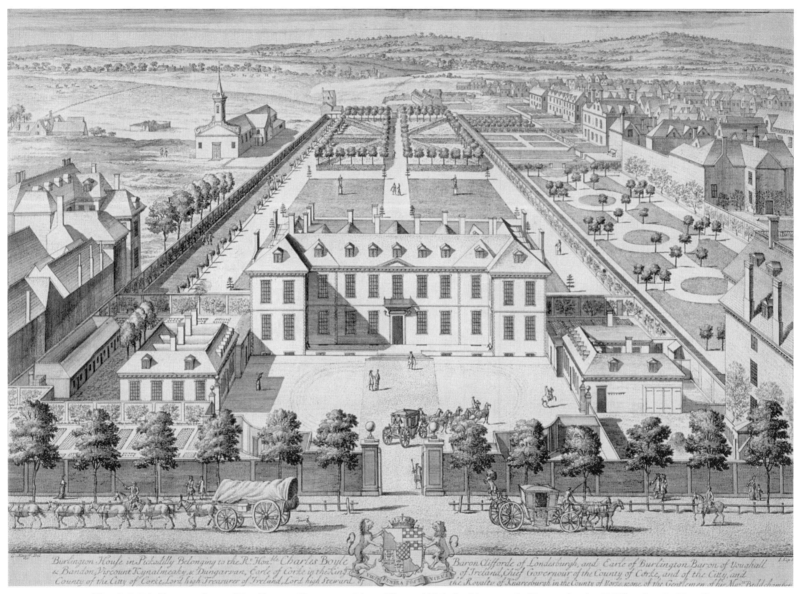

Fig. 2.5 Bird's-eye view of Burlington House on Piccadilly, *c*.1710, looking north (Engraving by J. Kip after L. Knyff)

Two examples of contemporary vehicles are shown in the foreground: a carrier's wagon (left), and a private coach (right). Also note the coach-house and stables to the righthand side of the courtyard.

Source: Guildhall Library.

were individually licensed and hired either separately or in gangs; fellowship (or Billingsgate) porters who dealt exclusively with corn, coal and salt on the waterfront; and finally, alien's porters who dealt with alien-owned commodities under the direction of the City's Packer and Porter of Alien's Goods.

Ticket porters were divided into two separate groups, uptown and waterfront. The uptown porters worked mainly in and around the various City markets and also provided a form of local messenger service. Waterfront porters were to be found working on the quays and wharves of the riverside. The City had jurisdiction for porterage not just within its usual administrative limits but also throughout the entire port of London, an area on both banks of the river extending a mile either side of London Bridge. Consequently the porters, of whom there were 5,000–6,000 by the 1690s, would have acted as conduits not only for goods, but also for news and information brought to London aboard the great variety of vessels at anchor in the Thames.[47]

Long distance carrying and coaching services

The focus of the long distance carrying and coaching trades were the inns, which provided much of the office, stabling and storage facilities required. Here carriers could unload, store or distribute goods by means of uptown porters working out of the inn yards. The coaching enterprises had developed greatly during the last few decades of the century. These services also focused on the inns but in this case many of the innholders undertook the direct management of the coaching enterprises.[48] Innkeepers were able to provide the traveller with a complete service, supplying refreshment and accommodation should it be required.

By the 1730s London's carriers served more than 200 routes, with over 300 services a week departing from some seventy-five different inns.[49] The carriers mainly transported goods but they also conveyed passengers, probably passengers of a lower rank than those who might ride in one of the vehicles of the rapidly expanding and, moderately faster, stagecoach services. Although the coaching enterprises served fewer routes — around 150 by the 1730s — the number of services was much greater, with over 450 per week. From these figures it might be suggested that on any given weekday London's streets would see some seventy-five to a hundred coaches departing for a wide range of near and far destinations.

Inns serving the coaching and carrying trades were found in the immediate suburbs and on the main roads approaching the commercial heart of the City (Fig. 2.6), with particular clusters of inns reflecting the regions served by the resident transport operators.[50] The overall distribution certainly seems to denote zones, characterised by warehousing and the transhipment of goods, which were peripheral to the congested commercial and riverside areas. While the carriers tended to crowd around the markets and warehouses of the City, the coaching inns were found in more diverse locations. The predominance of coaching services at the inns of Fleet Street, the Strand and Charing Cross is striking and suggests that there the prime concern was the transport of people, in all probability those of higher social standing, rather than the carriage of goods.

Hackney coaches

A person of standing who set out from Covent Garden to visit Maldon, Essex, for example, would probably have hired a Hackney coach to cross the city to Whitechapel where, on a Wednesday or Saturday, they could board a coach departing from the Blue Boar Inn.[51] Hackney coaches were numerous in London, and their numbers and fares were strictly controlled. In 1694 Parliament empowered commissioners to license and regulate Hackney and stagecoaches within the area defined by the Bills of Mortality. Seven hundred vehicles were allowed, suggesting that around 500 Hackney coaches operated in the regulated area at that time. Hackney coach licences cost £50 for twenty-one years, but with an annual charge of £4, while stage-coach licences were sold at £8 per annum. The basic hire rates for Hackney coaches were set at no more than 10s. per day or at an hourly rate of 1s. 6d. for the first hour, and an additional shilling for each successive hour of hire.[52] Given the estimated speed of coaches at this period of around six kilometres (four miles) per hour, such rates would make travel by Hackney coach comparable with conveyance by wherry, at least in terms of transport cost against distance, if not actual journey times.[53]

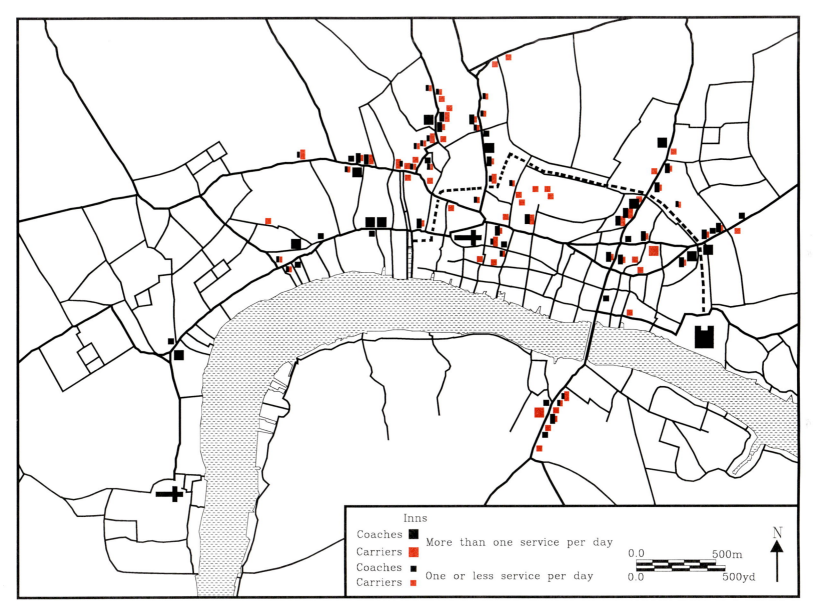

FIG. 2.6 The coaching and carrying inns of London, *c.*1730
Sources: Ogilby and Morgan (1676), Parish Clerks (1732), Rocque (1747).

By 1710 the demand for internal transport had mounted to such a level that Parliament raised the permitted number of licensed coaches to 800, with a new licensing charge of 5s. per week. This latter change, to a weekly rate, may indicate that the demand for Hackney coaches was becoming more seasonal. Conveyance by sedan chair, first noted in London in the early seventeenth century, was regulated by the same legislation with the number of licensed chairs being set at 200; the following year this figure was raised promptly to 300.[54]

The coach drivers, however, were the social élite of all the transport occupations. Eighty-one were assessed as eligible to contribute to the City poll tax of 1692, while the only other categories of transport worker assessed were fifty-six carriers and forty-five workers — watermen, lightermen, hoymen, mariners — occupied in water transport.[55] Many more watermen dwelt outside the City in the suburbs to the east and on the south side of the river, but these areas of residence themselves denote the relative poverty of the water-men.[56] The identification of transport workers assessed for the poll tax who also contributed to the four shilling aid provides some directly comparable measures of wealth. The mean rent per annum of stagecoachmen was found to be £25 while their mean stock holding was valued at £50; the next highest group were the Hackney coachmen with mean values of £14 rent and £24 stock. All other transport workers, apart from the closely associated stable-keepers, fell well below these levels.[57]

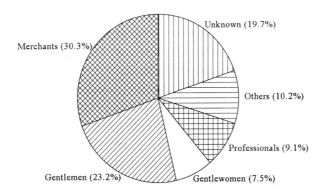

FIG. 2.7 The distribution of private coach ownership by social status within the City of London

Source: 1692 Poll Tax database.

Private horse and coach ownership

Horses and coaches were also privately owned, particularly in the wealthier parts of west London. Here there was space for stables and coach-houses and a greater incentive to use a horse or carriage to travel to property owned outside London. Coach ownership also helped to promote travel to outlying villages with recreational opportunities, such as Chelsea, Kensington, Hampstead, Islington and Hackney. The 1692 Poll Tax assessments provide a specific record of private and commercial coach ownership in the City, such coaches being the subject of a separate charge. The assessments reveal that there were 252 private and 112 commercial coaches. Thirty-seven of the latter belonged to Hackney coachmen, presumably an indication that most of London's 500 or so Hackney coachmen resided outside the City. Among the private owners

of coaches the overwhelmingly dominant groups were merchants and gentry (Fig. 2.7). Many of the latter may have been lawyers and the like, thus the proportion of coaches owned by those with professional occupations may have been greater than indicated.

The four shilling aid assessments of 1693–4 record a large number of coach-houses and stables. Many more such buildings probably existed but were not recorded since they were contained within the curtilage of the assessed household. The references nevertheless reveal certain localities which were distinctive for coach ownership and stabling. Coach-houses were especially prominent in the west of London and the maximum number for any ward, sixteen, was found in the relatively small Bedfordbury Ward in the parish of St Martin in the Fields (Fig.

TABLE 2.2
Stables assessed for taxation by aggregated area

Area	Stables	
	Number	Per cent
City within the walls	81	23.4
City without the walls	64	18.5
St Margaret Westminster	53	15.3
West End	92	26.6
Northern suburbs	38	11.0
Eastern suburbs	3	0.9
Eastern riverside suburbs	5	1.4
Metropolitan Middlesex	10	2.9
Total	346	100.0

Source: 1693–4 Aid database.

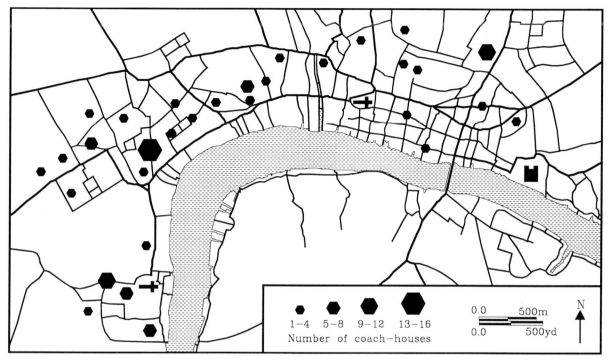

FIG. 2.8 The distribution of coach-houses assessed for taxation, grouped by ward

Source: 1693–4 Aid database.

Water transport

The alternative to land transport was to take to the Thames. The river was at this time possibly near its peak as a transport thoroughfare for London, movement by water being cheaper and often more easily accomplished than that undertaken by road. Despite the improvements in coaching services and road conditions through the formation of justice — and later turnpike — trusts, water transport remained supreme, with the majority of London's commercial imports and exports being landed or loaded at the wharves within the city. If ships were unable to land their cargoes directly at the London quayside, local lightermen would tranship their goods, upriver to the city, by barge. The lightermen also provided an illicit ferry service for mariners and others on the commercial stretches of the river, much to the anger of the Company of Watermen.[59]

The watermen provided what amounted to a water taxi service, transporting passengers from the north to south banks or from Westminster to the City and vice versa. Organised through the Company of Watermen they were, unusually, under the direct authority of the Corporation and Parliament. Despite earlier attempts at regulation it was not until 1696 that a well-organised system of licensing and control was introduced. Among these regulations were clauses ensuring that all watermen's wherries, and their hats, prominently displayed their licence number, and that they were only to wait for customers at the designated plying places. Eighty-eight such places were specified on both the north and south banks extending from

2.8). This area and the adjoining Charing Cross Ward held most of Westminster's recorded coach-houses and stables, some of which were built together in the form of mews. In Charing Cross Ward, for example, there were thirty-six separate payments of ground rent for space in the Blue Mews. This lay just to the south of Leicester Fields, and immediately north of the Royal Mews, which itself contained some 279 stable stalls and thirty-three coach-houses.[58] The total annual rent value for the Blue Mews was £147 5s. shared among twenty-six different tenants, giving a mean value of £4 2s.

each; thus mews stables were worth more than the overall mean rental value for London stables of £3 15s. The assessments record ninety-three coach-houses in all and 346 stables, not counting the stalls in either the Royal or Blue Mews. As with the coach-houses, the central area of Westminster contained most of the recorded stables, although the City within the walls was a close rival (Table 2.2). In both areas there is some evidence that concentrations of stabling tended to be located on the periphery of wealthy neighbourhoods, with relatively easy access to major routes or open ground.

Vauxhall in the west to Limehouse in the east. Their siting seems to reflect both the density of settlement and the public or private nature of the waterfront. The official rates to be charged by watermen were relatively comprehensive and were formally displayed at Westminster Hall, the Guildhall and the Royal Exchange, together with copies being posted at all public plying places (Table 2.3).[60]

TABLE 2.3
Some extracts from the rates of hire set by the Company of Watermen, 1671

Journey	Means of conveyance	
	Oars	Scullers
London to Wapping/Rotherhithe	6d.	3d.
Billingsgate to St Olave, Southwark	6d.	3d.
London Bridge to Westminster	6d.	3d.
Westminster to Lambeth	6d.	3d.
Temple/Blackfriars to Lambeth	8d.	4d.
London to Limehouse/Shadwell	1s. 0d.	6d.
London Bridge to Lambeth	1s. 0d.	6d.
London to Deptford/ Greenwich	1s. 6d.	–
London to Chelsea/Battersea	1s. 6d.	–
London to Blackwall	2s. 0d.	–
London to Woolwich	3s. 0d.	–
London to Gravesend	4s. 6d.	–
London to Kingston	5s. 0d.	–
London to Hampton Court	6s. 0d.	–
London to Windsor	14s. 0d.	–

Source: Humpherus (1887).

Ferries, such as the Horseferry at Westminster or that between the Isle of Dogs and Greenwich, served fixed routes at fixed prices (Table 2.4). A well-established ferry service operated by the watermen was the Long

Ferry or Tilt-Boat between Gravesend and Billingsgate Dock. Gravesend, just upstream of the Thames Estuary, was a more convenient anchorage for larger vessels or coastal transports wanting to avoid negotiation of the difficult and time-consuming upper reaches of the Pool of London. Hence a Tilt-Boat was to be found transferring passengers and commodities from Gravesend into the heart of the metropolis upon every tide.[61]

The end of the seventeenth century saw the commencement of significant changes in the pattern of urban transport. As was the case with many other craft organisations during this century, the watermen came to suffer increasingly from a steady growth in unlicensed competition. At the same time, a small but rapidly developing element of the water-borne trade was transferring to the roads in step with turnpiking and coaching improvements. Furthermore, the general increase in river traffic combined with the move to the roads introduced pressure for new bridge construction, a development the Thames watermen viewed with great alarm.

The passing of an Act in 1676 prohibiting Sunday traffic on the Thames was seen by the watermen as very detrimental to their trade. They had for most of the seventeenth century been fighting off what they saw as unfair and unlicensed competition. The Sunday ban was in many ways the last straw as it only worked successfully against licensed watermen; unlicensed operators could provide a Sunday service with little fear of prosecution. Once estab-

TABLE 2.4
Rates charged for ferry journeys, London, c.1708

Rates for the Horseferry between Westminster and Lambeth

Man and horse	2d.
Horse and chaze	1s. 0d.
Coach and two horses	1s. 6d.
Coach and six horses	2s. 6d.
Cart or wagon	2s. 0d.
Loaded cart	2s. 6d.

Rates for the Tilt-boat between Gravesend and London

Half a firkin	1d.
A whole firkin	2d.
A chest or trunk	6d.
One hundred weight of goods	4d.
A hogshead	2s. 0d.
Passengers	6d.
Hire of the whole boat	22s. 6d.

Source: Hatton (1708).

lished, illicit watermen were able to offer cheaper fares not only on Sundays but during the week, searches by the Company failing significantly to curtail their activities. The watermen's case against the prohibition of Sunday work was further strengthened in 1685 by a bill passed to regulate the services of Hackney coaches as this allowed 'a reasonable number' of Hackney coachmen to drive on a Sunday. It was not until 1700, however, that forty 'deserving' watermen were allowed to operate on Sundays, with a proportion of their enhanced fares going towards charitable purposes.[62]

The watermen suffered much depletion in numbers during the closing decades of the seventeenth century as a result of impressment for the Royal Navy. Although the watermen's apprentices were, by a statute of 1603, excused from the press this was, in practice, rarely observed. Consequently the Company of Watermen, through the offices of the mayor and aldermen, was forced to put pressure on the Crown to obtain effective protection. In 1694 William conceded and declared that no further licensed watermen should be pressed. Nevertheless the declining number of watermen resulted, in 1700, in the formation of the amalgamated Honourable Company of Watermen and Lightermen, a move that also recognised the economic problems watermen were experiencing as a result of much small-scale transport activity moving onto the roads.[63]

The increase in road traffic, particularly the regular local coaching services, was perceived by the watermen as having a deleterious effect on their occupation. The watermen to the west of London were particularly aggrieved; as early as 1673 one waterman was quoted as complaining that 'these [stagecoaches] are they that carry all the letters, little bundles, and passengers which before they were set up were carried by water'.[64] A further, and eventually far more damaging, threat they had to contend with was bridge building. In 1671 a bill was laid before Parliament to enable a bridge to be constructed at Putney. The bill was, albeit narrowly, rejected mainly through pressure from the watermen. An exchange in the Commons during the debate provides some indication of the interests both in favour and against new Thames bridges:[65]

| Mr Walker | If ill for Southwark, it is good for this end of the town where court and parliament are. At Paris there are many bridges — at Venice hundreds — we are still obstructing public things. |
| Mr Boscawen | If a bridge at Putney, why not at Lambeth, and more? And as for Paris where there are many bridges, there is no use for watermen at all … neither Middlesex nor Surrey desire it. |

Members of Parliament for the City remained ambivalent concerning the effect of new bridge construction upon the watermen, yet were keen defenders of the City's traditional monopolies which included the tolls gathered from London Bridge. Pressure to construct additional bridges in the metropolitan area became more intense in the early decades of the eighteenth century as movement by coach and carriage became commonplace and the dangers of water transport grew. The latter claimed to be a result of an increase in the activities of the press against the watermen, leaving only young boys and old men to operate the once numerous watermen's services. Eventually, between 1739 and 1748, a new bridge was constructed at Westminster, signalling the beginning of the end for the Thames watermen.[66]

London benefited from a topographic location and form that encouraged expansion towards the north and west, the increased population being amply supplied with wholesome water, most recently by the formation of a number of commercial waterworks undertakings. Drainage and waste disposal were dealt with to a greater or lesser degree of success by a variety of actions and innovations controlled through locally-based authority, while problems of transport congestion and regulation were approached in a similar, although more often metropolitan-wide, manner. London's infrastructure did, nevertheless, present a number of continuing problems, some of which would be resolved relatively soon after the 1690s while others remain a significant urban problem even today. The issue of transport by road or water, and the effect this might have on both metropolitan form and the employment of watermen, was gradually resolved throughout the eighteenth century as turnpike development and improvements in coach design changed the emphasis in passenger transport, moving transport issues away from questions of cost and re-focusing them upon issues of time. The problem of pollution, and specifically air pollution, however, remained unresolved into the twentieth century. Urban living was clearly recognised as a less healthy proposition than life in the countryside, but it is evident that the considerable social and economic benefits of metropolitan life, at least for the majority, outweighed any doubts citizens might have had concerning London's environmental quality.

Notes:

1. See Prince (1989), for an extensive and evocative description of the natural topography of the Thames and the London Basin.
2. Stow (1603), II, 200.

3. Evelyn (1661), 14.
4. The contour pattern was derived predominantly from the survey evidence detailed on the nineteenth-century Ordnance Survey maps; consequently the contours as mapped provide an indication of relative levels rather than any absolute measure.
5. Milne (1800).
6. Ray (1965), 6–8; Cox (1989), 3–11.
7. Reddaway (1940), 200–21.
8. Summerson (1978), 263.
9. Giuseppi (1908), 77–9.
10. Hollis (1978), 118.
11. The manner in which the public conduits were allowed to decay during the 1680s and 1690s was described by Mark Jenner in a paper ('Networks of water in London: 1500–1725') delivered to the Metropolitan History seminar, Institute of Historical Research, 1994.
12. Wilmott (1982), 3–5.
13. Stow (1603), I, 12–19.
14. Dickinson (1954), 9.
15. Rudden (1985).
16. Williamson (1936), 43–93.
17. Dickinson (1954), 24–8.
18. CLRO, Ms 40/62.
19. John Aubrey, in recounting the life of Sir Hugh Middleton, comments that the New River Company could supply houses with water for no more than two days a week. Clark (1898), II, 60.
20. The City's four laystalls were located at Dowgate, Puddle Dock, Whitefriars Dock and Mile End: Weinstein (1991), 31–2.
21. Weinstein (1991), 30–1.
22. Weinstein (1991), 29–40.
23. Rothstein (1961), 144–8.
24. Brimblecombe (1987), 22–6.
25. Evelyn (1661), 15–18.
26. Petty (1662), 41.
27. Graunt (1662), 10–11, 24.
28. Brimblecombe (1987), 58–60, analysing Gadbury (1691).
29. Bowler and Brimblecombe (1990), 159.
30. This assumes a walking pace of around six kilometres (four miles) per hour.
31. See below, pp. 31–4, regarding local carrying services.

32. Borsay (1989), 162; Pepys (1660–9), I, 53; Stow (1603), I, 90.
33. Shesgreen (1990).
34. Chartres (1977a), 30–1.
35. Bowen (1720), 1; Ogilby (1675), plate 1.
36. Hanson (1989), 37–9.
37. The majority of alleys and yards have been omitted from Fig. 2.3 for the sake of clarity.
38. Hanson (1989), 22–42, calculates a dead-end to thoroughfare ratio of 1:0.853 for the City of London, based on an analysis of Ogilby and Morgan (1676).
39. Masters (1974), 39–44.
40. Evelyn (1666), 33–4; Reddaway (1940), 288–94.
41. Pawson (1977), 341–3. The two turnpike roads to encroach upon the metropolis were: Enfield to Shoreditch, 1713; and London to East Grinstead, 1718.
42. Bennett (1952), 37; Maitland (1756), 453; Spence (1996), 9–26.
43. Mathias (1959), 6–9.
44. Bennett (1952), 78–9.
45. Baddeley (1921), 243–6.
46. Bennett (1952), 36–9. It is possible that certain aspects of this one-way system were modified by the widening of streets as part of the Great Fire rebuilding, however, it appears that the restrictions on empty carts entering Thames Street were not relaxed.
47. Stern (1960), 3–15.
48. Chartres (1977a), 34–7.
49. For a discussion of the problems encountered in attempting to establish the number and frequency of carriers' services for this period, see Gerhold (1988), 397–404.
50. Chartres (1977a), 29–33.
51. Parish Clerks (1732), 62.
52. Statute: 5 & 6 William & Mary c. 22 (1694); Parish Clerks (1732), 403–5.
53. Pawson (1977), 287–93.
54. Humpherus (1887), II, 86.
55. 1692 Poll Tax database. Although 135 porters were included within these assessments they were likely to be predominantly agents contracting-out porterage work. The assessed porters represented no more than two to three per cent of those employed within the sector, while the assessed coach drivers are considered to have represented some ten per cent of all such licensed drivers.

56. Boulton (1987a), 69–70.
57. Alexander (1989a), 216. The wharfingers and horse-coursers included by Alexander as transport occupations in his table 7.02, have been excluded from this calculation on the grounds that their higher rent and stock values were associated with property holding and dealing and not directly with transport activities.
58. Colvin (1976), 207–10.
59. Humpherus (1887), I, 303.
60. Humpherus (1887), I, 313–16.
61. Hatton (1708), 786; Humpherus (1887), I, 208–9, 232, 315, 353–4, 377–8.
62. Humpherus (1887), I, 351; II, 11–12.
63. Humpherus (1887), II, 6–8.
64. Humpherus (1887), I, 320.
65. The result of the vote being 54 in favour, 67 against: Humpherus (1887), I, 311–12.
66. Summerson (1978), 113–16.

3. Land Use and the Built Environment

The most immediate impact the late seventeenth-century metropolis had on any visitor was that of the almost unbroken expanse of buildings and structures extending some eight kilometres (five miles) or more along the north bank of the Thames. As Defoe put it,

> When I speak of London, now in the modern acceptance, you expect I shall take in all that vast mass of buildings, reaching from Blackwall in the east, to Tothill Fields in the west.[1]

That impressionistic statement, however, does not reveal the detailed forms and functions of the urban area, the differences between one part of the city and another, or the relationship of the urban core to its periphery and to the countryside beyond. One way of tackling those issues is by analysing the various uses to which London's land surface was put. By defining the broad outlines of the cityscape in this way, the detailed investigations of particular neighbourhoods will be more readily understood.

The uses to which land might be put were numerous, yet they can be grouped in five broad categories reflecting the functional processes of city life and its topographical identity: the built-up residential area; land devoted primarily to industrial use; areas devoted to intensive market-gardening; arable and pasture land; and areas of marsh liable to flooding. Most of these categories present problems of definition, partly on account of the available evidence, but more especially because in seventeenth-century London many buildings, sites and tracts of land were characterised by a combination of uses.

In an age when many people lived above, behind or close to their place of work most residential areas, whether densely built-up or more spaciously laid out, were characterised by an intermingling of residential, commercial and manufacturing uses. The degree of intermixture varied from area to area, but the detailed pattern, which could only be portrayed by a map of very fine calibre, is in any case only fitfully revealed by the available sources. A partial exception to this common picture is represented by those areas to the west of the City which, to an increasing extent over the seventeenth century, came to be characterised by fashionable streets of newly-erected houses occupied solely as residences by those of high social standing.[2] The four shilling aid provides some help in defining these neighbourhoods, which it should be noted often stood cheek by jowl with streets of a more heterogeneous character. Some industrial areas of more or less uniform functions also became increasingly evident in the later seventeenth century, most notably the riverside zones associated with shipbuilding and related trades.

By applying a broad definition which includes, or more accurately ignores, the relatively small spaces devoted to workshops, commerce and transport, some indication of the area potentially available for residential use can be given.[3] Maps dating from around the 1690s provide the main source for this delineation, which first defines the extent of the built-up area, and then eliminates those internal areas which had a predominantly non-residential use.[4] Among the identifiable sites in the latter group are rope walks, tenter grounds, burial grounds and other larger open spaces such as markets and squares. The resulting classification represents the net residential area, and is outlined in red on Fig. 3.1. While the total area of the built-up extent of the metropolis was in the region of 920 hectares (2,300 acres) the measure of net residential area for the same extent amounted to the smaller figure of some 740 hectares (1,830 acres).[5]

Other smaller open spaces cannot be identified when working at such a large scale; nevertheless, the extent of, and degree of access to, open space is important in understanding the particular character of any given district of the metropolis.[6] Much of this open space within the built-up area had a multiplicity of uses. Cheapside, for example, was a broad transport thoroughfare which gave access to houses and other streets, but also, to varying degrees at different times, served as a market and as a ceremonial way. Some open areas had a more restricted range of uses. These included Moorfields, designated by the City authorities for recreational

41

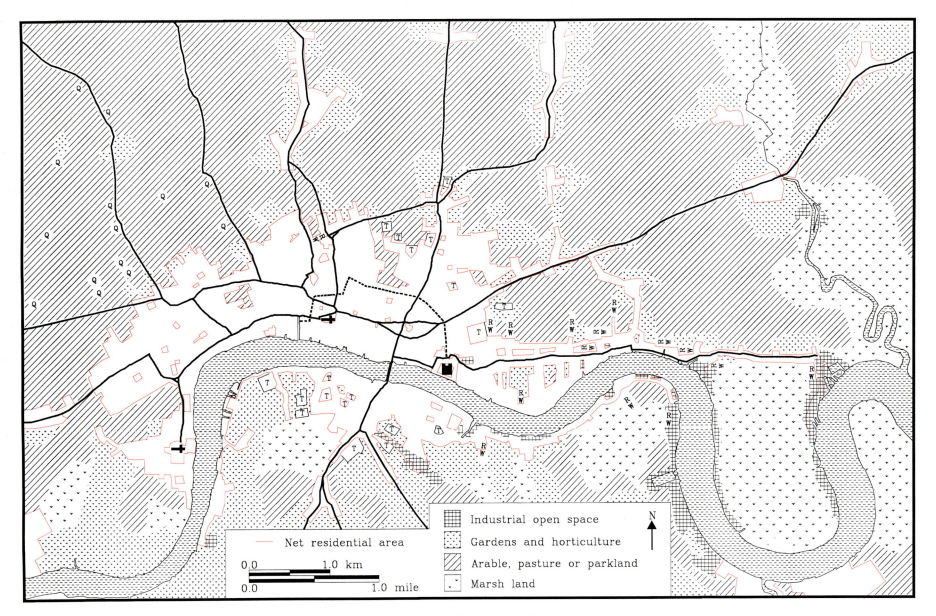

FIG. 3.1 Land use in the metropolitan area
Sources: Milne (1800); Ogilby and Morgan (1676); Rocque (1747). (Q=Quarry; RW=Rope walk; T=Tenter ground)

use, and those reserved areas such as St James's Park. Sites such as these might be loosely defined, in terms of contemporary land use analysis, as recreational open space.[7]

While those areas were in some senses public, other open recreational spaces, notably gardens, were more clearly defined as private.[8] Within the built-up area private gardens proliferated in the newer suburbs, particularly where planned property division had been undertaken with a more expansive attitude. In Spitalfields and other similar districts, gardens were restricted to the rear of houses, and in many cases probably served as little more than private yards. In the new, and more socially elevated, western suburbs gardens were found at the rear of houses, but also, significantly, immediately in front of the regular, imposing terraced facades. While these front gardens presented the intended appearance of openness, they were enclosed so as to prevent intrusion by people and animals. An emphasis on such fences and walls was a new fashion in the demarcation of urban space.[9] Good examples were to be found at Lincoln's Inn Fields and along the south side of Pall Mall.

Outside the built-up area the main source for defining land use has been Rocque's map of London in 1747. Rocque used a range of symbols to indicate different ground conditions or uses, and that information forms the basis of much of the cartographic identification of peripheral land use that follows.[10]

Two types of open industrial site immediately outside the central built-up area are readily identifiable on the maps: tenter grounds and rope walks. Tenter grounds were generally clustered close to cloth-manufacturing or cloth-finishing neighbourhoods, most notably at the limits of the built-up area to the north and east of the City and to the south and west of Southwark. Tenters — fixed frames on which cloths were stretched after fulling, dyeing or other processes — occupied long narrow strips of ground, known as runs, and were often grouped in parallel rows on larger square or rectangular plots. The particular siting of the most intensive groupings of tenter grounds might be explained by reference to the location of numerous clothworkers and dyers on the north bank of the Thames and in the eastern part of the city.[11] Some regard may also have been given to the direction of the prevailing winds in an attempt to avoid the contamination of cloth with coal soot.

Such considerations of pollution did not affect the location of rope walks, where hemp fibres were twisted and stretched into rope. This product was a major requirement of the maritime sector and hence most rope walks were found close to the river and to the east of the City, especially north of the Thames. The single rope walk identified to the north of the City in Clerkenwell may have produced the less substantial rope used in the packing or carrying trades rather than maritime cordage. Rope walks could be up to a quarter of a mile in length but tended to be no more than a few yards in width. Cartographic and pictorial evidence

suggests that the walks were often contained within one or more rows of trees, possibly to provide shade in the summer and to act as a wind break in winter.[12]

Moving downriver to the east and across the river to the south, a number of concentrated industrial sites could be identified: they are defined as industrial open space on Fig. 3.1. The most significant functional category within this group was that of shipyards and docks. Obviously such features lay on the waterfront but varied greatly in size from small-scale private yards nearer the built-up centre to large-scale industrial undertakings, such as the East India Company's Blackwall Yard, some ten kilometres (six miles) downriver from London Bridge. These installations often exploited marginal land at the water's edge, involving the construction of docks or reclamation. The frequent manifestation of waterfront timber yards provided a similar functional use for such land. Timber yards were important points in the supply and distribution networks for fuel and building material.

A range of other industrial land uses provide less tangible evidence. Glass works were found in small concentrations both to the east and west of the central urban area. Here, as in the case of foundries which are not easily identified from cartographic sources, it is likely that the noxious nature of the processes involved ensured that such activities were unlikely to be found in the city centre.[13] The highly noxious nature of tanning provides the final example of an industrial concentration, in this case forming virtually a dedicated industrial suburb lying in fields well supplied with water to the south-east of the built-up core of Southwark. Once again, the vicinity was strategically positioned down wind of the main residential area.[14]

From the main cartographic sources it is possible broadly to identify areas devoted to intensive market gardening and orchards, indicated as gardens and horticulture on Fig. 3.1. The supply of vegetables, fruit and other perishable horticultural products was an important undertaking for the many market gardening establishments found in the immediate hinterland of London, a practice with its origin in the Middle Ages.[15] By around 1700, cabbages, carrots, peas, beans, onions and asparagus were all grown for the London market in Surrey and that part of Middlesex to the west of the city.[16] Close to London, market gardens were mainly to be found in the areas of lighter and well-watered soils south of the metropolis. There were also less extensive areas of gardening on the heavier soils to the north and east. In all cases it was important that the markets of London were within easy reach, and the extension of market gardening further west in the eighteenth century stayed close to the line of water transport in order to maintain this temporal proximity.

Horticultural enterprise close to the built-up area benefited greatly from manuring with urban waste, by which means some hitherto intractable soils were made fertile. City refuse was also used to replace gravel extracted from beneath market garden sites predominantly to the south of the Thames. The gravel was sold to ships in the Pool as ballast before the resulting holes were backfilled with richly organic waste in order to manure the topsoil which was subsequently reinstated.[17]

Although Rocque's 1747 map can be used to identify areas of general agricultural land use, the scale of Fig. 3.1 prevents a more detailed differentiation of such use being undertaken. Arable fields, pasture and parkland cannot generally be distinguished, though some broad comment on such peripheral land use can be made. The heavier soils to the north and north-west of London were generally exploited for dairying. This pasture district extended from the City margins to the Hampstead-Highgate ridge, just to the north of the study area. Beyond, the agricultural use of land was more mixed with an increasing proportion of arable farming. The extent of the dairy pasture zone reflects both the soil conditions and its accessibility from the city. Although few beef cattle were reared within metropolitan Middlesex and Surrey, meadow land and marsh in the lower Lea Valley, the Isle of Dogs, Rotherhithe, and elsewhere were an important resource for the fattening of livestock which were to be sold in the City's markets.[18] These marshy areas also contained osier beds, supplying the raw material for the basketwork which was required in great quantity throughout the metropolis.

In the immediate metropolitan area the incidence of marginal land was relatively limited: land this close to London was in essence too valuable to be relegated to a marginal status. Two particular areas with a marginal character were nevertheless identified. An area of rough and boggy ground lay immediately to the west of the parish of St Margaret Westminster, and St George's Fields in Surrey presented similar ground conditions. Such areas would probably have been used for more general rough grazing before being engulfed in later urban expansion.

The enclosed parks associated with royal and aristocratic residences, but to an extent serving also as a resource for a wider community, were distinctive features of London's immediate hinterland. For the most part, however, they lay to the west of the metropolis, especially within reach of the Thames, and beyond the area shown in Fig. 3.1. It has already been stated that it is difficult within such a broad overview to distinguish such parkland from more general fields and pastures, though it can of course be argued that in terms of the form of land use such a differentiation would in any case be redundant.

One notable land use feature close to London was the extraction of clay and gravel by means of quarrying. The digging of brick-earth and clay for the manufacture of bricks took place first on the Taplow terrace, often close to the sites of construction.[19] Here as much as 1.2 metres (four feet) of brick-earth sub-soil would be removed to provide the raw material from which early bricks were made; as many as ten million per hectare (four million per acre) could be produced.[20] As the built-up area expanded, clay was obtained from further afield. Rocque shows that by 1747 a large number of quarry pits had been opened up to the north-west of the metropolis. These clay deposits contained the basic material from which bricks were manufactured, ash and other waste from London being added to the clay to improve its firing qualities.[21] Less is known about the extraction of gravel and sand. Nevertheless, gravel for use in construction appears to have been dug close to the city from an early date and by 1700, as we have seen, the removal of gravel was also associated with the extension of market gardening activity.

Londoners put the land of their city and its environs to a great variety of uses. Chief amongst these was obviously the built-up area of the urban core, although the identification in detail of particular land use within this area is problematic. Outside this core the uses of land are easier to define: industrial sites, market gardens, orchards and grazing were all present within the study area.

Near the limit of the built-up area open land intermixed with buildings on the urban margin. This zone was characterised by its wide variety of uses and its subdivision into small units. The urban fringe, as in the case of many other cities in many different periods, presented an untidy appearance which offended some contemporaries. Defoe, for example, identified such areas as in need of regulation, not to protect them from over building but in order that they might assume a neater and more symmetrical form:

for the better regulating the form of this mighty building [i.e. London] by forbidding the extent of the building in some particular places, where they too much run it out of shape, and letting the more indented parts swell out on the north and south side a little, to balance the length, and bring the form of the whole more near to that of a circle.[22]

Such suggestions were not taken up. Instead, London in the 1690s was a rapidly developing urban area where building was regulated to no more than a limited, yet growing, extent and where, for a variety of reasons, some open spaces inherited from earlier periods were preserved and increasingly valued. Overall, the metropolis appeared to have a well-balanced relationship with its immediate hinterland where the supply and servicing of its inhabitants created a distinctive landscape of agrarian, industrial, and recreational character.[23]

BUILDING DENSITY

Within the built-up area there were evidently wide variations in population and building density. The conjunction in most neighbourhoods of residences and workplaces within single buildings or plots makes it impossible to establish consistent measures of purely residential density. It is also clear that calculating densities based on population figures is only strictly possible for parishes within the City of London.[24] Nor is it feasible to establish a comprehensive measure of the density of houses or buildings across the metropolis. Nevertheless, the four shilling aid assessments provide material for calculating the density of households. Households,

of course, varied in both the number of their members and in the number of households per building.[25] Although such variables cannot be accounted for in any consistent manner, the distribution of the 57,315 households recorded in the 1693–4 Aid database does reveal important variations in the density of the social and physical fabric across the whole of the metropolitan area.

Household density

The density of households was calculated with reference to the net residential area (that is the built-up area less that occupied by squares, markets and other open spaces: Fig. 3.1). This was used to supply a figure of households per residential hectare (hh/ha) for most of the metropolitan area. Four of the analytical areas representing parts of rural Middlesex had to be eliminated from the exercise since calculating the built-up areas and defining households within their assessments proved too complex a process to provide reliable figures.[26] The mean household density for the study area was 84.7 households per residential hectare. While in general the highest household densities were to be found toward the centre of the metropolis and the lowest on the periphery, the pattern was not an uncomplicated concentric one (Fig. 3.2). The arrangement is probably at its least uniform at the level of highest density.

In the City and its immediate environs two types of areas of high concentrations of households can be identified. Areas on the periphery were evidently poor

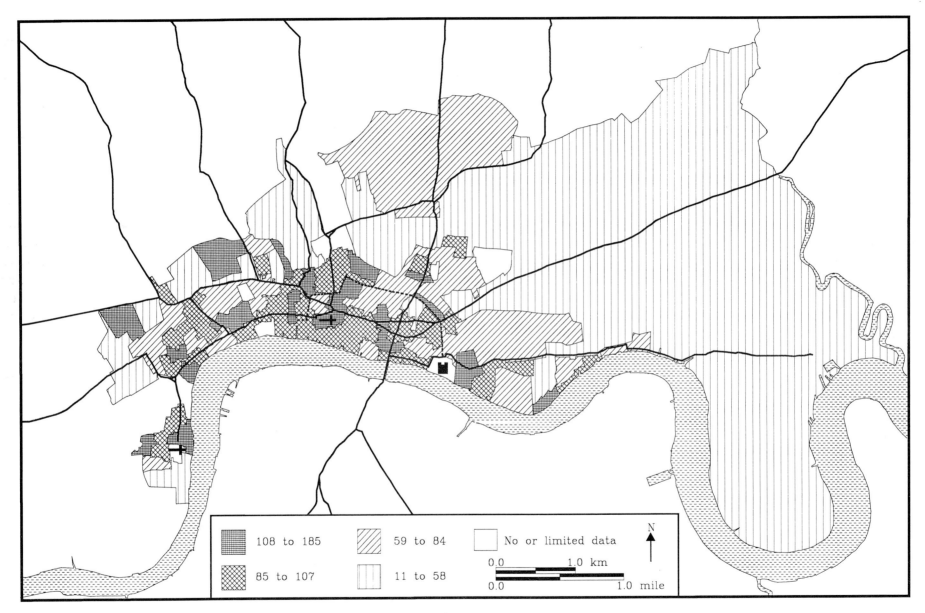

FIG. 3.2 Household density: number of households per residential hectare
Source: 1693–4 Aid database.

Legend:
108 to 185
85 to 107
59 to 84
11 to 58
No or limited data

0.0 — 1.0 km
0.0 — 1.0 mile

and contained both high densities of very small houses and many cases where several households would be crowded into a single building. The precinct of St Katherine by the Tower, with numerous small houses, had an extremely high density of 185 households per hectare. Other immediately extramural areas probably had a similar character: Houndsditch (135 hh/ha), outside Bishopsgate (158 hh/ha), outside Ludgate (131 hh/ha), and in the Smithfield area (122 hh/ha). In sharp social contrast, but with very similar densities, were several central districts within the City walls. These included the commercial neighbourhood around the Royal Exchange and Cornhill (112 hh/ha), where some of the City's most substantial mercantile households dwelled.[27] This area of high household density extended to include another along the line of Cannon Street and Eastcheap (113 hh/ha), a different type of commercial district probably characterised by the less substantial houses of prosperous merchants, retailers and manufacturers.[28] A similar social group probably predominated in the other intramural district of high household density which extends from around St Paul's (140 hh/ha) north to Cripplegate (115 hh/ha in the Wood Street area). Parts of this neighbourhood, however, included poorer, crowded households in the precinct of St Martin le Grand (153 hh/ha).

Areas within the walls characterised by low household densities tended to be peripheral to the main routes running through the City, although the area of lowest density in Bishopsgate Ward Within (57 hh/ha), is probably explained by the inclusion of Gresham College and the gardens and yards of a few substantial houses, company halls and churches. The areas around the Guildhall (77 hh/ha) and along Tower Street (76 hh/ha) probably had a similar character, in addition to which the latter area contained a significant number of warehouses. The riverside area around and to the east of Dowgate may have also owed its relatively low household density (79 hh/ha) to the occurrence of warehousing and perhaps industrial establishments such as breweries and dye-houses.[29]

To the east of the City there were several areas where household densities equalled those within the walls. The predominantly industrial district immediately east of St Katherine's precinct had a density (98 hh/ha) similar to that which prevailed over much of the City, although the extramural households may have been smaller.[30] Further east there was clearly an independent focus of dense settlement on the river at Wapping and Shadwell, the place of residence for many sailors and workers in the maritime trades. The area near Wapping Dock (110 hh/ha) was probably a focus for river-borne commercial activity.

In 1650 Shadwell comprised some 703 houses[31] while by the 1690s the number of households was 1,461,[32] a rise from fifty-two houses per hectare to a more densely settled level of seventy-three. What is significant in this comparison is the apparently limited impact that the more expansive rebuilding of large parts of the parish, following fires in 1673 and 1682, had on the density of inhabitation, despite an enlargement of the parish's built-up area over the intervening forty-five years.[33] It is clear that Shadwell and the adjacent Wapping waterfront formed an economically attractive district in which to settle.

To the west of the city in Westminster some similar patterns can be identified. There were areas of high household density which appear to have been focal points for commercial activity, most notably along Fleet Street and the Strand as far as Whitehall. Other high density areas were peripheral to these business-centred districts. The former included the mixed commercial and residential areas around Hungerford Market (110 hh/ha) and west of Covent Garden (Bedfordbury Ward: 118 hh/ha), the central part of St Margaret Westminster (111 hh/ha) and the crowded area around Aldwych to the east of Drury Lane (125 hh/ha). Several of these districts were adjacent to those in the next category with densities of between eighty-five and 107 households per hectare. Three areas can be identified: to the north and east of Covent Garden, a manufacturing and retailing area (90 hh/ha); further south centred on the mews area north of Whitehall (100 hh/ha); and an extensive part of St Margaret Westminster (87 hh/ha). In all these areas there was probably some intermixing of wealthier and poorer households.

Close proximity to the line of the unsavoury river Fleet, not unsurprisingly, provides high densities with Saffron Hill at 114 households per hectare and the area along the Fleet Ditch having as many as 131 households per hectare. Westminster also shows areas of overcrowded poverty: an area to the west of St Margaret Westminster (130 hh/ha), the commercial areas around Hungerford Market and Bedfordbury Ward (averaging 114 hh/ha), the commercial focus north of the Strand and into Drury Lane (averaging 125 hh/ha) and two concentrations lying to the north. These last two areas are difficult to explain but may represent areas of newer buildings constructed in a more concentrated form and providing housing for new tenants in a more intensive manner. They were in the northern half of St James Westminster (117 hh/ha) and the area around Lamb's Conduit Fields (124 hh/ha). The latter area was promoted by the developer Nicholas Barbon during the 1680s and early 90s. Each of his houses was furnished with at least six rooms, on three storeys, with the addition of a cellar.[34] It would seem that, despite a relatively low density of houses at the time of construction, such buildings were subject to a degree of multiple occupancy from the start.

Some parts of the western suburbs had particularly low household densities indicating either scattered housing of a semi-rural nature, as in the southern parts of St Margaret Westminster (35 hh/ha), or districts of more substantial or aristocratic houses as in Bloomsbury, near Montague House (29 hh/ha), and in the neighbourhood of Portugal Street and St James's Square (45 hh/ha). Districts such as Clerkenwell (29 hh/ha), Finsbury (39 hh/ha) and the more rural areas east of London (47 hh/ha), despite some localised concentrations of houses, had very low densities overall. It is noteworthy that in Hoxton and Shoreditch densities were somewhat

higher (72 hh/ha), this a result of the crowding of buildings close to the margins of the primary roads running north to Dalston and Hackney.

While no evidence is available for household densities in Southwark and Lambeth at the end of the seventeenth century, figures are available for 1678.[35] The built-up area, composed of St Mary's, St Olave's, St Saviour's and St Thomas's parishes, exhibited a low mean density of thirty-eight households per residential hectare.[36] Despite the poor quality of much land for building purposes, so limiting the settled area, it is evident that this district was among the least densely inhabited of London's suburbs.

Household densities thus provide a valuable indicator of the physical and social characteristics of neighbourhoods within the metropolis. Areas distinguished by above average density tended to be grouped around focal points of business and commerce, both in the City and the parishes of Westminster. These areas seem to have been characterised by relatively large households and generally high population densities. Some peripheral areas of high density were explained by poverty and the presence of low quality housing stock. Many such households would have been small so that in terms of population density these areas would not have ranked so highly. A new feature of the metropolitan landscape in the late seventeenth century, created largely during the building boom of the 1680s, were the outlying areas of high density where houses were concentrated in

terraced rows. Multiple occupancy of these sizeable properties acted to increase the household and population densities of these areas.

LAND VALUES

Each of the rack-rents listed in the four shilling aid assessments represents the value of a piece of land and the buildings standing on it, held by a single occupier or, in the case of multiple occupancy, the value of that part of a house in which a householder lived. Such values were determined by the underlying demand for the site and by the density and quality of the buildings which stood upon it, all factors which it is difficult to account for individually.[37] Here these values are defined collectively as 'land values'. By aggregating the rack-rents for each analytical area it is possible to determine the broad pattern of variation in land values within the metropolis in terms of value per hectare. These values can be considered in their wider context through the use of comparable valuations for the whole of England and for the adjacent county of Middlesex.

The value of London in a national and local context

The gross annual value of rent for all property within metropolitan London (calculated on the basis of those parishes within the study area for which four shilling aid assessments survive) was £994,643 16s. Over half that sum was represented by rents generated within the administrative limits of the City of London (£452,794 3s.). The gross

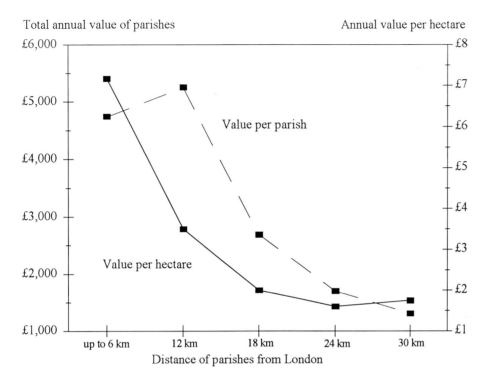

Fig. 3.3 Land values for Middlesex parishes grouped according to the distance of the parish church from London: values per parish and per hectare

Source: CLRO, Assessment Box 40 and 42.

a sharp fall off with increasing distance from the city in value per parish and even more so in value per hectare (Fig. 3.3). Grouped in bands of six-kilometre (four-mile) intervals these values ranged from £5,260 per parish to £1,305 per parish. But a more informative indicator of land value is that measured by hectares. These figures range from a high of £7 3s. 6d. per hectare (£2 18s. per acre), for parishes in the innermost band, to £1 12s. per hectare (13s. per acre) for parishes between eighteen and twenty-four kilometres (eleven and fifteen miles) away from London.[39]

Distance and transport cost from London probably had a marked impact on land values. A return journey to London of thirty or so kilometres (20 miles) was probably at the limit that could be accomplished within a single day, although the usual distance may have been less. The appearance of low mean land values, between one and two pounds per hectare, beyond a distance of twelve kilometres (seven miles) from London seems to support this. The slight increase in land values in the furthest band to £1 15s. per hectare (14s. per acre) may be explained by increased access to water transport, in the form of the rivers Colne and Lea, marginally reducing costs. Some further support for this view that London's impact on land values was especially strong within a day's journey of the city is provided by Milne's land use map of 1800, which places the westward limit of market gardening activity near Hampton Court, some twenty-one kilometres (thirteen miles) from the centre of the metropolis, presumably the furthest from which it

figure for metropolitan London represents twelve per cent of the total land value of England as assessed for the land tax (approximately £8,280,000). The value per hectare for the country as a whole was about 14s. (6s. per acre), and that for the metropolitan London study area was £1,356 (£549 per acre).[38] The value of the urban core of London's metropolitan area, comprising the contiguously built-up elements of the City of London, Westminster and a small part of Middlesex (see Fig. 3.1) was £960,034, or eighty-

two per cent of the value of the entire study area. The mean value per hectare of the urban core stood at £2,073 7s. (£840 per acre).

The metropolis had an impact on the value of all land in its vicinity, whether or not it was built upon. That impact can be measured in the four shilling aid valuations for the Middlesex parishes beyond the metropolitan area. These have been grouped according to their distance from London, and display

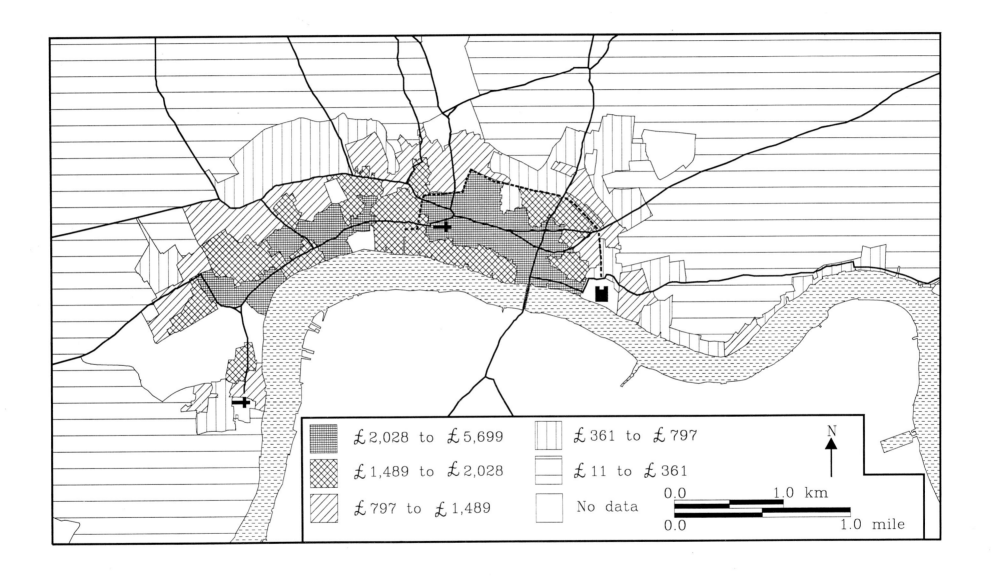

FIG. 3.4 Land values: rack-rent pounds per hectare
Source: 1693–4 Aid database.

£ 2,028 to £ 5,699	£ 361 to £ 797
£ 1,489 to £ 2,028	£ 11 to £ 361
£ 797 to £ 1,489	No data

was possible to have immediate access to the London markets with fresh produce.[40]

Metropolitan land/property values

Within the study area there was a wide range in the values per hectare calculated for the analytical areas, from £11 per hectare (£4 per acre) in the parishes of Bromley-by-Bow, Poplar and Blackwall to the east of London, to £5,699/ha (£2,306/acre) for the densely built-up central commercial district of Cornhill. The extramural district of Spitalfields had the lowest value for a built-up area forming part of the urban core at £462/ha (£187/acre), while the mean land value across the entire study area was £1,356/ha (£549/acre). The main factors determining the differences in land value were probably the density of buildings and the commercial value of the site, although the influence of these factors cannot be measured directly. In presenting an initial overview the values have been grouped by quintiles, to avoid skewing the picture toward the highest values (Fig. 3.4).

The map records a more clearly concentric pattern than that for household densities. The areas of highest value were associated in the main with busy commercial and retailing districts extending along major roads. There were two or three such areas, with several distinct foci: inside the City walls, and along Fleet Street and the Strand. Within the City walls, areas in the uppermost inter-quintile group were ranged along the main east-west axis extending from Newgate along Cheapside to Cornhill and Lombard Street, then down Gracechurch Street to London Bridge, and along Thames Street towards the Custom House and the Tower. The mean land value for this area was £3,290/ha (£1,444/acre).

The principal focus within this area was the neighbourhood of the Royal Exchange and Cornhill, the heart of the City's emerging central business district, where the highest land values in London were found, £5,699/ha (£2,306/acre). This high figure is partly explained by the presence of the largest single rent payment found within the metropolis, the sum of £1,458 p.a. for half of the Royal Exchange, which was bisected by a ward boundary. However, the desire of City merchants and dealers to occupy the densely-packed, high-quality houses within the immediate vicinity of the Exchange played a large part in generating the very high values.

A second major focus was Cheapside, especially towards its western end which was associated with the dealing and manufacturing activities of goldsmiths and luxury textile trades such as mercers, silkmen and haberdashers.[41] Here land values were found to be £3,767/ha (£1,524/acre). Values were slightly lower in the eastern part of the street, £3,465/ha (£1,403/acre), which was identified with those in the legal professions and warehousemen.[42] Values were also somewhat lower west of Cheapside towards Newgate and Aldersgate, £3,080/ha (£1,247/acre), an area of lower value retail trade and relatively crowded less valuable housing. A further area reached north from Cheapside to Cripplegate, which lay in the lower range of the highest quintile, £2,213/ha (£897/acre). This district was associated with fine metal working — gold- and silver-smithing, and wire-drawing — and the wholesaling of textiles around Wood Street, £2,215/ha (£897/acre), and Blackwell Hall, £2,285/ha (£925/acre).[43]

The Gracechurch Street axis was characterised by a high degree of commercial and retailing activity which provided slightly lower values, £3,270/ha (£1,324/acre), than those found along the eastern extent of Thames Street. Here high values were clearly associated with the handling of international trade and with the commodity markets at Billingsgate and elsewhere, £3,950/ha (£1,599/acre). This pattern of high-value areas within the walls broadly resembles that which can be calculated for 1638, with perhaps two notable differences which seem to reflect the enhanced role that large-scale commerce now played in the City's life.[44] Since 1638 the Wood Street area appears to have changed from being one of relatively low land value for the City to one of relatively high value, and the same development is more clearly apparent for Thames Street, downstream of London Bridge.

In the eastern part of the City, away from the central business area, land values declined sharply. A zone of land in the second highest inter-quintile group extending from Broad Street around to the south of Fenchurch Street displayed relatively homogeneous values with a mean of £1,792/ha (£726/acre). Apart from its lesser density of

FIG. 3.5 View of St Mary le Bow and Cheapside, 1757, demonstrating high commercial density of post-Great Fire rebuilding
Source: Guildhall Library.

buildings, it is noteworthy that in this zone the building stock was old, being the only area within the walls to have survived the Great Fire. This district also included the densely-settled strip of land outside the City wall along Houndsditch. The areas of lowest value within the walls were Coleman Street Ward, £785/ha (£318/acre), which also included open land beyond the walls, and to the south of Aldgate, £1,489/ha (£603/acre). This concentric fall off in values continued beyond the City walls to the north and east.

The riverfront district, upstream from London Bridge, handled river-borne trade within the walls and had a mixed industrial and residential character. The mean value of land in this zone was £1,748/ha (£708/acre). The Fleet valley area to the west of the City had a similar character, with a mean of £1,835/ ha (£743/acre). The marginally higher value for this extramural district, was a product of the notably higher value of land in the immediate vicinity of Smithfield Market, £1,989/ha (£805/acre).

Further to the west, along Fleet Street and the Strand, land values increased. Here there appear to have been two distinct areas of high values. The more easterly with an overall mean value of £2,500/ha (£1,012/acre) extended from Fetter Lane to Drury Lane, and additionally included the Covent Garden Piazza. The form of this area may reflect the influence of the Strand as an important commercial artery and also more localised concentrations of activity around the end of Chancery Lane, the church of St Clement Danes and Covent Garden.

The more westerly area, focusing upon the Strand Upper and Exchange Wards of St Martin in the Fields was of even greater value, with a mean of £3,114/ha (£1,261/acre). The area included the Royal Mews and Hungerford Market. It may in reality have extended south of Charing Cross to include neighbourhoods for which data are missing, but values nevertheless fell off in the direction of Westminster. The Earl of Salisbury's New Exchange, with shops on three floors and a total rental value of £5,363 13s. p.a., made an important contribution to the character of this quarter and its high values, which were similar to those in the eastern part of Cheapside in the City.

The zone which lay between these two commercial districts in the western suburbs had a lower value of £1,881/ha (£762/acre), probably owing to a more residential character. To the west of the Haymarket and around St James's Square land values were similar, averaging £1,768/ha (£716/acre). Despite the presence of individual houses of high quality and value, the lower density of building and a greater distance from the commercial centres clearly kept the overall value of land relatively low. Similar factors contributed to the character around the southern end of Whitehall, within St Margaret Westminster, where the mean value was £1,672/ha (£677/acre).

In general, areas with land values falling within the next class down, between £797/ha and £1489/ha (£322/acre and £603/acre), were found adjacent to those in the two highest classes, forming a circle around the metropolis. They clearly illustrate the principle that land values fell away with increasing

distance from the commercial centres, but nevertheless such areas differed in character. North of Westminster Abbey was a relatively densely settled district with an important local market, at £1,215/ha (£492/acre). To the north and south of Piccadilly, in St James Westminster, lay a spacious aristocratic neighbourhood, at £1,195/ha (£484/acre). In Soho and along the south side of High Holborn, despite variations in the density and age of buildings, and areas of lower social status, land values were relatively homogenous with a mean of £1,260/ha (£510/acre).

East of Gray's Inn Road was a further area in this class, extending from Hatton Garden, around Smithfield, and to Aldersgate and Cripplegate. This zone was near to the limit of the built-up area and its relatively high mean value of £1,144/ha (£463/acre) probably reflected a high density of housing. Further to the east, values within this class occur at the limit of the City between the high density area of Houndsditch and the lower values exhibited in Spitalfields. Here the mean land value was £1,158/ha (£469/acre). Further south the precinct of St Katherine by the Tower and the neighbourhood of East Smithfield had a relatively low mean value of £925/ha (£375/acre). This was despite a very high density of occupation, and presumably reflects the poor quality of housing in the area.

Areas found in the next most valuable category, £361/ ha to £797/ha (£146/acre to £323/acre), generally confirmed the concentric model and occupied the limits of the built-up area. The small district near Wapping Dock, £1,150/ha (£466/acre), was a notable exception, with a mean value twice that of the adjoining riverside district of Wapping Whitechapel and Shadwell (mean value £578/ha or £234/acre). The vicinity of Wapping Dock thus seems to have been a distinctive focus of maritime activity which was somewhat separate from London, despite lying within the continuously built-up area.

Other areas within this class had varying characteristics. To the north-east of the City lay Bishopsgate Street, with its numerous narrow alleyways running back to semi-rural tenter grounds, which had a value of £763/ha (£309/acre), while that for the recently-constructed suburb of Spitalfields was £500/ha (£202/acre). Further west, to the north of Holborn, was an extensive area with a mean value of £609/ha (£247/acre). This ran from the overcrowded environs of Saffron Hill, £640/ha (£259/acre), across partly open land to the newly built but densely occupied area of Lamb's Conduit Fields, £620/ha (£251/acre), and the prestigious developments north of Bloomsbury Market, £635/ha (£257/acre). There were two further blocks of similar value in the southern part of St Margaret Westminster parish, £648/ha (£262/acre) and, of somewhat lesser value, to the north of Golden Square in St James Westminster, £395/ha (£160/acre), areas of contrasting social character yet both engulfed in the process of new construction.

The four shilling aid data provide clear evidence for a model in which land values fall with increased distance from the centres of business, although a number of other factors were found to influence the picture in individual neighbourhoods. An area of well-built commercial street frontage on one of the city's major thoroughfares produced very high land values, but values almost as high might be obtained in a nearby high-status residential district. On the other hand poor quality housing and environmental factors, such as noisome activities, pollution and a tendency to flooding might drag values down. These influences can be readily identified in low-value districts to the east of the City. While certain types of overcrowding might tend to suppress land values, a large population occupying quality houses let at high rents would result in very high values per hectare. Here the underlying value of the site alone would tend to be high and there was, therefore, a strong incentive to maximise its use.[45]

In more general terms the commercial core of London, with separate foci in the City and in the western suburb, generated the highest land values, those in the City being pre-eminent. More highly residential areas surrounding these districts show similar, although slightly lower, values. There was then a disjointed but substantial buffer zone of middling value land. Land of lower value was found to encircle the core at the limits of the built-up area. The character of this outer zone varied. It included some long established districts of poor housing, and others — in the northern part of St James Westminster, St Anne Soho, and Lamb's Conduit Fields — which had recently been developed as 'green-field' sites with houses of some substance. In these latter areas the low value of the site alone, which was apparently not as yet significantly influenced by commercial or spec-ulative pressures, kept the overall value of property low.

THE GENERAL CHARACTER OF THE BUILT FABRIC

London's building stock

London's built fabric varied greatly from district to district across the city. While some areas were characterised by regular buildings of brick and stone others often comprised haphazard structures predominantly of timber construction. A continuing, and increasingly rapid, process of expansion and infilling meant that much of London's building stock was new and well appointed, but many older quarters of the metropolis endured decaying, squalid and insanitary housing conditions.

The City of London contained the largest extent of new buildings, constructed following the Great Fire of 1666 (Fig. 3.6). The new buildings were designed with regard to the regulations set out in the Rebuilding Acts of 1667: brick replaced timber and lath, wall thicknesses and heights were specified and numerous details of internal design and external form were defined.[46] Some older buildings were also substantially built, but many were rickety, overhanging, timber structures, often altered by tenants, or subdivided to provide shelter for many of London's poorer inhabitants.

In the newer suburbs, both east and west of the City, houses of a similar style to those defined in the City Rebuilding Acts were constructed. To the west these were often laid out in regular terrace rows in wide streets and squares. Interiors, often of a pattern-book character, varied with the wealth and status of the inhabitants yet retained a general uniformity of style within each rental band.[47]

An analysis of the estimated age profile of London's building stock provides a relative indication of the quality of housing within any given district of the metropolis (Fig. 3.7).[48] Buildings in the City were for the most part no more than thirty years old, having been rebuilt following the Great Fire. Similarly, much of the more recent construction to have taken place in the City without the walls was associated with post-fire reconstruction particularly in the ward of Farringdon Without. The areas just beyond the walls to the north and east of the City probably contained many older structures as there would be little incentive to rebuild in such densely inhabited poorer areas.

In the West End, despite the concentration of earlier seventeenth-century and older building stock in areas adjacent to the Strand and in Covent Garden, much new development had taken place. This was also the case in the parish of St Margaret Westminster where groups of new buildings were to be found adjacent to older, very crowded areas. Much of the most recent of this construction had been generated by semi-planned estate development ventures, notably under the auspices of speculative builders such as the Earl of Southampton (Bloomsbury Square, 1661),[49] Lord St Albans (St James's Square, 1665),[50] Richard Frith (King's —later Soho — Square, 1677)[51] and Nicholas

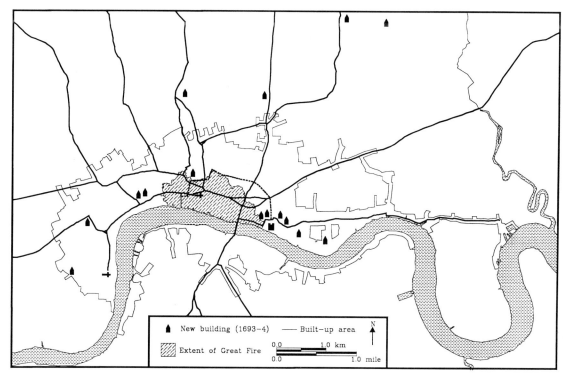

FIG. 3.6 New construction during 1693–4 and the extent of the Great Fire of 1666
Source: Ogilby and Morgan (1676); 1693–4 Aid database.

Barbon (Essex Street, York House, Red Lion Square, Lamb's Conduit Fields, and the Rugby Estate, among many other smaller undertakings, 1670–1698).[52]

In the older northern and eastern suburbs construction took two major forms: expansion and renewal. In the Spitalfields quarter extensive new building had begun around the 1660s.[53] These brick-built structures, although small and constructed sporadically, must have created a dramatic counterpoint to the older dilapidated tenements of Bishopsgate and White-

chapel which surrounded them. Renewal was mostly undertaken in areas characterised by a large stock of irregular older buildings. Among such areas were the precinct of St Katherine by the Tower, the neighbourhood of Aldgate both within and without the walls, and the vicinity of Drury Lane to the west of the city. Here, poorly constructed timber and brick buildings in great decay collapsed with monotonous regularity.[54]

The four shilling aid assessments record some properties as 'new' buildings or 'foundations', but

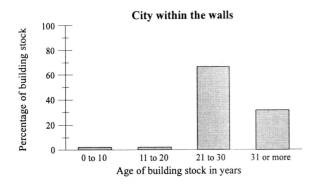

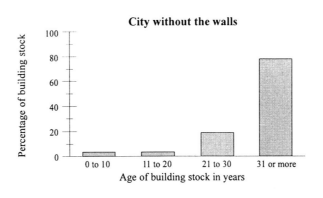

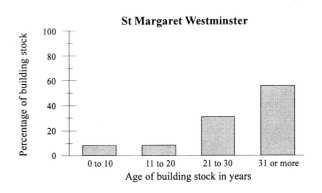

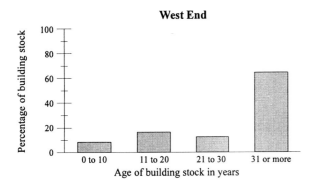

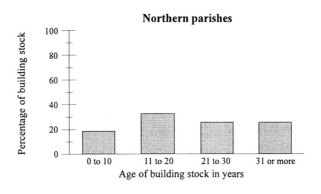

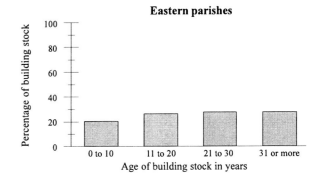

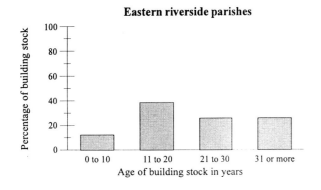

FIG. 3.7 Approximate age of London's building stock in the 1690s

Source: Brett-James (1935); Ogilby and Morgan (1676); Reddaway (1940); 1693–4 Aid database. For parish groupings see Fig. 1.7.

not in a regular or consistent fashion (Fig. 3.6). The new buildings tend to occur in suburban areas, where expansion and infilling were presumably taking place. Of the sixty-six new buildings recorded in the assessments, only twenty-six were found in the West End. Six of these were in the vicinity of Drury Lane, and Sir Francis Child, founder of the bank of Child & Co., was credited with the ownership of twenty in Sheere Lane Ward between Lincoln's Inn and Fleet Street — clearly a speculative venture.[55] Twenty-six new houses were located in the parishes immediately east of the City, possibly in replacement of earlier poor quality housing stock. Among their owners was a Mr Rogers, evidently a speculator in property with thirteen new houses and two foundations attributed to his name in King Street, Wapping. On the other hand, the aid assessments make no reference to new building in districts such as Spitalfields, Lamb's Conduit Fields and Soho, where it was certainly in progress in 1693–4.

Empty property

A metropolis the size of London, with well over 90,000 buildings, would at any one time have contained a substantial number of empty houses, reflecting the rapid turnover of occupants.[56] Vacancy rates would tend to be highest in the poorer areas, where length of occupancy was shortest, and perhaps in areas whose social make-up was changing. Gregory King estimated that 5.4 per cent of houses in London were empty by comparison with 3 per cent for the kingdom as a

Fig. 3.8 View of houses on the corner of Chancery Lane and Fleet Street, showing pre- and post-Great Fire buildings (William Capon, 1798)
Source: Guildhall Library.

whole,[57] while according to the Census of 1851 the vacancy rate for the City of London was 7 per cent.

The statute enacting the four shilling aid insisted that the tax be raised on all property whether occupied or not, with the result that many empty properties were recorded in the 1693–4 assessments. It seems probable from the mean vacancy figure obtained from the assessments (3.7 per cent) that not all empty property was noted. The number of entries for properties described as 'empty' was 2,224. This included a variety of property types, the most frequent category being the house or tenement. The 2,118 empty houses and tenements represents a vacancy rate of one empty dwelling for every twenty-seven households across the metropolis, and may be less than half the true proportion. This may, however, reflect the manner in which houses were often subdivided to accommodate more than one household. Nevertheless some general conclusions can be drawn as to the nature of urban vacancy from the distribution of empty houses (Fig. 3.9).

The highest vacancy levels were found in those areas that were generally peripheral to the districts of commercial significance. St Margaret Westminster had a comparatively high vacancy rate of 9 per cent. This mean figure conceals more detailed variations. The highest rate of empty houses, 10 per cent, was in New Palace Ward, an area of densely concentrated, older dwellings immediately north of the palace. The lowest levels were recorded in the wealthier areas to the south of Whitehall and to the west of the parish around Petty France, both 7 per

cent. A district similar in its mix of property types and open space was that of Aldgate and Mile End Old Town with a mean vacancy level of 7 per cent.

To the north of the city the greatest concentration of empty houses within any area of the metropolis was found in the liberty of Norton Folgate, with a rate of 13 per cent. The liberty contained many poorer quality buildings and its geographical position near the limit of the built-up area and on a major road approaching the City may indicate the presence of a substantial transitory population. Similar reasons may account for the high vacancy rates of 8 per cent in the more rural areas of Shoreditch, Hackney and Islington, though an increase in newly-built, but un-let, property may also be significant.

Poor, densely inhabited, areas provide consistently high numbers of empty houses. The precinct of St Katherine by the Tower, Houndsditch, the area north of Cripplegate, and Saffron Hill, all at 8 per cent, show clear signs of economic conditions influencing the level of vacancy.

Those areas that exhibit vacancy rates in the lowest class, under 1.3 per cent, include many for which no empty properties were recorded (Fig. 3.9). The strong possibility that this resulted from a failure by assessors to identify consistently such property suggests that this class does not provide information rigorous enough for further analysis. Those areas that fall in the class of 1.3 to 3.2 per

cent do, however, merit further comment. These areas represent some of the lowest levels of vacancy for the metropolis. The greater part of the City within the walls had relatively low levels of vacancy. Within this class the City of London can be divided into three districts: to the east of the Gracechurch Street-Bishopsgate axis (3 per cent), west of this axis to St Paul's Cathedral (2 per cent), and from the cathedral to the Fleet canal (3 per cent). The highly important commercial nature of these areas explain the relatively low levels of vacancy.

Extensive semi-rural areas to the north and east of the city, beyond the inner circle of poorer districts, had levels of vacancy similar to the urban core. Although the waterfront areas of Wapping and Ratcliff demonstrated average levels of vacancy, in districts away from the waterfront empty property was recorded at the lower rate of 2 per cent. The older part of Spitalfields, and the vicinity of Whitechapel High Street, had an equivalent rate of 2 per cent. Low levels of vacancy (2 per cent), were also found to the north-west of the city across a large part of Clerkenwell.

The very low levels of vacancy indicated for the West End may be unreliable. Much new construction was taking place to the north-west of this area, but the empty property this would inevitably generate does not feature in the assessments. Where empty houses are recorded, notably along the Strand and Drury Lane, the vacancy rate was 5 per cent. This marginally higher than average figure probably

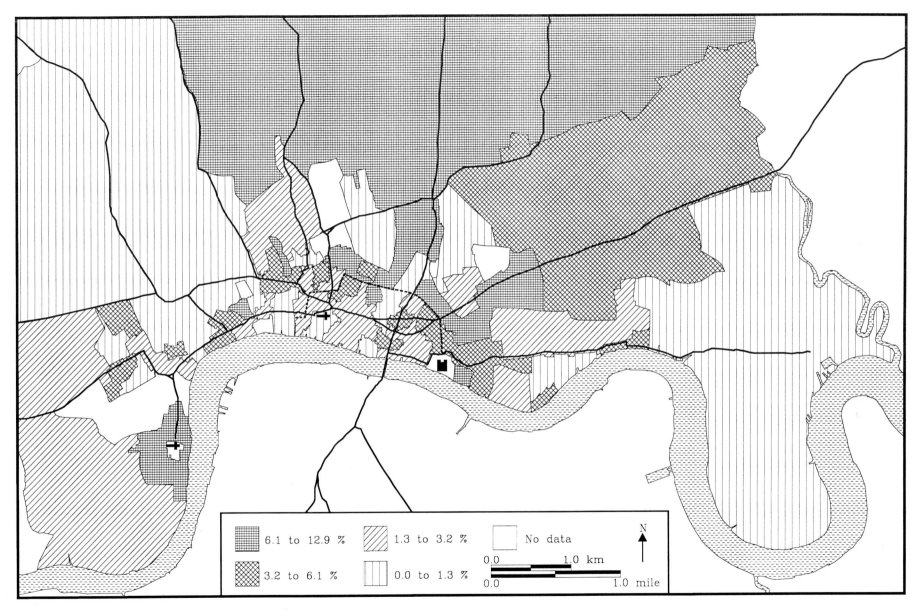

FIG. 3.9 Empty houses as a percentage of all households

Source: 1693–4 Aid database.

reflects both poor quality housing and new un-let buildings. It is notable that a comparable level of vacancy, 4 per cent, was recorded in the district of Aldgate, both within and without the walls, this area exhibiting a similar mixture of poorer housing and evidence of renewal.

The parish of St James Westminster demonstrates a pattern of vacancy that, unlike most of the West End parishes, seems to portray convincingly the underlying environmental and social conditions. The lowest levels of vacancy were recorded in the affluent neighbourhood of St James's Square and Pall Mall (1 per cent), and in the semi-rural, and relatively slowly expanding, area at the western limit of the parish (also 1 per cent). A vacancy rate somewhat lower than the metropolitan average was found in the more commercial area of Windmill Street and the Haymarket (2 per cent). The highest levels of vacancy were noted in the area to the immediate north-west of St James's Square (3 per cent), a marginally less wealthy quarter, and just south of Oxford Street (4 per cent), an area undergoing a process of rapid expansion and social adjustment.

In addition to the 2,118 empty houses identified in the 1693–4 Aid assessments, a smaller number of other types of property were recorded as vacant. Chief among these were thirty-four shops, many of which were grouped in retailing centres. Six shops in the Earl of Salisbury's New Exchange (some 5 per cent of all the shops in the Exchange), nine shops in Hungerford Market House, and fourteen shops which were probably associated with Clare Market, were all noted as empty. Among the 106 non-household properties the only other significant group of buildings were stables, nine of which were found to be vacant.

Members of the House of Commons were concerned at the potential loss of revenue from vacant properties:

> They came to the clause about empty houses whereon was a long debate. Some were for their paying; and others not and thought it punishment enough for the owners to have them empty, and therefore unreasonable to pay taxes for them. However, it was upon the question resolved they should pay; otherwise a great part of the tax would be lost.[58]

Yet vacancy was less significant for the loss of income than its incidence might suggest, presumably because the less valuable properties were more likely to be vacant. The total rent value of all empty property in London amounted to £18,818, no more than 1.8 per cent of the gross value of metropolitan rents.

London as a built environment

At the end of the seventeenth century some of the central characteristics of London's built environment were in the process of change. Within the City the Great Fire of 1666 had swept away the bulk of the overcrowded, timber-built, structures allowing relatively bold architectural renewal. Nevertheless, despite earnest attempts to promote more comprehensive redesign, the overall plan of the City was to remain essentially unchanged. Consequently, the City of London in the 1690s comprised many spacious brick-built edifices, which were allied to a range of piecemeal street improvements: paving, drainage, street signs and lighting. These changes undoubtedly made the City a more materially comfortable environment. For example, the customary, and often erratic, provision of street lights by individual City householders was replaced by the corporate efforts of the Convex Lights Company in 1694, householders being levied up to six shillings a year for the improved service.[59]

Outside the City there were, however, wide differences between rich and poor areas, old and new structures. The West End, through the seventeenth century, was the scene of much innovative construction, with a greater emphasis being placed upon uniformity of design and planning matters. In this area of the metropolis, however, the environment of the street was less well controlled. The erection of pedestrian bollards, street-name boards and public lighting, in the manner of the City, were, nevertheless, soon to follow.[60]

The retention of certain open spaces, in these expanding areas of the metropolis, enhanced the visual appearance of many new squares and streets. In a private context open space was employed to aid in the overall reduction of housing density, at least in the more affluent areas of the suburbs. Housing densities in the urban core and poorer quarters were often very high. No doubt such levels of density were influenced by the frequent occurrence of multiple occupation, but this cannot detract from the extremely close proximity that many Londoners would have been forced to endure with their neighbours.

Outside the central built-up areas, across the low value semi-rural periphery, land was employed in the service of London. Horticultural activity and dairying were a primary concern, while along the riverside industrial complexes and commercial installations were located. Workers employed in such operations were generally found to inhabit the more densely crowded, poorer quality housing that extended in a broken arc along the eastern and northern margins of the metropolis.

The differentiation between the highly sought after property in the commercial centre and the less desirable housing in the poorer districts of the metropolis had a profound effect upon the resulting land values. Affluent areas were often found juxtaposed to much poorer enclaves. For example, Hatton Garden, a relatively wealthy, well-built neighbourhood, stood in sharp contrast, to the immediately adjacent Saffron Hill, an area plagued by overcrowded and poor quality housing, factors which conspired to keep rent levels low.

This analysis of land use, housing density, land values and the quality of London's building stock shows that the metropolis possessed a highly valued commercial core surrounded by outlying districts and suburbs which contained environments characterised by spacious layouts and by those notorious for densely crowded poverty.

Notes:

1. Defoe (1724–6), 286.
2. See below, pp. 81–8, regarding household location and social status; Stone (1980), 173–7.
3. Best (1981), 29.
4. See Appendix II for list of maps consulted.
5. These figures refer to the contiguous built-up area north of the Thames.
6. See below, pp. 45–8, regarding household density.
7. Probably more accurately identified in terms of recreational land use was that space occupied by pleasure gardens, such as at Vauxhall. These, however, tended to be found in non-contiguous suburban situations and therefore must be excluded from any discussion of built-up land use.
8. Harding (1990a), 44–55.
9. Borsay (1989), 43.
10. Bull (1975–6) criticises Rocque's mapping, 'Although important for its early use of pictorial land use delineation [it] is cartographically flawed due to his limited survey methods', 3. Rocque's maps for land use analysis are however given more positive support by Weinstein (1990) and Harris (1990).
11. Boulton (1987a), 97–8; Forbes (1980).
12. For example, see the eastern riverside districts on Rocque's map (1747).
13. Rocque (1747); 1693–4 Aid database.
14. Rocque (1747); 1693–4 Aid database.
15. Galloway and Murphy (1991), 7–8.
16. Weinstein (1990), 83, 92.
17. Weinstein (1990), 90.
18. Bull (1975–6), 3–4.
19. See above, pp. 23–4, regarding the geology of the London area.
20. Bull (1975–6), 3.
21. Cox (1989), 3–5.
22. Defoe (1724–6), 300–1.
23. Also see Olsen (1982); Reddaway (1940); Summerson (1978).
24. See below, pp. 63–6, regarding population.
25. See below, pp. 88–93, regarding household structure.
26. The areas eliminated from the calculation of household density were the non-built-up area of St Martin in the Fields, St Marylebone and St Pancras, St Mary Islington, and St John Hackney. For simplicity density by acre has been omitted. The conversion factor is: 2.471 acres to 1 hectare.
27. See below, p. 70, for rent values in the Cornhill area.
28. See below, p. 137, regarding the occupational character of the Eastcheap area.
29. Alexander (1989a), 159–60, 199.
30. See below, pp. 88–93, regarding household size.
31. Power (1978a), 29.
32. 1693–4 Aid database.
33. Power (1978a), 43; Jones, Porter and Turner (1984), Table 3.
34. Summerson (1978), 48–9.
35. Boulton (1987a), 23–4.
36. The figure of 9,594 houses was derived from King's estimate for Surrey within the Bills and that for the total number of houses within the area of the bills (see Table 4.1). The net residential area was in the region of 250 hectares.
37. See below, pp. 66–70, for rental values per household.
38. Figures derived from Browning (1953), 318–22, and Best (1981), 14.
39. CLRO Assessment Boxes 40 and 42.
40. Milne (1800).
41. Alexander (1989a), 112–19.
42. Alexander (1989a), 99–100, 230–5.
43. Alexander (1989a), 172–5, 99–100.
44. See Dale (1931) and Jones (1980).
45. See below, pp. 70–5, for discussion of rents.
46. Reddaway (1940), 129–33.
47. Stone (1980), 205–8; Summerson (1978), 45; Power (1978b), 168–77.
48. The age profiles were based upon the following: the rate of rebuilding the City after the Great Fire, Reddaway (1940), 279–80; the changing extent of the built-up area during the course of the seventeenth century, Brett-James (1935); and map sources as in Appendix II. The 1693–4 Aid data were

used to provide the approximate number of households that were added by each stage of expansion. However, little can be known of the degree of renewal and infilling which might have taken place in the older quarters of the metropolis.

49. Summerson (1978), 39–41.
50. Survey of London (1960), 56–65.
51. Survey of London (1966), 42.
52. Summerson (1978), 44–51.
53. Survey of London (1957), 3–4.
54. George (1966), 83–5; Spence (1996), 40–1; 1693–4 Aid database.
55. *DNB*, IV (1917), 240–2.
56. See below, p. 65, Table 4.1.
57. Thirsk and Cooper (1972), 771, 793.
58. Luttrell (1691–3), 348.
59. Falkus (1976), 254–8.
60. Westminster attempted to force householders to provide street lighting by an Act of Parliament in 1690, but, following the example of the City, by 1704 the operation was in the hands of a private organisation, the Conic Lights Company: Falkus (1976), 256.

4. Metropolitan Social Structure

Man in his natural condition differs little from the rest of natures herd; As the rabbits increase new burrows are made, and the boundaries of the warren are enlarged. So it is with man, as he increaseth, new houses are built, and his town is made bigger.[1]

To analyse the underlying social structure of the late seventeenth-century metropolis a variety of sources have been utilised. As previously discussed in Chapter 1, principal amongst these are the 1693–4 Aid assessments and the returns for the 1692 Poll Tax. The aid assessments are here employed to examine population distribution, rental values, and patterns of gender and status among householders at a London-wide scale. The poll tax returns supply valuable information regarding household size and structure for the area of City of London. Detailed local studies of two aspects of London's housing structure, using the 1693–4 Aid assessments and focusing upon multiple occupancy of dwellings in Shadwell and the property-holding patterns of landlords in St Margaret Westminster, complement the broader picture already established. Finally, an analysis of rich and poor areas provides a further insight into the identification of different areas of the metropolis as either districts of exceptional poverty or those which housed predominantly wealthy inhabitants.

THE GENERAL PICTURE

London's population

There is little disagreement that the population of London at the end of the seventeenth century was in the region of half a million and probably well over that figure.[2] Some consideration, however, needs to be given to the manner in which the metropolitan population was distributed and was increasing. By the end of the seventeenth century the bulk of this population was not to be found within the area of the City, but to be dwelling in the suburbs where there had been a dramatic enlargement of the population (Fig. 4.1). It is, therefore, unfortunate that some of the more reliable measures of population are restricted to the geographically constrained area of the City of London, while estimates of the rapidly expanding suburban population can be supplied only from less systematic sources.

The most robust source for constructing a population estimate of the central area at the end of the seventeenth century is the marriage duty assessments

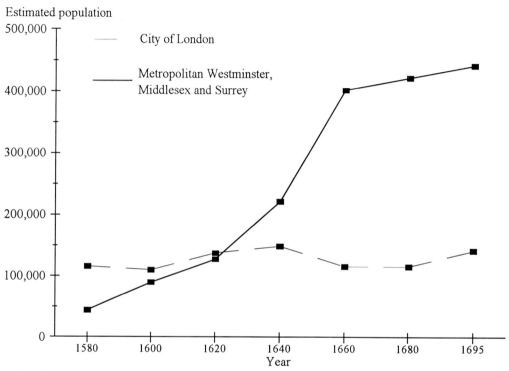

FIG. 4.1 Estimated population growth for metropolitan London during the seventeenth century
Source: Harding (1990).

63

for 1695. These suggest a population in the region of 70,000 inhabitants for the area within the walls, while the number resident in the City outside the walls is estimated to have been around 54,000.[3] Using these figures it is possible to calculate the shortfall in the coverage of inhabitants provided by the 1692 Poll Tax assessments for the City of London.[4] The 1692 figure of 81,824 lies far below the total of 124,000 indicated for the City by the combined marriage duty figures.[5] The difference in these figures reflects exemptions from the poll tax. As mentioned earlier, those not assessed included persons in receipt of poor rate or alms, the children of day labourers, and the children of those who had four or more children but less than fifty pounds worth of land, goods and chattels.[6]

Estimates for the wider metropolitan area are less certain. The problem is two-fold: a scarcity of source material and the uneven rate of suburban growth throughout the seventeenth century. A period of particularly vigorous increase is found, for example, between 1620 and 1660 (Fig. 4.1). A recent estimate of the population of metropolitan London in 1696–9 within the area covered by the Bills of Mortality (including 135 parishes in the cities of London and Westminster and in the adjacent counties of Middlesex and Surrey) suggests a range from 557,000 to 641,000 dependent upon the burial rate employed in calculation. The median figure, 596,000, may, however, be too high an estimate.[7] Gregory King's contemporary estimate of London's population in 1695 was some 528,000: that may have been too low.

Such global figures do not help to define the variation in population that might have occurred between one district of the metropolis and another. Such variations were influenced by many factors, including household density, but economic status probably had the most direct influence. For example it has been shown that the number of people within a household tended to reflect the economic position of its inhabitants.[8] Within the prosperous commercial core of the City in 1695, houses tended to contain in the region of 6.4 people, while houses in poorer areas within the walls tended to hold marginally fewer inhabitants, around 5.8 people.[9] In the wealthier areas houses would include more children, possibly more apprentices, and certainly more servants than elsewhere, and such houses also often held more lodgers or subordinate households.

Some estimates of population have been established by inflating the count of houses by the mean number of inhabitants per house, a method employed in the 1690s by Gregory King, who estimated that houses within the walls contained 5.5 persons, and those without 4.5 or less. Though simple, this technique is not entirely to be trusted. The close proximity, and even intermixing, of rich and poor accommodation within any particular area weakens the results of such calculations because of the effect such economic variables had upon household size. Also the sub-division of poorer property, and the tendency of the poor to be excluded from official records, in particular taxation assessments, further undermines any straightforward correlation between wealth, household size, and household numbers.

To give an example, using the 1695 Marriage Duty assessments Glass established population figures for both the notably poor parish of St Anne Blackfriars and the very wealthy parish of St Matthew Friday Street. The respective totals were 2,829 and 285. These figures indicated that the number of persons per house in St Anne's was 7.4, while the corresponding figure in St Matthew's was 6.2, both figures at odds with the more general pattern stated above.[10] A census undertaken during 1711 within the relatively wealthy and well-built parish of St Anne Soho provides a population figure of 8,113.[11] This indicates a mean population per house of 8.1 persons, similar to that calculated for St Anne Blackfriars despite clear differences in the underlying pattern of wealth that existed between the two parishes. Moreover, the population of St Anne Soho included many French Huguenot lodgers; if these lodgers are omitted from the calculation then the much smaller figure of 4.2 persons is obtained for the size of principal households, as opposed to the house as a whole. It is therefore clear that such varied means for the number of persons per house, or household, must be used cautiously in extrapolating overall population figures. This is particularly so without a proper consideration of the levels of household density and with limited knowledge of patterns of multiple occupancy.

While it is difficult to establish reliable estimates of population for different parts of London, the extensive nature of the 1693–4 Aid does allow a more dependable estimate to be made of household numbers across the metropolis. To some extent that can be adjusted to indicate the distribution of 'houses' (which in practice are difficult to distinguish from households) within the aggregated areas of the metropolis, which can be used to calculate an approximate pattern of population dispersal as shown in Table 4.1. This has been achieved by allocating population according to the proportion of houses found within each area.[12] An initial adjustment was made by utilising Gregory King's estimate of 15,000 houses for those parishes south of the river that were included within the Bills of Mortality. This figure was 14.3 per cent of King's total count for the metropolis of 105,000 occupied houses. Using the total household count obtained from the 1693–4 Aid as a more accurate basis, the 14.3 per cent for the Surrey parishes was found to equal 9,594 houses. Computations of population distribution were made using the population estimates obtained from the Bills of Mortality, the 1695 Marriage Duty for the City of London, and a combination of the two figures.

Regardless of the base figure used to calculate the distribution, it is clear that the most heavily populated of the aggregated areas were the West End and the City within the walls. Much of the West End probably had relatively high numbers of persons per house and consequently the resident population may have been even larger than these figures suggest. The distribution of households indicates that as many as a third of all dwellings in the metropolis were to be found in the City (31.7 per cent) and nearly a quarter within the boundaries of the West End and St Margaret Westminster (22.6 per cent). The figures for the City within and

TABLE 4.1

Estimated distribution of London's population in the 1690s

Area	Number of houses[1]	Percentage of total	Estimated population			
			Bills of Mortality	Marriage Duty	Marriage Duty/Bills of Mortality	Mean of columns 3, 4 and 5
City within the walls	11,722	17.5	104,300	80,018[.2]	80,018[.3]	92,159
City without the walls	9,540	14.2	84,632	61,534[.2]	61,534[.3]	73,083
St Margaret Westminster	2,851	4.3	25,628	19,148	28,612	24,463
West End	12,278	18.3	109,068	81,490	121,768	104,109
Northern parishes	4,692[.4]	7.0	41,720	31,171	46,578	39,823
Eastern parishes	5,729[.5]	8.5	50,660	37,851	56,559	48,357
Eastern riverside parishes	8,450[.6]	12.6	75,096	56,108	83,840	71,681
Total for aggregate areas	55,262	82.4	491,104	366,927	568,252	[453,675]
Middlesex within the Bills[7]	2,232	3.3	19,668	14,695	21,958	18,774
Surrey within the Bills	9,594[.8]	14.3[8]	85,228	63,678	95,152	81,353
Total for London within the Bills	67,088	100.0	596,000[.9]	445,300	596,020[.3]	[553,802]

Sources: 1693–4 Aid database, King (1696) in Glass (1965) and in Thirsk and Cooper (1972), Jones and Judges (1935–6) and Harding (1990b).

Notes:

[1] It is not easy to distinguish houses and households (of which the latter were presumably the more numerous): neither term is much used in the detailed local returns of the 1690s. Unless otherwise stated, the values in this column are based on the count of households in the 1693–4 Aid (see Table 4.2).

[2] The figures for the City within and without the walls are derived from the marriage duty assessments of 1695 in Jones and Judges (1935–6), inflated by 15 per cent to account for underenumeration. In order to estimate the figures for other areas, a median value was taken in which 1 per cent of the overall total is represented by 4,453 persons.

[3] The figures for the City within and without the walls are derived from the marriage duty assessments of 1695. The figure for the total population is derived from the Bills of Mortality (see below n.9). Subtracting the figures for the City from the total left 454,448, corresponding to 68.3 per cent of the total, and indicating that 1 per cent of the overall total is represented by 6,654 persons.

[4] The returns for St Giles Cripplegate are incomplete in the 1693–4 Aid, and so King's count of 'houses' in the parish has been used: Glass (1965), 175, 195.

[5] Includes King's estimate for Mile End New Town (Glass (1965), 177), missing from the 1693–4 Aid.

[6] For some parts of this district it is possible to identify instances of multiple occupancy, and so the count of 'houses' is lower than that for households (see Table 4.2).

[7] This district lay beyond the external boundary of the study area. The total covers the parishes of Islington and Hackney and parts of the parishes of Stepney and St Martin in the Fields: these values are derived from the returns for the 1693–4 Aid.

[8] Based on King's estimate that the houses within the Bills to the south of the river represented a seventh of the overall total within the Bills (Glass (1965), 188n.), and on the total of houses within the Bills north of the river indicated by the earlier figures in this column.

[9] Derived from estimates based on the Bills of Mortality for 1696–9: Harding (1990b), 121.

without the walls derived from the Bills of Mortality data alone would appear to be an over-estimate with reference to the more secure numbers derived from the marriage duty assessments. However, the calculated total population in the case of the marriage duty, 445,300, appears to be too low and might suggest that the figures for those areas outside of the City's jurisdiction need to be inflated. The mean population figures are considered to represent a more balanced view of the population structure, though the numbers for the City are probably still an overestimate. In this case the City and West End are found to share two thirds of the metropolitan population. The overall total for the area covered by the Bills of Mortality in this instance was 553,802.[13] Whatever figures are used, variations in multiple occupancy and the occurrence of lodgers, and their families, lie at the root of the problem of population appraisal.

To summarise, little evidence is available to supply accurate estimates of the population in those metropolitan districts outside the City of London at the end of the seventeenth century. Using the number of households or houses recorded in the 1693–4 Aid assessments does, however, allow a reasonable estimate to be made of the distribution of population between the districts of the metropolis. But, whatever the methods used to calculate population distribution, it is clear that the population of metropolitan London during the 1690s was indeed in excess of half a million people, most of whom lived within the central areas of the City and the West End.

SOCIAL GEOGRAPHY AS REVEALED BY HOUSEHOLD RENT VALUES

The overall pattern

The assessments for the 1693–4 Aid provide a relatively comprehensive picture of metropolitan rents. The primary measure upon which the Aid was assessed was the annual rack-rent value of real property. Generally such property would have been a single building — a house or tenement — however, subdivision would occasionally have directed the assessors' attention to the separate rents paid by the individual households within a shared property.[14] The assessed value of the annual rack-rent of a property rested upon an estimate of the full commercial rental value, irrespective of whether the property was held at will, by lease, or freehold.

Compared to the country as a whole, rents in London were high. As the lowest level of rent at which tax was levied was £1 per annum, it is likely that the majority of London households appeared within the 1693–4 Aid assessments. This assumption can be tested by comparing the numbers of households recorded in the 1693–4 Aid with the 1695 Marriage Duty returns, which were probably fuller in their coverage of the City. The surviving assessments for the marriage duty record a total of 22,038 households for eighty of the ninety-seven parishes within the walls of the City and for the thirteen parishes without. The 1693–4 Aid records 21,767 households for the corresponding area. The 271 fewer households noted by the 1693–4

assessments might be accounted for by exemptions on the grounds of low levels of rents. Given that this is only 1.2 per cent of the marriage duty total, the predominantly high values of London rents can be appreciated.[15]

Despite the lower limit for assessment of £1 rent per annum, the 1693–4 Aid assessments record twenty-one properties with values below this threshold. Such cases, and the large numbers of low value rents recorded in some poor areas suggest that in some districts, especially the riverside parishes to the east of the city, a significant proportion of households may have fallen below the minimum level for assessment. A study of housing in Shadwell, however, shows that even in a relatively poor riverside district there can have been few properties valued at less than £1. The parliamentary surveys of 1650–1 indicate that the mean value of 701 houses in Shadwell was £3 16s. per annum, with a mean value per room of £1 8s. per annum. Even if a broad adjustment is made to allow for multiple occupancy, at a rate of 121 households to every 100 houses, the resulting figure of £3 3s. rent per household per year is still well above the £1 minimum for assessment set some forty years later.[16] Indeed the mean rent value for Shadwell households recorded in 1693–4 was £7 15s. per annum. This suggests that, apart from those few households with exceptionally low rents, the great majority did in fact find their way into the 1693–4 Aid assessments.

The full range of individual rental values was large: there were 518 properties valued at the official

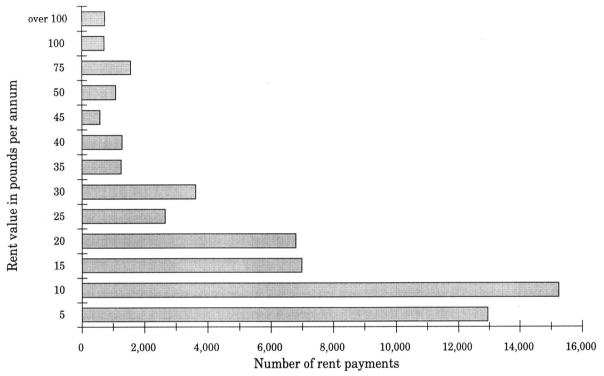

FIG. 4.2 The distribution of metropolitan rents by value
Source: 1693–4 aid database.

There are three ways in which the average household rent value for any given area can be represented (Table 4.2), and each method has limitations as a way of defining an area's characteristics. Nevertheless, they provide a quite sensitive indicator of the relative social composition of districts, as indicated by the rental value of households.

Mean values will represent the characteristics of an area best when the range of values within it is relatively small. In parts of the West End, for example, the presence of a few households worth £300 per annum among a much larger number of lesser households could significantly enhance the mean.

The mode — the most frequently occurring rent value — gives perhaps a better indication of the general character of rents within an area. Modal rent values are notably lower than the corresponding means. In most areas the modal value is approximately half that of the mean, demonstrating that the majority of rents in these areas were worth considerably less than the mean value.

The median — as the point above and below which half of all values in the group fall — provides some account of the distribution of values around the mean. The median values in Table 4.2 thus tend to fall between the figures for means and modes, indicating that in most cases the means were inflated by the presence of a small number of high value properties. Significantly this is not the case in the two highest value areas, the City within the walls

minimum of £1 per annum, while there were only some thirty instances of rents over £320 (for the overall pattern see Fig. 4.2). Rents of the lowest value occurred in an evenly distributed pattern across the metropolis. In an area at the western end of Ratcliff Highway, however, 20.1 per cent of rents were found to have been no higher than £1 per annum. The highest rents were invariably derived from property holdings of a mixed commercial nature or, less obviously, from tracts of non-urban land or property in the course of development. The

highest identifiable rental value for a single residential property was £320 per annum, for Burlington House in Piccadilly, the residence of Richard Boyle, Earl of Cork and Burlington (see Fig. 2.5). The next highest rent for identifiable single residences was £300. Eight noble houses were assessed at that value, all in the West End.[17]

Average household rent values for the metropolis as a whole inevitably conceal a wide range of variation between areas, and so are of limited utility.

TABLE 4.2
Total rent data for aggregated areas

Area	Household rents							Non-household rents[1]		
	No.	Total value	%	Mean value	Modal value	Median value	Range	No.	Total value	%
City within	11,722	£296,472	31.5	£25 6s. 6d.	£20	£19	10s.–£440	438	£26,245	47.7
City without	9,540	£129,089	13.7	£13 17s. 6d.	£6	£10	10s.–£300	127	£3,026	5.5
St Margaret Westminster	2,851	£33,842	3.6	£12 1s. 6d.	£6	£10	£1–£200	97	£1,215	2.2
West End	12,278	£275,271	29.3	£22 13s. 0d.	£20	£17	£1–£500	486	£9,518	17.3
Northern parishes	4,297	£59,344	6.3	£14 0s. 6d.	£10	£9 10s.	10s.–£342	70	£974	1.8
Eastern parishes	5,368	£43,688	4.7	£8 10s. 0d.	£5	£6 10s.	£1–£300	85	£1,427	2.6
Eastern riverside parishes	12,278	£55,546	5.9	£7 3s. 6d.	£3	£6	5s.–£150	114	£1,653	2.9
Metropolitan Middlesex	2,809	£46,932	5.0	£17 4s. 0d.	£3	£9	10s.–£600	297	£10,988	20.0
Total	61,143	£940,184	100.0	£17 7s. 3d.	£6	£10	5s.–£600	1,714	£55,046	100.0

Source: 1693–4 Aid database.
Note:
[1] This is rent from separately assessed non-household properties (e.g. warehouses); where single assessment was made of a mixture of household and non-household property such rents are included in household rents.

according to value. Each of the seven aggregated areas of the metropolis is then characterised according to the distribution of households within those groups (Fig. 4.3). The method provides a sensitive characterisation of the major differences between areas.

The City within the walls was distinctive for a predominance of high value households, particularly those in the top three groups representing rental values of £20 per annum and upwards. The West End had a similar profile, though the highest value households did not represent such a large proportion as was the case within the city walls. While the most valuable West End residences were worth more than those in the City, and occupied more spacious sites, the high value of many City households was a reflection of the value of the land on which they stood.

Surrounding the walled City was an area — the City without the walls — which demonstrated a more evenly distributed range of rent values. This distribution shows that a wide range of property values was to be found and that certain distinctive concentrations of high and low rents were present. The profile for the northern suburbs was the nearest to that for the metropolis as a whole, with the mean value for the district being closest to the overall metropolitan mean (see Table 4.2). In those areas to the east of the city there was a frequent occurrence of low value rents, especially those at or below £8. The eastern riverside suburbs show an even more dramatic concentration of very low

and the West End. Here the median values tended to be lower than the modes, indicating that higher value rents were in fact far more characteristic of the property found within these districts.

Even so, in most areas of London there was a wide range of household rental values. Furthermore, it was common for substantial residences to be found in close proximity to smaller ones. The social composition of an area is, therefore, better characterised by an indication of the relative significance within it of several different groups of household values, rather than by a single average figure. In order to adopt a standard approach, all the rental values which appear to represent residential units have been divided into ten groups of equal size

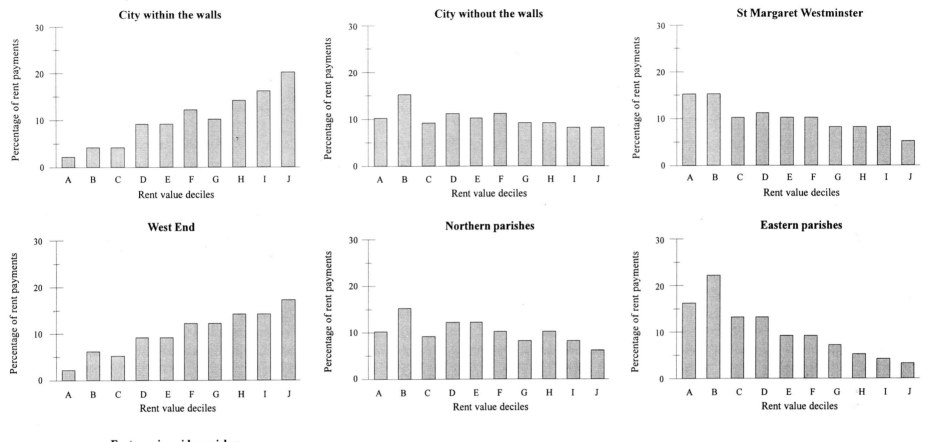

FIG. 4.3 The number of rent payments recorded within each rent value decile compared by aggregated area

Source: 1693–4 Aid database.

Decile values were as follows:
A = £1 to £4; B = £4 1s. to £5 5s.; C= £5 6s. to £7; D = £7 1s. to £8 10s.; E = £8 11s. to £11; F = £11 1s. to £14 10s.;
G = £14 11s. to £19 10s.; H = £19 11s. to £26; I = £26 1s. to £40; J = £40 1s. to £320.

value rents. In this case 46 per cent of the recorded rents were valued at or below £5. The mean and median averages for this district were the lowest in the metropolis at £7 3s. 6d. and £6 respectively.

Spatial distribution of rent values

While rent distribution profiles can also be used in the more detailed analysis of individual analytical areas, the pattern of social topography, as indicated by household rents, is most clearly revealed by the distribution of mean rental values by area. The values have been classified into four groups by the method of nested means: identified here as classes 1 to 4, in descending order of value (Fig. 4.4). The overall pattern in many respects resembles that for land values (see Fig. 3.4). The two central districts of high land value, the heart of the City and along the length of the Strand, appear once again, this time boasting the highest mean household rents of around £36. An important contrast between the pattern of land values and that for mean household rents is apparent in the district north of the Strand incorporating Covent Garden, where individual rents were very high, but values per hectare less so.

Areas in class 1

Within the study area those districts characterised by the highest mean household rents fell into two basic groups: commercial and high status residential. A third group of high-value properties lay outside the main built-up area. The commercial areas focused upon Cheapside and Cornhill. The latter area, including the southern district around

London Bridge, exhibited a mean household rent value of £36 2s. Moving west, away from the main centre of business, mean rent values gradually declined along the length of Cheapside, from £35 3s. for the area adjacent to the Stocks Market, to £33 15s. for the central Honey Lane Market and Guildhall area, and to £28 4s. for the district around St Paul's Cathedral and St Martin le Grand. The household rental distribution profiles of these areas show a frequent occurrence of high value rents, most likely along the commercial frontages, while in the western and central areas an increase in middle range rents acted to reduce the mean values.

Continuing towards the west, comparably high rents do not appear again until the parish of St Dunstan in the West at the limit of the City's jurisdiction. Here a mean rent value of £33 3s. was probably associated with the commercial function of Fleet Street. This area of high rents continued along the commercial axis of the Strand towards Charing Cross. The rent values throughout this area showed little variation, producing an overall mean of £31 4s. To the north of the Strand the mixed residential and commercial parish of Covent Garden demonstrated a mean household rent value of £30 6s. In this area it is possible to analyse the distribution of rent values by more specific location. The Piazza and the more significant streets such as Henrietta Street and King Street had mean household rent values of £74 5s., £45 19s. and £40 6s., respectively. Streets which were more distant from the central Piazza area had lower values; for example, Bedford Court, £33 1s.,

Maiden Lane at £23, and lowest of all the narrow passage of Hart Street, only sixty-five metres to the north of the Piazza, at £16 13s.

Other areas of the West End where mean levels of household rents were high were characterised by purpose-built residential accommodation of high status. The southern part of the parish of St Anne Soho had a mean household rent value of £27 13s. The rental distribution profile in that area demonstrates very few low value rents (only 8.6 per cent below £8 10s), while the remaining high decile groups hold generally similar quantities of households (ranging from 18.2 to 30.4 per cent). The parish of St James Westminster, on the western limits of the built-up area, was the second district within the West End to be significantly influenced by a concentration of purpose-built high status residential property. That part of the parish which lay to the south of Piccadilly demonstrated a particularly high mean household rent of £34 8s. This area included such prestige locations as St James's Street, £34 6s., Pall Mall, £95 14s., and St James's Square which displayed the exceptionally high mean of £205 11s.

To an even greater extent than the neighbourhood of Covent Garden, this part of St James Westminster parish was marked by the contrast between its high mean household rent value and its lower value per hectare (see Fig. 3.4). Moreover, the density of households per hectare was much lower than in Covent Garden, along Fleet Street and the Strand, and in the centre of the City.

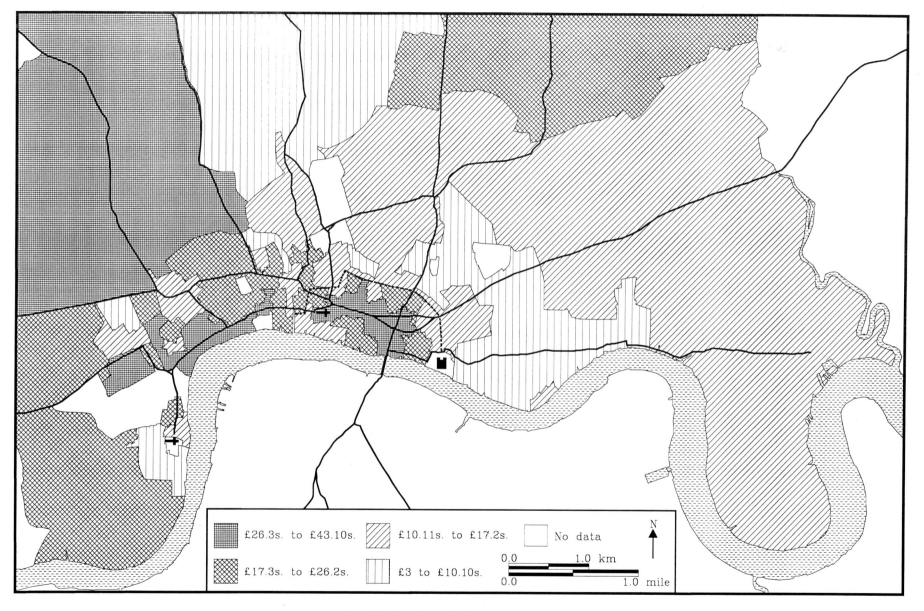

FIG. 4.4 Mean household rent value per annum
Source: 1693–4 Aid database.

The high value of rent thus provides only one indicator of the status of the resident. The apparently wealthy merchants and shopkeepers who lived in the central business district of the City occupied well-appointed houses but, residing in an area where population densities rose to 731 persons per hectare, they enjoyed very little space.[18] Conditions were marginally less crowded in Covent Garden, where the given rent could purchase a larger house than in the City, while the most spacious houses of all were to be found in St James Westminster.

The third area for high value properties was the more or less rural area to the north west of the built-up area. The high value properties of that area were not fully described, and probably consisted of extensive land-holdings and farm buildings. Such property may have derived its high value from the intensive use of the area for grazing.[19] The presence of some larger households, possibly associated with the more affluent district around the village of St Marylebone, may also have produced high levels of rent.

Areas in class 2
Much of the central area outside the highest value districts contained households with mean rent values above the metropolitan average. Inside the City walls one notable area of this type was that of the waterfront downriver from London Bridge, where the mean household rent value was £25 2s. That sum is low by comparison with the overall land value of the area, which reflected the high worth of the wharves and other specialised commercial property which occupied the riverside zone.

Other areas adjacent to the high-value core had an overall mean rent of £21 14s. Districts with such values were found within the City walls and near Smithfield, but mainly lay in the western suburbs, immediately north-east of Drury Lane and to the south of Whitehall. The Lincoln's Inn district and the area around the Southampton Estate were both characterised by a concentration of occupiers predominantly of the genteel or middling sort. The existence of such a social focus inevitably led to an increase in the value of rents, even though there was no commercial pressure. Consequently, the area bounded by the Strand, Drury Lane and Holborn had a mean household rent value of £21 7s., while the built-up area to the north of Holborn, including both the Southampton Estate and Hatton Garden, had a mean value of £21 14s. Further west the mean household rent of £20 13s. for the less developed northern half of the parish of St Anne Soho concealed some wide local variations. Thus the high status buildings of King's (now Soho) Square, with a mean household value of £73 1s., stood in sharp contrast to the newly-built properties along Dean Street, with a mean of £23 8s., and more humble structures in older thoroughfares such as Hog Lane, with a mean of £7 6s. Households at the southern end of Whitehall were in the same overall class (mean value £20 6s.). That reflected the presence, within the area, of the royal palace, government offices, and parliament, and the consequent demand for high status accommodation.

Two suburban or semi-rural areas at the limits of the metropolis were notable for rents above the metropolitan mean: to the west and south-west of Westminster (mean value £18 9s.). That was occasioned by the presence of a small number of high status households on the very western limits of the built-up area and in the adjacent suburban village of Knightsbridge. Households, or land units, in Hackney had a similar mean value (£17 18s.). Here a growing number of houses occupied by wealthy City merchants probably contributed to a general rise in property values.

Areas in class 3
Household rent values just below the metropolitan mean were found on the fringe of the western suburbs in areas that had recently been built or were in the process of development. Within the parish of St James Westminster, in the area just north of Piccadilly, the mean household rent value of £13 19s. probably reflected both the partially developed character of much of the area and its service role in relation to the wealthier element of the parish to the south. Similar reasons may explain the mean rent value (£16 11s.) of Bedfordbury Ward of St Martin in the Fields, which was low in relation to the surrounding neighbourhoods. Its residents may have provided a range of services for the higher status occupants of the nearby Covent Garden district.

In the northern part of the West End the ward of Cock and Pye Fields, within the parish of St Giles in the Fields, was in the process of construction during the 1690s. Under the direction of Sir Thomas Neale it would become the district known as Seven Dials. The 1693–4 Aid assessments do not mention the new streets created as part of this development, yet the mean household rent value of £15 10s. for this and adjacent areas probably reflects the character of this rapidly changing neighbourhood.

Much of the intra-urban length of the Fleet valley had mean household rent values that fell below the metropolitan average, despite the area occupying a central position between the higher value centres of the City and West End. The unsavoury social and environmental character of the area was probably reflected in lower rents: the district had an overall mean rent value of £14 1s. The riverside area from the mouth of the river Fleet eastward to Queenhithe also fell within this same rental category with a mean household rent value of £16. This was a commercial and industrial district, remote from the main centres of business in the City, so consequently its housing stock was probably of low standing.

Other marginal areas within the City had similar mean values. The district focusing on Aldersgate had a mean household rent value of £14 7s. within the City wall and a slightly lower value of £11 18s. immediately outside. Beyond the gate there was a mixture of high value commercial property fronting Aldersgate Street — most notably large coaching establishments such as the Red Lyon Inn — and poorer quality housing in the alleyways and lanes which branched from it.[20] Thus the mean value for Aldersgate Street was £15 18s., while Maidenhead Court and Cradle Court had means of £9 10s. and £7 15s., respectively. The rental distribution profile

for the extramural part of the Aldersgate area reveals the predominance of lower value households. Twenty-six per cent of the household properties fall within the two lowest decile groups (representing rents from £1 to £5 per annum), while the remainder were more or less evenly distributed among the other groups.

North of Aldersgate there was a broad arc of areas with mean household rents that fell within this class. Poor quality housing mixed with more substantial property and land holdings were characteristic of Clerkenwell (£12 4s.), the parish of St Leonard Shoreditch (£11 19s.), and the more rural districts of Bethnal Green and Mile End Old Town (£14 6s). On the east side of the City a district of similar values centred on Aldgate and Whitechapel High Street, with mean household rent values of £15 18s. inside the City wall, and £12 7s. outside. Those extramural areas to the north and south of Whitechapel High Street, yet still in the immediate vicinity of the City wall, had values that lay between these two figures. Thus Houndsditch, to the north, supplied a mean of £13 7s., while the area to the south-east of Aldgate had a mean value of £13 12s.

In the extensive area comprising the Isle of Dogs and much of the eastern part of the parish of Stepney extending to the river Lea (mean value £13 1s.), it is difficult to distinguish residential property from other types of holding, such as high-value grazing land in the marshes, and commercial and industrial sites on the Lea, near Blackwall, and in

Limehouse. High values for these holdings probably tended to counteract the effect on the mean of the many small houses that were to be found in this area. Similar factors may have brought the area around Wapping Dock into this class. Its mean household rent value was £11.

Areas in class 4

The districts with mean household rents less than £10 11s. lay predominantly to the east of the city. In the parish of Stepney the riverside hamlets contained a high number of poor quality houses, often in multiple occupation.[21] The built-up parts of these hamlets had many low value rents, with an overall mean of £7 7s., 46 per cent of them being worth £5 or less. The high density of low value houses gave the riverside strip a higher overall value per hectare than the area inland (see Figs. 3.2 and 3.4). The precinct of St Katherine by the Tower is an extreme example of this phenomenon. Here the very high density of households (185/ha) inflated the overall land value to £1,021 per hectare, while the poverty of the residents is apparent in the mean household rent value of £5 10s. — among the lowest for an intensively built-up area.

Just inland from this riverside zone lay a semi-rural district focused upon Wapping Marsh. The marsh area contained many small poor quality houses intermixed with open space of a low-lying and marginal character, used mostly for small-scale market gardens and pasture. The marsh district, which was bisected by Old Gravel Lane, had a mean rent value of £4 3s. The area to the north of the marsh, including the newly laid out Pennington Street, had the lowest mean rent value for any metropolitan area, £3 5s.[22]

Other areas of low value housing lay to the north of the City, principally outside Bishopsgate and in Spitalfields, which had mean household rent values of £7 5s. and £7 6s., respectively. These low rent levels probably reflected the overall poor quality of houses in the area, even if they had been recently erected, together with a degree of multiple occupancy. Nicholas Barbon, writing in 1689, felt that Bishopsgate was an improving area within which rents were rising in response to the demands of the increased population of nearby Spitalfields.[23] His statement that rents in the Bishopsgate district had risen to around £30 per annum, however, is not supported by the evidence of the assessments. In Bishopsgate Street itself the mean rent value was no more than £21 8s., even including the higher value area close to the City wall. The assessments show that in the northern half of the parish only 5 per cent of rents were worth £30 or more, while in the southern half of the parish, closer to the wall, 17 per cent of rents had this value. Rents were even lower off the main thoroughfare of Bishopsgate, for example in streets and alleys such as Widegate Street (£8 12s.) and Artillery Lane (£10 18s.) to the east, and Dunnings Alley (£5 4s.) and Skinner Street (£6 8s.) to the west.

Similar crowded environments of poor quality housing existed outside Cripplegate and in Saffron Hill. Immediately outside Cripplegate, houses were more valuable than at a greater distance, as was the case outside other City gates. Only a few yards to the north, however, houses in the area bounded by Grub Street to the west and Moorfields to the east had a mean rent value of £5 3s. — the lowest for any built-up area. Saffron Hill, with a mean rent value of £5 10s., was a poor enclave between two areas with much higher rental values, Hatton Garden (£21 4s.) and St Sepulchre without Newgate (£22 11s.).

On the west side of London only two areas fell within this class. They lay in the northern part of the parish of St James Westminster and in the parish of St Margaret Westminster, with mean values of £8 and £8 15s., respectively. These districts were characterised by sparsely situated buildings lying on the fringes of the built-up core. The northern part of St James Westminster in particular was in the process of being built upon for the first time. The area to the south and west of Westminster Abbey was also semi-rural in nature but included some pockets of crowded poor quality housing.

Conclusion

The 1693–4 Aid assessments provide a broad, if not totally inclusive, coverage of the values and distribution of household rent throughout the metropolis. The primary pattern revealed was of a major concentration of low value rents in the eastern suburbs of London, while high value rents were found clustered in the central, predominantly commercial, areas of the City and the West End. Several factors influenced the more detailed pattern within the wider distribution. An example of this was the focus of extremely high value rents in the parish of St James Westminster, south of Piccadilly. An investigation of the distribution of rents by individual streets was informative. In this case the potential for increased social status afforded by the ownership of visibly opulent property, most notably in Pall Mall and St James's Square, clearly provided a considerable spur to the levels of rent realised. This manifestation of wealth was comparable with other forms of conspicuous consumption exhibited during this period.

Such micro-analysis also helps in the explanation of the range of mean rent values obtained for districts on the periphery of the city, and in the eastern parishes. There the pre-eminence of property on the main commercial thoroughfares over the often crowded poorer quality housing stock to be found in the narrower streets and alleyways was immediately apparent in the differences in assessed rents. The proximity of industrial or commercial facilities could also influence rent, for example in the neighbourhood of Smithfield Market where a positive influence was seen, undoubtedly as a result of commercial opportunity. In parts of the riverside parishes, downriver from the Tower, however, the mean level of rent was negatively influenced, possibly as a combined result of intense industrial pressures, a polluted environment and a degree of property dereliction.

A person taking up residence in London during the 1690s clearly had a choice of district in which they might settle and within which they would expect to find rents of a certain character. When it came to choosing a specific property, however, it is evident that within each district they would have been able to find a range of rental values. The quality of such rents was dependent upon factors such as the commercial status of the location, the age and condition of the building, and the employment and social standing of their prospective neighbours. Such influences provided London with a wide range of household rents from the lowly £1 per annum to the much more extravagant, and usually aristocratic, figure of £320.[24]

SOCIAL STATUS OF HOUSEHOLDERS

The 1693–4 Aid assessments provide a limited range of information on the status of the householders themselves. The most consistent indicators are those of gender and those of aristocratic or gentry status. When linked to the value of the rental assessment these provide some insight into the social structure of the metropolis.

Women

By taking forenames or gender-specific titles as an indicator, it is possible to infer the gender of 92.9 per cent of all assessed householders. Of those, 84.1 per cent were male and 15.9 per cent were female, giving a gender ratio for householders of around fifty-three men to every ten women. As a proportion of all households (including those where the gender of the household head could not

be inferred), those certainly headed by women represented 14.7 per cent across the metropolis.[25]

While the distribution of households headed by males reveals no distinctive patterns, that of households headed by women is very striking (Fig. 4.5). There were very few female-headed households in the central area of the City. Within the area from Leadenhall to Ludgate and from the river to the north of Cheapside women headed only 9.7 per cent of all households. The single area within the walls to be most heavily weighted in favour of male householders was in the central part of Cheapside, near Honey Lane Market, where women were no more than 5.6 per cent of all householders. This was one of the key areas of the City for the undertaking of high-value business. Independent women — often widows — usually lacked the financial resources available to men and, consequently, tended to run smaller-scale businesses, so they would have been excluded from this district primarily upon economic grounds. The correlation between the high-value property of the central business area and the absence of women householders, however, was not entirely straightforward, for women were also a small proportion of householders in the lower value areas towards the river (10.6 per cent).[26] It may be that this reflects the occupational characteristics of that district, for the handling of commodities and the industrial activity which took place near the river may have created an environment which, for economic and social reasons, tended to exclude women as householders.

Women householders, however, occurred in higher proportions than the metropolitan average in several districts just outside the central area. There appears to have been a distinctive zone of such districts just within and just beyond the City walls. This stood in sharp contrast to much of the area within the walls: between Aldgate and Coleman Street, for example, 16.7 per cent of households were headed by women. It may be that the river frontage area of Vintry just to the east of Queenhithe, where the proportion of women householders, at 15.0 per cent, was also above average, was in a similar marginal position with regard to the main centres of business in the heart of the City. Beyond that zone, especially to the north of the City, the proportion of women householders fell, despite the low value of most of the houses there. This may point to the existence of a group of women householders who, probably for occupational or social reasons, chose to reside as close as they could to the heart of the City rather than simply in the cheapest accommodation available.

East of the City, near the river, the pattern was different. In a number of those crowded districts of small, cheap houses some of the highest proportions of women householders were to be found. The area with the highest percentage (26.2 per cent) was in the northern part of the hamlet of Ratcliff. This figure fell marginally to 23.3 per cent when the entire hamlet was considered. In the eastern part of Wapping Stepney and the riverside district of Wapping Whitechapel 21.3 per cent of households were found to be headed by women. Limehouse and the central part of Shadwell also

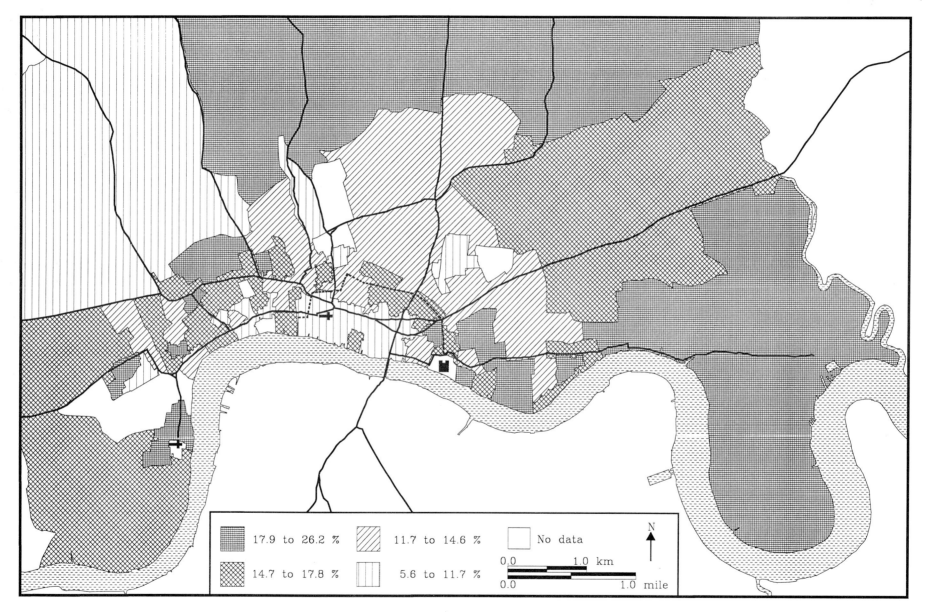

FIG. 4.5 Percentage of households headed by women
Source: 1693–4 Aid database.

demonstrated high numbers of women householders with 19.8 and 19.6 per cent, respectively. Other instances of high percentages were found on the eastern outskirts of the City. The precinct of St Katherine by the Tower had a percentage of 22.5. In Goodmans Fields and the southern part of Aldgate Ward the proportion was 17.9 per cent.

The pattern in the West End was somewhat less coherent. In most areas the proportion of women householders was close to the metropolitan mean. There were two areas where the proportion was notably low. Along the Strand, between Chancery Lane and Drury Lane, the low proportion of such households (10.6 per cent) probably reflects the commercial character of the street, in a similar manner to that of Cheapside in the City. The almost equally low percentage (11.2 per cent) for the south-eastern part of St James parish, south of Piccadilly, almost certainly arises from the substantial aristocratic character of the houses there. That particular area stands in sharp contrast to the immediately adjacent part of the parish where female heads of households were 20.7 per cent of the total. There is no obvious explanation for this sharp contrast, for those two parts of the parish seem to have been of similar social standing, though a tendency for women to live in close proximity to this high status area — yet not within it — might have developed for similar reasons to those noted in the City.

Several other parts of the West End had a high frequency of female householders, including the area between Hatton Garden and Gray's Inn Lane (20.1 per cent), the area to the north of Holborn and around the northern end of Drury Lane (18.1 per cent), and Bedfordbury Ward of the parish of St Martin in the Fields (17.9 per cent). Finally the entire built-up part of St Margaret Westminster, had a higher than average number of female house-holders, with a percentage figure of 19.5. In general terms the more outlying, semi-rural areas such as the Isle of Dogs, Stepney, Hackney and Islington were also characterised by an above average proportion of women householders.

To a considerable extent the distribution of female householders is to be explained by their relative poverty. They occurred relatively infrequently in the busiest commercial areas such as the Strand and in the heart of the City, and in some other areas where properties were valuable. They were most common where rents were cheap. Some other factors, however, were probably also influential. One may have been the nature of the work practised in the area, for example, silk throwing immediately to the east of the City. Another was certainly the tendency of some husbands to be absent, leaving their wife in control of their property. This probably contributed to the high proportion of women householders in riverside areas to the east of the city, especially in the hamlet of Ratcliff, where many men were employed in maritime activities.[27] That environment also offered special economic circumstances within which relatively poor single women operated victualling houses and provided lodgings for mariners.

Many of the women who headed households were described as widows and the distribution of these throws some light upon the pattern of female property ownership discussed above. It is almost certain, however, that more female householders were in fact widows than were so described. The extent to which widows were recorded as such in the returns varied from area to area, according to local custom and the efficiency of the assessors. Despite these limitations some useful conclusions emerge.

The 3,826 householders recorded as widows in the 1693–4 Aid assessments represent 47.9 per cent of all women householders. The most striking feature of the distribution of widows is that they represent a high percentage of female householders in those areas where women occur relatively infrequently as householders (Fig. 4.6). The City within the walls in particular stands out as an area where if women were heads of households then they were very frequently described as widows. Within the walls 67.2 per cent of female householders were widows. It was perhaps their status as widows continuing the operation of the businesses of their former husbands which enabled them to maintain households in that very expensive area. Other widows there may have been maintained by local charity, which often had the specific purpose of sustaining the widows of City traders and shopkeepers. That would have encouraged the perception of these single women as being 'widowed' and promoted their entry as such in the record. Even so, the distinctively male-dominated central part of Cheapside, near Honey Lane, was notable for its low proportions of both

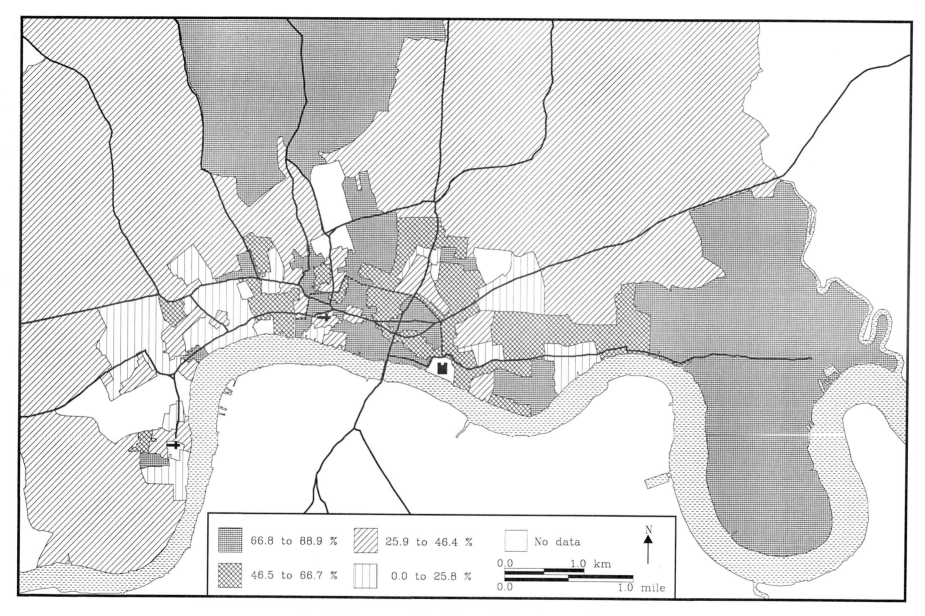

FIG. 4.6 Percentage of female householders who were widows
Source: 1693–4 Aid database.

TABLE 4.3
The distribution of female householders by social group

| Aggregated areas | Female householders defined as: | | | | | | Total | |
| | Aristocratic and gentry[1] | | Widows | | Other women | | Number | % |
	Number	%	Number	%	Number	%		
City within the walls	33	9.5	937	24.5	424	11.1	1,394	17.5
City without the walls	8	2.3	612	16.0	630	16.5	1,250	15.7
St Margaret Westminster	26	7.5	197	5.2	289	7.6	512	6.4
West End	195	55.9	434	11.3	1,162	30.5	1,791	22.4
Northern parishes	40	11.5	346	9.0	247	6.5	633	7.9
Eastern parishes	6	1.6	299	7.8	313	8.2	618	7.7
Eastern riverside parishes	4	1.1	795	20.8	547	14.4	1,346	16.9
Metropolitan Middlesex	37	10.6	206	5.4	199	5.2	442	5.5
Metropolitan total	349	100.0	3,826	100.0	3,811	100.0	7,986	100.0

Source: 1693–4 Aid database.
Note: [1] Countess, Duchess, Lady and Madam.

female householders and of widows among them. Outside the City, in less ordered and less close-knit areas of the metropolis, a woman's status as a widow may have had less social significance, at least in a formal sense, and consequently have been less rigorously noted by assessors.

Nevertheless, in the parishes to the east of the City, a high percentage of women householders were also described as widows. That probably reflects the cheapness of housing in the area, which enabled older women (often widows) who lacked a substantial income or a profitable business to find accommodation. It may also reflect the high rate of mortality among husbands employed in maritime occupations.[28] In Limehouse, Poplar and Blackwall

there was a very high incidence of widowed female householders (73.1 per cent of all women householders), and there was a similar proportion in Wapping (69.9 per cent). In that context, the parish of St Paul Shadwell is distinctive for its low proportion of widowed householders (17.2 per cent of all women householders), a figure which goes very much against the more general pattern observed across the eastern parishes; the reason for this anomaly is far from clear. Taken together, the eastern suburbs, with an overall incidence of widows among female householders of 55.7 per cent, were close to the metropolitan average. As in the City, there were some districts in the northern and eastern suburbs where a high incidence of widows was associated with a low incidence of female householders.

Overall, the West End presented a sharp contrast to both the City and the eastern suburbs in its comparatively low incidence of widows (24.2 per cent of female householders). Widows were a significant presence in the most commercialised parts of Fleet Street and to some extent the Strand, presumably for reasons similar to those proposed for the City within the walls. But in other parts of the West End, where women represented a relatively high proportion of householders, widows were notable by their absence. It may be that a woman's status as a widow was of less significance, and therefore less likely to be recorded, in the West End than in the City. Moreover, a relatively high number of female householders in the area were of aristocratic or gentry status so that if they were widows it was unlikely to have been stated in the returns (Table 4.3). However, it was also the case that the service trades of the West End allowed many women to conduct businesses and to set up households on their own account as single women.[29]

The status of women householders can also be characterised through an analysis of the levels of rent they paid. The total value of rent women householders were assessed for within the study area was £114,244 per annum, or just over 14.6 per cent of that paid by their male counterparts. Overall the mean household rent assessment for women was £14 6s. compared to a mean of £18 9s. for men. Despite the prevalence of widows within the higher value areas the large numbers of poor widows dwelling elsewhere reduced the overall mean household rent for widows to £12 1s.

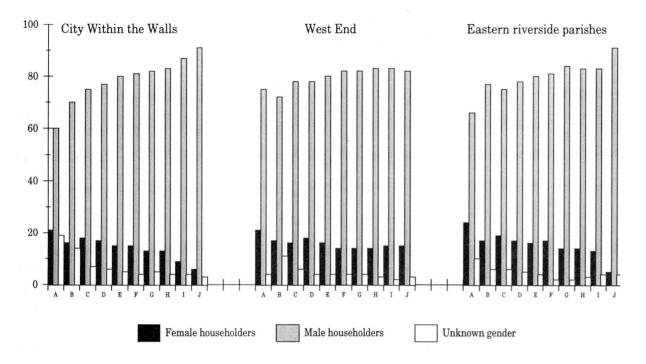

FIG 4.7 The percentage of household rent payments in each rent decile grouped by householders' gender
Source: 1693–4 Aid database. See Table 1.1 for deciles.

The rent distribution profiles for the three aggregate areas where the pattern by gender was most distinctive throw some light upon the nature of female property holding (Fig. 4.7). In the City within the walls low value rents tended to be associated with women householders, while the opposite is observed in the case of men. The rent values most frequently linked with women were those of the lowest group, from £1 to £3 15s. per annum, while female householders were rarely to be found associated with rents of high value.[30] Of the 109 women in the highest rental group, 54 per cent were described as widows and 18

per cent were of aristocratic or gentry status, which in the case of the assessments for the City almost entirely denoted the widows of knighted merchants. An even higher proportion of the seventy-four female householders in the lowest rent group were recorded as widows (72 per cent).

In the West End, female householders were also most prominent in the lowest rental group, but in contrast to the City they were also relatively significant in the higher value groups (Fig. 4.7). In the highest rent decile group 67 per cent of the 266

women householders were of aristocratic or gentry status, while only 7 per cent were widows. In contrast, within the lowest group 37 per cent were described as widows. The possession of landed income was clearly an important factor in explaining the relative significance of women (as opposed to widows) as high rental householders in the West End. Female householders of high aristocratic status do not occur in rental groups lower than group I (£26 to £39 4s.); the lowest rent paid by such a person being £36 per annum by the Countess of Montgomery for a property in Dean Street, St Anne Soho. Women householders who were not aristocrats, gentry or widows represent a much higher proportion in the West End (64.9 per cent) than in the City (30.4 per cent) or the eastern riverside suburbs (40.6 per cent). These figures support the suggestion that the working environment of the West End offered particular opportunities to independent women.

In the eastern riverside suburbs the rent distribution profile for women householders resembled that for the City, although their exclusion from the highest rental groups was not so marked (Fig. 4.7). In this area, however, the higher groups contained many fewer households than in the City, so that the six women in the highest group represented only 5 per cent of the total. The social character of this district differed significantly from that of the West End as only 0.3 per cent of the female householders in the eastern riverside suburbs had gentry status and none were aristocrats. The most prosperous woman house-holder was a Widow Swann, who was assessed for

£110 rent on property in the vicinity of East Smithfield. The lowest value group in this aggregate area had the highest proportion of women householders in any decile group for any part of London. Women made up just under a quarter (24 per cent) of all householders within the lowest decile group of the eastern riverside area. Of these 571 women 348 were widows, a figure which helped to generate the low mean rent value paid by such women for the metropolis as a whole.

The aristocracy and gentry

The 1693–4 Aid assessments identify a substantial number of householders by a title denoting social status. Those householders can be classified as aristocracy or gentry. The former is defined as all individuals with the title Baron, Count, Countess, Duchess, Duke, Earl, Lord or Marquis. The gentry group comprises those with the ascription Dame, Esquire, Sir — denoting baronets or knights — or Madam. The term Gent', or Gentleman, occurred very rarely within the 1693–4 Aid assessments, only fifteen cases being noted. Further, no examples of this designation were recorded for the City of London, although the Poll Tax assessments indicate that 383 members of the gentry were householders within that area. This possibly reflects a contemporary comprehension of the term as an occupationally-related title rather than one of social status alone. Consequently those giving the title Gentleman have been omitted from the following discussion of social structure.[31] The title Lady presents further complications: such women could

have been either the wives or widows of aristocrats or of gentry with the title Sir. Ladies have therefore been summarised separately in Table 4.4 and are omitted from the distribution patterns shown in Figs. 4.8 and 4.9. The titles Mr and Mrs have been excluded from this discussion as their overall distribution, to a certain extent, reflected the pattern among the other social groups. Moreover, these particular titles are a less reliable guide to status, mainly as a result of the recording peculiarities of assessors: in some cases, particularly in rural areas, almost all male householders were defined as Mr, while in other areas there were none at all. The title Mr, within the City, would appear to have been used to indicate those in charge of their own business, and therefore not necessarily of higher social status.

The aristocracy were assessed for 145 households with a combined rent value of £18,114 10s. (1.9 per cent of the metropolitan total).[32] The mean household rent was £124 1s., a value far greater than the metropolitan household mean of £17 7s., though the inclusion of a number of rent-generating properties within the calculation may have inflated the resulting mean. Aristocrats were often assessed for more than one property. It is clear that in addition to their residence they regularly held other houses or land from which they drew a rental income. Sometimes it is possible to identify them in their role as landlords, but often it is difficult to identify their place of residence from their other holdings. Where property of a non-household nature has been identified it has not been included in estimates of aristocratic household values. Nevertheless, the distribution of

aristocratic households demonstrates a clear pattern (Fig. 4.8).[33]

As might be expected, virtually all aristocratic households lay in the west of the metropolis and it was notable that no aristocrats were resident in the City of London. The greatest concentration of aristocratic households was in the parishes of St Anne Soho (22) and St James Westminster (42). In St Anne's parish aristocrats represented 2.0 per cent of all households, but their contribution to the rent value of the parish was £2,797 or 11.3 per cent of the total.[34] The most valuable properties (£300) were found in King's (Soho) Square, Carlisle House occupied by the Countess of Carlisle, and Leicester House, residence of the Earl of Leicester, situated on the north side of Leicester Fields (Square).[35] In St James Westminster aristocratic households accounted for 1.8 per cent of households with a combined value of £6,249, representing 13.1 per cent of the total rental value of the parish.[36] The most valuable property (£320) was Burlington House in Piccadilly, residence of Richard Boyle, Earl of Cork and Burlington (see Fig. 2.5). In 1668 the first Earl noted that the full cost of construction had been in the order of £5,000.[37]

Twenty-nine aristocratic households were located to the north of the West End in the parishes of St Andrew Holborn and St Giles in the Fields. Those households made up 0.5 per cent of the total number of households in the two parishes with a combined rent value of £3,085, 3.4 per cent of the total rent value for the area. Among the twenty aristocratic households that lay to the north of High Holborn were

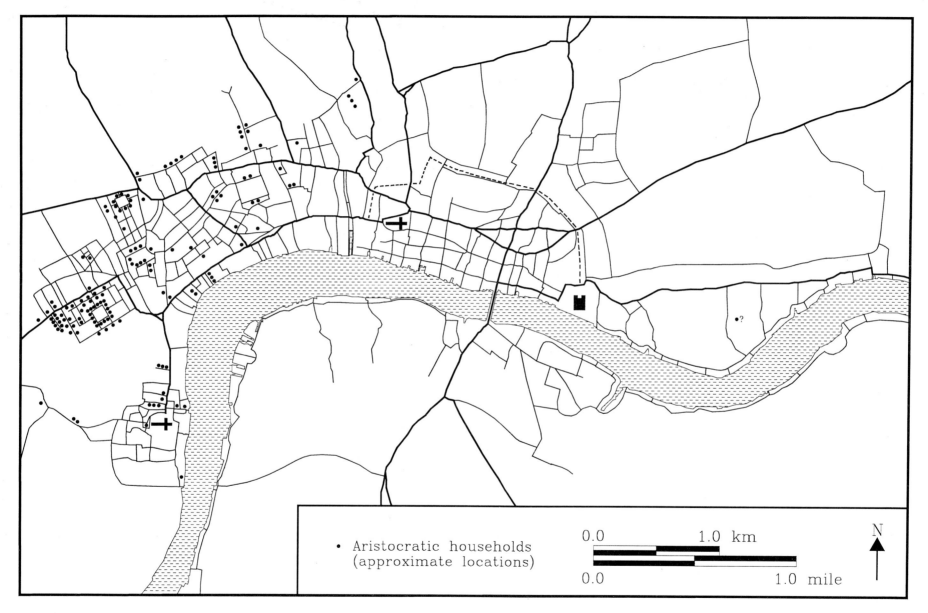

• Aristocratic households
(approximate locations)

0.0   1.0 km

0.0   1.0 mile

N

FIG. 4.8 Households headed by aristocracy
Source: 1693–4 Aid database.

TABLE 4.4
The distribution of aristocratic and gentry householders by social group

Aggregated areas	Aristocrats[1]		Ladies		Gentry[2]		Total	
	Number	%	Number	%	Number	%	Number	%
City within the walls	–	–	7	5.2	116	13.5	123	10.8
City without the walls	–	–	3	2.2	44	5.2	47	4.1
St Margaret Westminster	12	8.3	11	8.2	47	5.5	70	6.2
West End	101	69.6	89	65.9	421	49.0	611	53.6
Northern parishes	12	8.3	8	5.9	120	14.0	140	12.3
Eastern parishes	–	–	2	1.5	14	1.6	16	1.4
Eastern riverside parishes	1	0.7	1	0.7	15	1.7	17	1.5
Metropolitan Middlesex	19	13.1	14	10.4	82	9.5	115	10.1
Metropolitan total	145	100.0	135	100.0	859	100.0	1,139	100.0

Source: 1693–4 Aid database.
Notes: [1] Baron, Count, Countess, Duchess, Duke, Earl, Lord and Marquis. [2] Esquire, Madam and Sir.

the two great houses or palaces of Lord Montague and the Earl of Southampton. Lord Montague's house, originally designed by Robert Hooke had been destroyed by fire in 1686 and it is likely that by 1693–4 Montague was still in the process of rebuilding, the commencement of which had probably been delayed until 1688.[38] Nevertheless, the house, whatever its state of repair, was valued at £300 per annum, with the Earl of Montague noted as responsible for payment of the tax.[39] The neighbouring Southampton House, standing further to the east, was valued at £200 per annum, the inhabitant being Lady Russell. Southampton House was smaller and older having been constructed around 1657. It was the focal point of the wider development of the Southampton estate, the house standing in a dominant position across the entire northern side of Southampton (now Bloomsbury) Square.[40]

The area immediately to the west of the parish of St James Westminster — the outlying part of St Martin in the Fields — had seventeen aristocratic households. Such a position at the very edge of the built-up area took advantage of the open space and clean air afforded by the surrounding fields. The combined rental value of these properties amounted to £2,395, 20.7 per cent of the total household rental value for this predominantly rural area. The satellite settlement of Pimlico was also noteworthy as it contained property, probably an estate, belonging to the Earl of Devonshire that was valued at £500 per annum.[41]

Two further districts in the western half of the metropolis contained aristocratic households: St Margaret Westminster and an area from the Strand to the western end of Long Acre. St Margaret's, long

associated with the court and parliament, contained fourteen aristocratic households with a combined rent value of £1,166 10s., 3.2 per cent of the total rent value of the parish. The central district of the West End had twelve aristocratic households with a combined rental value of £1,211, 2.9 per cent of all household rents in the area.

One hundred and thirty-five women, probably mostly widows, had the title Lady. Either aristocrats or gentry, they could not be exclusively assigned to one group or the other and consequently they are discussed separately from those two groups. Ladies were responsible for £7,093 of household rent, 0.8 per cent of the metropolitan total or 6.2 per cent of all household rents paid by women. These high status women had an assessed mean rent value of £51 6s. This is much closer to the mean rent value for gentry households (£53 8s.) than the mean for aristocratic households (£124 1s.), and suggests that the majority of these ladies were probably the widows of knights or baronets. Overall, ladies comprised 11.9 per cent of all aristocratic and gentry householders, but in all areas except the West End their numbers were recorded below this average (Table 4.4). The greatest concentration of lady householders was in the West End, where eighty-nine women paid £5,239 in rent, with a mean value of £58 17s. Their situations varied, from Lady Russell who was assessed for £200 rent on her substantial residence in King Street, St Giles in the Fields, to Lady Mary Dashwood who paid £12 rent for a property in the Sheere Lane Ward of St Clement Danes parish. A further forty-six ladies

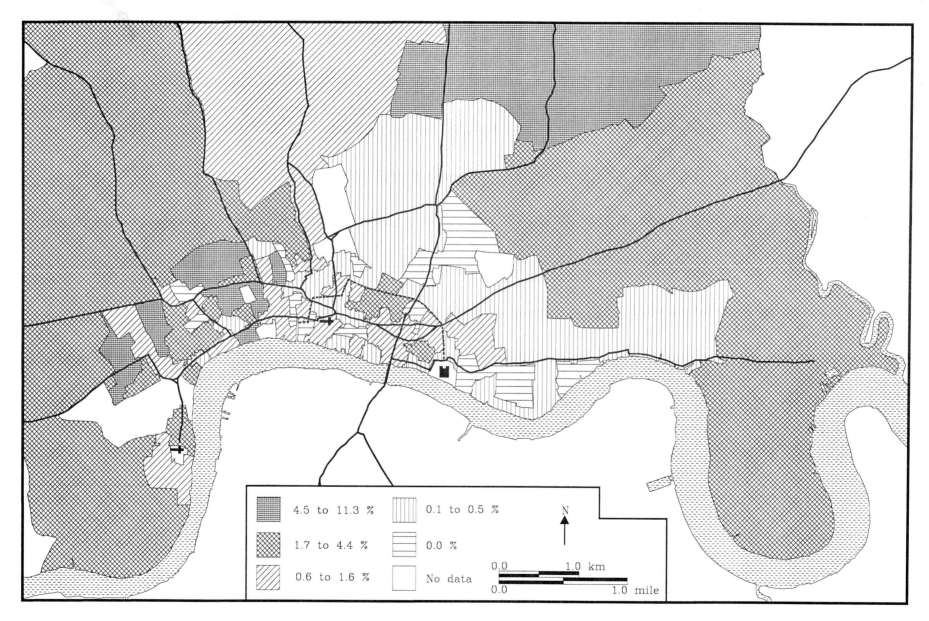

FIG. 4.9 Percentage of households headed by gentry
Source: 1693–4 Aid database.

were recorded as householders in other parts of London, with most resident in the western outskirts of the metropolis. Those recorded in St Margaret Westminster and on the edge of the West End were assessed for £764 rent, with a mean of £33 4s., while those dwelling in the remaining areas of the city were assessed for £1,108, which gave a mean rent value of £48 3s.

The gentry — that is, those householders with the title 'esquire', 'madam' or 'sir' — occupied property in more widespread locations than the aristocracy. Nevertheless, just under half of all gentry households were found in the West End (49.0 per cent). Other areas with high concentrations of such households were the northern parishes, which included the district of Hatton Garden, with a figure of 14.0 per cent, and the City of London within the walls, 13.5 per cent (Table 4.4). Overall there were 895 gentry households which represented 1.5 per cent of the total number of metropolitan households. The combined value of their assessed household rent was £46,264, 4.9 per cent of the total rent figure, with a mean household rent value of £51 14s.

The occurrence of gentry households at a neighbourhood level is displayed in Fig. 4.9. Those areas with the greatest concentration of gentry households were Hatton Garden, where thirty-eight households represented 11.3 per cent of all households in the area, and a district on the edge of the built-up area to the north of Holborn and Gray's Inn which housed forty-seven members of the gentry, 11.0 per cent of all households. The mean

rent for such households within the Hatton Garden area was £36 19s. The highest individual rent belonged to Sir George Treby, Lord Chief Justice in the Court of Common Pleas, who paid £60 per annum for a large house with a substantial out-building and private yard near the junction of Hatton Garden and Cross Street.[42] In the area adjacent to Gray's Inn gentry rents had a mean value of £55, with the highest single rent value being £100 paid by both William Smith esquire and Sir Richard Middleton for their properties near Lamb's Conduit. In this area, the association between gentry titles and those who practised law seems clear.

High numbers of gentry households were observed in three further areas of the West End: the western part of the parish of St James Westminster (7.3 per cent), the parish of St Anne Soho (8.3 per cent), and a fragmented district reaching from the Savoy through Lincoln's Inn Fields to the north of Holborn (8.2 per cent). An additional area with a high percentage of gentry households was the parish of St John Hackney where twenty members of the gentry made up 4.5 per cent of all the householders of the parish. The mean rent level for gentry resident in the western part of the parish of St James was £48 12s. Some of the highest value gentry properties found in a single concentration were those in Golden Square to the north of Piccadilly. Here rents ranged from Charles Chettwind esquire's £30 for a property on the south side of the square to £60 paid by three knights or baronets, two esquires and a colonel, for residences probably on the northern side of the square.[43] The

highest single gentry rent in this area was, however, located south of Piccadilly in King Street, where the northern magnate and one-time First Lord of the Treasury, Sir John Lowther, paid £120 for what was clearly a substantial property.[44]

In St Anne Soho the gentry occupied seventy-six households, some 8.3 per cent of the parish. Their mean household rent was £49 15s. per annum, and the value of their rents made up around 10.6 per cent of the total for the parish. The highest rent paid in this parish by a member of the gentry was £200 by Sir Samuel Grimstone, baronet, for a four-storey house on the south side of King's (Soho) Square positioned on the corner of Greek Street and adjacent to Monmouth House.[45] Between the western part of the parish of St James Westminster and the parish of St Anne Soho lay an area where very few gentry titles were recorded. From Oxford Street south to the area around Charing Cross gentry made up only around 1.0 per cent of all householders. The overall rental pattern for the area suggests that it probably had a commercial character and served the adjacent high status communities of both aristocracy and gentry.

A major concentration of gentry households was in the district extending from the newly developed area north of Gray's Inn, as described above, through Lincoln's Inn Fields and Chancery Lane, to the riverside around Essex Street adjacent to the Temple. This area was favoured by members of the legal profession and, in the case of the Inns of Court, by students of law. There were four districts

FIG. 4.10 Soho or King's Square, *c.*1720s, looking north (Sutton Nicholls)
Source: Museum of London.

in this area notable for a high number of gentry households, aside from that adjoining Gray's Inn. The 148 gentry households within these four areas had a mean value of £53 9s., represented 7.5 per cent of all households and accounted for £7,642 rent, 14.9 per cent of the total. Gentry households in the area to the north-west of Holborn had a mean value of £54 9s., represented 4.7 per cent of all households and accounted for £1,089 rent, 10.9 per cent of the total. Between Holborn and the Strand, including the surroundings of Lincoln's Inn Fields and Chancery Lane, gentry households with a mean value of £50 18s., represented 9.1 per cent of the total number, and accounted for £4,783 rent, 18.3 per cent of the total. Between the Strand and the Thames, immediately west of the Temple, gentry households with a mean value of £61 1s., represented 6.5 per cent of the total number, and accounted for £1,770 rent, 11.5 per cent of the total.

Four areas within the western suburbs were recorded with greater than average numbers of gentry households. Twenty-four such households in the district adjacent to the southern end of Whitehall in the parish of St Margaret Westminster had a mean rent value of £33 5s., represented 2.3 per cent of all households in the area and accounted for £813 rent, 4.4 per cent of the total. In the south-eastern part of St James Westminster gentry households represented 4.3 per cent of all households, had a mean rent value of £79 6s., and a total value of £1,665, 10.6 per cent of all household rents. An extensive central district of the West End covering an area from the riverside near Hungerford Market through the parish of St

Paul Covent Garden to the junction of Tottenham Court Road and Oxford Street contained sixty-one gentry households. Those households had a mean rent value of £82 10s., a total value of £5,145, representing 8.4 per cent of the total. The most valuable rent paid by the gentry households of this district was £350, recorded for three knights, two baronets and two esquires.[46] Among those seven was Robert Harley esquire, a resident of York Buildings, who would later become Earl of Oxford and 'first minister' during the reign of Queen Anne.[47] To the east of Drury Lane three areas with higher than average numbers of gentry households lay immediately adjacent to that district centred upon Lincoln's Inn Fields which had a very high occurrence of gentry, as described above. These three areas were the location for thirty-two gentry households with a mean value of £29 13s. and a total rent value of £948, 4.1 per cent of the total.

Further areas within which the proportion of gentry households was above the metropolitan average were mostly located in the western parts of the metropolis. The out-ward of the parish of St Martin in the Fields, to the south of Oxford Street, provided a semi-rural location for twenty-five gentry households. These had a mean rent value of £51 7s., with a total value of £1,284, 11.1 percent of all household rents. To the north-west of the built-up limit of the West End lay an area characterised by both high rent values and a relatively high percentage of gentry properties. The area, comprising the parishes of St Marylebone, St Pancras, and St James Clerkenwell, had an overall mean rent value of £23 10s. Land use information

suggests that high quality pasture might account for some of the high rents, though the incidence of gentry recorded within the combined assessments (5.5 per cent of all householders) suggests that large estates, possibly incorporating high value pasture, may have been a typical feature of the property-holding pattern within this district.[48]

In the City of London relatively few members of the gentry were specifically identified within the assessments for the 1693–4 Aid. Only 0.8 per cent of households were noted as headed by gentry, compared to 2.5 per cent indicated by the 1692 Poll Tax listings, though the latter identification relies upon the self-styled term gentleman, rather than the more formal attributions of sir or esquire as employed by the 1693–4 Aid assessments.[49] The City within the walls had a relatively low proportion of inhabitants with the titles esquire, madam or sir. It is likely that most, if not all, of these belonged to mercantile families. The mean value of these households was £76 6s. per annum, about three times the overall mean for the area. Despite this high mean rent for gentry resident within this area, the total rent paid by this group, £8,789, was only 3.0 per cent of the highly valuable total household rental figure for the City within the walls. Those areas with higher than average numbers of gentry lay away from the central district, which was characterised by a concentration of business activity. Two such peripheral areas can be identified. In the northern part of the City, Coleman Street Ward, part of Broad Street Ward, and the area around the Guildhall contained twenty-eight gentry households, 2.0 per cent of the total, with a mean rent of £79 6s., and accounting for £2,220, 6.9 per cent of the total. The second area lay on the east side of the City between Thames Street and Fenchurch Street, where nineteen gentry households were noted, 4.2 per cent of the total, with a mean rent of £63, and accounting for £1,210, 10.7 per cent of the total.

Gentry households occur in above average proportions in the parish of St John Hackney and in the areas of Mile End, Poplar and Blackwall, where they represent 3.3 per cent of all households, had a mean rent value of £44 14s., and accounted for £2,089 rent, 9.5 per cent of the areas' total value. The social standing of the gentry within this locality may have differed from the majority of those in the more built-up districts, as thirteen (half of the men assessed) were commissioners for the aid. The gentry in these areas possessed a variety of non-household property, particularly land holdings and groups of tenements, but some were clearly occupying residential property. In the parish of St John Hackney the gentry comprised 4.5 per cent of all householders and included the Jacobite conspirator Sir John Friend who possessed 'a fine country residence' with a rent value of £40 per annum.[50] Estates were also found in this area where Sir Thomas Cooke, a commissioner for the aid, owned a house and land worth £195; he was also assessed for a ferry, presumably across the river Lea, with a value of £12. To the south, in the hamlet of Poplar and Blackwall, the shipbuilder Sir Henry Johnson was found to be paying a rent of £600 for property which certainly included Blackwall Yard.[51]

He was clearly resident having been appointed as a commissioner for the aid within this area. Johnson also owned ten acres of the east marsh, valued at £15.

Some areas were noticeably lacking in inhabitants of higher social standing. The area between the parishes of St James Westminster and St Anne Soho in the West End has already been discussed, but a number of other districts, particularly to the north and east of the city, were notable for a complete absence of gentry households. Such districts included: the district of Acre Lane to the north of Covent Garden; the neighbourhood of Saffron Hill; most of the Fleet valley from Holborn Bridge to Blackfriars; an area within the walls between Thames Street and Cheapside; part of Cripplegate Ward Without; the northern part of the ward of Bishopsgate Without and the liberty of Norton Folgate; much of Spitalfields; and a large proportion of the eastern riverside area. All these districts tend to have been characterised by either low levels of rent or highly crowded environments, and in some cases both conditions were present. In some situations further social and environmental factors may have shaped particular neighbourhoods as inherently inferior in terms of social status when compared with those areas within which the majority of the gentry were resident. While these considerations may have influenced the location of gentry households the residential pattern of lodgers of gentry status, particularly as indicated by the 1692 Poll Tax assessments, needs to be considered before a clearer understanding of the overall pattern of gentry residence can be established.[52]

While complex in detail, the pattern of aristocratic and gentry residence overall is clear: such householders were overwhelmingly concentrated in the West End. The largest houses, which were often recently constructed, lay on the periphery of that area and appear to have been mainly occupied by members of the aristocracy. In the City and to the east those few who had gentry titles were predominantly of mercantile origin. An earlier pattern of aristocratic residence in London, in which a significant minority of those with a rank higher than that of knight were to be found in the City or in its northern and eastern suburbs, had been swept away as a result of the increasing concentration of court and fashionable life to the west and by a proliferation of industry and poor housing to the east. Thus the aristocratic residences of the West End became focused upon certain locations in which the high value of their rents could be exhibited as a form of conspicuous consumption.

SOCIAL STRUCTURE OF HOUSEHOLDS AND PATTERNS OF OCCUPANCY

Household structure

Two sources provide detailed information on household structure in the City of London during the 1690s: the records of the 1692 Poll Tax, and the marriage duty assessments of 1695. In this study extensive use has been made of the poll tax returns, since they include information on the occupations of householders which is lacking in the marriage duty assessments. Comparable information for districts

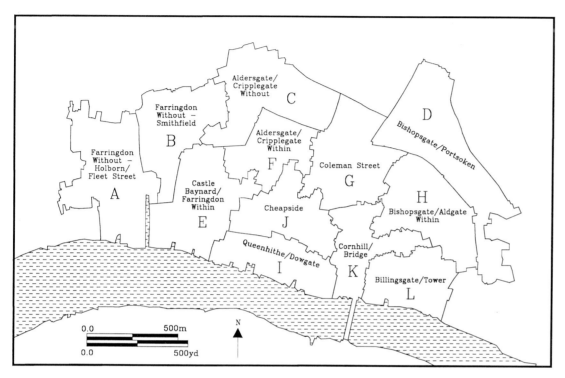

FIG. 4.11 Areas used for the analysis of the 1692 Poll Tax and aggregated from City ward boundaries
Source: See Appendix II; 1692 Poll Tax database.

walls (areas A, B, C, and D) are considered less representative than those within as a result of levels of exemption — as high as 75 per cent in the case of the western precinct of the ward of Cripplegate Without.[56] The overall mean for exemptions within the walls was 9 per cent when compared with the more extensive coverage of the 1693–4 Aid assessments, and 35 per cent for the area without the walls when compared with the 1695 Marriage Duty returns.[57]

Most published studies of household size and composition in late seventeenth-century London have been based on the 1695 returns.[58] Chief amongst these is the work by Glass whose conclusions, although based on a detailed study of only ten sample parishes, are worth summarising. The marriage duty returns for those parishes indicate a mean number of persons per house of 6.3, falling to 5.7 for the nuclear household and providing a mean size of 1.9 for subordinate, or lodger, households. Glass also supplies some measure of household structure, with a mean number of children per household of 1.1 and a mean number of servants per household of 1.5.

One problem associated with any such analysis, however, is the definition of household, which is most frequently taken to include the householder's family (that is, adults with or without children, and any additional resident kin), servants and apprentices. The exact composition and size of such households was dependent upon a number of economic, social and demographic influences.[59] The

outside the City does not exist, although the occurrence of wealthy lodgers across the metropolis as a whole can be traced from the 1693–4 Aid assessments.[53] From the 1692 Poll Tax database it is possible to derive standard sets of information on household size and composition for a number of social and occupational categories. Some categories of household were omitted, notably those receiving alms. Unlike some earlier poll taxes, however, the estimation of households which were covered was near complete for most central areas, and children

were generally not omitted, excepting those whose parents were themselves exempt or those of day-labourers.[54] Even so there will, of course, have been some under-enumeration. The poll tax returns have some advantage over the marriage duty assessments in that they survive for a greater area of the City, although in poorer quarters, mainly outside the City walls, a substantial minority of households were exempt.[55] In analysing the returns a series of aggregated areas has been employed (Fig. 4.11), although figures pertaining to the areas outside the

TABLE 4.5
Household size by aggregated area within the City, c.1692

City area[1]	No. of houses	Mean rent per house[2]	Principal households		Lodger households			Population of area	Mean no. of persons per house
			Mean size	Population	No.	Mean size	Population		
Without walls									
A	2,207	£18 10s.	3.38	7,461	1,052	1.56	1,641	9,102	4.12
B	1,527	£13 8s.	3.53	5,233	637	1.51	907	6,140	4.02
C	1,406	£13 14s.	3.00	4,213	311	1.34	416	4,629	3.29
D	1,725	£17 13s.	3.15	5,431	299	1.52	454	5,885	3.41
Sub total	6,865	£15 16s.	3.27	22,338	2,299	1.48	3,418	25,756	3.71
Within walls									
E	1,858	£24 17s.	3.84	7,138	1,157	1.52	1,764	8,902	4.79
F	1,334	£21 0s.	4.14	5,509	810	1.52	1,229	6,738	5.05
G	1,215	£27 18s.	4.43	5,388	908	1.56	1,413	6,801	5.60
H	1,444	£26 13s.	3.98	5,751	608	1.41	858	6,609	4.58
I	1,096	£22 3s.	3.51	3,852	483	1.63	788	4,640	4.23
J	1,322	£34 15s.	4.76	6,293	768	1.62	1,245	7,538	5.70
K	1,314	£41 12s.	5.09	6,687	698	1.58	1,102	7,789	5.93
L	1,118	£32 1s.	4.31	4,819	557	1.56	869	5,688	5.09
Sub total	10,701	£28 18s.	4.26	45,437	5,989	1.55	9,268	54,705	5.12
Whole City	17,566	£25 10s.	3.92	67,775	8,288	1.57	12,990	80,765	4.60

Source: 1692 Poll Tax database.

Notes: [1] For definition of areas, see Fig. 4.11.　　[2] Rent value for poll tax households linked to 1693–4 Aid assessments only.

status of lodgers, boarders or inmates in any given house is harder to determine; in some cases they will have been integrated within the main or principal household, at other times they may have maintained their own independent household within the principal householder's property. In the case of the 1692 Poll Tax returns lodgers are often explicitly recorded. Where this is not the case, the returns, in which entries are grouped by means of dividing lines, clearly indicate individual houses (although it

is far from clear that these units necessarily corresponded to the type of self-contained structure conventionally identified today as a house), identify members of the principal household together with their relationship to one another, and often also identify other persons resident within the unit. It can thus reasonably be assumed that those others were lodgers. These returns indicate that 47 per cent of houses contained subsidiary lodger households. Therefore, for the purposes of analysis three

categories have been employed: the number of persons per 'house'; the principal household (comprising servants and apprentices as well as family); and the lodger household.

The mean number of persons per house was 4.63 (the means for each aggregated area of the City are shown in Table 4.5 and displayed in Fig. 4.12). The Bishopsgate and Houndsditch area without the walls had the lowest mean (3.41 persons per house), while the highest was found in the central Cornhill and London Bridge area (5.93 persons per house).[60] A number of highly populated houses were found in the neighbourhood of Cornhill, an example of which is that of Richard William, a relatively wealthy packer. William's own household consisted of himself, two children, two male servants and a female servant. His house also contained three lodgers: Sir Robert Adams, who had a male servant; a merchant named Stephen Thormley; and Mrs Townes, who had a female servant. Thus the house, with a rent value of £100, contained eleven inhabitants. The number of persons in any given house was clearly influenced by the economic condition of the householders — wealthier households tended to be larger households — and to a lesser extent by the frequency of lodgers, but also by the physical size of the building. High numbers of persons per house could be a result of increased levels of subdivision. However, this must remain as speculation given the difficulty in forming an absolute definition for the terms 'house' and 'household' from the returns.

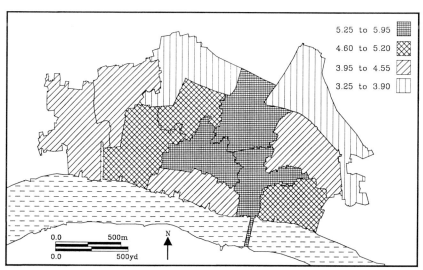

FIG. 4.12 Mean number of persons per house
in the City of London
Source: 1692 Poll Tax database.

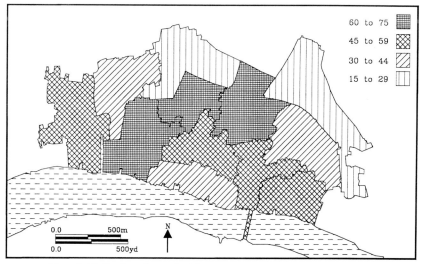

FIG. 4.13 Lodger householders as a percentage of all houses
in the City of London
Source: 1692 Poll Tax database.

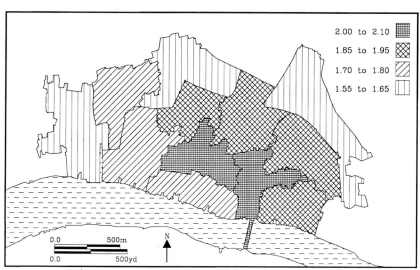

FIG. 4.14 Mean number of children per household
in the City of London
Source: 1692 Poll Tax database.

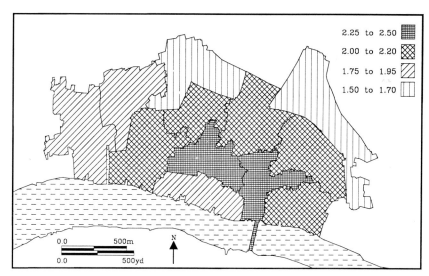

FIG. 4.15 Mean number of servants and apprentices per household
in the City of London
Source: 1692 Poll Tax database.

Nevertheless, while the pattern revealed in Fig. 4.12 indicates that the highest mean number of persons per house was to be found within the central wealthy commercial district of the City, an above average mean was found within the area adjacent to the downriver waterfront (5.09 persons per house). A similar mean was noted also across the entire western part of the City within the walls (4.92 persons per house). In the remaining areas within the walls (4.41 persons per house) and within the large extramural ward of Farringdon Without (4.14 persons per house) the mean number of inhabitants per house fell below the City-wide average. Areas to the north of the City walls had a relatively low mean number of persons per house (3.35 persons per house). Those areas were also characterised by low levels of rent.

In analysing the 1692 Poll Tax returns two types of household have been identified: the main or principal household held responsible for any rental payments, and lodger households.[61] The size of any given principal household varied with reference to a range of social, economic and environmental factors. The overall mean for the City of London was 3.92 persons per principal household (see Table 4.5). The area with the highest mean number of persons per principal household was in the district of Cornhill (5.09 persons per household). The area with the lowest mean number of persons per principal household was found to the north of the City walls in the area of Cripplegate (3.00 persons per household). There is a strong correlation between mean rent and the mean size of principal households — as one increases so generally does the other. This relationship resulted from a variety of factors; for example, the poorer peripheral areas of the City tended to present worse conditions for health and so increased mortality might be expected, particularly infant mortality, limiting the size of families. Those with households in wealthier areas tended to be larger, both through increased family size and the ability to employ more servants. So household size was a reflection of not only wealth but also underlying environmental and, to some extent, demographic factors; younger households were often smaller households.

The range of household sizes found within the City is shown in Table 4.6. Just over 24 per cent (4,284) of all principal households held only two people, 72.8 per cent (3,117) of those households comprised a married couple. In the case of the 3,501 households which contained three people 73.1 per cent (2,555) were headed by married couples. In 48.2 per cent (1,232) of those households the third person was a servant and in 36.7 per cent (938) a child. Just under half, 48.2 per cent (8,470), of all principal households held more than three people with 84.4 per cent (7,151) of these households being headed by a married couple.

The largest principal households in the City of London were the 435 (2.5 per cent) comprising ten or more persons. One of the largest was that of Sir Joseph Hearne in the parish of St Stephen Coleman Street which comprised himself, his wife, eight children, four male servants and nine female servants, a total of twenty-three people.[62] At the other end of the scale 1,311 households (7.5 per cent) consisted of the householder alone. The largest concentration of single person households was found in the Bishopsgate and Houndsditch district outside of the City walls (11.9 per cent of principal households), while the lowest concentration of such households was in the Cornhill area (3.4 per cent of principal households). The overall mean rent value of those principal households occupied by a single person was £6 19s., which stands in marked contrast to the £120 per annum rent assessed for Sir Joseph Hearne.

Principal households headed by men had a mean number of persons per household of 4.13, while women usually headed smaller households, with a mean of 2.6 persons per household. The first mean is inclusive of those households headed by a married couple where the husband would invariably have been recorded as the head of household for the purposes of the poll tax. In the case of principal households consisting of a single person a significant proportion (49.4 per cent) were female, just under half of these women being widows. Men comprised a slightly lower figure of 44.3 per cent of all such households. (The remaining 6.5 per cent of householders were of unstated gender.)

The households of lodgers were generally of a small size, with an overall mean of 1.57, while 61.7 per cent of these households consisted of no more than a single person (Tables 4.5 and 4.6). As a

TABLE 4.6
Household size

No. of persons	Principal households		Lodger households	
	Number	%	Number	%
1	1,311	7.47	5,118	61.74
2	4,284	24.39	2,238	27.00
3	3,501	19.94	587	7.08
4	2,778	15.82	220	2.66
5	2,063	11.75	68	0.82
6	1,440	8.20	35	0.42
7	922	5.25	9	0.10
8	514	2.93	5	0.06
9	313	1.79	2	0.03
10	194	1.11	3	0.04
11	106	0.61	1	0.02
12	53	0.30	2	0.03
13	29	0.16	–	–
14	26	0.14	–	–
15	14	0.07	–	–
16	2	0.01	–	–
17	5	0.02	–	–
18	5	0.02	–	–
19	3	0.01	–	–
20–23	3	0.01	–	–
Total	17,566	100.00	8,288	100.00

Source: 1692 Poll Tax database.

result of this high incidence of lodgers living alone, there was limited variation in the mean size of lodger households across the City. The largest mean size of lodger households was 1.63 in the Queenhithe and Dowgate area, the smallest mean household size was 1.34 outside the walls in the area of Cripplegate. Lodger households were found in all parts of the City (Fig. 4.13), though the greatest concentration was in the wards of Coleman Street and Broad Street (74.7 per cent), with the western intramural area having a similar high frequency (61.5 per cent). Areas which demonstrated the lowest incidence of lodger households were located beyond the City walls in the districts of Cripplegate (22.1 per cent) and Bishopsgate and Houndsditch (17.3 per cent). This distribution probably reflects the tendency for those of middling wealth to take in lodgers, as opposed to the poorest or richest householders who either could not accommodate or had no economic need of lodgers.

Where gender was indicated, men comprised 45.5 per cent of single lodger households and women 41.4 per cent. Within this group 10.9 per cent were noted as widows, a much lower proportion than that found for single female principal householders. In the 2,238 lodger households containing two people, 69.3 per cent comprised married couples. In 12.7 per cent of households of two people the second member of the lodger's household was a servant and in 10.0 per cent of such households the second person was a child. Relatively few lodger households exceeded two people (11.3 per cent of all lodger households), and most of these households held fewer than seven people, although two households as large as twelve were noted. One was the household of Thomas Preston who occupied part of the residence of Thomas Collett near to the church of St Magnus the Martyr in Thames Street.[63] Both men were relatively wealthy salters: Collett's rent stood at £50 per annum and his stock was worth £400, while Preston's stock was valued at £100.

Thomas Preston's household comprised himself, his wife, four children (increased to five by the time of the 1695 Marriage Duty assessment), four male servants and two female servants.[64] Collett's principal household was somewhat smaller: himself, his wife and two servants.[65]

Children were found in 8,576 (33.2 per cent) households — both principal and lodger — of the City of London (see Table 4.7). The overall mean number of children per household was 1.82, with 80.1 per cent of households with children having no more than two. Overall, the majority of children had at least one sibling, though when measured by household, 51.8 per cent of households contained a single child.[66] The mean number of children per household varied slightly across the extents of the City (Fig. 4.14). The highest mean number of children, 2.06 per household, was in the wealthy Cornhill area. The lowest mean number of children, 1.55 per household, was in the district of Cripplegate Without, though the high rate of exemption of both householders and especially children within this poor district requires a cautious reading of this figure. Nevertheless, the positive relationship between relative wealth and the number of children per household is clearly demonstrated with reference to mean rent value per house (Table 4.7) and to factors of occupational status (Table 4.10). Smaller numbers of children per household were probably an effect of life-cycle status, relatively high levels of infant and child mortality, or poverty which might force older children out of the household in search of work, for example, as domestic servants.[67]

TABLE 4.7
Number of children per household

Number of children	Principal households		Lodger households		Total number of children	Mean rent per house[1]
	Number	%	Number	%		
0	9,808	55.83	7,470	90.13	-	£ 22 1s.
1	3,855	21.94	591	7.13	4,446	£ 24 15s.
2	2,246	12.78	174	2.10	4,840	£ 29 8s.
3	931	5.30	33	0.40	2,892	£ 36 16s.
4	456	2.59	12	0.14	1,872	£ 38 6s.
5	168	0.96	4	0.05	860	£ 43 6s.
6	67	0.38	3	0.04	420	£ 46 6s.
7	24	0.14	1	0.01	175	£ 61 16s.
8	12	0.07	–	–	96	£ 65 8s.
9	–	–	–	–	–	–
10	1	0.01	–	–	10	£ 40 0s.
Total	17,566	100.00	8,288	100.00	15,611	£ 25 10s.

Source: 1692 Poll Tax database.

Note: [1] Rent value for poll tax households linked to 1693–4 Aid assessments only.

The greatest number of children in any one household was ten; this was in the household of Robert Curtis senior, a wealthy mealman of St Anne Blackfriars. Curtis's household comprised himself, his wife, one son, nine other children, and three servants.[68] Robert Curtis junior and his wife are also recorded as being resident in this house of seventeen people. The greatest number of children found within a lodger household was seven. This household situated near the junction of Cornhill and Lombard Street was headed by Joseph Marlow, a jeweller. Marlow's household comprised himself, his wife, seven children, a relative and a female servant. The principal householder was Isaac Marlow (Joseph's brother?), also a wealthy jeweller.

Isaac's household comprised himself, his wife, three children and a female servant.

The total child population for the City was 15,611, of whom 5,901 were recorded either as sons or daughters while the remainder were noted using the non-gender specific term child(ren). In those cases where gender was assigned (37.8 per cent) the ratio of boys to girls was 100:138. In those households (4,446) where a single child was noted this ratio increased to 100:147, though the sample with assigned gender fell to 34.1 per cent.

From the information in the poll tax returns it is possible to make some observations upon the structural organisation of families. The number of families with two parents and children was 6,755, or 78.8 per cent of all households with children.[69] Within such families the mean number of children was 1.87. Those households with children where only a single parent was present numbered 1,822, or 21.2 per cent. Of this group 65.6 per cent (1,196) were women, just under half (44.2 per cent) of whom were noted as widows. No estimate can be made of women temporarily heading a household as a result of the husband's absence on occupational grounds. Within families with a single parent the mean number of children was 1.64, a figure notably lower than the overall mean for the City. The returns indicate that at the time of assessment 19.2 per cent of children (2,990) had only a single living — at least resident — parent or guardian. Nevertheless this figure is a minimum with reference to the total experience of parental loss as it is impossible from the poll tax to establish the frequency, or incidence, of remarriage.

While the majority of households contained family members with a parent-child relationship, some households contained family members with other relationships. Such relations were usually adult siblings or the parents of adults; for example, in Cheap Ward John Whiteing, a glover, lived with his wife, their four children, three servants, and his sister Bess.[70] Overall, relatively few households, only 1,133 or 4.4 per cent, recorded such co-resident kin, although it is possible that a number of the multitude of servants and apprentices within the City may have been related to their head of household in various un-

TABLE 4.8
Number of servants per household

Number of servants	Principal households		Lodger households		Total number of servants	Mean rent per house[1]
	Number	%	Number	%		
0	7,494	42.66	7,527	90.82	–	£13 8s.
1	5,031	28.64	588	7.10	5,619	£22 15s.
2	2,587	14.73	126	1.52	5,426	£32 12s.
3	1,295	7.37	29	0.35	3,972	£39 11s.
4	641	3.65	13	0.16	2,616	£51 13s.
5	284	1.62	2	0.02	1,430	£67 17s.
6	106	0.60	2	0.02	648	£79 15s.
7	52	0.30	1	0.01	371	£90 5s.
8	38	0.22	–	–	304	£87 13s.
9	14	0.08	–	–	126	£82 10s.
10+	24	0.13	–	–	276	£118 17s.
Total	17,566	100.00	8,288	100.00	20,788	£ 25 10s.

Source: 1692 Poll Tax database.

Note: [1] Rent value for poll tax households linked to 1693–4 Aid assessments only.

recorded ways. In order to assess the frequency of extended family units, the number of households recording both children and other co-resident kin was calculated. Those 283 households which fell within this definition represented 1.1 per cent of all households, indicating that the extended family under one roof, of whatever pattern, was not a significant feature of the social structure of late seventeenth-century London.[71]

Households often included servants and/or apprentices: 10,834 households (41.9 per cent) recorded servants, while 2,434 households noted apprentices (9.4 per cent) (Tables 4.8 and 4.9). If, however, those few lodger households which employed servants and apprentices are subtracted from

this figure the percentages of principal households with servants or apprentices becomes 57.3 per cent and 13.5 per cent, respectively. Despite the use of these terms it must be noted that it is not possible from the poll tax returns effectively to distinguish domestic servants from those servants employed in connection with the householder's business.[72]

Where servants were present the overall mean number of servants per household was 1.92, this low figure reflecting the majority situation where, in 51.9 per cent of those households with servants, a single servant was retained. In most of those households the servant employed was female, 4,328 such women being found in a total of 5,619 single servant households.[73] There was a strong

correlation between increasing numbers of servants and higher mean rent values (Table 4.8). In those households (23.1 per cent) employing three or more servants the gender ratio showed a slight bias in favour of male servants, with ten male servants to every nine female.[74] The overall excess of male servants within wealthier households resulted from a number of influences: the greater incidence of male craft-workers, or journeymen, within wealthier businesses; the increased demand for male domestic servants to undertake the formal, or ceremonial, functions that wealthier householders often required; and the greater likelihood of coach ownership, and hence the need for coachmen, among such wealthy citizens.[75]

Those described as apprentices were found in fewer households (9.4 per cent of all households). Notably the mean rent values for those households with apprentices were relatively low; clearly apprentices had less utility for those with greater wealth (Table 4.9). Once again the majority situation, influenced by the City companies, was for householders to take only one apprentice at a time, the instance of householders taking on three or more apprentices was relatively rare, occurring in only 28.6 per cent of all households where apprentices were recorded.

Only 1,384 households (5.4 per cent of all households) contained both servants and apprentices. The largest combined group of servants and apprentices of any City household was that resident in the house of Joshua Vaux, a shoemaker in the parish of Holy Trinity the Less. Vaux's household of sixteen

TABLE 4.9
Number of apprentices per household

Number of apprentices	Principal households		Lodger households		Total number of apprentices	Mean rent per house[1]
	Number	%	Number	%		
0	15,197	86.51	8,223	99.22	–	£25 13s.
1	1,681	9.57	58	0.70	1,739	£22 7s.
2	611	3.48	6	0.07	1,234	£29 2s.
3	66	0.38	–	–	198	£36 12s.
4	11	0.06	1	0.01	48	£45 4s.
Total	17,566	100.00	8,288	100.00	3,219	£25 10s.

Source: 1692 Poll Tax database.

Note: [1] Rent value for poll tax households linked to 1693–4 aid assessments only.

consisted of himself, his wife, two sons, two daughters, six male servants, three female servants, and a single apprentice. It is difficult to separate those servants who worked on the manufacture of Vaux's shoes from those that were his domestic helps. In this particular case, without knowing the nature of Vaux's product, gender cannot be used as a possible indicator of the roles of those employed within this large household, as Collyer stated in 1761,

> The master shoemakers in London keep shop and employ many workmen and workwomen. ... The journeymen and the women who bind the shoes and sow the quarters together when they are made of silk, velvet, callimanco, etc., get but small wages.[76]

In the case of lodger households the largest combined servant and apprentice group was found within the household of Richard Rigby in the parish of St Bride's. Rigby appears to have occupied an extensive element of Thomas Webb's property. Rigby's household comprised himself, his wife, a child, two female servants, a further servant (of unknown gender), and four apprentices. Unfortunately the poll tax return fails to supply Rigby's occupation.[77]

The distribution pattern of households with servants and/or apprentices was found to have strong similarities with that of high rents (Fig 4.15). The area with the highest mean number of servants and apprentices per household (2.49) lay between the north end of London Bridge and Cornhill. High mean numbers of servants and/or apprentices were also found in those households in the vicinity of Cheapside (2.26 per household). Those households which provided a mean number of servants and/or apprentices of just over two (2.06) occupied an area within the City walls but away from the central riverside district. This commercial and manufacturing area had a mean figure just below two (1.97). The mixed rental environment of Farringdon Ward Without had a somewhat lower value at 1.78. Those areas with a small mean number of servants and/or apprentices per household (1.62) were positioned outside the northern and eastern parts of the City walls, in the Cripplegate, Bishopsgate and Houndsditch areas.[78]

Household size varied with occupational category, the largest households were those of victuallers, comprising principally innkeepers and alehousekeepers. The smallest were found within the transport sector.[79] The mean of 5.52 people per victualling household is almost twice the City mean of 3.12 per household. It was the nature of this occupation, with the necessity for numerous servants to cater to customers, and in the case of inns to coachmen and their horses, that underlay this high figure.[80] The largest such household belonged to a wealthy vintner, William Symonds of Exchange Alley. He employed eight male and three female servants who, together with his wife and four children, gave his household a total of seventeen inhabitants. Victuallers had both the highest mean number of servants per household, 3.40, and also apprentices, 1.82 (see Table 4.10).

With regard to family size those working in the mercantile and financial sector tended to have the largest numbers of children, with a mean of 2.44 per household. Of the thirteen households which contained eight or more children nine were headed by merchants or gentlemen.[81] The occupational sector with the smallest mean child group size was that of leather workers, at 1.57, though the size of

TABLE 4.10
Household structure and size by occupational group

Occupational group	Number of		Percentage of households with:			Mean size of household groups of:[1]			Mean size of households		Total population
	householders	lodgers	children	servants	apprentices	children	servants	apprentices	principal	lodger	
Building	752	46	45.2	35.2	23.7	1.70	1.52	1.35	3.63	1.89	2,814
Textiles & clothing	2,485	440	40.2	53.3	14.3	1.90	2.10	1.35	4.24	1.65	11,258
Wood/furniture	453	30	46.4	51.8	24.0	1.68	1.71	1.35	3.97	2.07	1,860
Leather	78	2	52.5	30.0	43.8	1.57	1.54	1.29	3.71	3.00	295
Metal	658	59	42.1	45.7	31.7	1.74	1.77	1.41	4.01	1.98	2,757
Misc. manufactures	464	44	46.7	45.1	29.9	1.73	1.74	1.32	4.01	1.68	1,936
Merchants & financial	939	334	43.8	73.4	5.6	2.44	2.63	1.30	5.83	1.70	6,039
Misc. dealing	1,752	75	45.0	62.3	11.8	1.79	1.70	1.25	3.90	1.92	6,980
Food & drink	1,195	83	49.1	63.7	20.7	1.85	1.86	1.30	4.31	2.12	5,329
Victualling	241	40	45.6	77.6	13.5	2.11	3.40	1.82	6.33	1.33	1,578
Gentry	383	417	33.5	60.5	1.0	2.09	2.50	1.63	5.56	1.86	2,908
Professional & official	600	198	37.0	60.0	5.0	2.15	2.11	1.25	4.49	1.53	2,999
Misc. services	438	204	28.8	35.8	7.2	1.75	1.71	1.28	3.55	1.39	1,841
Transport	356	65	24.5	26.4	4.0	1.60	1.56	1.35	2.86	1.58	1,120
Not stated	6,772	6,251	24.9	28.8	4.6	1.67	1.65	1.27	3.34	1.52	32,110
Overall	17,566	8,288	33.2	41.9	9.4	1.82	1.92	1.32	3.92	1.57	81,824

Source: 1692 Poll Tax database. See Table 5.7 for additional information.

Note: [1] Counting only households where the category is present.

this sample is relatively small. The poorer occupational groups, such as transport and manufacturing, generally had smaller numbers of children, and in many cases children were completely absent from their households. Thus only 24.4 per cent of households in the transport sector contained children. However, in the case of such poor households there was an increased possibility of children being exempted from the returns.

Transport workers also had a notably low mean number of servants per household at 1.56, only 26.3 per cent of such households containing servants. This compares with the largest servant groups, which belonged once again to victuallers, of 3.4 per household. It is not surprising, given the nature of their occupation, that some 77.5 per cent of victuallers' households were found to include servants. Other households with large mean numbers of servants were those of professionals, government and City officials and the gentry.

Apprentices were found most frequently attached to the households of leather workers — 43.7 per cent of such households had apprentices. Victuallers had the highest mean number of apprentices per household at 1.82. The lowest mean number was shared between those occupied in general dealing and professionals and officials with 1.25 apprentices per household. Those households least likely to include an apprentice were those of the gentry where only 1.0 per cent of households listed apprentices as part of their complement.

Overall, it is apparent that the size and form of households within the City were very much

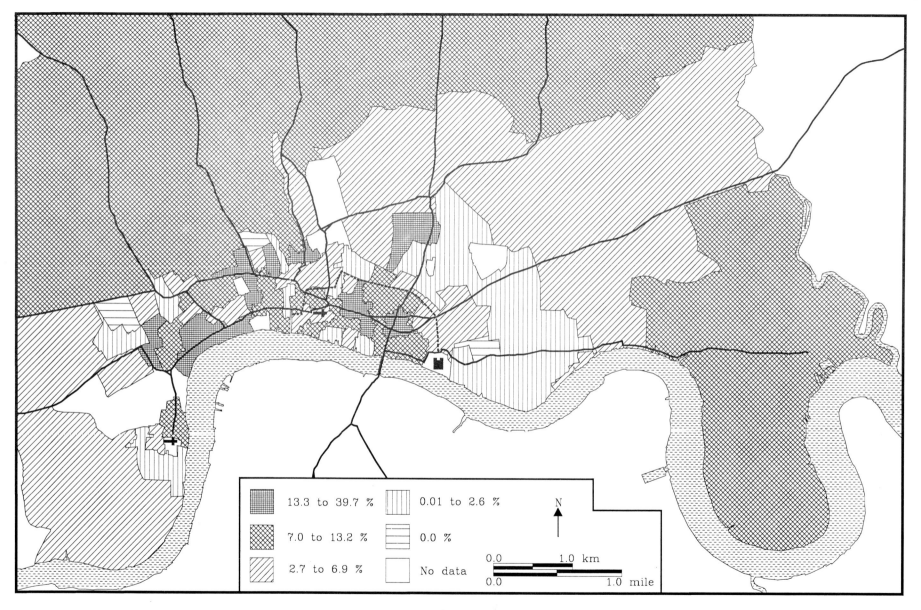

FIG. 4.16 Wealthy lodgers as a percentage of all households
Source: 1693–4 Aid database.

Legend:

- 13.3 to 39.7 %
- 7.0 to 13.2 %
- 2.7 to 6.9 %
- 0.01 to 2.6 %
- 0.0 %
- No data

N

0.0 — 1.0 km
0.0 — 1.0 mile

determined by economic conditions, although demographic, social and life-cycle factors all played a part. Source material to establish the size and form of those households found outside the area of the City is limited, and is certainly not available with the same abundance of information that the poll tax returns provide. Nevertheless, it is likely that even wider variation would be found in those areas, with the households of the very poor being comparatively small and those of the aristocratic rich being particularly large. One source of information related to household structure is, however, available for the wider metropolis. This is the incidence of lodgers whose personal wealth was in excess of £12 10s. and was thus considered taxable as part of the four shillings aid.

The number of wealthy lodgers assessed in each area is shown in Fig. 4.16 as a percentage of all households.[82] A simple visual comparison between this map and that of household rent values (Fig. 4.4) demonstrates a relatively strong link between high value rents and the presence of wealthy lodgers. Across the metropolis as a whole, wealthy lodgers were recorded in 6.9 per cent of households, and a number of disparate areas had values close to this figure. Of greater significance, however, were those districts where the number of wealthy lodgers far exceeded the London-wide mean. Wealthy lodgers were commonest in the parish of St Sepulchre within Middlesex, where 105 of them occurred across 39.7 per cent of the households. In the West End the three areas with a higher than average proportion of wealthy lodgers

also had high rents: the southern part of the parish of St Anne Soho (13.7 per cent), Covent Garden (24.6 per cent), and the area to the south of the Strand (18.2 per cent).

While most of the area within the City walls was above the metropolitan mean, two districts in particular were of note. In the area adjacent to Cheapside 21.4 per cent of households contained wealthy lodgers. Further east, in an area centred upon Cornhill and Fenchurch Street the figure was 15.8 per cent. As has already been demonstrated, the City gentry were disposed to occupy lodgings rather than becoming householders and it is therefore likely that many of the wealthy lodgers recorded within these City districts were members of this social group.[83] It is also possible that many of the wealthy lodgers resident within the parish of St Paul Covent Garden were part of a similar social group of mercantile gentry.

Within the City the members of certain mercantile and service groups tended more often to be lodgers than those practitioners of other trades. Thus of all those whose occupation is recorded, only 16 per cent were lodgers, while the corresponding figures for the 'mercantile and financial', 'professional and official' and 'miscellaneous services' groups were 26, 25, and 32 per cent, respectively (see Table 4.10). In more specialised service groups, the proportions of lodgers were even higher: 59 per cent of those providing clerical services were lodgers, 44 per cent of journeymen, and 36.5 per cent of the providers of medical services. This

pattern suggests a possible interpretation for the high percentages of wealthy lodgers to be found in certain areas outside the walls characterised by no more than middling levels of rent. In the area either side of the Haymarket in the West End, 21.3 per cent of households had lodgers assessed for the four shillings aid, many of whom may have provided high-status services to the aristocratic and gentry households in adjoining areas to the east and west. Further east, in an area extending from Gray's Inn to the Strand, 17.8 per cent of households had wealthy lodgers, while in nearby Hatton Garden the percentage was 18.9. In both these areas, and perhaps also in St Sepulchre's parish as mentioned above, the wealthy lodgers may have been associated with the legal profession. It is possible that in many such cases, principal householders who were not conspicuously wealthy but who lived in houses worth more than the average were supplementing their incomes by providing respectable accommodation for relatively well-off lodgers.[84]

Finally, one area shows a moderately large percentage of wealthy lodgers but rent levels below the metropolitan mean: the southern, urban part of St Leonard Shoreditch. This area had a lodger percentage of 13.8 but a mean rent value of only £12 12s. Apart from the numerous individual lodgers, who undoubtedly found a location on the periphery of the City combined with low rents advantageous, the area includes a group of twelve stock tax payers apparently lodging within the same house. The principal householder was one

FIG. 4.17 A view near Limehouse Bridge, 1751, looking down the Thames (John Boydell)
Source: Museum of London.

John Browne whose property in Holywell Street/Lane was worth £100, making him a relatively substantial landlord. That he was also one of the twelve parish assessors for the 1693–4 Aid may have been more than coincidental.

In those areas with low value rents few, if any, wealthy lodgers were resident. Such areas lay to the east of the City, along the upstream riverside district within the walls, in the district of Cripplegate Without, in Saffron Hill, to the north of the West End and in the southern part of the parish of St Margaret Westminster. These areas taken in combination provide a mean of 1.1 per cent of households giving accommodation to wealthy lodgers, though it is important to note that the incidence of lodgers too poor to be rated for the four shilling aid would have probably been high throughout these districts.

Occupancy and landlords

The 1693–4 Aid assessments do not routinely provide information concerning the type and arrangement of property occupied by individual householders, but sufficient indication is available in certain cases for instances of multiple occupation to be identified. The precise physical arrangements of such occupancy, the relationships between rent-sharing householders, and the nature of property within which several persons were noted as co-residents, are all questions to which the taxation sources can only provide general answers. Yet for certain parts of the metropolis, it is possible to supply some indication of the rates of multiple occupancy, with reference to location and rent value. The frequency with which freehold landlords were recorded within the 1693–4 Aid assessments was low, but once again in certain specific localities a far higher degree of reference occurred. Study of such areas provides some insight into the pattern of property holding by landlords within the metropolitan environment.

Multiple occupancy

Explicit instances of multiple occupancy are hard to identify in the 1693–4 Aid assessments, but in three areas it was clear from the textual arrangement of the entries, such as the systematic use of bracketing, that a large number of sub-divided dwellings was being assessed. In the ward of Bishopsgate Without, and the parishes of St Paul Shadwell and St Dunstan Stepney — all relatively poor neighbourhoods — a high frequency of multiple occupancy was encountered. In Bishopsgate a wide variety of household and non-household property, including some larger assemblages, was noted under single, or in some cases joint, ownership. Assessment entries often indicated properties which were under multiple occupation. Around 125 such properties were noted, some ten per cent of all residential property assessed within the Bishopsgate area. Generally within this area there were three or four tenants sharing any multiply-occupied property, though in a few instances more than six named occupiers were recorded. It is important to remember, however, that there are likely to have been other districts where multiple occupancy was common, but is not apparent in the record.[85]

In the parish of St Paul Shadwell 317 (26.3 per cent) of the total 1,204 households had more than one person listed as responsible for paying the tax upon rent. Of these households 211 named no more than one additional inhabitant, suggesting that dwellings under multiple occupation in Shadwell were usually apportioned between only two or three tenants. The smaller numbers of tenants per house was likely to be a reflection of the smaller size and lesser quality of many of the houses in this eastern riverside neighbourhood when compared with the relatively wealthier and more central district of Bishopsgate.[86]

It is possible in the case of Shadwell to measure the rates of multiple occupancy on a street by street basis (Figs. 4.18 and 4.19). The highest rate of multiple occupancy was found in Blewgate Fields in the north-western corner of the parish, where in a district of open fields and rope walks 72.2 per cent of houses were under multiple occupation. This location, well away from the commercial heart of the parish, also displayed the lowest level of rent per house at just £2 8s. per annum. The important thoroughfare of Ratcliff Highway, which ran through the parish from east to west (referred to in this location as Upper Shadwell), presented a very different housing character to that of Blewgate Fields and the other streets found in the north of the parish. Upper Shadwell had relatively low rates of multiple occupancy; 16.4 per cent on the south side of the road and only 10.5 per cent on the north. Despite this, it seems that many of these houses were substantial buildings, as indicated by their notably higher mean rents of £5 8s. and £7 14s., respectively.

The highest mean rents and the lowest recorded rates for multiple occupation in Shadwell were to be found in the highly commercialised area adjacent to the Thames. The 'water', or south, side of Lower Shadwell had the highest mean rent value for the parish of £15 2s., no doubt a product of the large size of the dwellings, often three stories, and their attached wharves and yards (for similar buildings, see Fig. 4.17).[87] Nevertheless, this street also had one of the lowest rates of multiple occupancy at just 9.0 per cent. To the west the similar situation of Wapping Wall provided the lowest rate for shared occupancy within the parish at 6.7 per cent. This riverside street also had high levels of mean rent, £13 13s. per annum. It is possible that these rates for multiple occupancy should be further reduced as a number of the riverside complexes may have been in the ownership of business partners rather than simple co-residents.

It has been established elsewhere that proximity to a commercial environment usually engendered higher levels of rent, but the evidence from Shadwell also indicates that such proximity did not necessarily encourage the sharing of dwellings.[88] This might suggest that those landlords who rented out large centrally-located properties tended to have little difficulty in obtaining tenants. Property of a less desirable nature or in a less attractive location appeared to have been more readily sub-divided, with the undoubted intention of maximising rental income. From the point of view of tenants, payment

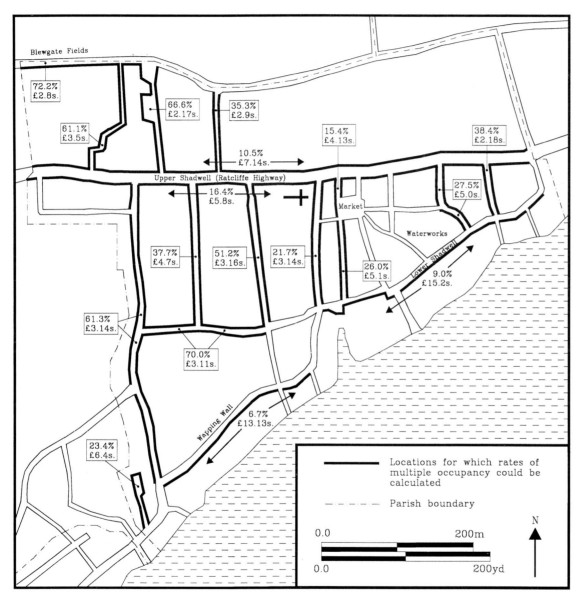

FIG. 4.18 Rates of multiple occupancy and mean rent values by street within the parish of St Paul Shadwell
Source: 1693–4 Aid database.

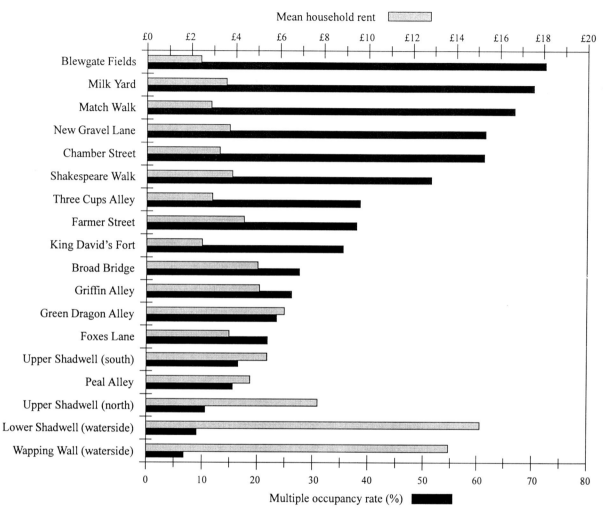

Mean household rent

Multiple occupancy rate (%)

FIG. 4.19 Multiple occupancy rates and mean rent values for selected locations in the parish of St Paul Shadwell
Source: 1693–4 Aid database.

of a low rent did not simply mean occupying a smaller property, but often resulted in the further hardship of having to share such a dwelling with one or more others.

Landlords

The 1693–4 Aid assessments generally do not provide comprehensive information with regard to landlords and the property which they might own. It is well known that, in the City, the Corporation, the livery companies and other institutions held much property and that in parts of the West End individual landlords possessed relatively large tracts of land upon which numerous buildings had been constructed. The assessments make little, if any, reference to such underlying freehold patterns, often identifying this type of landlord only if the property was empty. Nevertheless, in one or two districts something of the arrangement of property ownership by landlords can be deciphered. The informative area in this regard is the parish of St Margaret Westminster. Landlords were recorded in 1,943 cases, 61.8 per cent of all households. The only other area to have a comparably high percentage of recorded landlords was to the east of the City in the vicinity of Mile End and Bethnal Green, where 48.9 per cent of households had landlords listed in the assessments. This area was, however, less amenable to detailed analysis as much of the property was in the form of indeterminate parcels of land rather than clearly defined houses.

Although 613 separate landlords were recorded within the parish of St Margaret Westminster only about fifty were found to be substantial property-holders, defined as holding more than ten properties each. The most frequent ownership arrangements for such substantial landlords was for property to be grouped closely together in a single location, often an alley, court or yard. The degree to which such patterns represent sub-divided buildings is difficult to ascertain although, given the value of the assessed rents, it would seem likely that the bulk of such

TABLE 4.11

The estates of seventeen landlords in the parish of St Margaret Westminster

Landlord	Number of property units	Total value	Including
Edward Bossingham	8	£104	1 empty
John Cholmley	10	£281	
Henry Dagley*	16	£282	7 empty
Madam Delahey	35	£629	1 empty
Madam Farwell	27	£490	stable and 1 empty
Barbara Hutton	19	£239	4 empty
Mrs Kirke	22	£146	2 slaughter houses and a warehouse
Sir Roger Langley	26	£130 10s.	4 empty
Sir Robert Marsham*	10	£118	5 empty
Lord Ossulston	9	£63	2 empty
Thomas Perry	28	£598	1 empty
Alice Pluckenett*	3	£23	1 empty
George Pluckenett	1	£26	(received by guardian)
Dr Leonard Pluckenett*	6	£60	dyehouse and 2 empty
Thomas Pluckenett*	31	£274	shops, stables, gardens and 10 empty
Anthony Sturt*	20	£247	3 empty
Sir Edmond Wiseman	20	£654	Admiralty Office (£300), stable & 1 empty

Source: 1693–4 Aid database.

Note: for fuller details of these individuals, see text. *Property located on Fig. 4.20.

property was in the form of clearly distinct dwellings. (Table 4.11 summarises the holdings of the seventeen landlords mentioned in the following discussion.)

The property of landlord Thomas Perry exhibited this type of spatial organisation. Perry had eighteen property units in Bell Yard off King Street with a further ten in the adjacent Sea Alley and in King Street itself: these perhaps represent subdivisions of what had once been a single block of land. The property of others could be even more densely concentrated; Madam Delahey, for example, owned

thirty-five rent-generating properties all of which were located in George Yard, once again off King Street. The property-holding pattern of Anthony Sturt is shown in Fig. 4.20: most of his holdings lay in the area of Bell Alley, King Street and Thieving Lane. Though he had a few properties slightly further west, there is a clear focus to his property holding within the area to the immediate north-west of the abbey. Sturt was a wealthy City cornfactor and it is therefore likely that these rents provided additional rather than sole income (Table 4.11).[89]

More disparate patterns of property holding were also evident, particularly so in the case of the Pluckenett family (Fig. 4.20). Dr Leonard Pluckenett was a well-known physician and botanist dwelling in Old Palace Yard, where he died in 1706.[90] Alice, George, and Thomas Pluckenett who also held property in Westminster were presumably his relatives. The four of them held forty-one properties in all. Virtually all those belonging to Alice or Leonard lay in a group to the east of King Street. Thomas's were more widespread, being found both in the older parts of the parish and on the southern and western fringes where building had recently taken place. The Pluckenetts' holdings were diverse in character: Leonard owned a dyehouse in Rhenish Wine Yard, while Thomas had gardens in Great Almonry and Peter Street, stables in Chapel Street and two shops in Westminster Hall. Thomas also held property in Knightsbridge.

The property of Sir Robert Marsham was also relatively widespread; however, in this case much of his property was probably of new construction, located as it was on the very fringes of the built-up area (see Fig. 4.20). Sir Robert Marsham held property on Mill Bank, in Peter Street and in Marsham Street. The total value of the annual rental derived from Sir Robert's property was £118, although in real terms this income would have been reduced to £65 as a result of half of his property being vacant. Another landlord who may well have been taking advantage of new building activity was Henry Dagley who held property to the north and

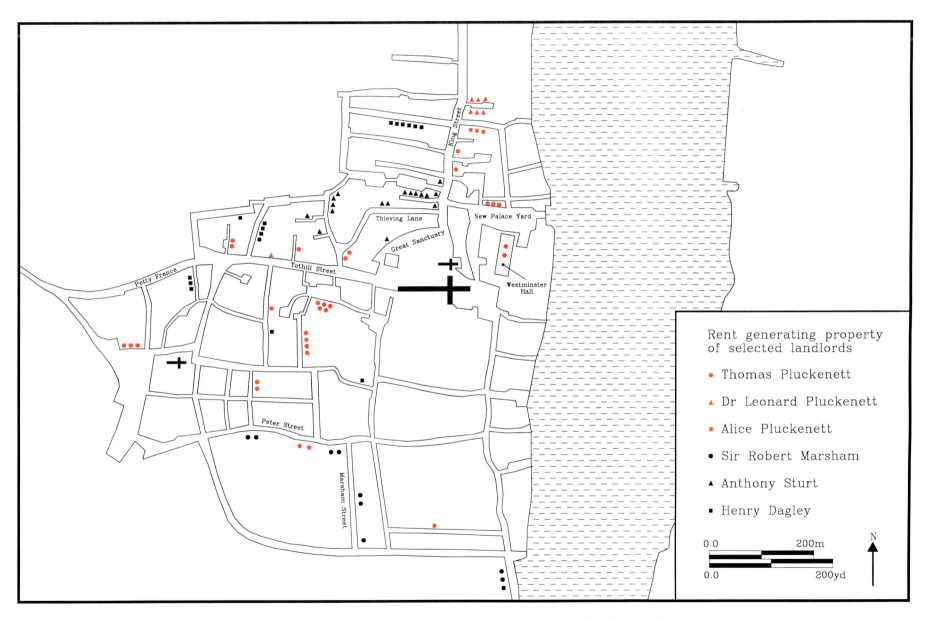

FIG. 4.20 Property holding patterns of selected landlords in the parish of St Margaret Westminster
Source: 1693–4 Aid database.

west of the parish, most notably possessing six high value properties in Charles Street with a combined rental of £146. Within the parish of St Margaret Westminster the greatest income derived from rents was that of Madam Delahey, whose thirty-five properties had a combined value of £629 per annum and would appear to have been well-managed with only one unit being recorded as empty.

Of those individuals who were recorded as landlords some 66.4 per cent were men, while 10.7 per cent were women.[91] It is likely these women actively chose to invest in property that would generate a rental income as only 26.5 per cent of them were given the title widow, indicating the possibility of property gained through inheritance. Though women were a small proportion of all landlords they, nevertheless, feature prominently among the most substantial property owners. Madam Delahey was joined by Madam Farwell, Barbara Hutton and Mrs Kirke in possessing a considerable amount of property which clearly provided their owners with significant levels of income (see Table 4.11).

It has been suggested that, in order to increase their income, landlords would sometimes let their own high status property while they themselves dwelt in rented accommodation of a lesser value.[92] The comprehensive nature of the 1693–4 Aid assessments make it possible to trace the residential location for a number of those landlords recorded within the parish of St Margaret Westminster. Of the fourteen landlords whose place of residence

could be ascertained, nine were resident in St Margaret's. Among these were Leonard and Thomas Pluckenett, occupying property in Old Palace Yard and Great St Anne's Lane, respectively. Madam Farwell lived in New Palace Yard 'in lodgings' worth £25 per annum, though she owned property in the same location valued at £120 per annum and let to the Earl of Caernarvon. Unfortunately, the assessments do not inform us who her landlord was. Others in St Margaret's lived in property that they owned: Madam Delahey dwelt in George Yard among her tenants. Edward Bossingham lived in a similar situation, next to three of his properties, in Bell Alley off King Street. Further west Sir Roger Langley dwelt in Green Dragon Court, off Tothill Street, in a property that was almost certainly his own.

Of the six landlords known to have been dwelling outside the parish of St Margaret Westminster, three were living in the West End, one had lodgings in the City, one had a property on the outskirts of London, and the last dwelt in Hertfordshire. Thomas Perry was living in Hampstead Court to the north of Hatton Garden in a house valued at £20 per annum. Anthony Sturt had a residence in nearby Bedford Walk to the north of Holborn valued at £70 in rent where he was assessed for £1,000 worth of stock. Mr John Cholmley, gentleman, was a lodger in the house of Henry Wood, a relatively wealthy wholesale hosier, in the eastern half of the parish of St Margaret Lothbury.[93] Lord Ossulston appeared to have shared a property in St James's Square

(worth £150) with the Earl of Bridgewater.[94] Sir Edmond Wiseman owned what must have been a relatively modest residence in Clapton to the north of London, valued at £12 per annum. Finally, Sir Robert Marsham, who had been born and married in the City of London, was probably living in Bushey, Hertfordshire in 1693–4.[95]

Although there is no consistent pattern, it is clear that some landlords did indeed rent property, or take lodgings, that had a lower value than that which they owned and in most cases rented out. In some instances this was probably to augment their income, in others the attraction of residence in a more salubrious location, such as St James's Square or Bedford Walk, was probably the deciding factor. Overall, it is likely that such substantial landlords were able to obtain a good level of return from their various properties, though the frequent occurrence of vacant property, possibly in itself an indication of poor management, must have reduced the income that was actually realised.

RICH AND POOR AREAS: AN OVERVIEW

This chapter has indicated some of the patterns which characterised London's social topography: the values of houses; the gender balance among householders; the incidence of aristocracy and gentry; and household structure. In many areas these patterns were complex, reflecting the variety of forces which determined both social composition and property values. In conclusion an attempt is made to demonstrate the broad pattern of wealth and poverty by highlighting those areas notable for one or the other.

In terms of the rent values of households this has been done by identifying areas where rents above and below the upper and lower quartiles respectively predominated (Fig. 4.21). For the metropolis as a whole rents above the upper quartile were those greater than £20 per annum, while those below the lower quartile ranged from £1 to £5 per annum.[96] The pattern is similar to that indicated by the distribution of mean rental values (Fig. 4.4), but displays a sharper differentiation between districts, which may well have corresponded with contemporary perceptions of the rich and poor areas of the metropolis.

In very broad terms, there was a significant, but not entirely exclusive, contrast between east and west. Areas where household rents above the upper quartile represented 30 per cent or more of the total were largely confined to the busiest commercial parts of the City, to the Strand and adjoining areas, and to the semi-rural district north of High Holborn and the road to Oxford. Areas where household rents below the lower quartile were comparably significant lay overwhelmingly to the east of the city, with some outliers in the northern suburbs and to the south and west of Westminster Abbey. Wealth was associated with the commercial foci in the City and the Strand, each of a different character, and with the aristocratic areas near Piccadilly. Poverty was associated with the industrial and maritime districts to the east and

with some of the more peripheral parts of the parish of St Margaret Westminster.

The areas with the greatest preponderance of rents above the upper quartile lay in four significant groups: within the City from the Bridge to the west end of Cheapside (65.0 per cent), from St Dunstan in the West to Covent Garden (55.2 per cent), immediately north of Charing Cross (50.3 per cent) and finally that part of St James Westminster south of Piccadilly (55.1 per cent). The City within the walls held the greatest single concentration of high value rents within the entire metropolis. In the district around Honey Lane Market and the church of St Mary le Bow three out of every four households paid a rent that was above the upper quartile (74.8 per cent). Other high rent concentrations were in the vicinity of the Stocks Market (73.1 per cent) and on, and adjacent to, London Bridge (71.3 per cent). Outside the City the Strand was again a focus of high value property. From the parish of St Dunstan in the West to Covent Garden just over half the households assessed had rents over £20 per annum (55.2 per cent). The highest single concentration of such rents to be found outside the City lay within this group in the West Division of St Paul Covent Garden (66.2 per cent).

Areas with lesser proportions of high rents lay adjacent to the central districts in a relatively clear concentric pattern. The areas between London Bridge and the Tower, either side of Bishopsgate Street within the walls, and to the south and west of Cheapside all fall within the 40–50 per cent class. A

similar pattern is apparent in the West End, where areas from Hatton Garden through Lincoln's Inn, St Anne Soho and Bedfordbury Ward of St Martin in the Fields, to the northern part of St Margaret Westminster formed a more disjointed pattern within the 30–50 per cent class. The area to the north of High Holborn and extending across the mainly rural parishes of St Pancras and St Marylebone, at 38.8 per cent, is harder to explain. As has already been indicated, some of these high rents were probably obtained from substantial houses, occupied in some instances by members of the gentry, while others may have been associated with high quality pasture or land with the potential for quarrying building clay.[97] The 1693–4 assessments provide no significant evidence regarding these aspects of land use.

The very poorest areas, where rents below the lower quartile represented more than half the total, lay at a little distance from the central districts of the City in a broad arc from Wapping Whitechapel, at the edge of the river Thames, to Saffron Hill in the west. Low value rents within the area from the eastern riverside to the north of Whitechapel High Street stood at 68.3 per cent. Other significant areas were: the precinct of St Katherine by the Tower (71.5 per cent); the northern part of Spitalfields (57.0 per cent); the area adjacent to Bishopsgate without the walls (54.9 per cent); St Giles without Cripplegate in the vicinity of Moor Lane (69.3 per cent); and finally Saffron Hill (60.3 per cent). The single area with the greatest occurrence of low value rents was south of East Smithfield and Ratcliff Highway: here four out

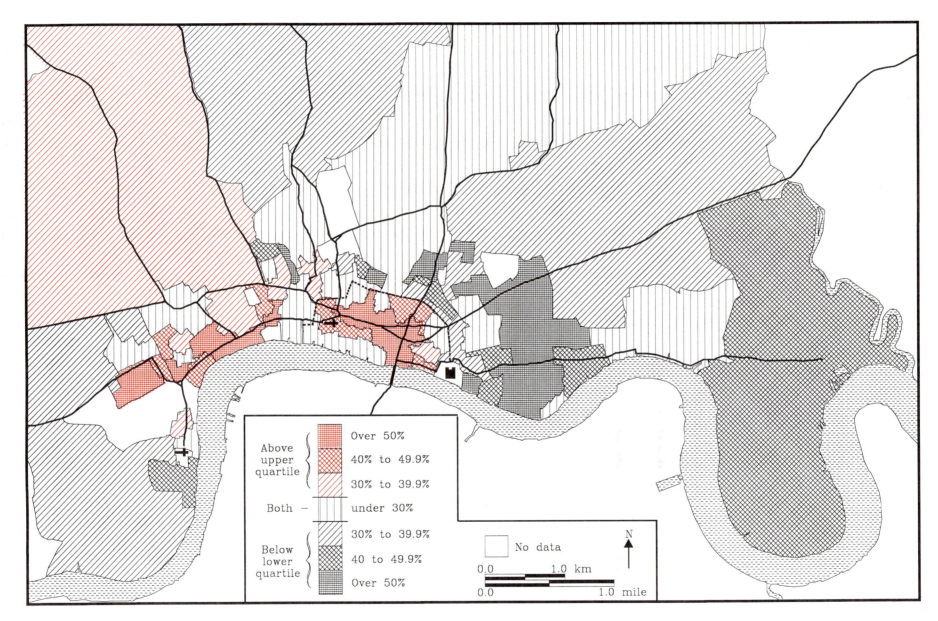

FIG. 4.21 Percentage of household rent payments falling within the upper and lower quartiles as derived from all rent payments
Source: 1693–4 Aid database.

of every five households paid a rent that fell below the lowest quartile (82.1 per cent). The neighbouring areas, from the Highway to the riverside also had high concentrations of low value rents, varying from 64.5 per cent to 77.0 per cent.

Areas with a lesser incidence of low rents mostly lay adjacent to the very poorest districts: Shadwell; part of the ward of Aldgate Without; the area north of Houndsditch; St Giles without Cripplegate; an area north of Hatton Garden; and the southern part of St Margaret Westminster. All those areas fell within the 40–50 per cent class. Large extents of the outlying rural area surrounding the metropolis had a relatively high incidence of low rents, with the Isle of Dogs and Poplar having a particular concentration, at 47.3 per cent. This was presumably because land in this area was cheap and houses and property plots tended to be small.

It is noteworthy that some of the areas where the lowest rents were most frequently encountered were quite close to the walled area of the City, suggesting that the poor inhabitants of those districts constituted the reserve of casual labour upon which the City's commerce depended. The corresponding group to the south of Westminster Abbey may have played a similar role in relation to the governmental and aristocratic quarters in the west of the metropolis.

For a variety of reasons mean rent values may not always be a true reflection of the underlying pattern of wealth or poverty. The occupation by an individual of a particular building within the metropolis undoubtedly related to a wide variety of factors, such as: building-use; period of residence; size of family; or the proximity of certain cultural or ethnic communities. Locational decisions based upon such a plethora of choices could, therefore, run counter to the simple relationship between high mean rents and the presence of wealthy inhabitants.[98] An analysis of the stock (revenue-generating personalty) of those assessed in the highest and lowest interquartile groups according to rent, however, indicates that rent was a positive reflection of wealth. A high percentage of upper interquartile rent payers were also possessors of stock assessed for the 1693–4 Aid (67.4 per cent), while in the lower interquartile the percentage was much lower (2.3 per cent).[99] Possession of stock thus tends to denote increased wealth.[100] Poverty can similarly be identified through an analysis of the distribution of funds for the relief of the poor.

The structure of poor relief was in a precarious condition at the beginning of the 1690s, the collection and distribution of the poor rate being based primarily upon the Elizabethan statutes of a hundred or more years earlier. Many parishes were engaged in bitter disputes concerning the issue of settlements, while overseers of the poor often took it upon themselves to define who should supply, and receive, the poor rate. In the 1690s the relief of the poor was, nevertheless, becoming more ordered. An Act of 1692 attempted to impose restraint upon the excesses of overseers, with vestries and justices of the peace receiving additional powers to monitor the poor.[101] Poor migrants also benefited from an improvement in the operation of settlements, while another statute, in 1697, yet further enhanced the status of poor migrant householders.[102]

It has been suggested that the poor relief raised within the area of the Bills of Mortality during the 1690s stood at around £40,000 per year, more than half of which was probably generated by rents on parish property.[103] This sum was distributed to the metropolitan poor — both within the parish of collection and elsewhere — by a well-established rate equalisation scheme operated by the Court of Aldermen.[104] Other relief came with the distribution of food and coals to pensioners and the indigent poor.

From the 1690s onwards, during times of special hardship, additional funds were raised and disbursed by means of collections 'taken upon the King's letter'. Early in 1694, with the dearth of the preceding year still painfully apparent, the City contrived to make such a collection.[105] The total received between 2 January and 8 April 1694 was £1,837 13s. 11d., including a gift of £1,000 from the king. During February and March 1694 the sum of £1,712 17s. was distributed, nearly all of it (95 per cent) to parishes outside the City walls.[106] Many of the parishes outside the walls were both contributors to and recipients of these funds. The status of parishes as net contributors or recipients provides some indication of contemporary perceptions of them as areas characterised respectively by wealth or poverty. When a net contributor was in receipt of a significant sum, that should indicate the presence of

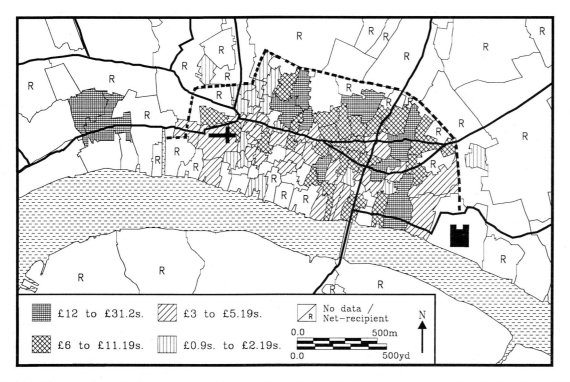

FIG. 4.22 Those parishes that were net-providers for the collection for the poor taken upon the king's letter in 1694
Source: CLRO 35.B.

parish was also the second highest net recipient. Almost all City parishes outside the walls and those adjacent to these areas were both givers and receivers of money. Predominantly, however, these parishes were net recipients of the fund. While Christ Church Spitalfields contributed only 7.8 per cent of the £90 it received, St Bartholomew the Great contributed 67.3 per cent of the £7 granted to it. The overall mean rate of contribution among these parishes was 22.3 per cent of the amounts they received. This indicates that pockets of wealth must have existed within a more general pattern of poverty across those districts that lay either side of the City boundary.

In terms of the largest amount of funds received by a single parish, St Giles without Cripplegate was granted £135 (to which it contributed 18.5 per cent), while St Olave Southwark received £130 (contributing 21.1 per cent) and St Botolph without Bishopsgate received £100 (contributing 24.0 per cent). Such large sums indicate that these populous parishes contained large numbers of London's poorer inhabitants. Seven areas which received money were absent from the list of contributors, they included: St James Dukes Place — the only such parish within the walls — (£7); St Giles in the Fields (£40); the hamlet of Wapping Stepney (£80); Wapping Whitechapel (£50); St Katherine by the Tower (£30); Mile End New Town (£20); and the parish of Poplar and Blackwall (£40). All of these areas lay to the east of the City, apart from St Giles in the Fields which lay to the north-west.

at least a pocket of deprivation within a predominantly prosperous area, and vice versa. The absolute size of the sums given or received reflect the population total of a parish as well as its wealth or poverty, a factor which, in this case, cannot consistently be allowed for.

The parishes which were net donors lay predominantly within the City walls (Fig. 4.22).[107] The largest sums were given by the larger and more populous parishes in the northern and eastern parts

of the walled City, rather than by the parishes of Cheapside, Cornhill and Gracechurch Street where households were more prosperous but less numerous. Only three areas outside the walls were net contributors: Holy Trinity Minories; St Bartholomew the Less; and, with a relatively generous contribution of £12, St Dunstan in the West together with the liberty of the Rolls.

In real terms St Olave Southwark provided the greatest single contribution, £36 12s., though this

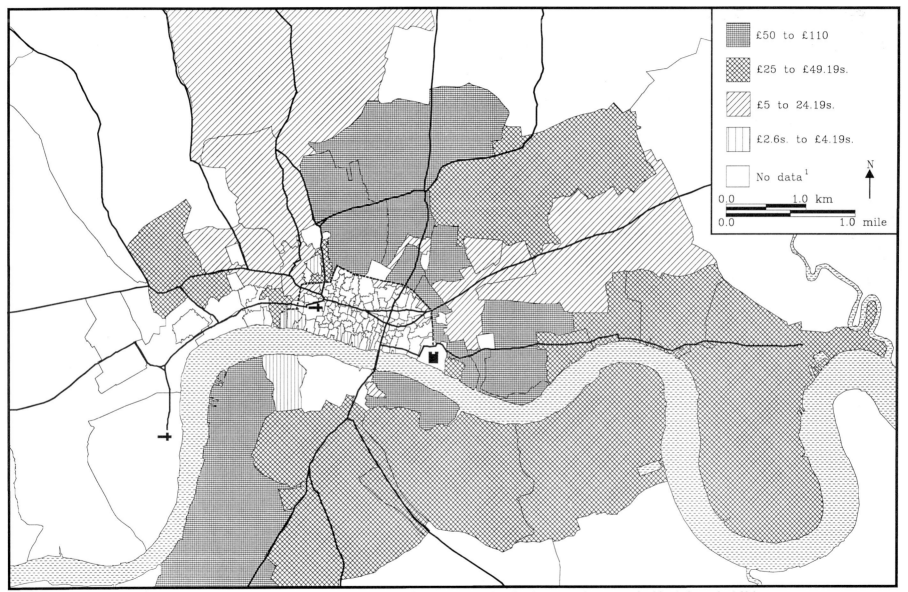

FIG. 4.23 Those parishes that were net receivers from the collection for the poor taken upon the king's letter in 1694
([1]For data on the City of London, see Fig. 4.22)
Source: CLRO 35.B.

Parishes that were recipients of the £1,712 17s. 6d. that was distributed to the poor during February and March 1694 are shown in Fig. 4.23. This pattern demonstrates that increased levels of poverty were focused on four distinct areas of the metropolis. As in the case of lower quartile rents attention is drawn to those areas lying immediately east of the City, but in this instance Houndsditch and Bishopsgate Without also show signs of increased poverty. The area to the north of the City includes St Giles without Cripplegate and St Leonard Shoreditch.[108] Finally two areas south of the Thames show increased levels of relief, St Olave Southwark and St Mary at Lambeth, both of which may have mirrored the poorer districts shown to have existed on the opposite side of the river in the area of Wapping and St Margaret Westminster, respectively.

The wealth of the City once again stands out, only those areas adjacent to the City walls or in the up-stream riverside zone were found to be net recipients, but even then at relatively low levels. To summarise, it is apparent that poverty was for the most part concentrated in the eastern parishes, with peripheral pockets in evidence within the western areas of the metropolis. The significance of the southern parishes in this instance is harder to define, though the similar pattern obtained from the measure of mean dwelling size by number of hearths, assessed in 1662–66, might suggest that these areas may have been equally important as centres of metropolitan poverty.[109]

Notes:

1. Barbon (1689), 4–5.
2. See Harding (1990b) for a comprehensive discussion of estimates of London's population during the early modern period.
3. Jones and Judges (1935–6), 54.
4. The number of households recorded in the 1693–4 Aid assessments for the City, 21,262, is very close to the marriage duty figure for households of 22,038. The number of households included in the poll tax was, however, much lower at 17,565.
5. If this figure is inflated by ten per cent, to allow for under-enumeration, a figure of at least 136,400 is suggested.
6. Arkell (1992), 144–5.
7. Harding (1990b), 121 (Table 3).
8. See below, pp. 88–101, regarding household structure within the City of London.
9. Glass (1966), xxiv (Table 3).
10. Glass (1966), xxvi.
11. Survey of London (1966), 7.
12. King suggested an inflation factor of three per cent to convert the number of houses into households. However, analysis of the 1692 Poll Tax data suggests that the proportion of houses with subordinate households (comprising two or more members) was much higher at eighteen per cent. The multiple occupancy rate of houses indicated by the 1693–4 Aid data for certain parts of the eastern parishes was 26.3 per cent. The mean of these figures is 15.8 per cent. The multiple occupancy rate is likely to have varied greatly from one part of London to another. Moreover, some of the totals of 'houses' in Table 4.1 are more likely to approximate to totals of households than of houses as generally understood today.
13. This figure is very close to Harding's figure of 556,710, calculated from the Bills of Mortality at the higher burial rate of 38 per 1,000, the use of which Harding suggests as more appropriate for calculating population in areas outside the City: Harding (1990b), 121, 124.
14. In most cases, however, such householders were assigned a single shared rent value within the assessments. See below, pp. 101–3, for further discussion of multiple occupancy.
15. Jones and Judges (1935–6), 61–2; Alexander (1989a), 21; 1693–4 Aid database.
16. Power (1978b), 178–82; Jones and Judges (1935–6), 53–5.
17. Countess of Carlisle (King's Square, Soho); the Earl of Leicester (Leicester House); Countess of Portland (Pall Mall); Marquis Halifax, the Duke of Ormond and Lord Dover (all St James's Square); the Earl of Nottingham (St James's Street) and the Earl Montague (Montague House).
18. Jones and Judges (1935–6), 60 (St Mary Magdalen, Milk Street).
19. See above, pp. 41–5, regarding land use.
20. See above, pp. 34–5, regarding coaching inns. The Red Lyon Inn had up to thirteen coach and waggon departures servicing some nine major destinations each week.
21. See below, pp.101–3, regarding multiple occupancy.
22. Power (1972), 240–1.
23. Barbon (1689), 20–1.
24. Those household rents assessed at below £1 per annum were almost entirely for empty, and possibly run-down, property.
25. This compares to figures of 14.1 per cent for Boroughside in 1622, Boulton (1987a), 128.
26. This figure relates to the riverside area from the River Fleet to Queenhithe.
27. Power (1990), 106–9.
28. Forbes (1971), 136–73; Power (1990), 109; Spence (1996), 15–26.
29. Earle (1989a), 158–60, 166–74.
30. As in other areas the pattern for householders of unknown gender resembled that for women. In the case of the City, however, the relative lack of association between male householders and the two lowest rent groups would be significantly altered if a large number of the 'unknowns' were men.
31. For a discussion of the distribution and social position of gentlemen, see below pp. 85–8, and pp. 98–101.
32. Defining the household of residence of aristocrats is difficult, therefore all references to households within this section of the text should not necessarily be considered to refer solely to those with resident aristocrats (see subsequent discussion).
33. Stone (1980), 196–205.
34. The following titles were noted in St Anne Soho: Baron, Count, Countess, Earl and Lord.
35. Survey of London (1966), 44 and 73; Sykes (1985), 24–6.

36. The following titles were noted in St James's parish: Countess, Duchess, Duke, Earl, Lord and Marquis.

37. Sykes (1985), 36.

38. Sykes (1985), 53–4.

39. The earldom was created in 1689, the dukedom in 1705: Powicke and Fryde (1961), 438.

40. Sykes (1985), 45–8.

41. William Cavendish, Earl of Devonshire, was created Duke of Devonshire in May 1694. In 1698 he abandoned plans to build a house in Lamb's Conduit Fields and instead purchased Berkeley House in Piccadilly on the western limit of the built-up area: Powicke and Fryde (1961), 425; Sykes (1985), 98.

42. Arlidge (1694).

43. Those paying £60 rent included: Sir Charles Hara, John How esquire, John Danvers esquire, Colonel Charles Cludd, Sir Peter Colleton (but see below, footnote 46), and Sir Robert Terrill.

44. Sainty (1972), 18, 138. Sir John Louther (Lowther) was also assessed for £4,000 stock at this address.

45. The account book of Sir Harbottle and Sir Samuel Grimstone records the payment of £92 9s. 10d. to 'Sir Thomas Stamp [landlord?] for half a years rent for the house at SoHo; taxes deducted', on 24 November 1693. HMC Verulam Ms, ff. 209–16, cited in Browning (1953), 470–4.

46. The seven were: Sir Mathew Andrews knt, Sir Thomas Clarges knt, Sir Benjamin Newland knt, Sir Samuel Barnardiston bt, Sir Peter Colleton bt, Paul Foley esquire, and Robert Harley esquire.

47. Sainty (1972), 19, 131, 276.

48. See above, pp. 41–5, regarding land use.

49. Green (1990), 176.

50. DNB, VII, 716–17.

51. Survey of London (1994), 558–9.

52. See below, pp. 99–101, for discussion of gentry lodgers.

53. Wealthy lodgers were defined as those assessed for stock tax but not for rents in the 1693–4 Aid assessments.

54. Arkell (1992), 144–50.

55. The marriage duty assessments are missing for seventeen of the ninety-seven parishes within the walls. Glass (1966), xviii. For the percentage of marriage duty households assessed for the poll tax, see Alexander (1992), 186–9.

56. Alexander (1992), 186.

57. See above, pp. 8, 14–15, for discussion of the quality and extent of the poll tax data.

58. Glass (1966), xxviii–xxxiv; Jones and Judges (1935–6), 51–6.

59. Goose (1980), 363–70.

60. See below, Appendix IIIB, for the means of individual City wards.

61. The measure of household size includes all family members, plus servants and apprentices.

62. Sir Joseph Hearne (Herne) held a number of notable positions both in government and commerce: Woodhead (1965), 88–9. He was: Commissioner of the East India Company, 1678–93, 1698–9; Governor of the East India Company, 1690–2; Alderman of Broad Street Ward 1686–7; admitted to the Mercers' Company 1687; knighted, 1690; Commissioner for the 1693–4 Aid; and was Member of Parliament for Dartmouth, 1689–99. He died in February 1699 'with a bleeding nose', leaving a fortune said to have been worth £200,000. Hearne's residence contained twenty-four people in total as a merchant named Richard Munford is recorded, within the poll tax assessment for Coleman Street Ward, as occupying part of Hearne's property.

63. The 1693–4 Aid assessment records that Thomas Collett's property in the parish of St Magnus the Martyr included a back-house; it may have been this element of Collett's property that was occupied by Thomas Preston.

64. The 1695 Marriage Duty assessment records: Thomas Preston; his wife (not named); three sons, Thomas, John and William; and two daughters, Sarah and Mary. Glass (1966), 239.

65. The 1695 Marriage Duty assessment records: Thomas Collett; his wife (not named); and his son, Robert. Glass (1966), 68. Thomas was a Common Councillor for Bridge Ward: 1674–76; 1678–83; 1689–91; (1692–8 Deputy); and 1702–3. He was also a member of the Vintners' Company. His wife was named Sarah. Woodhead (1965), 51.

66. The use of the term sibling in this context does not preclude the possibility that there may have been no biological relationship between the children found in any given household, as such details cannot be ascertained from the poll tax assessments.

67. Goose (1980), 370–3.

68. The 1695 Marriage Duty assessment records: Robert Curtis; his wife, Ann; four sons, Henry, Francis, Charles and Joseph; and four daughters, Ann, Phenicia, Susanah and Katherine. Glass (1966), 80.

69. 'Family' was defined as responsible adults (for example husband and/or wife/widow), and sons, daughters and/or other children, although the adults need not necessarily have been the biological parents of any or all of the children present in the 'family'.

70. The 1695 Marriage Duty assessment records: John Whiteing; his wife, Elizabeth; one son, Jason; and three daughters, Elizabeth, Rebecca and Mary. Glass (1966), 316.

71. Identifying extended family units is a very difficult process within the complex neighbourhood structures of early modern London as relatives may often have lived in separate yet nearby property. In addition, there are significant methodological problems in applying family reconstitution techniques to the rapidly changing and mobile populations found in urban environments.

72. See Earle (1989a): for a discussion of servants within middling households, see pp. 212–29; for a discussion of apprentices in middling households see pp.100–5.

73. The actual figures were 4,328 female servants, 772 male servants and 519 servants of unstated gender.

74. The actual figures were 4,409 male servants, 3,974 female servants and 1,360 servants of unstated gender.

75. The increased tendency for male servants to undertake formal functions within households was noted by Tim Meldrum in a paper ('Domestic servants in London, 1660–1750') delivered to the Economic and Social History of Pre-industrial England Seminar, Institute of Historical Research, 1992. The mean rent paid by those in possession of private coaches was £61 2s.; 1692 Poll Tax and 1693–4 Aid database.

76. Collyer (1761), quoted in George (1966), 197.

77. Interestingly, the name Richard Rigby is recorded a second time within the poll tax returns, in that case as a lodger living alone in the parish of Christ Church and having the occupation of shoemaker.

78. See below, pp. 144–5, for a discussion of servants and apprentices as an occupational group.

79. See below, pp. 128–46, for a more detailed discussion of the occupational structure of the City of London.

80. In addition to the forty-six coach, or stagecoach, men listed in the 1692 Poll Tax there was one stagecoach woman: Elizabeth Moulen was a resident of the Holborn area in the ward of Farringdon Without and operated a single coach.

81. Included in this nine were: John Berry, gentleman; Thomas Booke, merchant; Sir John Brown; Elias Dupuy, merchant; Jaques Gonsales, merchant; Sir Joseph Hearne; Sir John Houblon; Samuel Lock, merchant; and Richard Mountney, gentleman.

82. Because of the nature of the 1693–4 Aid assessments a very small number of those taxpayers included within the category of wealthy lodgers were co-resident kin and not independent lodgers. Further, it has not been possible to allow accurately for the incidence of more than one lodger per household within the gross calculation of lodger percentages. The relative numbers of lodgers per house was, however, estimated for three sample areas: St Paul Covent Garden, St James Clerkenwell, and Bridge Ward Within (see Table below). Overall 77.5 per cent of houses that included lodgers had only a single lodger, 13.0 per cent of houses had two lodgers, and 9.5 per cent of houses held more than two lodgers.

Lodgers per house	St Paul Covent Garden		St James Clerkenwell		Bridge Ward Within	
	no. of houses	%	no. of houses	%	no. of houses	%
One	92	76.0	22	73.3	25	83.3
Two	23	19.0	2	6.7	4	13.3
Three	5	4.1	3	10.0	1	3.3
Four	1	0.9	1	3.3	-	-
Five	-	-	1	3.3	-	-
Nine	-	-	1	3.3	-	-
Total	121	100.0	30	99.9	30	99.9

83. See Table 4.10. The poll tax returns record gentry as lodgers in 52.1 per cent of cases.

84. Earle (1989a), 209.

85. See above, pp. 45–8.

86. Power (1978a), 30–3.

87. Power (1978a), 32.

88. See above, pp. 70–2, for a discussion of high rents in commercial districts.

89. Chartres (1986), 185–6. Sir Anthony Sturt was also Member of Parliament for Stockbridge, 1695–1701, and for Hampshire, 1713–15. Woodhead (1965), 126.

90. *DNB*, XV, 1318.

91. The remaining 22.9 per cent of landlord entries did not provide enough information to allow gender to be assigned, although in 15 per cent of these cases corporate bodies were cited as landlords which can be taken to infer control of such property by men.

92. Jones (1993), 25.

93. Alexander (1989a), 121–2.

94. Lord Ossulston was also noted as owning a further adjacent property in St James's Square worth £200 per annum.

95. *DNB*, IX, 1139; GEC, *Complete Peerage* (1983 reprint), III, 383.

96. The lowest quartile group represented 23.4 per cent of all assessed households while the upper quartile group comprised 24.6 per cent of all assessed households.

97. See above: pp. 41–5, for a discussion of land use; pp. 70–5, for a discussion of mean rents; and pp. 85–8, for a discussion of gentry households.

98. This problem is recognised by geographers as the 'ecological fallacy'.

99. See below, pp. 149–60, for a fuller discussion of the holding of assessed stock.

100. See below, pp. 160–3, for a description of the overall pattern of wealth.

101. Slack (1990), 45.

102. Slack (1990), 36.

103. Pearl (1981), 122, 130–1. Pearl indicates that 6.7 per cent of the housing stock was in parochial ownership. Using the household rent total from the 1693–4 Aid, such a proportion amounts to approximately £62,000 per annum. It is likely, however, that this figure is inflated by the presence of a few very high value rents derived from properties of a type unlikely to have belonged to the parish.

104. Pearl (1981), 125.

105. Hoskins (1968), 2.

106. As with any fiscal enterprise, whether charitable or not, there were administrative costs. Of the total funds raised Sir Leonard Robinson, Chamberlain of the City of London, claimed £11 2s. 6d. for coach hire and other expenses incurred in obtaining the gift of money from the King. Three other gentlemen of the City claimed amounts totalling £70 for unspecified purposes. A more apparent expenditure, of £43 14s. 3d., was for coal supplied by Mr Samuel Throswell of Brick Hill Lane, Thames Street. This would have purchased twenty-eight chaldrons of coal (785 cwt), at 1691–1702 prices. CLRO Assessment Box 35.B. 1692 Poll Tax database. Hatcher (1993), 569, 588–9.

107. CLRO Assessment Box 35.B.

108. This might suggest that the incomplete nature of the 1693–4 Aid data for the parish of St Giles Cripplegate may have had a negative effect upon those totals of low to moderate rents for the metropolis as a whole.

109. Power (1986), 203.

5. Metropolitan Economic Structure

At the end of the seventeenth century London was England's most concentrated site of manufacturing and the focal point of its import and export trade. The growing consumption of both basic and luxury commodities by the metropolitan population furthered the expansion of London's commerce. The economic structure and commercial operation of the metropolis can be explored through the principal sources of the 1693–4 Aid assessments and the returns for the 1692 Poll Tax. The aid assessments record many industrial installations, storage and distribution facilities, and wholesale and retail outlets, the distribution of which throws some light on London's commercial geography. The returns for the poll tax indicate the occupations of many householders and so provide a more detailed picture of the distribution of trades within the City. Furthermore, the stock tax element of the 1693–4 Aid can be used to indicate patterns of commercial wealth across the metropolis. These three approaches provide a background against which more general accounts of London's, and England's, commercial life can be set.[1]

THE PHYSICAL STRUCTURES OF COMMERCE

Many commercial structures, perhaps shops above all, were an integral part of residential buildings and so were not routinely recorded by the assessors for the 1693–4 Aid.[2] Nevertheless the assessments provide some indication of the variety, value and location of commercial installations across the metropolis and certain coherent patterns emerge (Figs. 5.1, 5.4–5.6).

TABLE 5.1

Manufacturing properties assessed for the 1693–4 Aid

Property type	Total number	Number individually assessed	Total rent value[1]	Mean rent value[2]	Range of rent values	Number individually assessed for stock	Total stock value[3]	Mean stock value[4]
Tenter runs	91+	76	£286	£3 15s.	£1–£5	–	–	–
Brew houses	23	17	£785	£46 4s.	£6–£120	5	£1,200	£240
Powder houses	14	14	£192	£13 14s.	£2–£110	–	–	–
Slaughter houses	12	11	£70	£6 7s.	£4–£13	–	–	–
Rope walks	9	8	£119 10s.	£14 19s.	£4 10s.–£30	–	–	–
Dye houses	4	3	£36	£12	£4–£16	–	–	–
Mills	4+	–	£164	–	–	–	–	–
Melting [tallow] houses	3	3	£10	£3 7s.	£2–£5	–	–	–
Glass houses	2	1	£18	£18	–	1	£1,000	£1,000
Printing houses	2	2	£90	£45	£10–£80	–	–	–
Sugar houses	2	2	£55	£27 10s.	£15–£40	1	£200	£200
Napping house	1	1	£14	£14	–	–	–	–
Still house	1	1	£14	£14	–	–	–	–
Tannery	1	1	£8	£8	–	1	£200	£200
Total	169+	140	£1,861 10s.	£13 6s.	£1–£120	8	£2,600	£325

Source: 1693–4 Aid database.

Notes:

[1] Total rent value of individually assessed property only.

[2] Mean rent value of those properties for which individual rent values were recorded.

[3] Only includes stock associated with individually assessed manufacturing properties.

[4] Mean stock value of those properties for which associated stock values were recorded.

Sites of manufacture and processing

The aids record a number of manufacturing properties, ranging from sites of industrial production

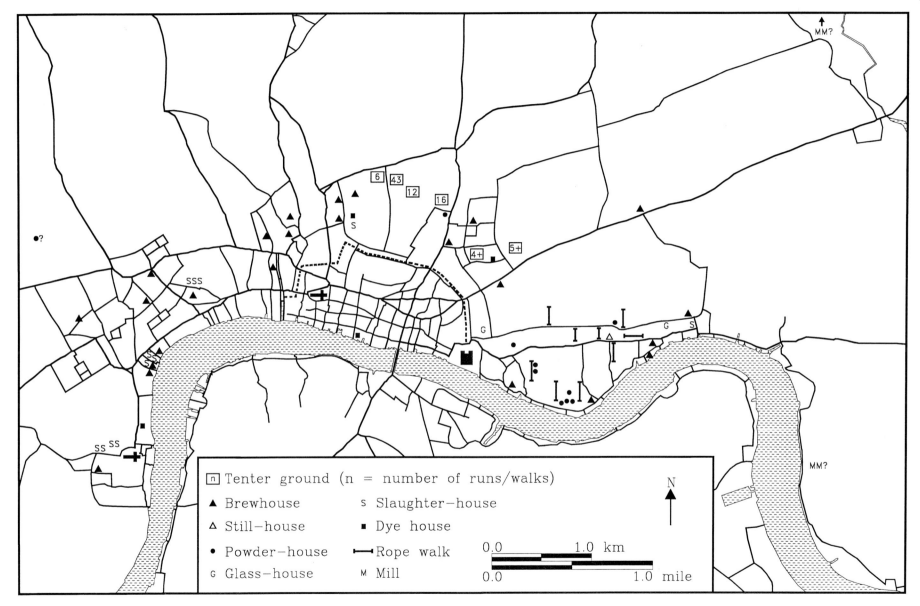

FIG. 5.1 Manufacturing property assessed for the 1693–4 Aid (approximate locations)
Source: 1693–4 Aid database.

such as (gun) powder-houses and glass-houses, to those of processing activities such as slaughter-houses and tenter grounds (Table 5.1). More than 169 manufacturing properties were mentioned by the assessors, of which 140 were individually assessed. The latter had a combined rent value of £1,861 10s. and a mean value of £13 6s. Mean rents ranged from £3 7s., for tallow melting-houses, to £46 4s., for brewing establishments.

The most frequently occurring manufacturing property to be individually valued was the tenter run, or walk, a narrow extent of ground furnished with posts and rails upon which cloth was stretched. Tenters were, however, found clustered in six discrete groups on open ground to the north and east of the City walls (Fig. 5.1). Tenters had the second highest combined rent value, £286, which reflected both their large number and their physical separation from housing.

The highest combined value was that of the brew-houses, £785. Brewing took place in a wide variety of establishments from the domestic environment of the alehouse to the major industrial complexes of the Common Brewers. It is likely that those larger, and physically distinctive, properties most frequently drew the attention of the assessors. At least half of the twenty-three brewhouses assessed were close to the Thames or other main water-courses, while the remainder presumably derived their water supplies from wells or streams.[3] Few assessed brewhouses were found in central areas, most occupying positions in the suburban areas to

FIG. 5.2 View of the river Thames, looking west and showing York Buildings and the industrial nature of the waterfront, c.1752 (John Boydell)
Source: Guildhall Library.

the north, east and west of the City. The most valuable brewing establishment was the Red Lion Brewery, located in the vicinity of St Katherine's Street Wapping, and in the ownership of Sir John Parsons and his partner, with a rent value of £120.[4] Brewhouses were also assessed for associated stock more frequently than any other manufacturing property (Table 5.1). The high level of investment required for such enterprises can be gauged by assessed stock values of £100 to £500, though these figures certainly underestimate the true value of the equipment and materials that a large brewery would require. Parsons and his partner, for example, were jointly assessed at his residence in Well Close (rent value £117) for stock valued at £3,200, much of which was probably connected with his brewing activities as no stock was assessed at the Red Lion Brewery site.

Fourteen powder-houses were assessed, mainly in the eastern riverside suburbs away from the built-up area (Fig. 5.1). The group includes a saltpetre storehouse which was, however, located in Gun Yard, perilously close to the busy thoroughfare of Bishopsgate Street without. The mean value of these installations was £13 14s., a figure inflated by the presence of a single powder-house worth £110, located in Hangman's Acre off Ratcliff Highway. Their mean value excluding the Hangman's Acre powder-house was only £7 2s. The only other manufacturing properties to be assessed in any significant numbers were rope walks. Exclusively located in the eastern riverside suburbs, close to the focus of maritime activity — the main market for the

product — these establishments had a mean rent value of £14 19s. Two owners stand out, Joseph Todd and David Bushall. Todd possessed two rope walks, one worth £10 near Virginia Street in Wapping Stepney, the other with a value of £30 in Wil(t)shire Lane in Wapping Whitechapel.[5] Todd was assessed for stock worth £200 at his residence adjacent to his Stepney rope walk which had no separate assessment for stock. David Bushall on the other hand appears to have concentrated his production on one site, at the eastern end of Great Hermitage Street, where his rope walk and ware-house had a combined rent value of £80, with associated stock to the value of £300.[6] Bushall himself lived in nearby Collett's Yard in a property valued at £12.

Other manufacturing properties were recorded in lesser numbers. Four dye-houses were assessed with a mean rent of £12; a number of mills were recorded on the river Lea and on the Isle of Dogs, probably windmills in the latter case; three melting-houses, concerned with the production of tallow, were noted; two glass-houses, two printing-houses, and two sugar-houses were also assessed. The glass-houses were both located in the eastern suburbs, the one nearest the City was the higher valued at £90 with £1,000 worth of 'glass house stock'. This property, clearly identifiable on Rocque's 1747 map, was owned by Michael Rackett, who was assessed for a further £1,000 in cash, apparently in association with the glass-house property. The printing-house of Joshua Hoskinds in Coleman Street Ward was valued at £10, but the

King's printing-house in Printing House Yard, in the parish of St Anne Blackfriars, was valued at the higher level of £80. No stock was recorded for either property. Of the two sugar-houses, one, owned by Jerome Collins, was in the parish of St Anne and St Agnes near Aldersgate and had a rent value of £15; the other, valued at £40 and owned by William Matson, was in the parish of St Mary Somerset near the Thames waterfront.[7] Matson's sugar-house was assessed for stock to the value of £200, probably an indication of both the capital-intensive nature of this type of production and the high value of the raw material itself. Significantly, the sugar-houses, together with one of the dye-houses, were the only industrial installations that the assessors recorded within the City walls, probably in recognition of the high value of the products and the specialised and innovative nature of the production processes.

Twelve slaughter-houses were noted, with a mean assessment value of £6 8s. They seem to have been recorded erratically — for example, none of the slaughter-houses known to have been sited behind the butchers' houses in Aldgate High Street appear. Nevertheless, there were clusters in the crowded areas near Clare Market and Hungerford Market, and another cluster on the fringes of Westminster.

Storage and warehousing

London's pre-eminence as a trading centre is best delineated with reference to the immense quantity

FIG. 5.3 View of the Custom House and other buildings fronting the river in the Port area, *c.* 1750 (John Maurer)
Source: Guildhall Library.

TABLE 5.2
Property associated with storage or supply and assessed for the 1693–4 Aid

Property type	Total number	Number individually assessed	Total rent value[1]	Mean rent value[2]	Range of rent values	Number individually assessed for stock	Total stock value[3]	Mean stock value[4]
Warehouses	180+	97	£1,419 10s.	£14 13s.	£1–£70	13	£3,350	£257 14s.
Vaults	79+	50	£424	£8 10s.	£3–£30	–	–	–
Cellars	56+	26	£334	£12 17s.	£1–£60	9	£791 13s.	£87 19s.
Barns	21+	15	£68	£4 11s.	£1–£10	–	–	–
Quays (Keys)	18	3	£740	£246 14s.	£16–£72	1	£200	£200
Wharves	14	8	£552	£69	£1–£400	3	£350	£116 13s.
Store houses	9+	5	£236	£47 2s.	£4–£200	–	–	–
Timber/wood yards	6	3	£9	£3	£1–£5	–	–	–
Granaries	4	3	£18	£6	£1–£8	–	–	–
Total	387+	210	£3,800 10s.	£18 2s.	£1–£400	26	£4,691 13s.	£180 9s.

Source: 1693–4 Aid database.

Notes:
[1] Total rent value of individually assessed property only.
[2] Mean rent value of those properties for which individual rent values were recorded.
[3] Only includes stock associated with individually assessed storage/supply properties.
[4] Mean stock value of those properties for which associated stock values were recorded.

of goods brought into the metropolis, there to be stored, re-packaged, sometimes additionally processed, and eventually sold, distributed elsewhere in England or re-exported (Fig. 5.3). The assessments for the 1693–4 Aid provide some useful information concerning the physical infra-structure for this vigorous commercial activity. More than 387 properties associated with the storage or distribution of goods were noted by the assessors. The 210 individually assessed properties in this category had a total rent value of £3,800 10s. (Table 5.2).

Warehouses were the category of storage property most commonly recorded. Warehouses could be occupied and used separately, but were often part of residential properties and so not explicitly recorded by the assessors. Of the 180 warehouses mentioned, ninety-seven were assessed separately, while the remainder were valued in conjunction with quays, cellars, stables and vaults. The separately-assessed warehouses had a mean rent value of £14 13s. Apart from the massive storage undertakings of the East India Company and other similar enterprises, the most valuable warehouse in the possession of an

individual, worth £70, was owned by William Westwood and lay just to the south of Aldgate inside the City wall. In this half of the City, to the east of the Gracechurch Street/Bishopsgate axis, 41 per cent of all the recorded warehouses were located (Fig. 5.4).[8] The great concentration of warehouses within this relatively small area was clearly a product of the close relationship between warehousing and the import-export trade carried on through the adjacent Port of London. Only 8 per cent of warehouses were found within the built-up area to the west of the City walls. In a few cases, especially in the western part of the City and in the West End, separate warehouse properties also probably served for the display and sale of goods and as workshops rather than purely for the bulk storage of the commodities of international trade. Despite the obvious connection between goods and warehouses, only thirteen warehouses had their contents separately assessed, resulting in a mean stock value of £257 14s. It is likely that most owners had the contents of their warehouse included within the assessment of personal wealth undertaken at their place of residence.

The second most frequently mentioned structure associated with storage was the vault, most likely to have been a cellar below a house, warehouse, or public building, possibly constructed with a brick- or stone-vaulted roof. At least seventy-nine vaults were noted, of which fifty were individually assessed, with a mean rent value of £8 10s. A close similarity of function between warehouses and vaults in the City is indicated by the presence of 58 per cent of all

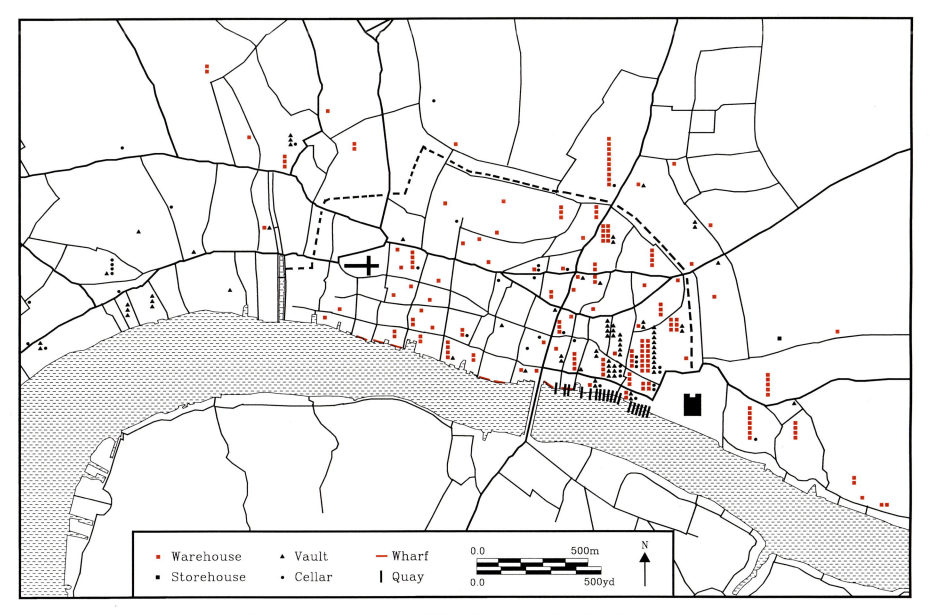

Fig. 5.4 Storage and supply property assessed for the 1693–4 Aid in and around the City of London (approximate locations)
Source: 1693–4 Aid database.

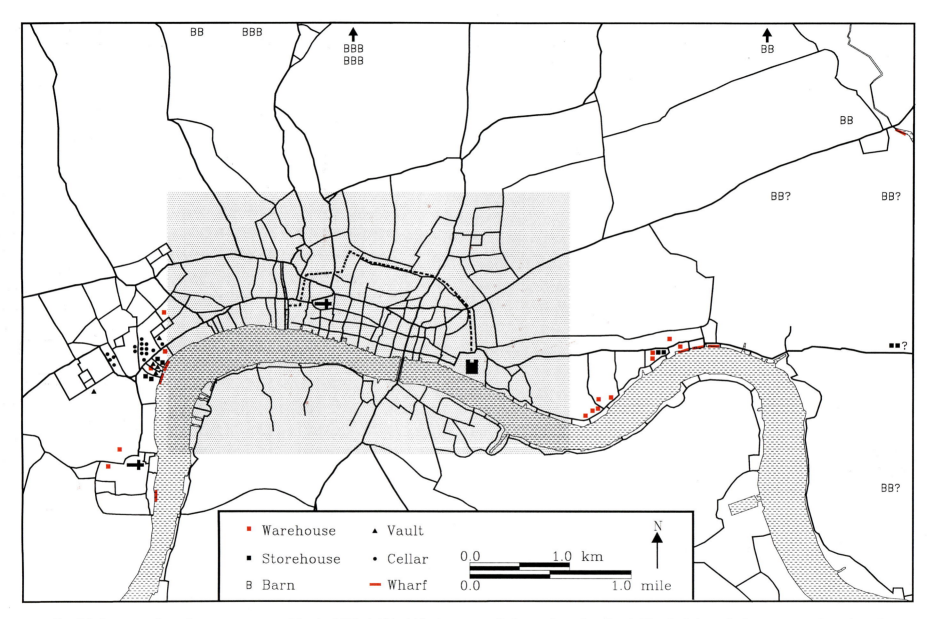

FIG. 5.5 Storage and supply property assessed for the 1693–4 Aid within the metropolis (approximate locations). The shaded area is that represented on Fig. 5.4.

Source: 1693–4 Aid database.

vaults to the east of the Gracechurch Street/ Bishopsgate axis and within the City walls. The assessors also noted cellars, a term that may often have referred to a structure identical to a 'vault', and so have denoted a storage facility, although in some instances people may have been using cellars as dwellings. At least fifty-six cellars were recorded across the metropolis. The twenty-six with individual assessments had a mean rent value of £12 17s.[9] Unlike vaults, cellars were not clustered in the commercial area of the City; their greatest concentration, 29 per cent of the total, was in the West End, particularly in the vicinity of St Martin's Lane, where they may have served as dwellings (Fig. 5.5).

The warehouses and vaults, especially those in the eastern half of the City, were supplied primarily from the quays and wharves of the Thames waterfront. All eighteen of the quays recorded in the assessments lay between London Bridge and the Tower. Together with New Fresh Wharf (see below), they made up the statutory 'Free Keys' of the Port of London (See Fig. 5.3).[10] Only three quays were individually assessed but, with a combined rent value of £740, and a mean value of £246 14s., they were clearly of great economic importance. The wealthiest owner according to the assessments was Richard Meriweather, who with his partners held Custom House Key, Wool Key, Hartshorne Key and several warehouses, with a total rent value of £970.[11] His nearest rivals were Joseph Ashton and partners, who owned properties to the value of £840, including Botolphs Wharf and Lion Key, and Peter Cartwright, a merchant, who owned Wiggins Key, Ralphs Key,

Youngs Key and sundry warehouses and cellars, with a combined value of £750.[12] The total assessed rack-rent value of the nineteen 'Free Keys' (including New Fresh Wharf) and the properties associated with them was £6,480 per annum. The capital value of the 'Free Keys', including the waterfront, cranes and other equipment, is estimated to have been in excess of £70,000.[13]

Fourteen wharves, including New Fresh Wharf, were assessed for the 1693–4 Aid. Eight had separate valuations giving a mean value of £69, though if the very high rent value of New Fresh Wharf (£400) is omitted the mean falls to £21 14s. The terms quay (or Key) and wharf meant much the same thing, but the former had, by the seventeenth century, become associated with the busy sites of international trade in the port. Of the wharves, only New Fresh Wharf and Botolphs Wharf, both names with very long histories, lay downstream of London Bridge, while most of the others lay upstream, principally in Queenhithe and Dowgate Wards. Five wharves lay further west, servicing the Hungerford Market area and the parish of St Margaret Westminster, and three wharves were recorded in Shadwell and Ratcliff. The wharf of lowest value, £1, was some distance from the centre, on the river Lea, in the parish of St John Hackney.

Beyond the built-up area the predominant storage structure was the barn, more than twenty-one of which were noted in the assessments, fifteen with individual valuations. Barns, though generally large buildings, had a relatively low mean rent value of

£4 11s., reflecting their location on land of lower value. Just over half of the barns were recorded in the parish of St Mary Islington, with the remainder on the low-lying farmland of Hackney, Stepney and the Isle of Dogs.

A small number of other properties associated with storage or supply were noted. The nine storehouses assessed, though similar in function to warehouses, appear to have been predominantly associated with maritime or market activities. Two storehouses lay in the hamlet of Poplar in the parish of St Dunstan Stepney, and two others in Mariners Street, Shadwell. Those storehouses noted in the west of the metropolis were in the vicinity of Hungerford Market. Six timber or wood yards were assessed, three were individually valued giving a low mean rent of £3. Three timber yards lay in the parish of St Botolph without Bishopsgate: one near Moorfields, another in Globe Yard, and the third in Gun Yard. A fourth timber yard was situated in Shoe Lane in the parish of St Bride. Two wood yards were located in the parish of St Giles Cripplegate, one on Fore Street, the other off Grub Street. There were four granaries — in the parishes of St Leonard Bromley, St John Hackney and St Sepulchre in Middlesex. None can be more precisely located, but they were perhaps associated with milling.

Shops and markets

Supplying Londoners with both essential and luxury goods fell to the shops and markets of the metropolis. Many thousands of street hawkers,

123

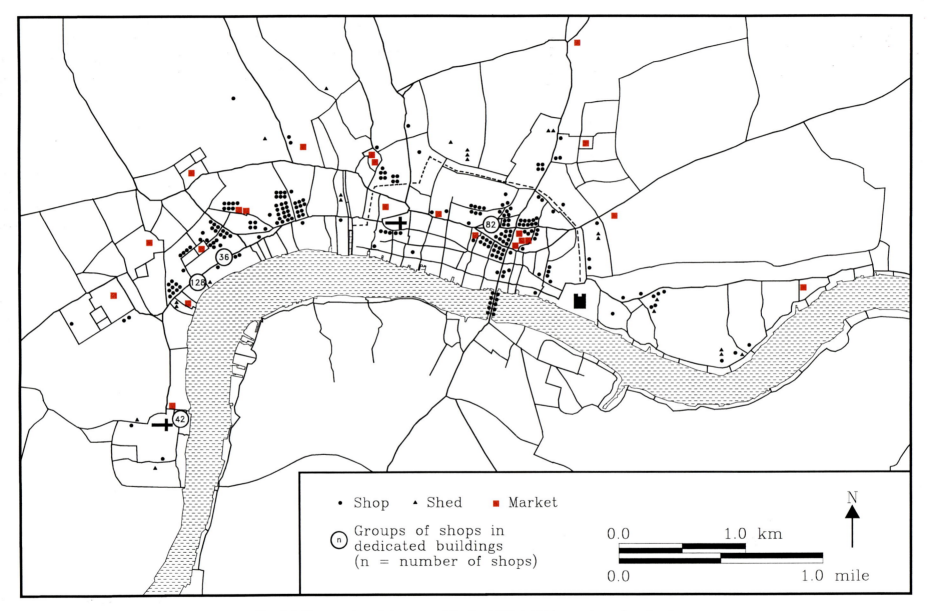

FIG. 5.6 Shops and markets assessed for the 1693–4 Aid (approximate locations)
Source: 1693–4 Aid database.

TABLE 5.3
Shops and markets assessed for the 1693–4 Aid

Property type	Total number	Number individ-ually assessed	Total rent value[1]	Mean rent value[2]	Range of rent values	Number individually assessed for stock	Total stock value[3]	Mean stock value[4]
Shops	254+	175	£1,699 10s.	£9 14s.	£1–£46 13s.	33	£2,225	£67 8s.
New Exchange	128	128	£3,677 8s.	£28 15s.	£10–£100	110	£13,058 3s.	£118 14s.
Royal Exchange	82	81	£1,977	£24 8s.	£12–£100	1	£50	£50
Exeter Exchange	36	36	£368	£10 5s.	£6–£15	22	£1,450	£66
Westminster Hall	42	42	£174	£4 3s.	£3–£10	2	£50	£25
Total shops	542+	462	£7,895 18s.	£17 2s.	£1–£100	168	£16,833 3s.	£100 4s.
Sheds	42	35	£64 10s.	£1 17s.	5s.–£15	–	–	–
Markets	23	16	£2,744	£171 10s.	£20–£631	–	–	–
Total	607+	513	£10,704 8s.	£20 17s.	5s.–£631	168	£16,833 3s.	£100 4s.

Source: 1693–4 Aid database.
Notes:
[1] Total rent value of individually assessed property only.
[2] Mean rent value of those properties for which individual rent values were recorded.
[3] Only includes stock associated with individually assessed shop/market properties.
[4] Mean stock value of those properties for which associated stock values were recorded.

stallholders, and shopkeepers were scattered across the built-up area. The integral nature of residences and shops was such that assessors omitted in many instances to record their presence. The assessments, nevertheless, mention well over five hundred shops, of which 254 lay in scattered locations, while 288 were recorded in four distinctive groups: at the purpose built emporia of the Royal Exchange, the New Exchange, Exeter Exchange, and in Westminster Hall (Fig. 5.6).

Individually assessed shops had a total rent value of £1,699 10s., giving a mean figure of £9 14s.

(Table 5.3). The highest assessment for an individual shop was £46 13s., for one of three shops 'under the Dutch Church' at Austin Friars.[14] The lowest was £1, for an empty shop in Shovel Alley, Whitechapel. Rents of £3 to £5 were common for shops of the lowest values. Thirty-three shops were recorded with individual stock valuations, the mean being £67 8s.

Although widely scattered, some of the assessed shops were recorded in loosely clustered groups discernible in Fig. 5.6. A large number of shops, at least thirty-six, were noted in the area of Lombard

Street and Cornhill, close to the Royal Exchange. Many of these shops provided services or luxury goods for the wealthy, predominantly merchant, clientele who daily circulated in the area. Within the City three other clusters of shops can be defined: London Bridge, with its haberdashers, hosiers, cutlers, and booksellers; St Paul's precinct, occupied by stationers, bookbinders, drapers, and cabinet-makers; and the vicinity of the Leadenhall markets where fishmongers, poulterers, and upholsterers were located.[15] At the western limits of the City's authority another large group of shops (twenty-seven) were clustered around the southern end of Chancery Lane.[16] Such shops were probably occupied by specialist metal workers and retailers of luxury goods. Shops were also recorded in smaller groups along Drury Lane, around Covent Garden, and at the southern end of St Martin's Lane. Conspicuously absent are records of shops in Cheapside, perhaps because the many shops there, in contrast to the other areas, tended to be run by the inhabitants of the houses of which they were part.

Of the four notable assemblages of shops, that of greatest assessed value was the New Exchange, constructed in 1612 to the south of the Strand by the Earl of Salisbury, and valued at £3,677 8s. in rent in 1694.[17] The 128 individually-assessed shops of the Exchange were grouped on two levels, and had a mean value of £28 15s. Shops on the upper floor (fifty-nine) were worth slightly less than those at ground level (sixty-four) with mean rents of £27 11s. and £29 19s., respectively. The further five shops recorded 'under the exchange' probably faced the street at ground level and had an even higher mean rent at £34 16s. Stock was valued for 86 per cent of the shops in the Exchange, the mean per shop being £118 14s. The New Exchange was built to provide a wide range of retailing outlets in which the inhabitants of the West End could buy both luxury and commonplace articles. The Royal Exchange, on the other hand, incorporated shops only as a secondary function, its main purpose being to serve as a site for mercantile business (see Fig. 5.18). The physical structure of the retail units gathered on the first floor galleries, or 'pawns', of the Royal Exchange, must have been relatively flexible as in twenty-two cases fractions ranging from a quarter of a shop to one-and-a-half shops were assessed. The mean rent of a single shop unit was £24 8s., slightly less than for a shop at the New Exchange. There is no indication that the shops recorded at the Royal Exchange included any of those known to have been built into its outside walls facing the street. Those shops were probably more valuable than those within the Exchange, and they may have been separately assessed. Exeter Exchange, which lay on the north side of the Strand, contained fewer shops than the other purpose-built assemblages, with a lower mean value of £10 5s. per shop. Stock valuations were, however, recorded for 61 per cent of those shops, with a mean value of £66. Westminster Hall was not a purpose-built retailing structure, yet since at least the fifteenth century a number of stalls, or shops, had been set up within it on a formal and regular basis. Forty-two shops with a combined value of £174 were assessed for the 1693–4 Aid. The low mean rent value of £4 3s., together with a number of

FIG. 5.7 Interior of Westminster Hall, *c*.1730, showing the courts of law and women shopkeepers
Sources: Guildhall Library.

126

TABLE 5.4

Shopkeeping by gender among those assessed for the 1693–4 Aid

	Total number	Shops kept by women (%)	Shops kept by men (%)	Gender of shopkeeper unknown (%)	Total rent value[1]		Rent paid by women (%)	Rent paid by men (%)	Rent paid by those of unknown gender (%)
Shops	254	6.1	76.6	17.3	£1,699	10s.	4.5	83.8	11.7
New Exchange	128	50.0	46.9	3.1	£3,677	8s.	45.6	51.7	2.7
Royal Exchange	82	46.6	49.7	3.7	£1,977		44.7	52.8	2.5
Westminster Hall	42	40.5[2]	59.5	–	£174		60.9	39.1	–
Exeter Exchange	36	38.9	44.4	16.7	£368		38.9	44.8	16.3
Total	542	27.9	61.8	10.3	£7,895	18s.	36.6	58.3	5.2

Source: 1693–4 Aid database.

Notes:

[1] Total rent value of individually assessed property only.

[2] A number of women in Westminster Hall were assessed for more than one shop.

contemporary illustrations, suggest that these were small stalls, predominately occupied by booksellers, rather than the more substantial shops characteristic of the Exchanges. Seventy-eight per cent of the total assessed rent value of shops (£7,895 18s) was made up by those concentrated into the Exchanges and Westminster Hall, though such units only represented 53 per cent of the total number of retail outlets recorded.

Women were especially significant as shopkeepers at the three exchanges and Westminster Hall, where they occupied at least 39 per cent of shops (see Fig. 5.7). By contrast, women can be identified as occupiers of no more than 6 per cent of the other shops scattered across the metropolis (Table 5.4). The Exchanges perhaps provided the sheltered environment within which could flourish the small-scale retailing activities associated with women trading on their own, independently of their husbands or other men. Strype noted that in the New Exchange there were 'shops on both sides of the walks, both below and above stairs, for milliners, sempstresses and other trades that furnish dresses'.[18] Outside the Exchanges, shops were perhaps more likely to have been run as family businesses, where the male head of household would have been perceived as the responsible shopkeeper, even if a woman had day-to-day care of the shop. Moreover, small shops run by women were probably often subsumed within a general household assessment. Independent women probably had less access than men to the resources needed to employ servants or apprentices, to maintain a large stock, and to acquire

the elaborate fittings which were characteristic of the more substantial retail establishments.[19]

The distribution of rents between men and women within the Exchanges was roughly comparable with that of the percentages of shops kept. In the case of Westminster Hall, however, women were noted as paying 61 per cent of the rent for only 41 per cent of the shops. This indicates that the twelve women who operated seventeen shops within the Hall had the greater share of the financial investment involved, an unusual situation within the retailing networks of late seventeenth-century London.

The forty-two sheds recorded within the assessments are likely to have been structures from which goods were sold.[20] Nineteen of them, for example, were located in Hungerford Market. The mean rent value of £1 17s. for those structures suggests that they were probably small and of slight construction. The lowest rent value for such a property was a total of £1 10s. for 'six small sheds' in Hungerford Market House.

Markets were noted by the assessors, though there was little consistency in the manner in which they were identified or valued — values, for example, were associated with market-traders' rents, tolls, or buildings. Twenty-three separate market valuations occur but these range from a full £631 rent 'for the 3 markets' at Leadenhall — the responsibility of Sir Leonard Robinson, Chamberlain of the City of London — to an ambiguous value of £30 attached to the haymarket at Smithfield, which was in the control of one John Wind. The assessments, nonetheless, provide some useful information regarding the markets of the metropolis, as, for example, in the case of Hungerford Market. That market was in the joint ownership of Sir Stephen Fox, one of the wealthiest men in England, and Sir Christopher Wren, and is said to have been worth £1,488 5s. per annum in 1686.[21] Though the assessment of 1693–4 gives no absolute rent value for Hungerford Market it is possible to formulate an assessed rent value of £1,997 for properties associated with the Hungerford Market estate, a figure not dissimilar to that of 1686.[22] Most other market valuations, however, were much lower: for example, Covent Garden Market, known to have been more successful than Hungerford Market during this period, had an assessed rent value of just £250.[23] Nevertheless, the assessments do appear to record all of London's significant markets and their locations are indicated in Fig. 5.6. These include markets on long-established sites such as Leadenhall, Smithfield, and Covent Garden, and others that were relocated following the Great Fire of 1666, such as Newgate. A number of more recent additions were also noted: to the east at Shadwell and Spitalfields; and to the west the market of King Street Westminster, and Newport Street, St James, and Clare Markets. The 1693–4 Aid assessments suggest that the greater part of the metropolis was well served by convenient markets, except in those areas characterised by low rents and high densities to the north and east of the City walls and around Fleet Street, where there was a notable lack of market facilities.

OCCUPATIONAL STRUCTURE AND PATTERNS

The sources

The social and economic structure of the metropolis has a clear and direct association with the occupations undertaken by its citizens. Defining, quantifying, and establishing the inter-relationships of the hundreds of different trades, crafts and callings that Londoners followed is a difficult undertaking. At its simplest it involves establishing the individual occupations that were followed, and quantifying their numerical occurrence, particularly with regard to geographical distribution. Constructing acceptable economic and functional aggregates to reflect the occupational structure of the metropolis as a whole is, however, a more complex task.

The initial problem in defining adequately those occupations pursued within late seventeenth-century London is somewhat more prosaic; it is in the location of suitable source material. The returns of the 1692 Poll Tax supply occupational labels for nearly 13,000 of those who dwelt within the City of London and were liable for the tax, mainly as heads of households.[24] Two significant further categories of records have, however, been successfully exploited. Some parish registers indicate occupations, but — despite contemporary drives to improve the recording of occupational titles — this coverage is intermittent through both time and space.[25] Nevertheless, such material has been used by Power, Forbes, and Beier, to indicate occupational

structures for Stepney and Shadwell, St Giles Cripplegate, and the wider extents of London, respectively.[26] Legal records in the form of church court depositions have also been analysed, most notably by Earle, and provide information concerning the occupational patterns of men and, most usefully, women.[27] One further occupational source was analysed as part of the present study, a list drawn up in 1677 of all the inhabitants of St James Clerkenwell, a parish to the north of the city, which includes an assessment of rent and provides an indication of the occupations followed by 71 per cent of those recorded.[28]

Occupations in the City of London

The 1692 Poll Tax returns provide occupational information for 12,831 householders of the City of London, half of all taxpayers (Fig. 5.8). The returns also record the servants and apprentices within households. Analysing the distribution of such individuals in relation to the occupation of heads of household provides an important insight into the nature of the London labour market.

Three important points need to be made concerning early-modern occupational labels and the poll tax as a source. Firstly, many who professed a single occupation in fact undertook several; secondly, discrepancies might occur between the actual form of employment and the formal occupational title noted by the assessors; and, thirdly, the overall occupational pattern may have varied according to the season.

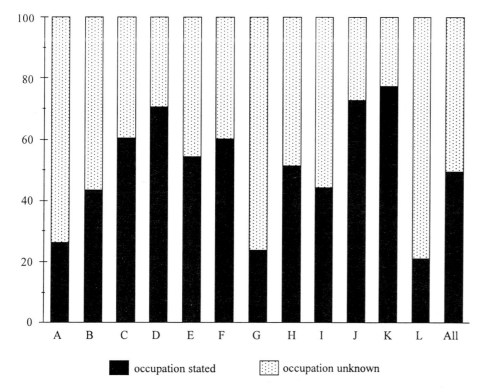

FIG. 5.8 Percentage of taxpayers stating occupations in the 1692 Poll Tax returns grouped by aggregated areas

Source: 1692 Poll Tax database. See Fig. 4.11 for extent of areas.

■ occupation stated ▒ occupation unknown

returns are a reasonably good guide to the occupational structure of the City so far as it is revealed by the primary occupations of householders.

TABLE 5.5

Those occupations attributed to more than one hundred individuals in the City of London, c.1692

Occupation	Rank	Number of individuals	% of all occupations
Gentry	1	800	6.2
Victualler	2	759	5.9
Merchant	3	753	5.9
Tailor	4	449	3.5
Weaver	5	241	1.9
Shoemaker	6	239	1.9
Joiner	7=	194	1.5
Barber	7=	194	1.5
Haberdasher	9	168	1.3
Cooper	10	156	1.2
Carpenter	11	154	1.2
Linen trades	12=	150	1.2
Goldsmith	12=	150	1.2
Attorney	12=	150	1.2
Apothecary	15	148	1.2
Grocer	16	143	1.1
Wire trades	17	136	1.1
Porter	18	131	1.0
Butcher	19	130	1.0
Vintner	20	129	1.0
Baker	21	112	0.9
Mercer	22	108	0.8
Silk trades	23	107	0.8
Tobacco trades	24	104	0.8
Total		5,792	45.2
All stated occupations		12,831	100.0

Source: 1692 Poll Tax database.

From the poll tax returns alone it is difficult to estimate whether a taxpayer had more than one occupation, although it is probable that most would have stated their primary means of employment to the assessors, leaving lesser activities unstated. Also it is undoubtedly the case that in some contexts and records individuals were identified by their company affiliation rather than by a term that accurately defined the means by which they earned a living. In the case of the poll tax, however, Alexander has demonstrated that actual occupations were regularly stated: for example, 70 per cent of the 753 poll tax payers who gave their occupation as 'merchant' appear in the London port books as active merchants. A similar comparison was made between those poll tax payers listed as 'victuallers' and the ward returns of licensed victuallers for 1691–2. This indicated that of the 759 poll tax payers described as 'victuallers', 77 per cent (584) were found within the ward returns and that of them 91 per cent were actually employed in victualling or allied trades.[29] Such correlations suggest that the occupational labels in the poll tax

TABLE 5.6
Rent and stock by occupational group in the City of London, c.1692

Occupational group	Total number stating occupation	%	Rent payers			Stockholders		
			Percentage linked to the 1693–4 Aid	Mean value of rent	Rank	Percentage linked to the 1693–4 Aid	Mean value of rent	Rank
Building	798	6.2	74.9	£14 12s.	14	45.1	£56 7s.	13
Textiles and clothing	2,925	22.8	68.7	£27 17s.	5	67.5	£125 2s.	5
Wood/furniture	483	3.8	75.6	£18 17s.	9	56.6	£58 6s.	12
Leather	80	0.6	78.8	£16 6s.	12	55.4	£60 8s.	11
Metal	717	5.6	70.7	£15 7s.	13	54.5	£71 3s.	8
Miscellaneous manufactures	508	4.0	71.1	£18 1s.	10	60.0	£67 1s.	9
Merchants and financial	1,273	9.9	63.6	£46 14s.	2	91.5	£248 3s.	2
Miscellaneous dealing	1,827	14.2	78.0	£26 9s.	7	66.1	£88 6s.	7
Food and drink	1,278	10.0	77.4	£27 8s.	6	71.2	£112 7s.	6
Victualling	281	2.2	78.3	£74 13s.	1	87.4	£126 1s.	4
Gentry	800	6.2	35.3	£41 7s.	3	84.4	£273 14s.	1
Professional and official	798	6.2	51.9	£32 13s.	4	71.9	£184 12s.	3
Miscellaneous services	642	5.0	47.8	£17 10s.	11	42.9	£64 12s.	10
Transport	421	3.3	52.0	£21 0s.	8	35.3	£55 16s.	14
Sub total	12,831	100.0	66.8	£28 10s.	–	66.9	£113 14s.	–
Not stated	13,023	–	37.1	£20 16s.	–	46.2	£44 15s.	–
Total	25,854	–	51.8	£25 10s.	–	59.5	£171 3s.	–

Sources: 1692 Poll Tax database, 1693–4 Aid assessments.

The seasons directly affected many of the diverse crafts and trades pursued in London with some — particularly construction and manufacturing activities — prone to a considerable decline in available work during the winter months. Other occupations suffered in the summer, notably the service and luxury trades associated with the London 'season' which came to an end in June of each year. However, the termination of the 'season' had a greater impact in the West End than in the City. The varying seasonal demands upon the port have been outlined by Schwarz who noted a peak of activity during the summer and autumn months. It is likely that unoccupied mariners followed alternative land-based employments during the winter and spring.[30] In this case any such occupational shift would have been confined to the eastern parishes and was probably little felt in the City or West End. The effect upon the analysis that any seasonal fluctuations within the administrative boundaries of the City were

likely to have had has been reduced as a result of the seasonal variation among those returns used to compile the poll tax database.

In all, 773 different occupational descriptions were recorded by the assessors for the poll tax, ranging from accountant to yeoman. The most frequently stated title, in this instance given in lieu of an occupation, was that of gentleman or gentlewoman: 800 members of the gentry were listed, 6.2 per cent of all those with an occupational description (Table 5.5). The next most common occupations were those of victualler (759) and merchant (753). The fourth, fifth and sixth most frequent occupations were associated with the textile and clothing sector, principally tailors, weavers and shoemakers. A further eighteen occupations had more than one hundred individuals recorded in the poll tax returns. They included: joiners, carpenters, goldsmiths, porters, bakers, and tobacconists or tobacco workers. Overall, 39.3 per cent of all those stating occupations (5,361 individuals) shared just twenty different occupational titles, with a mixture of manufacturing, dealing and service functions, in a descending order of prominence.

To provide a clearer picture of the overall occupational structure, the 773 occupational titles were aggregated into fourteen major groups, based upon economic function or product-type (see Tables 4.10, 5.6 and 5.7). A few large groups cannot fully represent the great occupational diversity and dynamism of a city as large and prosperous as London, yet the technique is necessary to provide a

TABLE 5.7
Servants and apprentices by occupational group in the City of London

Occupational group	Percentage of taxpayers in group	Servants									Apprentices			Servants and apprentices		
		All servants			Male		Female		Unknown gender		no.	no. per taxpayer	%	no.	no. per taxpayer	%
		no.	no. per taxpayer	%	no.	%	no.	%	no.	%						
Building	6.2	681	0.9	4.7	181	3.4	199	2.6	46	3.0	255	0.3	10.4	936	1.2	5.5
Textiles and clothing	22.8	3,266	1.1	22.4	1,271	23.7	1,728	22.4	267	17.6	565	0.2	23.0	3,831	1.3	22.5
Wood/furniture	3.8	427	0.9	2.9	199	3.7	158	2.1	70	4.6	157	0.3	6.4	584	1.2	3.4
Leather	0.6	37	0.5	0.3	13	0.2	21	0.3	3	0.2	45	0.6	1.8	82	1.0	0.5
Metal	5.6	582	0.8	4.0	247	4.6	300	3.9	35	2.3	320	0.4	13.0	902	1.3	5.3
Misc manufactures	4.0	399	0.8	2.7	167	3.1	207	2.7	25	1.7	201	0.4	8.2	600	1.2	3.5
Merchants and financial	9.9	2,461	1.9	16.9	792	14.7	1,310	17.0	359	23.7	92	0.1	3.7	2,553	2.0	14.9
Misc dealing	14.2	1,940	1.1	13.3	643	12.0	1,135	14.7	162	10.7	268	0.1	10.9	2,208	1.2	12.9
Food and drink	10.0	1,515	1.2	10.4	525	9.8	816	1.6	174	11.5	344	0.3	14.0	1,859	1.5	10.9
Victualling	2.2	741	2.6	5.1	431	8.0	270	3.5	40	2.6	69	0.2	2.8	810	2.9	4.8
Gentry	6.2	1,210	1.5	8.3	344	6.4	672	8.7	194	12.8	13	0.02	0.5	1,223	1.5	7.2
Professional and official	6.2	1,012	1.3	7.0	317	5.9	623	8.1	72	4.8	50	0.1	2.0	1,062	1.3	6.2
Misc services	5.0	394	0.6	2.7	151	2.8	198	2.6	45	3.0	59	0.1	2.4	453	0.7	2.7
Transport	3.3	173	0.4	1.2	90	1.7	61	0.8	22	1.5	23	0.5	0.9	196	0.5	1.2
Sub total	100.0	14,583	1.1	100.0	5,371	100.0	7,698	100.0	1,514	100.0	2,461	0.2	100.0	17,044	1.3	100.0
Not stated	–	6,208	–	–	1,690	–	3,400	–	1,118	–	758	–	–	6,966	–	–
Total	–	20,791	0.8	–	7,061	–	11,098	–	2,632	–	3,219	0.1	–	24,010	0.9	–

Source: 1692 Poll Tax database. See Table 4.10 for additional information.

manageable overview of the pattern of employment.[31] The occupational groups have been characterised with reference to the values of rent and stock (Table 5.6), and associated numbers of servants and apprentices (Tables 4.10 and 5.7).[32]

The building sector comprised relatively few occupations, mainly carpenters, bricklayers, stone-masons, glaziers, and a number of other related trades such as plumbers, plasterers and painters. The overall numbers employed within this sector were probably much greater than the 798 individuals listed, as day-labourers were likely to have been exempted from the tax and so do not appear within the returns. In addition, many building workers probably dwelt in the poorer areas of London, outside the administrative boundaries of the City. Within the City, building workers tended to live away from the commercial centre, outside the walls to the west, north, and east, and along the poorer, western section of the intramural river-frontage (Fig. 5.10). Their greatest concentration was outside Aldersgate and Cripplegate, where they comprised 9.5 per cent of all those with stated occupations. In

131

Bishopsgate Without they represented 8.0 per cent of those giving occupations. The area of Tower and Billingsgate Wards housed the least number of building workers, only two individuals being resident within the area — Charles Essington, a plumber, and John Ayliffe, a glazier. Those in the building sector paid the lowest mean rent of any group, £14 12s. They also had a very low mean stock value, which at £56 7s. was well below the overall mean of all those who stated an occupation (see Table 5.6). The craft nature of their work is indicated by their low number of servants (0.9 per household), and by an above average number of apprentices (0.3 per household) who were present in 23.7 per cent of households.

Those working in the textile and clothing sector (2,925 individuals) comprised two functional groups: manufacturers and finishers, and dealers. The first group included a relatively large number (241) of weavers, as well as dyers, clothworkers and calenderers. Prominent among the textile dealers were linendrapers, mercers, drapers, and both men and women who dealt in silk or lace. Clothing or apparel makers represented the largest single group of workers within the City, comprising 1,075 individuals. This group included tailors (an exceptionally large body of 449), sempstresses and hatters, among a wide range of other more specialised garment manufacturers such as bodice-makers, mode-makers, manufacturers of periwigs, and the somewhat singular calling of glove-perfumer. Clothing dealers included haberdashers, milliners, salesmen, and hosiers.

FIG. 5.9 *The Fellow 'Prentices at their Looms* (William Hogarth, 1747)
Source: Guildhall Library.

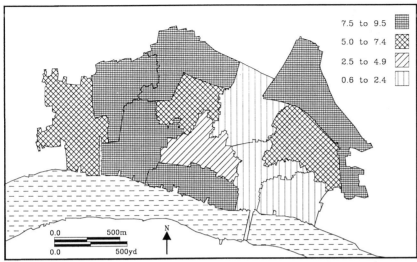

FIG. 5.10 Building occupations as a percentage of all stated occupations
in the City of London
Source: 1692 Poll Tax database.

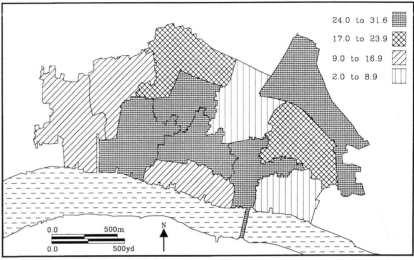

FIG. 5.11 Textile and clothing occupations as a percentage of all stated
occupations in the City of London.
Source: 1692 Poll Tax database.

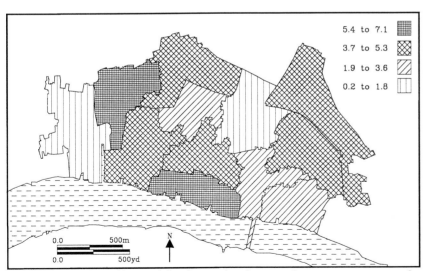

FIG. 5.12 Wood-working and furniture related occupations as a percentage of
all stated occupations in the City of London.
Source: 1692 Poll Tax database.

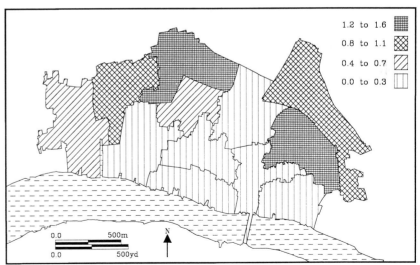

FIG. 5.13 Leather-working occupations as a percentage of all stated
occupations in the City of London.
Source: 1692 Poll Tax database.

The dual nature of the textile and clothing sector, is further demonstrated in Fig. 5.11. Two concentrations can be observed, the central and western area within the walls, mostly containing dealers and apparel manufacturers, and the district of Bishopsgate Without, which comprised mostly textile manufacturers or finishers. The greatest concentration of textile and clothing workers was found at the western end of the City around St Paul's, where 31.6 per cent of all those stating occupations fell within this sector. In the district of Bishopsgate Without 28.1 per cent of the taxed householders had employment associated with textiles or clothing. The district of Tower and Billingsgate Wards had the lowest occurrence of textile and clothing workers at just 2.0 per cent. It is probable that the occupancy of centrally-located high value property influenced the mean rent value of this sector, £27 17s. being just above the overall mean. The mean value of stock held by those in the sector was £125 2s., somewhat below the overall mean, though the textile and clothing group had the second highest total value of stock at £177,889 3s.

The manufacture and finishing of textiles and clothing employed large numbers of servants in a productive capacity. Consequently, this sector accounted for the greatest percentage share of all male and female servants, 23.7 and 22.4 per cent, respectively, although in terms of servants per householder this sector was equal to the overall mean (see Table 5.7). With regard to the binding of apprentices, the picture is similar: 14.3 per cent of householders within this sector took apprentices,

equal to the overall rate of apprentice take-up in the City of London among all those stating occupations (Table 4.10), and the number of apprentices per householder was also close to the mean (Table 5.7). As a result of this the sector contained the largest occupational group of the City's apprentices: 3,831 individuals (see Fig. 5.9).

Coopers, turners, cabinet makers, carvers, and chair makers comprised the majority of those working in the specialised wood and furniture sector. Four hundred and eighty-three individuals stated occupations associated with this group (Table 5.6). The greatest concentration was found in the neighbourhood of Smithfield in the ward of Farringdon Without, where 7.1 per cent of those stating occupations worked with wood or furniture (Fig. 5.12). The riverside area from Queenhithe to Dowgate Wards also had a high number of wood-workers. In this instance the particular demands of the commercial activity of that neighbourhood influenced the detailed occupational composition, thirty-seven (84.1 per cent) of the woodworkers in the area being coopers. The lowest incidence of wood- and furniture workers, 0.2 per cent, was in the Coleman Street and Broad Street Wards. The mean rent value paid by those within this sector was a low £18 17s., while the mean value of stock was close to the lowest of all the occupational groups at £58 6s. (Table 5.6). The craft-based nature of this sector encouraged the taking of apprentices: a relatively high 24 per cent of woodworkers acted as masters, and the number of apprentices per master was above the mean (Table

4.10). On the other hand, householders in this sector had below the mean number of servants, most of whom were probably employed in domestic capacities.

Leather workers were a small occupational group within the City, for many of London's tanneries occupied sites in the semi-rural parishes south of the Thames. Particular occupations stated for the eighty workers within this group included currier, saddler, leather-dresser, and harness- and bridle-maker. These leather workers were almost exclusively located in the periphery of the City, with the greatest concentration, 1.6 per cent, resident in the area of Aldersgate and Cripplegate Without (Fig. 5.13). The central district of Cheapside, and Tower and Billingsgate Wards, housed no leather workers. The group had a noticeably low mean rent at £16 6s. and a similar low mean stock value of £60 8s. (Table 5.6). The sector also had the second lowest mean number of servants per household, 0.5. Leather workers, however, took more apprentices than any other group: 43.8 per cent of households accommodated apprentices, with an overall mean of 0.6 per household (Tables 4.10, 5.7).

The metal trades included both basic manufacturers and those skilled in working with fine metals, 717 taxpayers in all. Among the manufacturers were smiths, founders and braziers. The fine-metal workers included wiredrawers, silversmiths, jewellers, engravers, and a variety of more specialised occupations. Those in the metal-working sector made up 16.5 per cent of all those

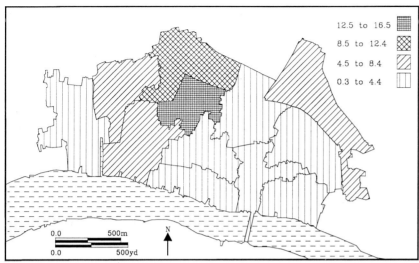

FIG. 5.14 Metal-working occupations as a percentage of
all stated occupations in the City of London
Source: 1692 Poll Tax database.

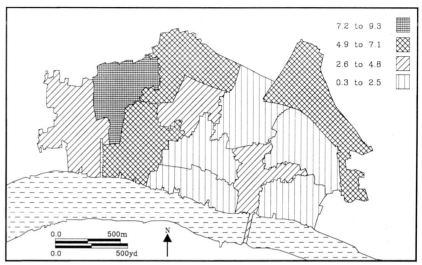

FIG. 5.15 Miscellaneous manufacturing occupations as a percentage of
all stated occupations in the City of London.
Source: 1692 Poll Tax database.

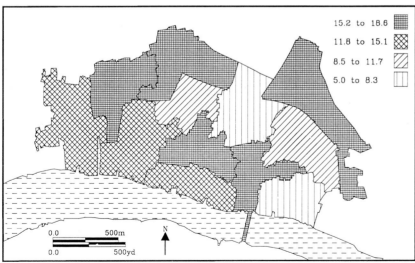

FIG. 5.16 Miscellaneous dealing occupations as a percentage of
all stated occupations in the City of London.
Source: 1692 Poll Tax database.

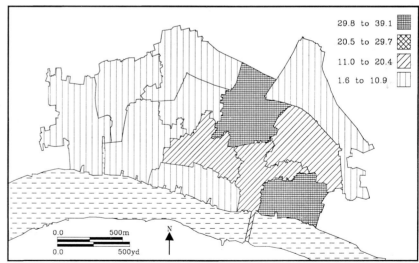

FIG. 5.17 Mercantile and financial occupations as a percentage of
all stated occupations in the City of London.
Source: 1692 Poll Tax database.

stating occupations in the area of Aldersgate and Cripplegate Within Wards, a long-standing location for metal working (Fig. 5.14). Among the metal trades in this district, 61.3 per cent were either silversmiths or wiredrawers. Adjacent areas, mainly outside the City wall, also had relatively high numbers of metal workers. In Bishopsgate Without and Portsoken Wards the group represented 10.8 per cent of all occupations, of which thirty-three individuals (40.7 per cent) were braziers or founders. In the central and eastern parts of the City within the walls those in the metal trades were resident in low numbers, 2.2 per cent overall. The metal-work sector had the second lowest mean rent value of any occupational group, £15 7s., though the inherently high value of their raw material contributed to a mean stock value of £71 3s., eighth overall (Table 5.6). Like other manufacturing sectors, metal workers had below the mean number of servants, but were well above the mean in terms of those who took apprentices (31.7 per cent), and in apprentices per household (0.9) (Table 5.7).

The miscellaneous or general manufacturing category included a wide range of production-based occupations, for example, watch- and clockmakers, printers, bookbinders, gunsmiths, wheelwrights, and soap makers. Many in this sector undertook the construction or assembly of mechanical devices ranging in complexity from pumps and looms to scientific instruments. The greatest concentration of these manufacturers was in the vicinity of Smithfield in the ward of Farringdon Without, where 9.3 per cent of those stating occupations were

in this group (Fig 5.15). Other districts on the western side of the City had a high proportion of manufacturers, as did Bishopsgate and Portsoken Wards. The least occurrence (0.3 per cent) was in the wards of Billingsgate and Tower. Some manufacturers formed specialist groups which demonstrate evidence of geographical clustering. Thirty-three clockmakers were noted within the returns, thirteen of whom dwelt in Farringdon Without. Among that group was the renowned clockmaker Thomas Tompion, who occupied a substantial property called, appropriately, the 'Dial and Three Crowns' on the western corner of Water Lane and Fleet Street. Tompion was the wealthiest of all such manufacturers paying a rent of £55 and holding stock valued at £200.[33] The mean rent among clockmakers was £16, their mean stock value £53 11s.

Manufacturers of watches evidently possessed a variety of skills comparable to those of clockmakers, indeed the two terms were often interchangeable, yet their geographical distribution differed in one particular way.[34] Sixty-four per cent of clockmakers occupied property outside the City walls, mainly to the west of the City, whereas only 28 per cent of watchmakers dwelt beyond the walls. A significant number (twelve) were located in the ward of Farringdon Without, but the largest group (fifteen) dwelt inside the walls in the adjacent ward of Farringdon Within. The labour markets within which these two interconnected groups operated go some way toward explaining their geographical patterns. Clockmakers frequently engaged skilled

furniture makers, of the sort more often encountered in the western half of the metropolis, to produce cases and stands for their timepieces. They also required access to the expanded market for luxury household goods that the élite inhabitants of the West End provided. Watchmakers, on the other hand, employed jewellers, enamellers, and the like, to complete the elaborate cases that held the mechanisms they had engineered. A high proportion of individuals with those particular skills dwelt within the City walls, as did the merchants and many of the gentry who formed an important element of the market for watches. The sixty-seven watchmakers listed in the returns were marginally wealthier than their clockmaking counterparts, with a higher mean rent of £19 10s., but a similar mean stock value of £52 4s. There were, nonetheless, large disparities of wealth within the group. The innovative watchmaker Daniel Quare paid a considerable rent, £90, and had a stock value of £100, at his property in the parish of St Mary Woolnoth.[35] Yet on the corner of Black and White Court on the west side of Old Bailey dwelt John Higgs, holding stock valued at £25 and paying a rent of only £5.

A further field of specialist manufacturing was that of printing and bookbinding. The poll tax returns record fifty-one printers and thirty-three book-binders. The printers were located principally in the western part of the City, 51 per cent dwelling in the wards of Farringdon Within and Castle Baynard. These wards encompassed the traditional centre of London's printing community — St Paul's

Churchyard. Bookbinders had a similar distribution, but a smaller proportion of their number, 39 per cent, was located in those particular wards. With regard to rent and stock values there was little difference between the two callings. Combined, this group had a mean rent value of £16 6s. and a mean stock value of £68 11s. The wealthiest member of the group was a printer, Roger Norton, whose property in Little Britain, just outside the City wall, had a rent value of £35 and whose stock was valued at £300. In 1668 Norton is known to have had three presses, one apprentice and seven workmen employed in his premises. He was an influential member of the Stationers' Company who, as Master in 1684, enabled the stationers to become the first City company to obtain a new charter from Charles II following the *Quo Warranto* episode.[36] Bookbinders appear often to have undertaken printing work, as was certainly the case with the two most prosperous members of that group. The brothers Ralph and Richard Simpson had adjacent properties at the signs of the 'Harp' and the 'Three Trouts' in St Paul's Churchyard, with rent values of £40 and £30 respectively. Their combined stock value was £225. Both are noted as printers within the literature but Ralph, significantly, was referred to in a contemporary reference as a particularly accomplished bookbinder.[37]

The mean rent value of the miscellaneous manufacturing group as a whole was a relatively low £18 1s., reflecting the diverse nature of their occupations (Table 5.6). Rents ranged from the £3 per annum paid by Adrian Newth, a relatively poor maker of mousetraps living in the northern part of the parish of St Botolph Bishopsgate, to the wealthy spectaclemaker, William Longland, who lived near the junction of Lombard Street and Cornhill and was assessed for an annual rent of £100.[38] The low mean value for stockholding, £67 1s., possibly reflected the undertaking of productive work primarily on a commission basis and the service nature of much of the sector. Manufacturing households in this sector contained a small proportion of all servants (2.7 per cent) yet had a relatively high percentage of apprentices (8.2 per cent: Table 4.10).

The miscellaneous dealing sector incorporated occupations which ranged from suppliers of raw materials and fuel, such as woodmongers and coal merchants, to those who provided small household goods, such as waxchandlers and toy sellers. The highest concentration of dealers was in the Smithfield district of Farringdon Without, where they represented 18.6 per cent of all occupations (Fig. 5.12). The areas of Aldersgate and Cripplegate Without and Bishopsgate Without and Portsoken Ward also had high percentages (14.7 to 17.7). The Cheapside, Cornhill and London Bridge district had a high frequency of minor dealers and a noticeable concentration of sixty-five apothecaries and thirty-eight druggists (40.6 and 69.1 per cent, respectively, of all apothecaries and druggists in the City of London). The mean rent paid by dealers was £26 9s., just above the City-wide mean (Table 5.6). Their mean stock value was relatively low, £88 6s. Yet this figure conceals wide disparities of wealth among those assessed for stock. For example, Richard Chiswell, probably the most renowned publisher of the period, was noted as a bookseller at the 'Rose and Crown' in St Paul's Churchyard, a property he had occupied since 1666. Chiswell's household included four servants and he was assessed for £600 of stock, undoubtedly including valuable printed material.[39] Representing the less wealthy elements of the sector was one Richard Heyard, a cutler in the parish of St Katherine Cree, who was one of six less wealthy dealers each of whose stock was valued at only £12 10s. As dealers rather than manufacturers, members of this group employed servants rather than apprentices, who were present in 62.3 and 11.8 per cent of households, respectively. It was unusual for those in this sector to engage more than one apprentice, and of the 268 apprentices working within dealing households only 17.2 per cent shared a master.

Merchants, and those who worked in occupations concerned with financial dealing and services, were amongst the wealthiest of the City's inhabitants. Their mean rent value was £46 14s., their mean stock value £248 3s. (Table 5.6). Stockholding was particularly widespread among the members of this group with 91.5 per cent of those linked to the 1693–4 Aid being assessed for stock. Merchants and financial workers represented 9.9 per cent of all stated occupations, making it the fourth largest occupational sector within the City, yet this group was responsible for 20.9 per cent (£220,600) of the City's total stock value. Two major concentrations of such individuals existed (Fig. 5.17). In the wards of

Fig. 5.18 Bird's-eye view of the Royal Exchange's south front, *c*.1700 (Johannes de Ram)
Source: Guildhall Library.

Billingsgate and Tower the sector represented 39.1 per cent of all occupations, and almost all of them were engaged in overseas trade (97.1 per cent). In the area of Coleman Street and Broad Street Wards 36.9 per cent were categorised in this sector. However, in this instance more (13.4 per cent) were associated with financial activities (see Fig 5.18).

The mercantile and financial sector was a very significant employer of servant labour. Householders had the highest mean number of servants (1.9) and the lowest mean number of apprentices (0.1). Female, most probably domestic, servants predominated, with 17.0 per cent of all female servants employed by those within the sector. Yet this group also returned the highest percentage of servants whose gender was unknown, 23.7 per cent. In these cases the servant's name is not recorded — perhaps a sign of a relatively weak identity within a large and wealthy household and an indication that this population of servants was more transient than in other sectors (see Tables 4.10 and 5.7). Individuals identified as apprentices, on the other hand, were rarely encountered within such households: only 5.6 per cent of households were noted by the poll tax returns as including an apprentice. Furthermore, of the ninety-two apprentices within this sector thirty-five, 38.0 per cent, were engaged by goldsmiths, some of whom were manufacturers as well as providers of financial services.

Bakers, brewers, confectioners, fishmongers, milkwomen, pastry-cooks, sugarbakers and tripesellers were included within the forty-one occupations followed by those in the food and drink sector of the City's economy. The majority were involved in the production or processing of foodstuffs, but a number were more concerned with the sale and supply of specific commodities. The greatest concentration of such workers was in the wards of Queenhithe, Vintry, and Dowgate on the upstream waterfront (Fig. 5.19). The most frequently cited occupation in that district, within this sector, was salter (twenty-five), followed by grocers (twelve), distillers (eleven), and cheesemongers (ten). The presence of the river, as a means of transport and as an abundant water supply, provided the primary attraction for such high numbers of salters, both suppliers of the raw material — who had for centuries been associated with the Queenhithe area — and those who salted meat and fish, and for the distillers. The area of Bishopsgate Without and Portsoken Ward also had a relatively high proportion, 11.9 per cent, of food and drink occupations. In this instance the thirty-five butchers formed the most prominent group. Chandlers (thirty), bakers (eighteen), and cooks (eighteen), were also recorded in high numbers among the total of twenty-eight different occupations stated. That focus upon butchery and cooking activities is explained by the particular characteristics of the location, being on the outskirts of the City where livestock were received and where there was space for trades using large ovens, yet adjacent to the heavily populated areas of the eastern parishes.

Mean rent for the food and drink sector was £27 8s., just above the overall mean for all those who stated an occupation and were linked to the 1693–4 Aid assessments (Table 5.6). Most paid relatively small rents reflecting the low economic remuneration of much of this form of activity. Nevertheless, high rents were encountered occasionally: Thomas Wickham, a wealthy distiller, occupied property in the parish of St Botolph Billingsgate with a rental value of £360, and was further assessed for £200 of stock. The mean stock value for the sector as a whole was £112 7s., a result of the relatively high value of certain of the commodities that were dealt with, including sugar and coffee. Households in this sector had just above the mean number of apprentices, and the size of the sector meant that it contained the second largest group of apprentices within the metropolis. A relatively large proportion (63.7 per cent) of households included servants, although the number per household was close to the mean (Tables 4.10, 5.7). This profile perhaps reflects the presence in the sector both of dealers and of manufacturers or processors.

The victualling trades were represented by a relatively small number of householders yet were associated with both large numbers of employees, needed to attend to the needs of customers, and the high levels of rent related to larger properties. Innholders and vintners, who made up the greater part of this sector (76.5 per cent), retained a greater proportion of servants and apprentices than any other single occupational category, with mean numbers of servants and apprentices at 3.01 for innholders, and 3.84 for vintners where households included such individuals. In the victualling sector

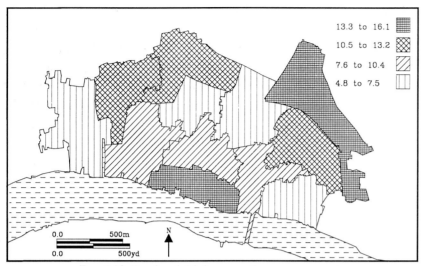

FIG. 5.19 Food and drink occupations as a percentage
of all stated occupations in the City of London
Source: 1692 Poll Tax database.

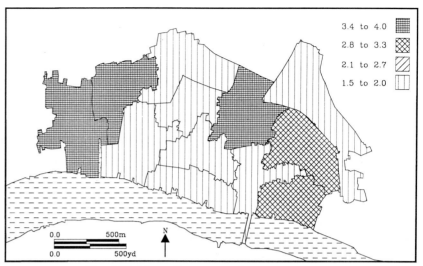

FIG. 5.20 Victualling occupations as a percentage
of all stated occupations in the City of London
Source: 1692 Poll Tax database.

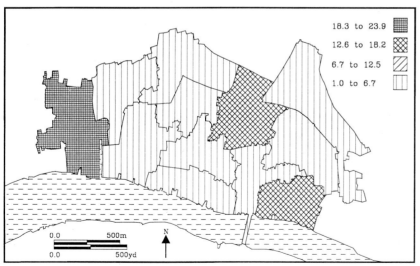

FIG. 5.21 The gentry as a percentage of all stated
occupations in the City of London
Source: 1692 Poll Tax database.

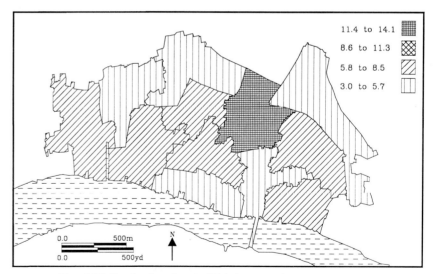

FIG. 5.22 Professional and official occupations as a percentage
of all stated occupations in the City of London
Source: 1692 Poll Tax database.

overall, the mean total of servants and apprentices per household (2.9) was higher than for any other sector, and the mean number of servants (2.6) was substantially higher, while the mean number of apprentices was no more than average (Table 5.7). Those in the victualling trade were well distributed across the City, the highest number being in the Broad Street and Coleman Street area where they represented 4.0 per cent of all stated occupations. In no area, however, did they fall below 1.5 per cent of all occupations (Fig. 5.20). Much of the victualling trade was intrinsically associated with substantial property-holding, in the form of inns, taverns and the like, and rents were consequently high. Innkeepers paid a mean rent of £84 3s. per annum, with innholders and vintners paying mean rents of £79 16s. and £79 10s., respectively. Half of all innkeepers, innholders and vintners had rent values in excess of £70, while rents below £50 were only noted for 21 per cent of that group. The highest rent related to victualling was £269 paid by Thomas Traunter for the Saracen's Head Inn and associated tenements, just outside Newgate on Snow Hill. The significance of the Saracen's Head was noted as early as 1598 by Stow who described it as 'a fayre and large Inne for receipt of travellers'.[40] The sector as a whole had a mean rent value of £74 13s., the highest of any occupational category (Table 5.6). Stock values were not exceptionally high: the sector had a mean value of £126 1s., with the highest individual stockholding, of £600, belonging to Edward Cooke, a vintner of the parish of St Bartholomew by the Exchange. Vintners as a group had a relatively high mean stock value of £153 12s.,

probably a reflection of the valuable stocks of wine they held, a situation substantiated by numerous inventory accounts.[41]

The gentry, 497 gentlemen and 303 gentlewomen, formed an economic, social, and consequently occupational, group of some significance within the City. Those in this sector were located principally in three areas: Broad Street and Coleman Street Wards (17.2 per cent of all stated occupations), Billingsgate and Tower Wards (18.5 per cent), and the western half of the ward of Farringdon Without (23.9 per cent) (Fig. 5.21). In the last area 102 of the 212 gentry recorded dwelt in the parish of St Dunstan in the West, a location — immediately adjacent to the Temple, Chancery Lane, and Lincoln's Inn — which points to some members of this group being employed in the law. The gentry held the highest mean stock value of any occupational sector at £273 14s., they also paid relatively high levels of rent, with a mean rent value of £41 7s. (Table 5.6). Membership of this group was primarily a reflection of wealth and as such a variety of occupational callings were represented. For example, the highest rent paid by a member of the City gentry was £140 by Thomas Frederick, gent, of the parish of St Olave Jewry, who added to his father's already substantial wealth and gained yet more by his advantageous marriage.[42] The largest stock assessment, £2,000, was for Jeffrey Jefferies, gent, who owned property, including a warehouse, near the junction of St Mary Axe and Leadenhall Street. In 1688 Jefferies inherited much of his wealth from his uncle, John Jefferies, with whom he had been a partner in the tobacco trade.[43]

The wealthiest gentlewoman was Madam Elizabeth Barron, a gentleman's widow of St James Garlickhithe.[44] She was assessed for a rent of £68 and for stocks valued at £1,000. Frederick, Jefferies, and Barron each owned a private coach.[45] Gentry households were often large, bolstered by a significant number of servants. With a mean of 1.5 servants per household, the gentry were exceeded only by the mercantile and victualling groups, although among the gentry the servants were more likely to hold domestic positions. Apprentices, however, were extremely rare, the returns indicating only eight households (1.0 per cent) in which apprentices were resident.

The early modern City was the venue for a wide variety of professions and the focus of much officialdom, both major and petty. The greatest concentration of professionals was in the Coleman Street and Broad Street Wards to the north of the City, where 14.1 per cent of all those stating occupations could be categorised within this sector (Fig. 5.22). The distribution in all other areas was broadly even, from 3.0 per cent in the wards of Bishopsgate Without and Portsoken, to 8.5 per cent in Billingsgate and Tower Wards. The group as a whole had a mean rent value of £32 13s., and held stock with a mean worth of £184 12s., just above the City-wide mean (Table 5.6). Occupations within this sector ranged widely from toothdrawers to surgeons, from sextons to bishops, from bailiffs to excisemen, and from under-beadles to judges. Each of those groups represents a broad professional field — medicine, religion, administration (local or state), and the law — and as such provide a finer measure of relative levels of wealth as demonstrated by rents and stocks.

Those in the medical professions had a mean rent value of £23 14s., and a mean stock value of £47 8s. The wealthiest individual within this group was a physician, Dr Brown, who dwelt in a property in or near Fleet Street with a rental value of £70, and who also held £500 of stock. While seventy-five men within this group of 178 held high status positions as physicians or surgeons, it is likely that the sixty-one providers of primary healthcare — midwives, nurses, and nurse-keepers — were all female (though only forty-seven could be positively assigned gender).[46] It is also important to recognise that much routine medical care was likely to have been undertaken by a large number of women in their role as domestic servants. While few apprentices were resident in the households of professionals as a whole, surgeons and barber-surgeons were notable for the significant number of apprentices they retained, twenty-four apprentices identified within nineteen such households. Clerics, and those with associated occupations, in both the established church and dissenting groups, had a mean rent value of £31 17s., and a mean stock value of £664 2s. Nevertheless, such figures are deceptive as clergy frequently lived in property attached to their church, and the value of their stock was estimated by means of a calculation based upon the income derived from their livings. The mean rent and stock values for those occupied within civil administration was a more direct measure at £38

11s. and £103 15s., respectively. However, many members of that group also received official salaries, which though liable to assessment are imperfectly recorded in the returns. Those in the legal profession had a mean rent value of £33 13s. and a mean stock value of £150 9s. The wealthiest member of this group was Sir Salathiel Lovell, sergeant-at-law and Recorder of London. Lovell owned property valued at £65 near the Guildhall in the parish of St Michael Bassishaw, and was also assessed for an official salary worth £1,200.[47] The notable wealth of the legal group was further indicated by the mean number of servants per household, a relatively high 2.34. Overall 57.6 per cent of all servants working for those in the professional sector were engaged within the households of legal professionals. Those in the legal professions, scriveners and attorneys in particular, also retained a significant number of apprentices. Twenty-two apprentices found such employment within seventeen households.

The sector defined as miscellaneous services included a wide variety of occupations which occurred infrequently across the City. Services were provided by chimney-sweeps, dancing-masters, herald-painters, laundresses, mathematicians, musicians and school teachers, among many others. The only two service activities to be recorded in large numbers were those of barbers (198), and clerks (109). The area of the City with the greatest concentration of occupations within this sector was to the west of the river Fleet (Fig. 5.23). There 9.8 per cent of all stated occupations were of a service

nature, compared to a City-wide mean of 5.5 per cent. Among that group twenty-five (28.7 per cent) were clerks, while fourteen weavers, four glovers, two hempdressers, a pinmaker, and a tailor, were all resident as instructors within Bridewell.[48] The mean rent value for this sector was £17 10s., though the highest value rent, £300, was paid by an individual named Batteton, not for a residential property but for a playhouse in the southern part of the parish of St Bride (Table 5.6). This was undoubtedly the Dorset Garden (or Duke's) Theatre, constructed on the Thames waterfront after the Great Fire, which is known to have been under the control of the actor/manager Thomas Betterton.[49] Representing the other end of the rental spectrum, John Ravern, a barber residing in Cock Yard near to the church of St Giles Cripplegate, was responsible for a rent of £4. The sector contained below average numbers of servants and apprentices, while the mean stock value of the sector was a relatively low £64 12s. (Tables 5.6, 5.7).

While those employed in long-distance transport activities can be expected to have dwelt in the periphery of the built-up area, and in the vicinity of major access points or routes, others concerned with internal circulation would have been located nearer to the commercial core of the City. Consequently, relatively few transport workers (421) were recorded by the poll tax returns (Table 5.6). The distribution of those poll tax payers with transport-related occupations within the City confirms the foregoing observation (Fig. 5.24). The greatest concentration of such workers was in the wards of Queenhithe and

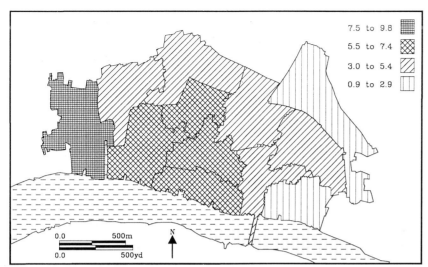

FIG. 5.23 Miscellaneous service occupations as a percentage
of all stated occupations in the City of London
Source: 1692 Poll Tax database.

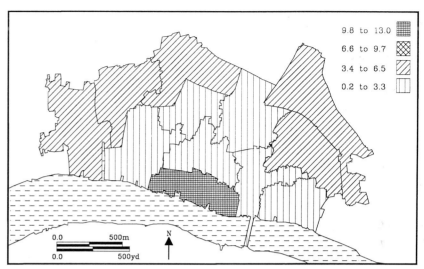

FIG. 5.24 Transport occupations as a percentage of
all stated occupations in the City of London
Source: 1692 Poll Tax database.

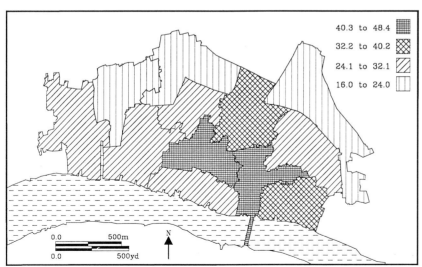

FIG. 5.25 Servants as a percentage of the adult population
within the 1692 Poll Tax returns
Source: 1692 Poll Tax database.

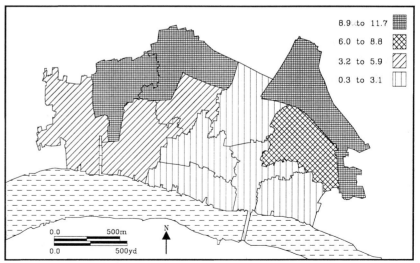

FIG. 5.26 Apprentices as a percentage of the adult population
within the 1692 Poll Tax returns
Source: 1692 Poll Tax database.

Dowgate, an area which was the water-land transport interface for the greater part of the upriver trade. In that district 13.0 per cent of all workers were employed in transport related activity, of which thirty (33.0 per cent) undertook occupations associated with water transport, as lightermen (eighteen), watermen (ten), and wharfingers (two). The only other districts to have a relatively greater frequency of transport workers were those which lay predominantly outside the City walls (and, in the case of water transport, predominantly south of the river). That extramural area was the location for 191 transport workers; in this case thirty-five (18.3 per cent) were directly associated with the movement of goods or people in vehicles: thirty-eight coachmen, twenty-four hackney-coachmen and one hackney-coachwoman, seventeen carmen and one carwoman, four stagecoachmen and one stagecoachwoman, and one drayman. The most frequently stated transport occupation for the City as a whole was that of porter or messenger, with 198 such workers being recorded, though it is likely that many more porters were too poor to be eligible for the poll tax. Transport workers had a mean rent value of £21, just below the City-wide mean (Table 5.6). Their mean stock value was the lowest of any occupational sector, £55 16s., as was the percentage of those actually holding stock, 35.3 per cent. However, it should be noted that coaches were subject to separate taxation within the poll tax, and that coach and cart operators were obliged to pay annually for licences. The relative poverty of the transport sector was further emphasised by the low numbers of servants employed, 173 in total. Apprentices were also infrequently bound

to transport workers, creating one of smallest apprentice groups, twenty-three individuals or 0.9 per cent of all apprentices (Table 5.7). That transport workers employed so few servants and apprentices was reflected by the lowest mean household size of any sector, at only 2.86 (see Table 4.10).

Servants and apprentices

Two particular groups of workers within the overall occupational structure of the City are comprehensively illustrated by the household summaries that make up the poll tax returns: servants and apprentices. While those two groups have already been discussed in relation to household structure and within their more specific occupational contexts, both groups form trans-occupational categories that merit some further investigation.[50]

Servants made up the largest single occupational category within the City of London, accounting for 20,791 people, or 31.4 per cent of the total adult population recorded in the poll tax returns. Of this number, 53.4 per cent was female, 34.0 per cent male, with a further 12.6 per cent whose gender was unknown (Table 5.7). While the majority of servants would have been engaged in predominantly domestic tasks, many were undoubtedly employed within the commercial activities of their household. The two occupational groups where this arrangement was most likely were, as indicated above, the victualling sector, and the textile and clothing sector, although it also seems likely that in the mercantile and dealing

sectors households tended to rely on servants rather than apprentices in the conduct of their business. The greatest density of servants, irrespective of occupational group, was within the Cornhill and bridgehead areas, where servants made up roughly half of the adult taxed population (48.4 per cent). A similar figure of 43.5 per cent was recorded for the central Cheapside area (Fig. 5.20). Both of these areas fall within those districts where households in the textile and clothing sector were most prominent and where merchants and dealers were also significant (Fig. 5.7). Servants made up between 32.2 and 40.2 per cent of the adult population of the Coleman Street and Broad Street area and of Tower Ward, districts which are significant for having high concentrations of both merchant and gentry households (Figs. 5.13 and 5.16). The City without the walls was notable for housing very few servants. In the area of St Giles Cripplegate servants made up only 16.0 per cent of the adult population. Despite having a very high occurrence of textile and clothing sector households the ward of Bishopsgate Without also had a small servant presence at just 16.3 per cent of the adult population, though the status of those junior members of households employed in such work was probably more likely to be that of apprentice than servant. This profile reflects the fact that in Bishopsgate Without the textile and clothing sector was represented by manufacturers and finishers rather than dealers.

Apprentices were present in all occupational sectors with most, 23 per cent, working in the textile and clothing sector (Table 5.7).[51] Three out of every five apprentices (60.1 per cent) were involved in production or manufacturing activities, a reflection of the great emphasis placed upon the learning of practical skills throughout the course of an apprenticeship. Among all poll tax paying householders, regardless of whether an occupation was stated, 9.4 per cent took apprentices. In those households where there were apprentices, the mean number per master was 1.32. Most apprentices (1,739 or 54 per cent) were the sole representatives of that status group within their master's household, the situation in 71.5 per cent of all households with apprentices (see Table 4.10). Six hundred and seventeen masters (25.4 per cent) had two apprentices, sixty-six (2.7 per cent) three, and twelve (0.5 per cent) four. These twelve included three joiners, a linen draper, an upholsterer, two vintners, three wiredrawers, and two masters of unknown occupation. Aside from regulatory restrictions imposed by certain livery companies, wealth would appear to have been a significant factor when considering the number of apprentices that might be taken. Those masters who had a single apprentice were assessed for a mean rent value of £18 and a mean stock value of £51 1s., figures very close to the City-wide means of £18 10s. and £52 18s., respectively.[52] Those twelve masters who took four apprentices each, had a much higher mean rent value of £42 13s. and a mean stock value of £156 5s.

Apprentices were present in all areas of the City (Fig. 5.26), though in the district of Cornhill and immediately to the north of London Bridge apprentices were sparse, representing only 0.3 per cent of the total adult population recorded by the poll tax. The central area of the City also had low numbers of apprentices, generally below 3.2 per cent of the adult population. Those areas outside the City wall, however, had a much higher incidence of apprentices. In the area of Bishopsgate Without and Houndsditch apprentices constituted 11.7 per cent of the adult population. That distribution pattern was clearly influenced by the nature of the occupations followed within each district. Manufacturing activities located outside the walls accounted for the greatest concentrations of apprentices, while the mercantile character of the central area was associated with a lower incidence of apprentices and a much higher incidence of servants (Figs. 5.25, 5.26).

Independent women with identified occupations

The 1692 Poll Tax returns for the City of London refer to 31,017 women, of whom 15,001 (48.4 per cent) were the spouses of male heads of households, 11,097 (35.8 per cent) were servants, probably mostly domestic, and 4,919 (15.8 per cent) had the status of independent heads of households. Of this last group the returns provide occupational information for 987, a fifth of all female householders. It is important to note, however, that the records give no indication of the type of paid or unpaid work that may have been undertaken by the wives of male heads of households.[53] Nevertheless, even such limited occupational information is valuable as it casts some light upon the variety of paid employment that independent women, whether spinsters or widows (388 of the total), pursued in the metropolis.[54]

The 987 independent women shared some 178 different occupational descriptions, covering a wide spectrum of activities from apothecaries to worsted-sellers. The most frequently cited occupational or status title was that of gentlewomen (294), with sempstresses or tailors comprising the next largest, and more clearly occupational, group (99). After them came victuallers (90), chandlers (40), and those who traded in coffee (33).[55] With regard to distribution across the occupational sectors, independent women, aside from those in the gentry group, were found to be most frequently engaged in textile and clothing manufacturing and dealing, 21.5 per cent (Table 5.8). That group was followed by those engaged in a variety of dealing activities, 15.4 per cent, and by those working in the food and drink sector, 11.9 per cent. The only other group of note was that of professionals and officials, 4.8 per cent, which comprised thirty-one nurses, fifteen midwives, two nursekeepers, and the matron of Bridewell Hospital.

While many independent women with stated occupations, particularly widows, had servants and/or apprentices (522), a large number (465) had neither. It is probable that such women stated an occupation in which they were personally engaged or one in which they acted as employers, sub-contracting workers on a daily basis. Within the building trades, for example, eight women found remuneration. Four were widows, two of whom had apprentices who were probably actively performing the stated functions of glazier and plasterer; a third had both a male servant and an apprentice engaged in the trade of joiner. The fourth widow stated her occupational title as plumber's widow, and since she had no servants or apprentices she may not have been carrying on her husband's trade, although she may have employed day-labourers. Of the four other women one, a painter, had an apprentice, while another employed a male servant, probably as a joiner. The final two women in this group had no servants or apprentices and thus were either physically engaged in the occupation given or were directly employing journeymen or day-labourers; they were Ann Evans, bricklayer, of Bishopsgate Without, and Elizabeth Ming, plumber, who dwelt just inside the City wall in the parish of St Olave Silver Street.

In summary, the City of London had a complex occupational structure within which most manufacturing, dealing and service occupations were represented. The status and numbers of those finding work in each sector varied across the extent of the City. In economic terms the most dominant group was undoubtedly that of merchants and financial workers. That sector was assessed for a total of £258,437 of rent and stock, 18.5 per cent of all rent and stock recorded by those poll tax payers linked to the 1693–4 Aid. With regard to overall numbers, the population dependant upon textile- and clothing-related employment was the largest at 11,258 or 13.8 per

cent of the total population recorded by the poll tax (81,824). As noted above, locational distinctions were also clearly evident in relation to certain occupations, particularly in the case of metal workers, merchants and financial workers, professionals and officials, and those in the transport sector. Other occupations were found widely dispersed across the City. Notwithstanding the fine detail provided by the poll tax returns, the City housed just under one third of metropolitan London's total population (see Table 4.1). It is, therefore, necessary to consider the range of economic activity followed in areas beyond the boundaries of the City if a fuller picture of London's occupational structure is to be revealed.

TABLE 5.8
Occupations followed by independent women householders in the City of London

Occupational group	Number of widows	Number of non-widows	Total number	Percentage
Building	4	4	8	0.8
Textiles and clothing	74	138	212	21.5
Wood/furniture	11	6	17	1.7
Leather	2	1	3	0.3
Metal	18	10	28	2.8
Miscellaneous manufactures	7	9	16	1.6
Merchants and financial	8	17	25	2.5
Miscellaneous dealing	91	61	152	15.4
Food and drink	58	59	117	11.9
Victualling	12	10	22	2.2
Gentry	80	214	294	29.9
Professional and official	10	37	47	4.8
Miscellaneous services	6	27	33	3.3
Transport	7	6	13	1.3
Total	388	599	987	100.0

Source: 1692 Poll Tax database.

Occupations in the wider metropolis

A number of studies have investigated the occupational structure of metropolitan London during the seventeenth and eighteenth centuries. As a result of the imperfect coverage of the available source material, much of that work has been limited in geographical scope. Nevertheless, a brief consideration of that material provides some indication of occupational patterns in districts outside the City.

The activities of those resident in London's eastern suburbs were heavily influenced by the river Thames and the ubiquitous nature of its maritime trade. In the riverside parish of St Paul Shadwell, in 1650, 59.8

per cent of male inhabitants were employed in the marine sector as sailors, lightermen, or watermen. A further 10.7 per cent of those dwelling in Shadwell were involved in shipbuilding.[56] In the neighbouring but much larger parish of St Dunstan Stepney an analysis of those occupations recorded in the burial registers between 1610 and 1690 indicated that 35.0 per cent could be categorised as marine carriers — sailors and the like — while 6.0 per cent had employment associated with shipbuilding.

Away from the waterfront, the eastern suburbs were more notable for textile production, with 17.0 per cent undertaking that activity in both the parish of Stepney (1610–90), and further west in the parish of St Giles without Cripplegate (1654–93).[57] These areas thus bore some resemblance to the City ward of Bishopsgate Without, which adjoined them. The area to the north of the city, for obvious reasons, demonstrated less occupational specialisation than the conspicuously marine character of Stepney. In Cripplegate parish significant numbers were found in all occupational sectors, with only the marine trades being poorly represented. In addition just over a quarter of all occupations (26.0 per cent) were categorised as miscellaneous.[58] As a general observation (based upon a study of legal records for the period 1695–1725), there were few dealers or professionals in the eastern and northern parishes, with most employment being found in manufacturing or petty distribution.[59]

The parish of St James Clerkenwell lay directly to the north of the Middlesex part of the parish of St Sepulchre and to the north-west of Cripplegate, and encompassed both a heavily built-up southern district and an extensive area of semi-rural land to the north. The range of occupations followed by the householders of the parish recorded in the list of householders in 1677 reflect its topography.[60] While 204 were engaged in the ten most frequently cited occupations — victualler (seventy-two), butcher (twenty-four), labourer (nineteen), carpenter (eighteen), gentlemen (sixteen), tailor (fifteen), brewer (twelve), baker (ten), smith (ten), and cooper (eight) — a further 173 householders shared eighty-nine different occupational titles. Included in that group were forms of employment most often associated with urban environments, such as porters, tobacconists, apothecaries, looking-glass makers, and printers, but also those which were clearly of a rural nature, such as cowkeepers, gardeners, a grazier and a hogman.

When allotted to groups of a similar constitution to those used to analyse the 1692 Poll Tax data, the most prevalent occupation followed in Clerkenwell was victualling, 21.0 per cent (Table 5.9). The manufacture and provision of food and drink employed 17.0 per cent of householders, with 10.9 per cent working in the textile and clothing sector, and 10.3 per cent employed in the building trades. Particularly small occupational groups in the area included those of mercantile and financial workers (0.5 per cent), professionals and officials (1.6 per cent), and the leather and transport occupations (2.4 per cent each). Victualling apart, there was a significant lack of occupational specialisation

within Clerkenwell pointing to it being a peripheral area in economic as well as geographic terms. The agricultural sector (a group not represented among those occupations listed in the poll tax returns) had the highest mean rent of £20 11s., undoubtedly a reflection of the holding of large tracts of land on the metropolitan periphery. The victualling group had a mean rent of £15 1s., while the leather-working sector, though small in numbers, had a significantly high annual rent value of £10 2s., probably linked with the supply of valuable harness goods to the land transport trade. Of individual occupations, innkeepers were the wealthiest in this area with a mean annual rent of £116 14s., followed by yeomen (£80), innholders (£41), cowkeepers (£22 17s.), and bridlemakers (£22 10s.). Overall the mean rent for the parish in 1677 was £10 4s., based on the rents of 529 householders. By 1693–4 the metropolis had expanded and household numbers had risen to 810, although the mean rent value was only slightly higher at £12 10s.[61]

During the period 1695–1725 the West End of the metropolis had a diverse occupational character, although certain types of employment were more prominent than others. Servicing and supplying the needs and demands of the gentry and aristocracy provided work for many, especially domestic servants, coachmen, furniture makers, the makers of clothing (tailors, dressmakers, peruke-makers, and glovers), lawyers, sword-cutlers, and — a sure sign of consumer activity — locksmiths. Those who found employment in the service of the state frequently dwelt in the west of the metropolis: army

TABLE 5.9
Occupational structure of St James Clerkenwell, 1677

Occupational group	Number stating occupation	Percentage	Mean value of rent	Rank by value of rent
Building	39	10.3	£5 17s.	11=
Textiles and clothing	41	10.9	£6 13s.	9
Wood/furniture	18	4.8	£7 3s.	8
Leather	9	2.4	£10 2s.	4
Metal	16	4.2	£6 12s.	10
Miscellaneous manufactures	17	4.5	£5 17s.	11=
Merchants and financial	2	0.5	£5 0s.	13
Miscellaneous dealing	23	6.1	£8 2s.	6
Food and drink	64	17.0	£9 18s.	5
Victualling	79	21.0	£15 1s.	2
Gentry	16	4.2	£13 15s.	3
Professional and official	6	1.6	£7 16s.	7
Miscellaneous services	28	7.4	£4 4s.	15
Transport	9	2.4	£4 9s.	14
Agriculture	10	2.7	£20 11s.	1
Sub total	377	100.0	£9 10s.	–
Not stated	152	–	£11 19s.	–
Total/mean	529	–	£10 4s.	–

Source: BL, Ms. Sloane 3928.

officers, soldiers, and government functionaries. Those who maintained themselves upon their estates, either by means of investment or rental income, also predominated in that district at the beginning of the eighteenth century.[62] Significant numbers from that particular group were still present in the west of London at the end of the eighteenth century. A study of voter occupations in the Westminster constituency, in 1784, indicates that 14.9 per cent of voters (representing four-fifths of all male householders) were categorised as rentiers. That analysis also demonstrated that 31.5 per cent of voters found employment under the general heading of dealing occupations, while 29.6 per cent worked in the manufacturing sector.[63]

In the early seventeenth century (1604–25) Southwark had a highly structured occupational character.[64] The central area of Southwark, the Boroughside, was notable for the high numbers engaged in the production and retailing of food and drink (29.7 per cent), probably related to the busy nature of the bridgehead area and the road to the south. Upstream from London Bridge the liberties of the Clink and Paris Garden were the location for a large group of transport workers, mainly watermen (46.7 per cent), their presence linked to the high demand for their services above London Bridge and to the South Bank playhouses, a topographic feature absent from the later seventeenth-century metropolis. Finally, in the downstream parish of St Olave the most predominant occupational groups were sailors (15.3 per cent) and textile workers (26 per cent) — most significantly, feltmakers contributed 16 per cent of this latter figure. The productive importance of this district is reinforced by the known concentration of leather workers who resided in an area rich in exploitable water supplies, some distance from, and downwind of, the main settlement.

Metropolitan London was, therefore, characterised by a great variety of occupational specialisation and also significant geographic concentrations within certain occupational sectors. Inside the City walls the occupational grouping which held most wealth was that which comprised merchants and financial workers. The majority of those following such occupations dwelt in two narrowly defined areas, the downriver port area and the district immediately north of Cornhill. Wealthy merchants and financiers also proved to be a focus for the employment of large numbers of servants and so they too occurred in large numbers within those areas. A substantial proportion of the population relied upon the textile and clothing trades to provide income. Many were engaged in that activity in the central and western areas of the City within the walls, predominantly dealers of apparel or those undertaking tailoring work, and in the eastern and northern wards beyond the walls, where textile-finishing activities were of greater importance. That form of work was also followed by a large proportion of Londoners who dwelt beyond the City boundary, particularly in the northern and eastern suburbs. In the parishes of Stepney and St Giles without Cripplegate almost a fifth of all identifiable employment was associated with textiles, while south of the river Thames the proportion of the population so employed was just over a quarter. Away from the central area, transport activities were more significant. Marine transport supplied the occupational focus for a considerable proportion of those employed in the eastern and southern suburbs. Around 70 per cent of all workers in those areas were engaged either as mariners or in shipbuilding activity. To the north and west of the City a smaller yet still significant group found employment in both general dealing activities and manufacturing. That form of employment was also important to the west of the metropolis. The West End was also the location of many domestic servants, frequently employed by wealthy householders, a significant number of whom gained their income from rents alone.

These readily identifiable local concentrations of specialised activity were set within an overall pattern characterised by diversity and intermixture of trades. They arose from the interaction of many factors, including the physical and social environment, the level of rent, access to raw materials and suppliers, and access to consumers and to specialised markets, some of which had become fixed in particular localities centuries before.

ECONOMIC INTERESTS AND GEOGRAPHY AS REVEALED BY STOCK VALUES

The stock valuation element of the 1693–4 Aid relied upon an assessment of net wealth in the form of money, investments, raw materials, and stock-in-trade, which were deemed to be the source of the assessed person's income.[65] Not all Londoners were assessed for stock tax, and in practice the tax was not imposed on wealth valued at less than £12 10s. The higher stock values, however, could conceal varied patterns of wealth holding, ranging from the aristocrat with a plethora of investments, to the financier holding large sums of cash and bonds, to the merchant with large stocks of commodities, and to the craftworker with quantities of valuable raw materials. For the assessors to make an accurate assessment of stock value was consequently a complex, and inevitably subjective, undertaking. Stock values tended to be stated in round whole numbers, of which the most frequent was £50, recorded 5,413 times. Other commonly stated sums were £100 (4,832), £25 (3,848), £200 (2,244), and £300 (1,094), only eighty-four other values were noted among the remaining 3,281 stock assessments.[66]

By comparing inventories from the City of London's Court of Orphans with the corresponding assessments for individual stock tax payers, Alexander established that the stock tax valuations involved a considerable degree of under-assessment.[67] Where comparison was possible stock assessments were worth between three to nine per cent of the inventory evaluation, although it should be noted that the inventories included personal goods — which were exempt from the stock tax calculation — and involved a much more detailed assessment of wealth than could be undertaken by the 1693–4 Aid assessors. As a very rough rule of thumb, stock tax valuations should perhaps be multiplied by twenty to convert them to values equivalent to those given in the Orphans' inventories. Nevertheless, the degree of under-assessment was generally consistent and so the stock tax valuations stand as a good indication of relative wealth among those assessed.

The overall pattern

Within metropolitan London 20,712 individuals were assessed for stock tax and the total value of that stock was £3,034,669 (Table 5.10).[68] The greatest concentration of stockholding was within the walls of the City, where just over one million pounds of stock was assessed (34.4 per cent of the total). The only other area to demonstrate significant stock holding was the West End with just under one million pounds of stock (31.5 per cent). The aggregated area of lowest stockholding was the parish of St Margaret Westminster, where only 3.1 per cent of London's total stock value was held (£92,550).

There was no property holding requirement for those liable for stock tax assessment, and so 3,831 lodgers

TABLE 5.10
Total stock data by aggregated area

Area	Total stockholding					Householder stockholding			Householder to lodger ratio	Lodger stockholding		
	Number	Total value	%	Mean value	Range	Number	Total value	Mean value		Number	Total value	Mean value
City within	7,427	£1,043,575	34.4	£140 10s. 3d.	£12 10s.–£15,000	6,293	£827,563	£131 10s. 3d.	5.5:1	1,134	£216,012	£190 10s. 0d.
City without	2,972	£287,907	9.5	£96 17s. 6d.	£12 10s.–£1000	2,547	£244,466	£96 0s. 0d.	6.0:1	425	£43,441	£102 4s. 3d.
St Margaret Westminster	635	£92,550	3.1	£145 15s. 0d.	£25–£3,000	495	£55,017	£111 3s. 0d.	3.5:1	140	£37,533	£268 2s. 0d.
West End	5,315	£956,704	31.5	£180 0s. 0d.	£8 6s. 6d.–£5,000	4,039	£664,013	£164 8s. 0d.	3.2:1	1,276	£292,691	£229 7s. 9d.
Northern parishes	1,323	£226,987	7.5	£171 11s. 6d.	£12 10s.–£20,000	951	£153,262	£161 3s. 3d.	2.6:1	372	£73,725	£198 4s. 0d.
Eastern parishes	1,043	£121,424	4.0	£116 8s. 6d.	£25–£2,000	887	£99,600	£112 6s. 0d.	5.7:1	156	£21,824	£139 18s. 0d.
Eastern riverside parishes	1,429	£149,781	4.9	£104 16s. 6d.	£13 6s. 6d.–£3,200	1,305	£135,323	£103 14s. 0d.	10.5:1	124	£14,458	£116 12s. 0d.
Metropolitan Middlesex	568	£155,741	5.1	£274 4s. 0d.	£25–£5,000	364	£106,575	£292 16s. 0d.	1.8:1	204	£49,166	£241 0s. 0d.
Total	20,712	£3,034,669	100.0	£146 10s. 6d.	£8 6s. 6d.–£20,000	16,881	£2,285,819	£135 8s. 3d.	4.4:1	3,831	£748,850	£195 9s. 6d.

Source: 1693–4 Aid database.

were assessed for stockholding amongst the total of 20,712 stock tax valuations. Overall, there were 4.4 householders to every lodger paying stock tax. In terms of value, householders held 3.1 times the value of stock held by lodgers, although the mean value of stock was consistently higher for lodgers than for householders, except in metropolitan Middlesex where the lodger mean fell some £52 short of that for householders. The generally high mean stock values for lodgers may indicate some deficiency in the identification of stockholders amongst that group, with only the more obviously wealthy attracting the assessors' attention.[69]

Analysis of taxpayers by aggregated area indicates that, while in most areas the number of stockholders was closely related to the overall number of householders, in the City and the eastern parishes the two factors diverged (see Table 4.1). The City within the walls contained 35.9 per cent of all metropolitan stockholders, but only 17.5 per cent of all households, a striking indication of the City's commercial vitality. In the West End there was a similar — though less marked — disparity, 18.3 per cent of households compared to 25.7 per cent of all stockholders, the combination of aristocratic residence and commercial activity helping to explain this variance. Different influences held sway in the eastern parishes of the metropolis where high housing density and low rent levels were contributory factors in accounting for the low frequency of stockholders encountered. The eastern parishes held 5.0 per cent of all stockholders but 8.5 per cent of households, while in the riverside districts the disparity was even greater, with 6.9 per cent of stockholders and 12.6 per cent of households.

The mapping of stockholders as a percentage of all households by analytical areas demonstrates the density of stockholding across the metropolis in finer detail (Fig. 5.27). Overall, the mean frequency for London stockholding was 38.7 per cent. High numbers of stockholders existed in the central part of the City within the walls (overall 74.8 per cent), in the area south of the Strand adjacent to the Temple (66.8 per cent), in Covent Garden and again south of the Strand (72.0 per cent), along the Haymarket in Westminster (72.2 per cent), and in the Middlesex part of St Sepulchre parish. That district had the greatest frequency of stockholders of any part of the metropolis at 104.5 per cent (and was the only

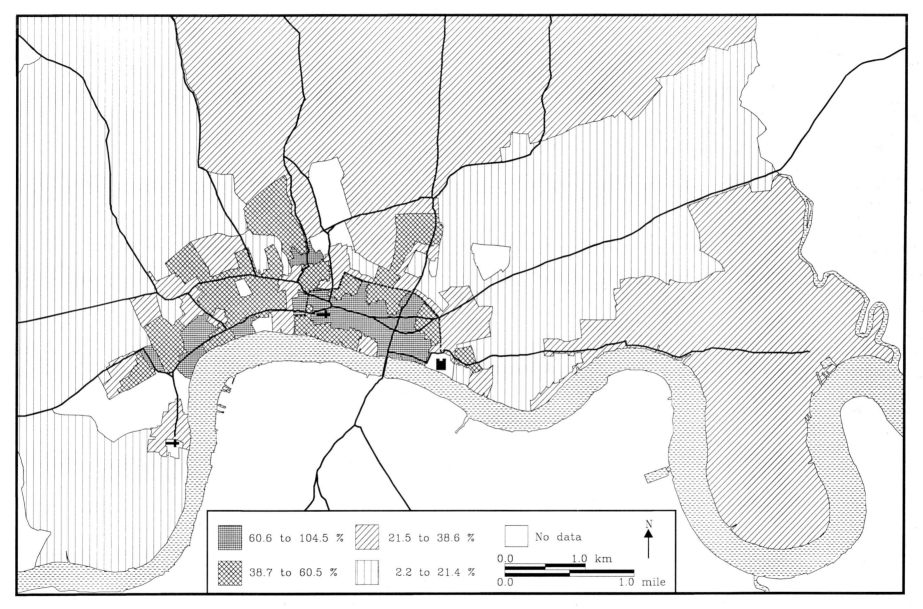

FIG. 5.27 Number of stock tax payers as a percentage of all householders
Source: 1693–4 Aid database.

analytical area to possess more stockholders than householders). Most of these areas were centres of commercial activity, often with associated high value rents. The Middlesex part of St Sepulchre parish may have been associated with lawyers and gentry lodgers, holding substantial financial investments.[70] Low densities of stockholding occurred in most of the unbuilt-up areas that surrounded the centre and in neighbourhoods characterised by low rents and high household densities. For example, St Katherine by the Tower (16.5 per cent), part of the ward of Cripplegate Without (10.9 per cent), Saffron Hill (5.4 per cent), the area of Seven Dials which was in the midst of building activity at this time (19.6 per cent) and, the area with the lowest frequency of stockholders, the northern semi-rural part of the parish of St James Westminster (2.2 per cent).

Not all assessable wealth, however, was held by individuals. Presaging the impending financial revolution, much wealth was vested in the hands of joint stock companies. The operational scale of these organisations required a distinct approach to stock tax assessment, with companies making special assessments based upon their yearly dividends or profits. Among those companies for which 1693–4 Aid data is available, the wealthiest was the East India Company which, on 14 March 1694, presented its own separate assessment document to the assessors of Lime Street Ward. According to that document the company had an assessed stock value of £900,000.[71] By contrast, East India House, in Leadenhall Street, was valued at £191 rent, and the Company's major warehouses

at £270. An analysis of the Posting Book of the Chamberlain of London, however, shows that the East India Company actually contributed £11,700 in tax toward the 1693–4 Aid which, allowing for the value of the company's real property (a figure derived from the main series of property assessments), points to the value of its stock being £974,996.[72] The next wealthiest joint stock organisation was that of the Royal African Company which had real property valued at £200 rent and a stock value of £171,666. The Greenland Company was taxed on rents of £20 and stocks of £49,667. It is unclear exactly how the rent and stock elements of the Hudson's Bay Company's 1693–4 Aid payment of £1,200 were structured, but, assuming that most of the assessment was based upon stockholding, a value of around £100,000 is indicated. Given that these valuations were based upon declared dividends it is unlikely that they suffer from the degree of under-assessment that affected the valuation of private stockholding. Nevertheless, the diverse nature of joint stock company holdings, in goods, shares, moneys, and more tangible assets such as ships, mean that the figures should be treated with some caution.[73]

Spatial distribution of stock values

While the incidence of stock tax payers by area presents a relatively simple concentric pattern (Fig. 5.27), the pattern revealed by the distribution of mean stock values is more complex (Fig. 5.28). The values have been classified into four groups by the method of nested means, identified here as classes 1

to 4 in descending order of value. The general pattern has a broken outer band of high value means, much of which derived from a relatively small number of wealthy individuals dwelling in those outlying areas. That outer band surrounded an inner area, predominantly comprising the City without the walls, which had low mean values. High value areas occurred in the neighbourhoods of Covent Garden, Lincoln's Inn Fields, within the City of London and in the hamlet of Wapping in the parish of Stepney. The overall metropolitan mean, derived from the area mean values, was £137 3s.

Areas in Class 1

Eight distinct districts can be identified within the highest class of mean stock values — between £212 15s. and £423 17s. These include large tracts of predominantly rural land on the periphery of the built-up area. To the west of the metropolis the out-ward of St Martin in the Fields together with the northern parts of St James Westminster and St Anne Soho had a mean stock value of £309 17s. The highest individual stock valuation in this district, £5,000, was recorded three times for Lord Pawlett and a Mr Rosoe, both resident in King's Square, Soho, and Lord Mulgrave, who held property in Dover Street off Piccadilly. Immediately north of the West End, the area around Lamb's Conduit Fields, which included the new estates being developed by Nicholas Barbon, had a mean stock value of £324 4s. The highest single stock assessment there was £10,000 held by Anthony Sturt esquire, a resident of Bedford Walk.[74] A large extent of land to the north of Holborn, including

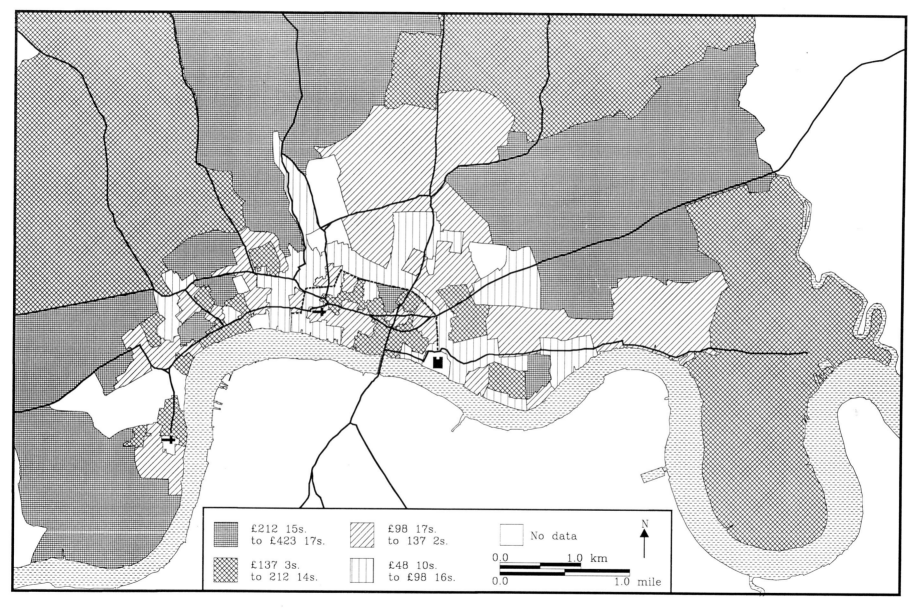

FIG. 5.28 Mean stock values
Source: 1693–4 Aid database.

Clerkenwell and Islington, had a mean stock value of £326 4s. This area included the London residence of the Earl of Clare who had the highest recorded stockholding of any individual, £20,000 in cash. To the east of the metropolis, the hamlet of Mile End Old Town also had a high mean stock value, £300 1s., three quarters of which was derived from householder stocks. Near to the river a part of the hamlet of Wapping in Stepney had a mean stock value of £241 19s. This high mean was the result of only twenty-three individuals sharing £5,564 10s. of stock. The list included five men with the title Captain, probably sea captains.

Within the more built-up areas of the metropolis three districts had high values. In the West End the parish of St Paul Covent Garden had a value of £272 13s. That district undoubtedly housed many whose stocks were in the form of material stock-in-trade, goods, or merchandise. Others, particularly lodgers (184 in a total of 492 stockholders) and women (seventy-seven of the total), may have held wealth in less tangible forms, such as money, stocks, bonds, or mortgages.[75] The highest individual stockholding in that parish was £4,500 held by the estate owner, the Earl of Bedford. To the east of the Drury Lane corridor the neighbourhood of Lincoln's Inn Fields had a high mean stock value, £269 16s. In that area men with the title Esquire were a significant element, accounting for 19.8 per cent of all stockholding by value. The highest individual holdings were two instances of £5,000 held by the dowager Countess of Northumberland and by Madam Elizabeth Pierpoint. Within the City

walls only one area had a particularly high mean stock value: this was a part of Broad Street Ward at £274 4s. which included both 'The Governor and Company of ye King and Queens Corporation of the Linnen Manufactory' with stock of £8,000, and 'The Governor and Company of the Lute String [lustring] Makers' whose stock was assessed at £15,000.[76] Below these high levels the greatest value of stockholding was £1,000 held by both Charles Duncomb esquire, a prominent goldsmith-banker, and by a lodger of George Fry named Edward Bovey, both resident in the parish of St Benet Fink.[77]

Areas in Class 2
Areas within this class, £137 3s. to £212 14s., differed widely in character, from highly commercialised districts in the City and West End to relatively poorer neighbourhoods in the eastern and western suburbs, and also incorporated three outlying districts. Those districts were: the parishes of St Marylebone and St Pancras, £200 17s., which had high land values but few stockholders (thirty-four); the parish of St John Hackney, £174 17s., characterised by property owned by wealthy City merchants; and the parish of Bromley by Bow and the hamlet of Poplar and Blackwall, Stepney, with a combined mean of £148 6s. The highest value stockholding in that district was that of the shipbuilder Sir Henry Johnson, whose stock in the commercially successful Blackwall Yard must undoubtedly have exceeded its assessed value of £1,000.[78]

Within the built-up parts of the metropolis a number of districts fell within this class. In the

parish of St Margaret Westminster, the area around King Street at the southern end of Whitehall had a mean stock value of £159 16s., whereas the Tothill Street North Division to the west of the parish had a mean stock value of £139 15s., and notably lower levels of mean rent.[79] At the northern end of Whitehall, the area of Spur Alley Ward, and part of Exchange Ward in the parish of St Martin in the Fields had a mean stock value of £196 6s. That area included a number of holders of high value stock; for example, £3,000 was held by John Pretty, a lodger with Thomas Pattle of York Buildings, and £1,500 was held by Noah Lavecke of Villiers Street. Samuel Pepys esquire, also of York Buildings, was one of nine individuals assessed for £1,000 stock, although since Pepys was noted as a 'non-swearer' or non-juror he may have been obliged to pay double the rate of taxation.[80] Further along the Strand, a large area from Cecil Street to the Temple had a mean stock value of £183 8s. To the north of the Strand an area of St Clement Danes parish, adjacent to the Liberty of the Rolls, had a mean stock value of £160 17s. A slightly lower level of mean stockholding, £147 7s., was recorded on the eastern side of Drury Lane near its junction with Long Acre. Two areas in the periphery of the West End fell within this class, the southern part of the parish of St Anne Soho, and the district from Hatton Garden to Gray's Inn Lane. The first of those areas, St Anne, had a relatively high mean stock value of £200 19s. The highest individual stockholdings in the district were those of Colonel Cornwell and the Countess of Suffolk, who were each assessed for £2,000. The Hatton Garden area had a similar mean stock value of £184 12s., again the highest individual stockholding was £2,000, held by a Mr Horne esquire, and a Colonel Guy, both of whom lived in Hatton Garden Street.

Most of the commercial core of the City had mean stock values that lay within class 2. A small area from the eastern end of St Paul's Cathedral to the north of the Guildhall had a mean stock value of £145 3s. The greater part of the City, however, from the east end of Cheapside to just west of the Tower, and from London Bridge in the south to the City wall at Bishopsgate in the north, had a mean stock value of £157 8s. The highest individual stockholding within those two areas was £1,200, held jointly by the merchants Peter and Peire [sic] Henriquez who, with their families and six servants, occupied a property valued at £150 in the parish of St Gabriel Fenchurch Street.[81] The next highest value of stockholding in that district was £1,000. Such relatively low values combined with a high density of stockholders, as shown by Fig. 5.27, indicates that stockholding in the City was characterised by large numbers of stockholders in possession of relatively small amounts of assessable stock.[82] To the east of the City two areas were within class 2. The district from Rosemary Lane, through Goodmans Fields and Whitechapel High Street, north to Wentworth Street had a mean stock value of £173 10s. The highest individual stockholding was that of James King of Wentworth Street, £2,000. King also owned a number of properties with a combined value of £100.[83] Between the Highway and the river, an area of Wapping Whitechapel had a mean stock value of

£138 10s., one of the lowest values recorded within this class.

Areas in Class 3
Areas with mean stockholding between £98 17s. and £137 2s. were scattered widely throughout the built-up part of the metropolis and also included districts extending into rural areas to the north and east of the city. Within the western part of the metropolis four areas had mean stock values within this class. The entire southern half of the parish of St Margaret Westminster had a mean stock value of £114 16s. The highest value of individual stockholding in that area was that of Lord Ashburnham, and Tobias Ruskatt, a lodger of William Capow, who each held £1,000 of assessed stock.[84] To the north of Whitehall an area from the Strand through Charing Cross and the Haymarket to Pall Mall had a mean stock value of £120 1s. That area included the 128 shops of the New Exchange, 86.0 per cent of which were assessed for stock. The mean stock value per shop, £118 14s., was close to the area's overall mean. The highest individual stockholding, £4,000, was held by one Hester Tandin (Taudin), probably the widow of a noted Huguenot pewterer, who dwelt in a property valued at £54 per annum near the southern end of St Martin's Lane.[85] Two areas at the northern and southern ends of Drury Lane had mean stock values of £119 3s., and £123 9s., respectively. Just at the western limit of the administrative area of the City, the district centred upon Chancery Lane, St Dunstan in the West, and Gray's Inn had a mean stock value of £127 10s. The contiguous area to the north of Hatton Garden and down Saffron Hill had a

marginally higher mean value of £129 10s. In that area only fifty stockholders shared £6,477 of stock, the highest individual holding being the £500 of Madam Hind, who was located in Black Bull Yard off Saffron Hill. In the case of the Chancery Lane-St Dunstan-Gray's Inn district, however, stockholding was much more widely enjoyed with 624 individuals sharing a total of £79,927 9s. worth of stock.

Three areas adjacent to western parts of the City wall had a mean stock value of £118 3s. Within the central part of the City an area from St Paul's Cathedral in the west to the Stocks Market in the east had a mean stock value of £122 3s. The wealthiest stockholder in this district was the merchant Abraham Dolin(g)s esquire, who held £2,000 of stock and was resident in the parish of St James Garlickhithe.[86] The Leadenhall area and a large section of the eastern part of the City had a relatively low combined mean stock value of £107 9s. The largest individual stockholding was £2,000 held by Jeffrey Jefferies, whose stock apparently consisted mostly of goods lodged in a warehouse near the junction of St Mary Axe and Leadenhall Street.[87]

A large district to the north-east of the City, including part of Bishopsgate Without and most of the neighbourhood of Spitalfields, had a mean stock value of £119 13s. That area's maximum stock value of £1,000 was noted three times by the assessors for Sir Samuel Dashwood, Noah Housay, and Thomas Bates with Widow Kiddar. Dashwood occupied property in Devonshire Square valued at £102 rent which straddled the boundary between Bishopsgate

Without and Portsoken.[88] Housay dwelt in Vine Court, Spitalfields, in property valued at £18 per annum. Bates and Kiddar shared a property of the same value in Rose Lane off Wentworth Street.

To the north of the City an area of mainly rural land lay within this class, having a mean stock value of £113 16s., the area mostly comprised the northern part of the parish of St Leonard Shoreditch. The highest assessed stock value in that district was £2,000 held by Derick Wittenome and his partners, Wittenome lived in the White Cross Street precinct of St Giles Cripplegate and was perhaps a vinegar maker.[89] Further to the east an extensive tract of land from Well Close to Limehouse had a mean stock value of £130 7s. The highest individual stock assessment in this area was £1,400, for two residents of Dolphin Yard in the hamlet of Ratcliff. In the Wapping waterfront district two areas in this class had a combined mean stock value of £105 12s., the lowest within Class 3.

Areas in Class 4
The class of least value shown in Fig. 5.28 comprises mean stock values between £48 10s. and £98 16s. The major geographical focus for low-value means was the near entire extent of the City without the wall, together with some adjacent areas just inside the City wall. Two parts of the West End fell within this class, with six further districts to both the north and the east of the city having similar mean values. The area associated with the northern half of St Martin's Lane, its extension into Hog Lane, northward across Broad Street St Giles, and

into the developing area of the Southampton Estate, had an overall mean stock value of £80. The area immediately north of the church of St Clement Danes centred upon Clement's Inn had a mean stock value of £71 3s. The highest value of stock-holding in this area was £300, held by eight individuals, three of whom were lodgers.

The eastern part of the parish of St James Clerkenwell had a mean stock value of £74. The highest individual stockholding was that of £500 held both by Sir Thomas Rowe and Mr Edward Godfrey, respectively, commissioner and assessor for the 1693–4 Aid. To the north of the city, an area including Moorfields, the liberty of Norton Folgate, and the northern part of Spitalfields, had a combined mean stock value of £68 18s. The lowest mean value for any single analytical area of the metropolis was Norton Folgate which had a mean stock value of £48 10s.[90] One hundred and five individuals were assessed for stock in that liberty, 24.9 per cent of all those noted in the assessment document. The value of stockholding in the area ranged from £25, held by thirty-five people, to a single holding of £500. The modal value for stockholding in this instance was £50.

To the east of the city four areas fell within this class. A district from the eastern end of Whitechapel High Street to the settlement of Mile End Old Town had a mean stock value of £90 4s. The greatest individual stockholding in this area was that of Michael Yoakley who was assessed for £700 of stock and was resident in a property on the

south side of Whitechapel High Street valued at £16 rent per annum. An area of similar character, extending from the precinct of St Katherine by the Tower east along Ratcliff Highway, had a mean stock value of £71 10s. The nearby Wapping waterfront area had the slightly higher mean stock value of £93 13s. Further downstream the parish of St Paul Shadwell had a mean stock value of £80 11s. The highest individual stockholding within the parish was that of Richard Wigg of Lower Shadwell waterside. Wigg's assessed stock value, at £1,000, was far in excess of the modal value for the area of £50.[91]

Almost the entire area of the City without the walls fell within this class. The mean stock value for that area as a whole was £75 10s. The values of the various neighbourhoods within the area ranged from a low of £53 9s., for the northernmost part of Cripplegate Without, to a high of £97 10s., for Coleman Street Ward — though that area was partly within the City wall. The highest single stock valuation for the City without the walls was £1,100, held by the brewer Sir John Friend and his company in the Tower precinct of Portsoken Ward. Friend also owned property at that location valued at £200 per annum, probably the 'stately' Phoenix Brewery he is known to have constructed in the Minories.[92] Three areas immediately within the City walls had mean stock values within class 4: the southern half of Coleman Street Ward (already discussed), a large area to the west of the City, and the waterfront district centred on Lower Thames Street. The western area extended from Monkwell Street in the north around the inside of the City wall to the river and then along the upstream waterfront as far as Queenhithe. The mean stock value for that area was £82 18s., the highest single assessment being for £3,500, the value of the stock held in Stationers' Hall. The greatest stock-holding of any individual in this district was £1,000 held by Sir Richard Levitt, a commissioner for the 1693–4 Aid living in the parish of St John Zachary.[93] In the south-east corner of the City, the area around Lower Thames Street had a mean stock value of £91 10s. Given its large number of ware-houses, and the quantities of goods within them, this area might be expected to have generated a higher mean stock value. It is likely, however, that those goods were frequently rated at the residential addresses of the merchants who owned them and so they were not assessed against the wharfingers and warehouse keepers within whose property those goods may have been kept. The highly commercial nature of the waterfront and its buildings evidently precluded the residence of those with greater wealth.

Conclusion

Stockholding — the possession of assessable amounts of wealth not in the form of real estate — was relatively widespread throughout the metropolis at the end of the seventeenth century. Among householders 27.6 per cent of those recorded by the 1693–4 Aid assessments had such amounts of wealth. A further 3,831 lodgers also had their wealth evaluated for the purposes of taxation, possibly somewhere in the region of 13 per cent of all lodger households within the metropolis.[94] The greatest concentration of stockholders was in the City and West End, with a lower incidence in areas characterised by low rents and crowded living conditions, such as Saffron Hill and St Katherine by the Tower. The pattern of stockholder distribution, shown as a percentage of all households in Fig. 5.27, has marked similarities to that of mean household rent value (Fig. 4.4).

Overall, the value of metropolitan stock was comparable from one neighbourhood to another, though the use of rounded assessment figures and a high degree of under-evaluation point to problems with the utility of individual stock assessments. Nevertheless, the neighbourhood pattern of mean stock values shown in Fig. 5.28, indicates high value areas around the outskirts of the built-up core, with the lowest value district concentrated in the area of the City without the walls. The mean stock value in the area of the City within the walls was just below the wider metropolitan mean. When considered with the information for stockholding density this would support the conclusion that though individual stock values were not particularly high within the City, stockholding itself was relatively widespread. In the western and northern parts of the metropolis stock values were somewhat higher but in these areas fewer individuals enjoyed the privilege of being assessed for notable levels of wealth as a part of the 1693–4 Aid assessment mechanism.

SOCIAL STATUS OF STOCKHOLDERS

As was the case with rent values it is possible to gain an insight into the social structures of stock-holding, and hence patterns of personal wealth, using the social indicators of gender and aristocratic or gentry status. Such manifestations of social group identity are found throughout the 1693–4 Aid assessments.

Women

The gender and related social status of the majority of stockholders were determined from an analysis of gender-specific titles and forenames recorded within the 1693–4 Aid assessments. The gender of 98.1 per cent of stockholders was inferred by that method. Of that group 89.8 per cent were male and 10.2 per cent female, yielding a ratio of approx-imately nine male stockholders to every one female assessed for stock. In aggregate, men held £2,581,054 (85.0 per cent) of stock, and women £372,290 (12.3 per cent, see Table 5.11). Consequently, the mean value of stock held by women, £179 14s., was somewhat higher than that for men, £141 10s. That women had a higher mean assessed stock value than men may be a result of their often secondary position within the structure of any given household. In other words, it would appear that women only attracted the attention of assessors when they held noticeably high values of stock, much in the same way as only the wealthier lodgers may have attracted the assessors. A further explanation of this differential may be that the wealth of many women was held in the form of paper titles, such as bonds, and so could be valued more accurately than that which comprised much male wealth, most notably stock in trade.

TABLE 5.11
Stockholding by gender

Gender	Number of householders	Number of lodgers	Total number of stockholders	Percentage of stockholders	Mean value			Range	Total value	Percentage of of all stock
Men	15,385	2,857	18,242	88.1	£141	10s.	0d.	£8 6s. 6d.–£20,000	£2,581,054	85.0
Women (incl. widows)	1,273	799	2,072	10.0	£179	14s.	0d.	£12 10s.–£9,000	£372,290	12.3
Widows	*533*	*95*	*628*	*3.0*	*£89*	*0s.*	*0d.*	*£12 10s.–£1,000*	*£55,883*	*1.8*
Unknown gender	223	175	398	1.9	£204	6s.	6d.	£12 10s.–£15,000	£81,325	2.7
Total	16,881	3,831	20,712	100.0	£146	10s.	6d.	£8 6s. 6d.–£20,000	£3,034,669	100.0

Source: 1693–4 Aid database.

TABLE 5.12
Stockholding by gender and aggregated area

Aggregated areas	Men				Women				Unknown		Area total	%
	Householders	Lodgers	Total	%	Householders	Lodgers	Total	%	Total	%		
City within the walls	5,828	910	6,738	36.9	387	160	547	26.4	142	35.7	7,427	35.9
City without the walls	2,315	326	2,641	14.5	177	77	254	12.3	77	19.3	2,972	14.3
St Margaret Westminster	432	106	538	2.9	57	30	87	4.2	10	2.5	635	3.1
West End	3,669	868	4,537	24.9	335	363	698	33.7	80	20.1	5,315	25.7
Northern parishes	856	277	1,133	6.2	83	76	159	7.7	31	7.8	1,323	6.4
Eastern parishes	811	130	941	5.2	62	17	79	3.8	23	5.8	1,043	5.0
Eastern riverside parishes	1,169	97	1,266	6.9	114	19	133	6.4	30	7.5	1,429	6.9
Metropolitan Middlesex	305	143	448	2.5	58	57	115	5.5	5	1.3	568	2.7
Metropolitan total	15,385	2,857	18,242	100.0	1,273	799	2,072	100.0	398	100.0	20,712	100.0

Source: 1693–4 Aid database.

One social group among female stockholders often had a more prominent standing within the household — widows. The 628 widows assessed for stock tax comprised just under one third of all women stockholders (Table 5.11). However, widows were not noticeably wealthy, their total stock value amounting to only £55,883, just 15.0 per cent of the total value of stock held by women. The City within the walls was the place of residence for the largest group of taxable widows, 272 in number. As in the case of those widows recorded as heads of household within the area of the City, wealthy widows were found in greatest numbers in districts that lay just inside the City walls.[95] The next largest group of widows dwelt in the area of the City without the walls where ninety-nine widows were assessed. In combination those two areas of the City held 59.1 per cent of all London widows assessed for stock tax. Across the remainder of the metropolitan area 257 further widows, 40.9 per cent, were noted in connection with this element of the 1693–4 Aid. However, the use of other titles and the apparent routine omission of the title 'widow' in areas beyond the jurisdiction of the City may have influenced the number of wealthy women identified as widows by this method in those areas.

TABLE 5.13
Stockholding by social status

Title	Number of householders	Number of lodgers	Total number of stock holders	Percentage of all stockholders	Mean value			Range	Total value	Percentage of all stock value
Aristocracy										
Baron	3	–	3	–	£208	6s.	6d.	£25–£300	£625	–
Countess	6	3	9	–	£1,522	4s.	3d.	£200–£5,000	£13,700	0.5
Duchess	1	1	2	–	£750	0s.	0d.	£500–£1,000	£1,500	–
Earl	13	3	16	–	£3,000	0s.	0d.	£500–£20,000	£48,000	1.6
Lord	21	14	35	–	£1,331	13s.	3d.	£100–£5,000	£46,600	1.5
Sub total	44	21	65	0.3	£1,698	17s.	0d.	£25–£20,000	£110,425	3.6
Lady	53	59	112	0.5	£587	10s.	0d.	£50–£5,000	£65,775	2.2
Gentry										
Esquire	271	154	425	2.1	£475	16s.	6d.	£25–£10,000	£202,241	6.7
Madam	98	165	263	1.3	£354	3s.	3d.	£25–£5,000	£93,066	3.1
Sir	136	72	208	1.0	£646	13s.	3d.	£25–£5,000	£134,424	4.4
Sub total	505	391	896	4.4	£479	12s.	3d.	£25–£10,000	£429,731	14.2
Total	602	471	1,073	5.2	£564	14s.	0d.	£25–£20,000	£605,931	20.0
Other stock holders	16,279	3,30	19,639	94.8	£123	13s.	6d.	£8 6s. 6d.–£15,000	£2,428,738	80.0
Total	16,881	3,831	20,712	100.0	£146	10s.	6d.	£8 6s. 6d.–£20,000	£3,034,669	100.0

Source: 1693–4 Aid database.

Analysis of the gender of stockholders by aggregated areas indicates major deviations from the overall metropolitan gender ratios in only two districts, the City within the walls and the West End (Table 5.12). The City was the location for 6,738 male stockholders, 36.9 per cent of the metropolitan total; women stockholders within that area numbered only 547, 26.4 per cent of all those women assessed for stock. Once again the subordinate economic position of women within the particular social structure of the City is apparent. In the West End the reverse was apparently the case

with 698 women, 33.7 per cent, being assessed for stock tax, compared to 4,537 men, 24.9 per cent of all male stockholders.

The aristocracy and gentry

Sixty-five individuals with aristocratic titles were assessed to pay the stock tax (Table 5.13). Two thirds of that group (forty-four) were householders, the rest lodgers. Overall, aristocrats held stock with a mean value of £1,698 17s., and a total value of £110,425. With reference to stockholding alone, the wealthiest

individual among this group of high social standing was, as already noted, the Earl of Clare. The highest amount of stock held by any female with an aristocratic title was the dowager Countess of Northumberland, also previously discussed. While aristocrats only represented 0.3 per cent of all stockholders they held stock which amounted to 3.6 per cent of the total metropolitan value. Women with the title Lady could have been the wives or widows of aristocrats or of gentry who held the title Sir, and so have been considered separately from either of those social groups. There were 112 stockholders

159

with the title Lady, the combined value of whose stock was £65,775. The mean stockholding for that group was £587 10s. The largest single stockholding was that of one Lady Arabella (possibly a relation of the Duchess of Newcastle) who was assessed for £5,000 of stock at a property in Bowling Alley, Clerkenwell, at which she was a lodger.

The gentry held £429,731 of metropolitan stock, distributed among 896 individuals. The mean value of stockholding within that group was £479 12s., with the greatest single holding, £10,000, being that of Anthony Sturt esquire, a resident of Bedford Walk in the parish of St Andrew Holborn.[96] Two men with the title Sir held stock with a value of £5,000, the highest amount recorded for those with that title. These were Sir Nicholas Sherburne, also of Bedford Walk, but who as a 'reputed Papist' may have been charged double the rate of taxation, and Sir Walter Plummer, a resident of Southampton Buildings in the parish of St Andrew Holborn, who was also a commissioner for the 1693–4 Aid. Among those women considered to have been of gentry status, Madam Elizabeth Pierpoint, of the Lincoln's Inn neighbourhood, held stock valued at £5,000. Overall, the gentry held 14.2 per cent of the total metropolitan value of assessed stock. That the same group (which comprised 57.4 per cent of all those of gentry status recorded by the 1693–4 Aid assessments) made up only 4.4 per cent of all stockholders indicates the generally high level of wealth enjoyed by Londoners within that social rank.[97] The aristocracy, ladies, and gentry combined held one fifth of all metropolitan stock (20.0 per cent);

in number however, they comprised little more than one twentieth of the stockholding population (5.2 per cent).

THE OVERALL DISTRIBUTION OF WEALTH

Measuring broad patterns of wealth in the early modern city relies upon two significant measures, levels of rent and the value of personal wealth — in this instance quantified through the assessment of stock. Attempts to define the general quality of an area by incorporating other, non-economic, measures such as household density or age of building stock, are not widely applicable at the metropolitan level. For example, while increased household density may be a sign of reduced living standards in one area, it is likely to reflect a vigorous commercial demand for space in the more business-oriented parts of the city. Such measures are far more pertinent when used in comparative studies undertaken at a direct inter-neighbourhood or district level.

Surtax assessments

The stock valuations made as an element of the 1693–4 Aid assessments, however, provide a valuable insight into the relative levels of wealth that existed within the metropolis. One approach to defining such levels of wealth is through a consideration of contemporary indicators of prosperity. Both the 1692 Poll Tax and the 1695 Marriage Duty imposed a range of surtaxes upon those who were deemed of higher social or economic standing. Poll tax payers whose estates were

estimated at £300 or above were liable for a variety of surtax charges dependent upon their social status, while the marriage duty applied a surtax to those whose personal estate was not less than £600, or whose real estate was valued at or above £50 per annum.[98] It has been demonstrated that individuals subjected to surtaxes can be equated with those listed by the 1693–4 Aid assessments as holding stock with a value of £100 or more. Such wealthy stockholders are likely to have had real wealth, as indicated by inventoried appraisals, of £2,000 or more.[99] Metropolitan London had 10,947 wealthy stockholders, representing just above fifty per cent of all stockholders within the London area (Table 5.14).[100] The levels at which taxpayers became liable for surtax were established with reference to national patterns of wealth and status. The exceptionally high proportion of Londoners holding significant amounts of wealth is therefore indicative of the great concentration of prosperity within the capital, compared to the rest of England's population.

The distribution of wealthy stockholders within the metropolis is also significant. Aggregated areas where more than fifty per cent of all stockholders can be categorised as wealthy in this way were the City within the walls, the West End, and the parish of St Margaret Westminster — though that latter area had the lowest share of all metropolitan wealthy stockholders at just 3.2 per cent. Metropolitan areas just beyond the built-up extent of London had a very high proportion of wealthy stockholders, 79.9 per cent, probably a result of extensive stockholding of

TABLE 5.14

The distribution of wealthy stockholders, based upon contemporary indicators of wealth (see text for explanation), and non-stockholding households

Area	All stockholders		Wealthy stockholders				Non-stockholding households		Ratio of wealthy stockholders to non-stockholders
	Number	Percentage	Number	Percentage within area	Percentage of wealthy stockholders	Mean value of stock	Number	Percentage	
City within the walls	7,427	34.4	3,981	53.6	36.4	£228 14s.	5,746	14.8	1:1.4
City without the walls	2,972	9.5	1,253	42.2	11.4	£174 7s.	6,574	16.9	1:5.3
St Margaret Westminster	635	3.1	345	54.3	3.2	£234 6s.	2,342	6.0	1:6.8
West End	5,315	31.5	3,099	58.3	28.3	£279 14s.	8,373	21.5	1:2.7
Northern parishes	1,323	7.5	670	50.6	6.1	£304 8s.	3,308	8.5	1:4.9
Eastern parishes	1,043	4.0	484	46.4	4.4	£204 8s.	4,088	10.5	1:8.5
Eastern riverside parishes	1,429	4.9	661	46.3	6.0	£181 3s.	5,898	15.1	1:8.9
Metropolitan Middlesex	568	5.1	454	79.9	4.2	£331 2s.	2,608	6.7	1:5.8
Total	20,712	100.0	10,947	52.9	100.0	£242	38,937	100.0	1:3.6

Source: 1693–4 Aid database.

an agricultural nature and the presence of a number of aristocratic residences. The greatest concentration of wealthy stockholders was in the City of London which housed 36.4 per cent of all such individuals. In the City, the ratio of wealthy stockholders to non-stockholders was 1:1.4, by comparison with 1:3.6 for the metropolis as a whole. The widespread character of wealthy stockholders in the City is indicated by the relatively low mean value of stock held by wealthy stockholders, £228 14s., by comparison with a metropolitan mean of £242. The aggregated area with the highest mean value of wealthy stockholding was that of the northern parishes, with a value of £304 8s. The area with the lowest ratio of wealthy stockholders to non-stockholders was the eastern riverside district (1:8.9). This area also had a low mean value of wealthy stockholding (£181 3s.), although the lowest mean value overall was for the City without the walls (£174 7s.).

An aggregate valuation of wealth

The value of rents also contributed to the general profile of metropolitan wealth. An aggregate measure of the spatial distribution of wealth can be achieved by combining the rent value of properties (which notionally represented 6 per cent of the capital value of the property) with that of the stock, and mapping the total, as expressed in pounds per hectare, by net residential area (Fig. 5.29).[101] This measure denotes the relative density of capital assets and so highlights those neighbourhoods which would have been characterised by the presence of a substantial body of wealthy inhabitants, regardless of the form which their wealth took. Overall, the pattern has some similarity to that obtained for land/property values alone, but there is a degree of variance from that model (see Fig. 3.4).

The mean value of wealth per hectare for the metropolitan area as a whole was £5,115 12s., increasing to £5,597 8s./ha when those especially low value areas beyond the built-up limits are excluded. The wealthiest metropolitan district by this measure was just to the south of the Strand, with a value of £18,167 8s. per hectare. That area was characterised by property with high rents and high values of personal stockholding. The western half of the parish of St Paul Covent Garden exhibited a similar social character and had a notably high aggregated value of £14,988 14s./ha. When compared with the pattern of land/property values across the metropolis the pattern of wealth in the West End was seen to be more dispersed. Within the City walls the mean value per hectare among those districts which fell within the highest value class was £14,495. The highest value of any individual district within the City was £17,831 8s./ha for the neighbourhood of the Royal Exchange

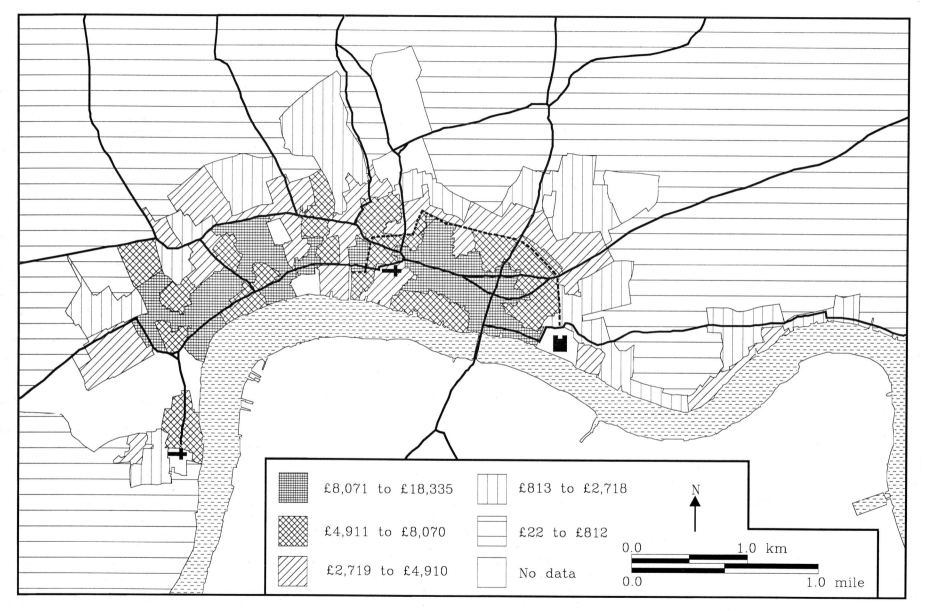

FIG. 5.29 Aggregated rent and stock values (£/ha [NRA]) for the central metropolitan area
Source: 1693–4 Aid database.

extending westward to include the eastern end of Cheapside. The pattern of aggregate wealth within the City appears to indicate a somewhat more concentrated distribution than that indicated by property values alone, with areas adjacent to either the City wall or the riverside — barring the downriver port district — having notably lower densities of wealth.

Two districts in the periphery of the built-up area had notably low concentrations of wealth. To the west of the metropolis the northern part of the parish of St James Westminster had a low value of £310 2s./ha, an area which was nevertheless in the process of development. To the east of the metropolis the neighbourhood of Ratcliff Highway had a similarly low value of £362 2s./ha. The neighbourhood exhibiting the lowest density of wealth yet located most clearly within the built-up area was the eastern part of the parish of St Giles Cripplegate with a value of £1,039 10s./ha. This area, between Grub Street and Moorfields, was exceptionally poor partly on account of its high population density.

The configuration of wealth within metropolitan London has been indicated through an analysis of the value of rents and stockholding, considered both in terms of real value (by calculated means) and density (of both stockholder occurrence and the aggregated value of rent and stock by hectare). The general picture is one of increased wealth in the centre and poverty in the periphery of the built-up area. The pattern, however, is not uniform with some central areas having lower concentrations of wealth, probably as a result of specific environmental conditions or occupational structures, and some apparently high densities of wealth representing widespread possession of more moderate levels of individual prosperity. That circumstance was a particular characteristic of the City within the walls, a situation compounded by a high number of wealthy lodgers. The very poorest districts lay on the edges of those wealthy areas and were distinctive for their very low levels of rents, low incidence of stockholding, virtual absence of wealthy lodgers and increased density of households.

Notes:

1. See Beier (1986), Chartres (1977b, 1986), Clay (1984), Coleman and John (1976), Coleman (1977), Corfield (1982), Dietz (1986), Earle (1989a), Fisher (1971), Schwarz (1992), Weatherill (1988), Wrigley (1966).
2. See above, p. 13, regarding the relationship between residential and commercial property.
3. In 1699 London had 194 Common Brewers, but estimates of the number who were substantial operators range from thirty-seven to fifty-eight: Mathias (1959), 6–9.
4. Sir John Parsons was Commissioner for Victualling the Navy 1683–8; Alderman of Bassishaw Ward from 1689–1717; admitted to the Brewers' Company 1688, Master 1689; knighted, 1687; Sheriff of the City of London, 1687–8; Lord Mayor, 1703; and Member of Parliament for Reigate, 1685–98, 1701–8, and 1710–5: Woodhead (1965), 126; Ball (1977), 128. His daughter married Sir Anthony Sturt, see above, pp. 104–6 and below p. 151. His Red Lion Brewery was identified as 'Parson's Brewery' on Rocque's map of 1747: Mathias (1959), 5.
5. The first of these properties is clearly visible on both Morgan's map of 1682 and Rocque's map of 1747 labelled as 'James's Rope Walk', parallel to Virginia Street.
6. Bushell's rope walk and warehouse are shown as a substantial installation on Rocque's map of 1747.
7. In 1692 Jerome Collins was recorded as being a distiller. 1692 Poll Tax database.
8. The East India Company was assessed for a rent value of £270 on warehouses in the Great St Helens precinct of the ward of Bishopsgate Within. See below, p.152, regarding stock assessments for the various joint stock companies.
9. Although nine cellars were assessed for stock the difficulty in assigning storage or residential functions to these properties makes comparison with warehouse stock impractical.
10. An Act of 1558, amended in 1663, limited the number of 'Free Keys' between London Bridge and the Tower to nineteen, a total which included New Fresh Wharf: Chartres (1980), 30.
11. The most valuable of the Free Keys was Wool Key, with an estimated capital value of £8,000: Chartres (1980), 31.
12. For Ashton, see Chartres (1980), 33. Between 1675 and the 1690s Cartwright had been a lesser partner among a group of four owners, Mark Mortimer, John Mathew, and Richard Linney; following Mathew's death in 1680 it appears that Cartwright rose to prominence within the partnership; Mathew had probably become related to Cartwright through his marriage to Olive Cartwright: Chartres (1980), 33–4; Woodhead (1965), 113; Glass (1966), 54–5.
13. A sum calculated from entries in the Fire Court Minutes c.1670: Chartres (1980), 31.
14. The assessment entry was actually a single charge of £28 (£140 rent value) for all three shops.
15. Alexander (1989a), 277–308.
16. Ten of these shops were recorded within the churchyard of St Dunstan in the West.
17. Stone (1980), 203. 1693–4 Aid database.
18. Strype (1720), II, Book VI, 75.
19. Walsh (1995), 96–106.
20. Bennell (1989), 190. Walsh (1995), 108–9.
21. Clay (1978), 181–83, 195 (Table XI).
22. This value is not given in Table 5.3 as it is not for separately-assessed market property and includes some assessment entries which can only be inferred as having a possible association with the market estate.
23. Strype (1720), II, Book VI, 76.

24. Alexander (1989b). See also Glass (1969), 373–89.
25. The value of burial registers as a source for occupations is discussed by Beier (1986), 142–46.
26. Power (1990), 103–20; Forbes (1980), 120–7; Beier (1986), 141–67.
27. Earle (1989b), 328–53.
28. BL, MS. Sloane 3928.
29. Alexander (1989a), 25–8.
30. Schwarz (1992), 103–23.
31. Creating an aggregate structure that will adequately reflect the nature of early modern occupations is a problematic and in many ways questionable undertaking. A number of authors have discussed this methodological problem, for example: Beier (1986), 141–67; Corfield (1987), 38–61, and (1990), 207–30; Dingwall (1994), 127–32; Glennie (1990), 4–19; Green (1990), 164–81; Keene (1990), 1–16; and Patten (1977), 296–313.
32. In Appendix IIIc totals are given for a different scheme of occupational classification using a greater number of categories.
33. Thomas Tompion's workshop produced some 6,000 watches and 550 clocks during his lifetime (1638–1713). Tompion was a close associate of Robert Hooke and Sir John Flamsteed, for whom he manufactured a number of scientific instruments. Tompion was admitted to the Clockmakers' Company in 1671, became free of the company by redemption in 1674, and was elected Master in 1703. Though never married he had a particularly large household of eighteen, which included his sister, a journeyman (?George Graham), and a number of apprentices and servants: Symonds (1951), 10–39, 237; Baillie et al (1956), 276–9; *DNB*, XIX, 947–8.
34. It is noteworthy that Thomas Tompion is listed as a clockmaker in the poll tax returns, yet he produced almost eleven watches for every one clock he manufactured.
35. Daniel Quare is credited with designing the first repeating watch mechanism in 1688 following his victory in a patent contest; he was elected Master of the Clockmakers' Company in 1708; he is known to have had three daughters and a son, but in 1692 his household comprised himself, his wife Mary, a single child, seven male servants and two female servants: Baillie et al (1956), 280–1; *DNB*, XVI, 534–5; Glass (1966), 242; 1692 Poll Tax database.
36. Roger Norton became Younger Warden of the Stationers' Company in 1671, following a bitterly contested election during which he uttered 'several menaces'; he was Master of the company in 1678, 1682, 1683, 1684 and 1687; his household in 1692 comprised himself, his wife, two children, one male servant and three female servants: Rivington (1883), 49; Plomer (1922), 140; Blagdon (1960), 158, 168, 172; Myers (1990), 207; 1692 Poll Tax database.
37. Richard Simpson became free of the Stationers' Company in 1661, Ralph in 1676. Between 1704 and 1706 Richard served as Master of the company. Ralph's household comprised himself, his wife Sarah, daughter Mary, and two servants, one male and one female. Richard's family in 1695 consisted of himself, his wife Elizabeth, son Benjamin, daughters Anne and Elizabeth, and adult son John, in 1692 he employed two male servants: Rivington (1883), 50; Plomer (1922), 271–2; Howe (1950), 85–6; Glass (1966), 267–8; 1692 Poll Tax database.
38. William Longland was Master of the Company of Spectacle Makers in 1686 and 1694–5; in 1692 his household comprised himself, his wife Sarah, three children, including his daughter Sarah and son William, a male servant and two female servants: Law (1979), 93; 1692 Poll Tax database; Glass (1966), 188.
39. Chiswell published mainly theological works but also had licences to publish government information. His household comprised, himself, his wife Mary, his son John, and two male and two female servants. He was Common Councillor for the ward of Farringdon Within, 1689: *DNB*, IV, 256; Plomer (1907), 45–6; Glass (1966), 60; 1692 Poll Tax database; Woodhead (1965), 46.
40. Stow (1603), II, 34.
41. Possibly the same Edward Cooke who became Master of the Vintners' Company in 1706: Crawford (1977), 288. For vintners' inventories, see Alexander (1989a), 138–9.
42. In 1687 Frederick, son of Sir John Frederick, was, briefly, Alderman for Aldgate Ward (paying a fine of £420 he was discharged of the position after twelve days); he was also a Commissioner of the East India Company, 1687–8, 1689–91, becoming Deputy Governor of the Company in 1698–1700; he invested his inherited fortune in stocks (Bank, South Sea Company, and Exchequer), but, after falling out with his children he bequeathed £9,000 to London hospitals in his will of 1720: Woodhead (1965), 73; Roseveare (1987), 4–9; Imray (1991), 262–3.
43. Jefferies and his uncle were said to have lost tobacco worth £20,000 in the Great Fire of 1666; Jefferies was Member of Parliament for Brecon Boroughs in 1690–8 and 1701–9; he was a knight and alderman in 1701, and was considered to have wealth amounting to £300,000; his household was large, comprising himself, his wife Sarah, two sons, three daughters, nine male, and five female, servants, twenty-one people in all: Woodhead (1965), 97–8; Glass (1966), 165. See also below, p. 154.
44. Glass (1966), 18.
45. 1692 Poll Tax database.
46. The increasing role played by apothecaries in the provision of primary health-care during the late seventeenth century underlines the problems encountered in formulating accurate boundaries between economic activities based upon occupational title alone. See p. 137 above for apothecaries. See also Earle (1989a), 71–2.
47. Sir Selathiell Lovell is noted as 'recorder and his majesty's serjeant-at-law', in the assessment for the 1695 Marriage Duty, for which he was a commissioner; his family comprised himself, his wife Mary, and their four daughters, Mary, Elizabeth, Penellope, and Jaine; the 1692 Poll Tax returns indicate that his household included two sons and three daughters, two male servants and two female servants; in 1696 he became a judge on the Welsh circuit and devoted the next eleven years of his life to 'the discovery and conviction of criminals'; he sat on the bench of the Exchequer in a decrepit condition until his death, aged ninety-five, in 1713: Glass (1966), 189; 1692 Poll Tax database; *DNB*, XII, 175.
48. The Bridewell instructor who claimed to be a tailor was one William Atkins, who in a deposition to the Prerogative Court of Canterbury identified himself as a teacher of carpentry to the children of Bridewell: 1692 Poll Tax database; Earle (1994), 25.
49. Betterton and his wife Mary are known to have taken up lodgings in an apartment over the porch of Dorset Garden Theatre in 1671; by 1694 the company he managed had moved its headquarters to Drury Lane; Betterton clearly retained financial responsibility for the playhouse in St Brides parish, although by the 1690s the United Company

of players (formed in 1682) rarely performed there; in 1695 he established a new company in the Old Lincoln's Inn Fields Tennis Court: Highfill et al (1973), 73–99.

50. See above, pp. 95–7, regarding household structure.

51. These figures refer to apprentices within households where the householder stated an occupation.

52. These City-wide means were calculated using the more comprehensive 1693–4 Aid assessments, rather than the higher means derived from poll tax linked individuals alone as shown in Table 5.6. The higher means obtained from the smaller sample might suggest that those with greater wealth were more likely to state an occupation to the assessors.

53. For a discussion of married women's employment, see Earle (1989b), 336–44, and (1994), 107–23, 130–55.

54. See Earle (1989a), 166–74, regarding independent business-women.

55. The sixth to tenth most frequently cited female occupations were: nurse/nursekeeper (32), butcher (16), midwife (15) and schoolmistress (15), vintner (12), and cook (10).

56. Power (1978a), 36.

57. Power (1990), 105.

58. Forbes (1980), 120–26.

59. Earle (1994), 273–77.

60. BL, MS. Sloane 3928.

61. 1693–4 Aid database.

62. Earle (1994), 273–77.

63. Green (1990), 169–70.

64. Boulton (1987a), 65–73.

65. See above, p. 10, for a detailed description of the operation of the stock tax element of the 1693–4 Aid.

66. The median figure for stock values was £466 12s.

67. Alexander (1989a), 29–35.

68. Multiplied by a factor of twenty a more 'realistic' figure of around £60,700,000 is indicated.

69. See above, pp. 99–101, for a discussion of the distribution of stock tax paying lodgers.

70. See above, p. 87.

71. CLRO Assessment Box 29/15.

72. CLRO Assessment Box 40/62.

73. For further information, see: East India Company — Chaudhuri (1978), Keay (1991), Lawson (1993); Royal African Company — Davies (1957); Hudson Bay Company — Newman (1985); and joint stock companies generally —

Scott (1951).

74. See above, pp. 104–6, for Anthony Sturt's property holdings.

75. See Earle (1989a), 143–57, for a discussion of the investment patterns of the middling sort.

76. Without these two high stockholdings the mean stock value for the area fell to £192 17s., this places the district in class 2 like much of the rest of the eastern half of the City within the walls. Lustring was a special form of glossy silk fabric.

77. Charles Duncombe, a goldsmith and banker, whose business address between 1672 and 1695 was at 'The Grasshopper' in Lombard Street, was Alderman of Broad Street Ward, 1683–6, and Bridge Within Ward, 1700–9; Prime Warden of the Goldsmiths' Company 1684; Member of Parliament for Hedon, 1685–7, for Yarmouth on the Isle of Wight, 1690–5, Downton, 1695–8, 1702–5, 1705–11, and Sandwich, 1701; knighted, 1699; Lord Mayor, 1708; a mint official, 1700; Receiver General of the Excise, 1698; and Colonel of the Green Regiment, 1702–7; the return for the 1692 Poll Tax shows him living in the parish of St Peter le Poor, with three servants; he retired from banking in 1695, buying the estate of Helmsley in Yorkshire for around £90,000, in what was reputed to have been the largest single land transaction ever known; he died at his house in Teddington in 1711, said to be worth £400,000: Woodhead (1965), 63; 1692 Poll Tax database; *DNB*, XI, 175–7.

78. Survey of London (1994), 558–9.

79. See above, p. 74, for mean rent values.

80. Pepys (1660), Preface, xxxix.

81. The Henriquez ?brothers are recorded in the 1695 Marriage Duty as follows: Peter, gentleman, his wife Sarah, son Abraham, and daughters Rachel and Cleare, and Peter, gentleman, his wife Easter(?), and sons Abraham, Isaac and Aron: Glass (1966), 144.

82. The median value of stock holding for the class 2 area of the City was £300, that for the entire metropolis was £467.

83. James King was noted in the 1693–4 Aid assessments as holding property from three different landlords; Bulstrode, Staphurst, and Harman.

84. Lord Ashburnham occupied Ashburnham House in the 'Deanery' [Little Dean's Yard] valued in 1693–4 at £100. Built during the 1660s the interior of that palatial house,

particularly the magnificent staircase (c.1665), remains substantially unaltered to the present day: Pevsner (1973), 476–7, plate 60; Sykes (1985), 36–9.

85. Hester was probably the widow of James Taudin, a Huguenot refugee pewterer who introduced an improved pewter alloy, containing antimony, to the English craft. He is known to have occupied a house on the west side of St Martin's Lane directly opposite the church. Taudin suffered much harassment by the Worshipful Company of Pewterers, who in 1655 entered his house in St Martin's Lane and battered his pewter with hammers and poleaxes. Taudin, however, obtained the protection and support of Oliver Cromwell, and later Charles II for whom he produced pewter goods by appointment. He died in 1680: Murdoch (1985), 138; Hatcher and Barker (1974), 225–7; Homer (1989), 13–14.

86. Dolin(g)s wife was named Anne, their household included three servants: Glass (1966), 90; 1692 Poll Tax database.

87. See above, p.141, and footnote 43.

88. Sir Samuel Dashwood held a number of important positions both in City government and commerce; he was made free of the Vintners' Company in 1663 and became Master in 1684; Alderman of Cheap ward, 1683–7; Alderman of Aldgate ward, 1688–1705; member of the Committee of the East India Company, 1684–6, 1690–5, 1698–1703; Deputy Governor of the East India Company, 1700–2; Assistant of the Levant Company, 1680–91; Assistant of the Royal African Company, 1672–4, 1677–9, 1682–4, 1687–9, 1692–3, 1698–9, 1701–3, 1705; knighted, 1684; Sheriff of London, 1683–4, Lord Mayor, 1703; Commissioner for Lieutenancy, 1688; Commissioner for the 1693–4 Aid; Member of Parliament for London, 1685–7, 1690–5; he died in September 1705; Dashwood's household comprised, himself, his wife, Alice, three children, five male and five female servants: Woodhead (1965), 56–7; 1692 Poll Tax database.

89. Rocque's map of London (1747) shows a large industrial installation immediately to the north of Upper Moorfields labelled 'Mr Witanoom's Vinegar Yard'.

90. The boundary of the analytical area coincides with that of the non-parochial Liberty of Norton Folgate.

91. For rental patterns in St Paul Shadwell, see above, pp. 66, 101–3, and Power (1978a), 34.

92. *DNB*, VII, 716–7. See also above, p. 88.

93. Sir Richard Levitt was an Alderman in 1690 and became Lord Mayor in 1699. He was in partnership with the wealthy tobacconist Francis Levett (his brother?); his household comprised himself, his wife Mary, two sons, two daughters, five male and seven female servants: Woodhead (1965), 108. Glass (1966), 184; 1692 Poll Tax database.

94. The 1692 Poll Tax returns for the City of London indicate that 47 per cent of principal households had subsidiary lodger households, Therefore, 47 per cent of the total household count derived from the 1693–4 Aid assessments (61,143) would suggest a figure in the region of 28,750 possible lodger households for the metropolis as a whole.

95. See above, pp. 77–81, for a discussion of widows as heads of household.

96. See above, pp. 104–6, for Anthony Sturt's other property holding.

97. In total those recorded by the 1693–4 Aid assessments with the title Esquire, Madam, or Sir, comprised 1,561 individuals within the metropolitan population.

98. Arkell (1992), 144–51, 166; Glass (1966), xx.

99. Alexander (1992), 197–200.

100. Wealthy stock holders who were householders comprised 51 per cent of all householders who held stock.

101. The capital value of property was not calculated as the 6 per cent value fluctuated across both time and space. The values in Figure 5.29 have been classed in quintiles to avoid the high value of certain individual stockholdings distorting the underlying pattern.

6. Conclusion

I do not pretend to give a full account of all things worthy to be known, in this great city, or of its famous citizens, for that would make an huge volume but only of the most eminent which have occurred to my reading or observation.[1]

Just over three hundred years later De Laune's disclaimer still holds true. It is inevitable that providing a fully comprehensive account of the London metropolis of the 1690s is as difficult now — even with the benefit of modern technology — as it was then. But, with the use of that late twentieth-century technology it has been possible to investigate some aspects of the character of the early modern metropolis in ways that few contemporaries would have thought possible. Nonetheless, striving to flesh out all the social and topographic bones of that premier of English cities at a distance of some three centuries inevitably leaves many questions unanswered. In order not to lose sight of the general objective of the current work great pains have been taken to present as broad a picture of London as possible. While such an approach tends toward generalisation, the great volume of material under study ensures that it does not detract from the principal findings. The foregoing pages contain a wealth of information upon which certain substantive observations can be made and that pose a number of intriguing questions.

It is now clearer than ever that any study of the seventeenth-century metropolis needs to be just that, a study of the whole metropolis. One way to bring the various parts of the whole together is in a review of those topographic elements that performed that connecting function at the time. Thus a focus upon the infrastructural nature of the river Thames and the capital's road network has proved of value. Here a significant feature of London's development stands out, the pattern of east-west expansion along the line of the river, with only limited growth northward before the later eighteenth century. The informal, yet evidently effective, integration of river with road transport is found in the comparability of the fare-pricing systems enforced by Parliament and those governing the City for both means of transport. The clarity of the land-transport system is further exemplified by the well-differentiated distribution of the capital's coaching and carrying inns. By combining such infrastructural information with an overview of the area's geomorphology it is possible to differentiate more clearly London's various parts: that is, not simply the well regulated area within the walled City or those newly planned elements of the West End, but also the more organically developing suburbs to the east and north, and (though lacking substantial data for the period) those to the south of the Thames.

Having made some inroads in identifying the major spatial components of the city, one of the key objectives of the current work has been to reassemble critically the early modern metropolis from its several parts. While engaging with the customary concepts of urban core(s) and suburban peripheries, the analysis has drawn upon information from the lesser and more diverse areas of parishes, wards and precincts to develop an understanding of social and economic neighbourhoods. Such an approach was made practicable through the innovatory formulation of 'analytical areas' across the extents of the metropolis, each containing an approximately equal number of households. This technique has helped to maintain the primacy of the wider metropolitan picture yet has done so without detriment to the more closely grained contextual information with which that picture has itself been drawn.

The contextual detail upon which the study is based is that provided by the records of contemporary taxation. The taxation regime of the 1690s reached new levels of rigour as the pressure to finance continental warfare intensified. The records themselves — the poll tax, marriage duty and four-shilling aids — provide detailed household listings of various compositions. The survival of those documents for most areas of the metropolis has allowed a number of measures to be determined and importantly mapped across the extents of the city's neighbourhoods. As a result the broad social position of some 65,000 households has been ascertained and somewhere in the region of 300,000 individuals have been located both spatially and with regard to status, in relation to their head of household.

London in the 1690s was a city of great differences. It is clear that a simple reading of the data showing a commercially prosperous core and a poverty-stricken periphery would overlook the finer contours of that diversity. The population of the metropolis at the time was just over 500,000. Those people were distributed across a densely built-up urban core and a rapidly growing suburban periphery yet it is significant that, when mapped, an even more variegated picture emerges. The density of London's population, based upon the incidence of households, was found not to have been a simple pattern of ever decreasing concentric contours. Instead pockets of intense habitation — up to 185 households per residential hectare — could just as well convey commercial vigour as abject poverty. Within the City, demands for commercially valuable property led to increased densities in just the same way that the poor crowded together in the search for cheap rents in districts such as St Katherine by the Tower, Saffron Hill and St Giles without Cripplegate.

Establishing an average rent value for the metropolis has proved difficult. While an overall mean value of £17 7s. 3d. per annum was indicated, the modal value lay at a much lower £6 per annum. It was the presence of a limited number of very high value properties among a sea of lesser ones that produced such a divergence; nonetheless those higher rentals and the social cachet they conveyed upon a particular neighbourhood could not be ignored. Measuring the modal value of rents area by area showed that the majority of rents within most areas were worth much less than the mean. However, in the City and West End this was not the case. In those districts a comparison of the various methods of averaging indicated that higher value properties were far more likely to be the norm. Individual rent values ranged from £320 — as in the case of Burlington House in Piccadilly, occupied by the Earl of Burlington — to the £1 per annum value of the property in New Fish Street inhabited by John Allen, a combmaker, and his family. Overall, the taxation records indicate that the majority of Londoners occupied property with rental values of £15 or less.

Land values provide a more expansive view of the value of metropolitan property. By aggregating rents and calculating the values in pounds per hectare it was possible to elaborate upon the distribution of metropolitan wealth as it was embodied in real estate. In this instance the traditional core-periphery pattern of contours of declining value held true. Within the heart of the City and West End values just short of £6,000 per hectare were noted, yet within the built-up periphery values of less than £400 per hectare were recorded. Such generalised figures provide a useful corrective for the previously stated rental averages, and as such help to stress the importance of maintaining a London-wide overview.

The various neighbourhoods of the metropolis exhibited signs of social differentiation just as marked as those indicated by property or rental values. Women, for example, were found to be responsible for some 16 per cent of all London households. Yet in some districts women house-holders were almost entirely absent. Most notable in this regard were various parts of the City within the walls. There commercial pressures and the traditional male dominance of governance and property holding conspired to eliminate virtually all women householders, unless they held the status of widow. In other areas women made up as many as a quarter of all householders: in this case the maritime neighbourhoods to the east of the City and some parts of the West End were significant. Nevertheless, whatever the incidence of women householders, they were generally found to occupy property of lower rental value than that of their male counterparts.

The West End was also notable for housing virtually all of London's noble élite, the taxation records indicating at least 145 such individuals in areas such as St James's, Leicester, and Soho Squares. Gentry householders, both male and female, supplied a further 1,000 or so members of London's population though their distribution was marginally more widespread. When both élite groups were combined, just over half of their households were located in the West End, with around a tenth each in the City, the northern parishes and metropolitan Middlesex. While such individuals may have been relatively few in number the values of their property were significant, as was their contribution to the metropolitan economy through both personal levels of consumption and the employment they created.

Work in London ranged from domestic service through manufacturing activity to a variety of specialist and professional occupations. While sources for the late seventeenth century fail to provide a good overview of metropolitan work, the 1692 Poll Tax for the City does help to delineate some of the patterns of employment for as much as a fifth of the population. The poll tax assessors recorded 773 different occupational titles, the most frequently occurring being gentleman or gentlewoman, victualler or merchant — all titles which could conceal a variety of actual economic activity. Among those callings with clearer economic purpose were those engaged in the clothing and textile trades, which comprised nearly a quarter of all those who stated an occupation. The same activity was of significance in areas outside the City, such as the northern suburbs, while maritime trades almost entirely monopolised the working population in some eastern districts. The West End apparently had a more mixed occupational profile, though an increase in the numbers in that area who relied upon rental income was perhaps significant.

On closer inspection, occupational variety in early modern London was found to be greatest at the micro level: when grouping of occupations was carried out, certain locational concentrations became apparent. Domestic servants, for example, were found to occur in high numbers in those households located along Cheapside, around Cornhill and down to London Bridge — areas within which they supplied as much as half of the adult population. Apprentices, on the other hand, were found only rarely in those areas but were far more numerous in those wards outside the City walls. Other occupation groups demonstrated gross clustering, such as metal workers who were mostly located in the north-western quarter of the City, while merchants and financial workers were to be found occupying property almost exclusively towards the east of the City.

The poll tax provides similar information concerning the internal social structure of London households. It was possible to separate principal from lodger households, the former having a mean household size of 3.92 people and the latter a lower value of 1.57 people. Nonetheless, when considered overall, and irrespective of type, the most frequently encountered household was that comprising one or two people, mainly lodgers living alone or married couples. It is interesting, especially in light of the information on women householders, that just over 40 per cent of single lodgers within the City were women (though that figure fell to around 20 per cent in the case of wealthy lodgers distributed across the wider metropolis). Children were present in just under half of all principal households within the City, but occurred in only 10 per cent of lodger households. The mean number of children per household, whatever its type, was 1.87, and it was relatively unusual for households to contain more than two children. Very few lodgers, less than 10 per cent, maintained servants as part of their household. Servants were, however, much more widespread among principal households, just over ten thousand of which included servants. The most common situation was for a single servant to be retained: in seven out of ten cases this would be a female. Extended multi-generational families under one roof were a very rare occurrence in the City, with probably less than 1 per cent of all households having such a structure.

Londoners with no familial ties did, however, frequently share property, whether in the formal arrangement of principal and lodger householders or more simply as co-resident inmates or tenants. Investigating this aspect of housing occupation across the metropolis proved difficult and resort had to be made to certain sample districts. Key among these were the ward of Bishopsgate Without and the parish of St Paul Shadwell. Records from these areas helped to demonstrate that in the more built-up neighbourhood of Bishopsgate multiple occupancy could include a high number of inmates sharing a single rental, while in Shadwell such occupancy rarely extended beyond two or three tenants. It was clear from both cases that there were economic benefits associated with shared occupation. In Shadwell the street with the lowest mean level of rent was Blewgate Fields, at £2. 8s. per annum; this was also the area with the highest incidence of multiple occupancy, with multiple tenancy apparent in 72.2 per cent of properties. Nevertheless, such figures can also be read as indicative of an insidious combination of poverty and overcrowding. Streets with higher value rents within the parish had a proportionally lower incidence of multiple occupancy: for example, Wapping Wall with a mean rent value of £13 13s. exhibited a level of multiple occupancy of just 6.7 per cent. Even less information was available at a metropolitan level concerning the nature of landlordship, but it was evident that some individuals, often of gentry status, were able to obtain substantial incomes as rentiers.

Establishing the non-property based wealth of Londoners was also problematic — not in this case because of a shortage of data but because such data was difficult to interpret. The stock tax element of the 1693–4 Four Shilling Aid provides a good comparative measure of individual wealth, but the assessed values are known to under-estimate the actual level of wealth held by any given individual. However, the tax levied on stocks does allow two particular observations to be made: first, the spatial distribution of stockholding; and second, its relative value. Wealthy taxpayers were distributed across the metropolis in roughly circular bands radiating from two main centres: the central core of the City, and the Strand and Covent Garden area of the West End. In both these cases well over half the taxable population were noted as having stock worth at least £12 10s., the minimum taxable amount. Those built-up areas where less than 20 per cent of taxpayers had such wealth included St Katherine by the Tower, Spitalfields and Bishopsgate Without, St Giles without Cripplegate, Saffron Hill, and the northern part of St James Westminster. By turning to the value of the stock assessed it is possible to review the general pattern of non-property based wealth. It is evident from the mean values calculated for the analytical areas that those dwelling within the City walls usually had relatively moderate levels of wealth, but that such wealth was widely distributed. In the case of the West End and northern suburbs such distribution was more restricted, though the

level of individual wealth appeared higher than that of the City. In those areas noted above with few stockholders, the level of wealth held was also relatively low.

It has also been possible to combine the measures of property and non-property based wealth in order to formulate a measure of the distribution of substantive capital across the metropolis. Such values have been quantified in terms of wealth per hectare. By this method the wealthiest London neighbourhood was found to be immediately north of Whitehall and to the south of the Strand, with a value of £18,167 per hectare. The higher value areas of the City within the walls were found to have a mean wealth value of some £14,500 per hectare, while the built-up area with the lowest value was a heavily populated part of St Giles Cripplegate where wealth was measured at just over £1,000 per hectare. Formulating such measures of wealth is perhaps pushing the evidence to its demonstrable limits, but it has a pragmatic basis in helping to characterise individual districts and in the comparative study of certain neighbourhoods.

The present study has shown metropolitan London at the end of the seventeenth century to have been a city of great wealth and diversity, yet also to have comprised districts of densely populated poverty. Londoners occupied a range of property types and lived in a variety of domestic social units. While married men were the predominate type of householder others, such as single lodgers of either sex, widows, and joint tenants, all contributed to the

capital's pattern of occupancy. Rents were generally high, especially when compared with other parts of the country, but only a few dwelt in property of the very highest value. While the scope of metropolitan employment was extensive, a few occupational sectors made up the bulk of work opportunities, particularly those of domestic service, the clothing and textile trades, mercantile and financial activities, various forms of provisioning, and the maritime trades. The city's streets and markets were the focus for a retail trade characterised by both increasing levels of complexity and affluence, with the new exchanges taking pride of place in that system. Against such conspicuous consumption pockets of relative poverty did exist but they were, in the main, spatially circumscribed and attempts were made, if intermittently, to redistribute a certain measure of London's wealth to them. The predominant intention of this text has been to describe the social and economic matrix of the metropolis in the decade of the 1690s. In that, the work has been broadly successful. In some areas, however, certain questions have arisen and other remain unresolved.

Our critical knowledge of the origins of the West End is still somewhat murky, but it is possible to suggest two key issues around which future study might concentrate. Firstly, general work which will further elaborate those forces that encouraged the remarkable development of the western suburbs — be it the presence of royal and aristocratic households, the capacity of gentry money, or a cosmopolitan mix of disparate cultural and social factors. Secondly, and at a finer level of analysis, studies of property holding patterns and tenancy forms — let alone the poorly understood household and occupational structures — across the entire western half of the metropolis are sorely needed. Elaborating the broader distribution and status of lodger households in this regard would also be useful. Moving eastward, the relationship between the City and the eastern suburbs and the nature of life and labour in that area, especially with regard to the port and seasonal patterns of occupation also deserves further investigation.

Finally, this study has concentrated upon the decade of the 1690s, but there is clearly scope for comparative work on, for example, the 1660s or 1720s. Such studies would be well placed to address the somewhat intractable issues of the internal mobility of the resident population and the concomitant question of rates of tenancy transfer. Other future work might undertake useful comparative studies between metropolitan London and the other great cities of Europe, or even further afield, at the same or similar times. Despite the range of the current work many questions remain unanswered, but any city of the size and complexity of London will predictably and persistently provide cause for investigation for, it might be confidently expected, at least another three hundred years.

Note:

[1] De Laune (1690), preface.

Appendix I. Sources used to construct the principal databases

A. THE ASSESSMENTS FOR THE FOUR SHILLINGS IN THE POUND AID

Ward	Date	CLRO assessment box reference
CITY OF LONDON:		
Aldersgate Ward Within:	2nd qtr 1694	9/7
St Martin Le Grand	2nd qtr 1694	9/2
Aldersgate Ward Without	2nd qtr 1694	9/11
Aldgate Ward	2nd qtr 1694	9/4
Bassishaw Ward	2nd qtr 1694	15/4
Billingsgate Ward	2nd qtr 1694	36/7
Bishopsgate Ward Within	4th qtr 1693	13/40
Bishopsgate Ward Without	2nd qtr 1694	11/14
Bread Street Ward	4th qtr 1693	13/13
Bridge Ward Within	4th qtr 1693	13/22
(for comparison	*2nd qtr 1694*	*38/2)*
Broad Street Ward		
& Excise Office	2nd qtr 1694	9/10
Candlewick Ward	2nd qtr 1694	9/6
Castle Baynard Ward	2nd qtr 1694	11/19
Cheap Ward	2nd qtr 1694	9/8
Coleman Street Ward	2nd qtr 1694	9/5
Cordwainer Ward	[no date]	9/9
Cornhill Ward	2nd qtr 1694	6/9
Cripplegate Ward Within	2nd qtr 1694	6/12
Cripplegate Ward Without	2nd qtr 1694	9/14
Dowgate Ward	2nd qtr 1694	9/12
Farringdon Ward Within	2nd qtr 1694	9/13
Farringdon Ward Without:		
Smithfield	2nd qtr 1694	}
St Bartholomew the Less	2nd qtr 1694	} 6/19
Church	2nd qtr 1694	}
St Andrew Holborn	2nd qtr 1694	35/9
St Martin Ludgate	2nd qtr 1694	38/1
St Bride	2nd qtr 1694	6/11
Old Bailey	2nd qtr 1694	}
Whitefriars	2nd qtr 1694	} 22/4

Bridewell	2nd qtr 1694	}
St Dunstan in the West	2nd qtr 1694	}
St Bartholomew the Great	2nd qtr 1694	15/5
Holborn Cross	2nd qtr 1694	15/17
Langbourne Ward	2nd qtr 1694	17/4
Lime Street Ward	2nd qtr 1694	17/3
Portsoken Ward	2nd qtr 1694	17/6
Queenhithe Ward	2nd qtr 1694	17/5
Tower Ward	2nd qtr 1694	4/5
(inc. Custom House and		
Navy Commission)		
Vintry Ward	2nd qtr 1694	17/4
Walbrook Ward	2nd qtr 1694	38/4
Inns and Liberties:		
Barnard's Inn	2nd qtr 1694	}
Gray's Inn	2nd qtr 1694	} 3/10
Staple Inn	2nd qtr 1694	}
Duchy Liberty		
(St Mary in the Savoy)	2nd qtr 1694	3/16
Liberty of Norton Folgate	2nd qtr 1694	42/11
Liberty of the Rolls		
and Offices	[?] qtr 1693	42/5
Tower Liberties	2nd qtr 1694	40/7
Westminster Offices	2nd qtr 1694	3/16
MIDDLESEX:		
St Andrew Holborn	[?] qtr 1693	46/1
Bromley by Bow	[?] qtr 1693	43/21
St Botolph Aldgate	2nd qtr 1694	42/2
St Dunstan Stepney:		
Bethnal Green	2nd qtr 1694	43/22
Limehouse	2nd qtr 1694	42/18
Mile End Old Town	2nd qtr 1694	42/15
Poplar and Blackwall	2nd qtr 1694	42/7
Ratcliff	2nd qtr 1694	42/6
Spitalfields	2nd qtr 1694	40/12
Wapping	2nd qtr 1694	40/5
St Giles Cripplegate	2nd qtr 1693	89/1
St Giles in the Fields	[?] qtr 1693	42/1

St James Clerkenwell	1st qtr 1693	89/2
St John at Hackney	2nd qtr 1694	40/25
St Katherine by the Tower	2nd qtr 1694	40/24
St Leonard Shoreditch	2nd qtr 1694	40/23
St Mary Islington	2nd qtr 1693	83/9
St Marylebone	2nd qtr 1693	42/16
St Mary Whitechapel:	[?] qtr 1694	40/21
Wapping	[?] qtr 1694	40/4
St Pancras	2nd qtr 1694	40/20
St Paul Shadwell	2nd qtr 1694	40/19
St Sepulchre	[?] qtr 1693	18/16
Stratford, Bow and Old Ford	2nd qtr 1694	40/11
WESTMINSTER:		
St Anne Soho	2nd qtr 1693	83/2
St Clement Danes	2nd qtr 1694	15/11
St James	2nd qtr 1693	18/5
St Margaret	2nd qtr 1694	40/22
St Martin in the Fields	2nd qtr 1694	83/5
St Paul Covent Garden	2nd qtr 1694	38/7

B. THE RETURNS FOR THE QUARTERLY POLL TAX

Note: The main elements of the database were derived from the returns for the first quarter of 1692. When that return did not survive, the surviving return nearest to that date was used. Other returns were also used, as indicated below, to supply information on the occupations of householders in the database. See also Alexander (1989a).

CITY OF LONDON:		
Aldersgate Ward Within:	1st qtr 1692	34/12
	4th qtr 1692	35/13
	1st qtr 1694	60/1
St Martin Le Grand	1st qtr 1692	34/11
	4th qtr 1692	8/15
	2nd qtr 1698	69/8

Aldersgate Ward Without	1st qtr 1692	33/1
	2nd qtr 1692	8/8
	4th qtr 1694	60/9
	2nd qtr 1698	69/10
Aldgate Ward:	1st qtr 1692	33/2
	3rd qtr 1692	5/5
	4th qtr 1694	71/8
St James Dukes Place	1st qtr 1692	34/14
Bassishaw Ward	1st qtr 1692	34/15
	3rd qtr 1692	112/2
	4th qtr 1692	36/17
	1st qtr 1694	60/2
Billingsgate Ward	1st qtr 1692	35/3
	2nd qtr 1692	56/11
	3rd qtr 1692	56/16
	4th qtr 1692	32/11
Bishopsgate Ward Within	2nd qtr 1692	32/26
	4th qtr 1692	35/14
	3rd qtr 1692	71/4
Bishopsgate Ward Without:	1st qtr 1692	34/21
	2nd qtr 1692	9/9
	3rd qtr 1692	113/11
	4th qtr 1692	36/11
Second Division	3rd qtr 1694	35/25
Bread Street Ward	1st qtr 1692	14/13
	2nd qtr 1692	56/1
	4th qtr 1692	38/32
Bridge Ward Within	1st qtr 1692	19/20
	4th qtr 1692	71/7
Broad Street Ward	1st qtr 1692	33/3
	2nd qtr 1692	110/7
	4th qtr 1692	33/6
Candlewick Ward	1st qtr 1692	32/9
	2nd qtr 1692	71/6
	4th qtr 1692	35/4
	4th qtr 1694	20/15
Castle Baynard Ward	1st qtr 1692	22/3
	4th qtr 1692	41/1
Cheap Ward	1st qtr 1692	33/5
	4th qtr 1692	34/18
	1st qtr 1694	60/3
Coleman Street Ward	1st qtr 1692	34/13
	2nd qtr 1692	56/4
	4th qtr 1692	33/7

	1st qtr 1694	113/1
	4th qtr 1694	60/11
	2nd qtr 1698	113/7
Cordwainer Ward	1st qtr 1692	33/4
	4th qtr 1692	32/12
	1st qtr 1694	70/14
Cornhill Ward	1st qtr 1692	35/12
	4th qtr 1692	2/13
	4th qtr 1694	20/1
	2nd qtr 1698	71/5
Cripplegate Ward Within	1st qtr 1692	32/10
	4th qtr 1692	32/14
	4th qtr 1694	60/13
	2nd qtr 1698	60/13
	3rd qtr [?] 1698	113/8
Cripplegate Ward Without:	4th qtr 1692	32/15
	2nd qtr 1698	18/1
Fore Street & Grub Street	1st qtr 1692	41/2
	2nd qtr 1692	8/20
Red Cross Sreet & White Cross Street	1st qtr 1692	8/21
	2nd qtr 1692	110/8
	4th qtr 1694	113/15
Dowgate Ward:	2nd qtr 1692	8/24
	1st qtr 1694	60/4
	4th qtr 1694	113/12
Western Division	2nd qtr 1698	113/9
Farringdon Ward Within:	4th qtr 1692	24/12
	1st qtr 1694	60/5
	4th qtr 1694	60/15
	2nd qtr 1698	69/3
Monkwell	1st qtr 1692	35/21
St Anne Blackfriars	1st qtr 1692	71/3
	2nd qtr 1692	35/24
St Martin Ludgate	2nd qtr 1698	69/5
Farringdon Ward Without:		
Bridewell	4th qtr 1692	38/11
St Andrew Holborn	1st qtr 1692	14/20
	1st qtr 1694	60/17
	2nd qtr 1698	69/4
St Bartholomew the Great	4th qtr 1692	41/3
St Bartholomew the Less	1st qtr 1692	56/17
	2nd qtr 1692	18/10
	2nd qtr 1698	56/17
St Bride	4th qtr 1692	34/16

	3rd qtr 1694	60/7
	2nd qtr 1698	71/5
St Dunstan in the West	2nd qtr 1692	112/7
	4th qtr 1692	38/28
St Martin Ludgate	1st qtr 1692	33/12
	4th qtr 1692	38/29
	4th qtr 1694	113/3
St Sepulchre — Church	2nd qtr 1692	56/2
	4th qtr 1692	38/14
	3rd qtr 1694	60/7
St Sepulchre — Holborn Cross	2nd qtr 1692	8/21
	4th qtr 1692	33/8
St Sepulchre — Old Bailey	2nd qtr 1692	56/20
	4th qtr 1692	38/13
St Sepulchre — Smithfield	1st qtr 1692	33/9
	2nd qtr 1692	8/21
	4th qtr 1692	33/8
Whitefriars	4th qtr 1692	38/12
	4th qtr 1694	112/5
	2nd qtr 1698	69/6
Langbourne Ward	1st qtr 1692	32/5
	2nd qtr 1692	20/17
	4th qtr 1692	36/12
	3rd qtr 1694	20/2
	2nd qtr 1698	71/9
Lime Street Ward	1st qtr 1692	112/3
	2nd qtr 1692	32/18
Portsoken Ward:	2nd qtr 1692	18/12
	4th qtr 1692	32/16
Houndsditch	2nd qtr 1698	18/4
Tower Hill	2nd qtr 1698	18/4
Bars	3rd qtr 1698	112/4
Covent Garden	2nd qtr 1698	112/4
High Street	2nd qtr 1698	112/4
Queenhithe Ward	4th qtr 1692	41/4
	3rd qtr 1694	60/8
	4th qtr 1694	60/20
Tower Ward	1st qtr 1692	33/10
	4th qtr 1692	4/3
	3rd qtr 1694	113/2
Vintry Ward	1st qtr 1692	71/14
	4th qtr 1692	34/17
Walbrook Ward	4th qtr 1694	60/21
	2nd qtr 1698	113/10

Appendix II. Sources used to construct the maps

Arlidge, A. (1694), *A Survey of Hatton Garden* (Facsimile edition, London Topographical Society Publication 128, 1983).

Bowles, J. (1736), *London Surveyed or a New Map of the Cities of London and Westminster and the Borough of Southwark* ... (copy held at Guildhall Library).

Faithhorne, W., and Newcourt, R. (1658), *An Exact Delineation of the Cities of London and Westminster and the Suburbs Thereof...* (Facsimile in J. Fisher, *A Collection of early Maps of London, 1553–1667*, Harry Margary in association with Guildhall Library, 1981).

Four Shillings in the Pound Aid assessments, 1693–1694, Corporation of London Records Office (See Appendix I).

Gascoigne, J. (1703), *An Actual Survey of Poplar Parish in Stepney* (Facsimile in H. Green and R. Wigram, *Chronicles of Blackwall Yard*, London: Whitehead, Morris & Loew, 1881. Also facsimile edition, London Topographical Society Publication 150, 1995).

Hollar, W. (1658), *West Central London (part of The Great Map)* (Facsimile in J. Fisher, *A Collection of Early Maps of London, 1553–1667*, Harry Margary in association with Guildhall Library, 1981).

Horwood, R. (1799–1819), *Plan of the Cities of London and Westminster, the Borough of Southwark, and parts adjoining ...* (Facsimile edition, P. Laxton, *The A to Z of Regency London*, London Topographical Society Publication 131, 1985).

Laxton, P. (1990), 'Richard Horwood's plan of London: a guide to editions and variants, 1792–1819', *London Topographical Record*, **26**: 214–63.

Leake, J. (1669), *An Exact Surveigh of the Streets, Lanes and Churches Contained Within the Ruins of the City of London...* (Facsimile in J. Fisher, *A Collections of Early Maps of London, 1553–1667*, Harry Margary in association with the Guildhall Library, 1981).

Lewis, S. (1842), *The History and Topography of the Parish of St Mary, Islington, etc.* (Includes a facsimile of a survey map of Islington by (?)Rocque dated 1735.)

Loftie, W.H. (1884), *History of London*, London: Edward Stanford. (Includes four maps based on Rocque's map of *The Environs of London* but with parochial boundaries indicated.)

London Topographical Society (1959), *The City of London showing Parish Boundaries prior to the Union of Parishes Act 1907*, London Topographical Society Publication 92.

Masters, B. (1974), *The Public Markets in the City of London Surveyed by William Leybourne in 1677*, London Topographical Society Publication 117.

Milne, T. (1800), *Milne's Plan of the Cities of London and Westminster, circumjacent towns and parishes....* (Facsimile edition, *Thomas Milne's Land Use Map of London & Environs in 1800*, London Topographical Society Publication 118–119, 1975–6).

Morgan, W. (1682), *London &c. Actually Survey'd...* (Facsimile edition, Harry Margary in association with the Guildhall Library, 1977).

Mylne, R.W. (1856), *Map of the Geology and Contours of London and its Environs* (Facsimile edition, London Topographical Society Publication 146, 1993).

Ogilby, J. (1685), *Plan of the Precinct (Eastern Part) of the Hospital of St Katherine by the Tower* (Facsimile edition, London Topographical Society Publication 90, 1957).

Ogilby, J. and Morgan, W. (1676), *A New and Accurate Map of the City of London, Distinct from Westminster and Southwark ...* (Facsimile edition, R. Hyde, *The A to Z of Restoration London*, London Topographical Society Publication 145, 1992).

Ordnance Survey (1864–1914), *1:2500 Scale Survey Maps, 1864–1914*. (Centre for Metropolitan History and facsimile editions, Alan Godfrey, various dates.)

Parish Clerks (1732), *New Remarks of London: or, a Survey of the Cities of London and Westminster, of Southwark, and Part of Middlesex and Surrey, Within the ... Bills of Mortality...*, London: E. Midwinter. (Includes textual descriptions of parochial and sub-parochial boundaries.)

Port, M.H. (ed) (1986), *The Commissions for Building Fifty New Churches, The Minute Books, 1711–1727, A Calendar*, London Record Society, **23**. (Includes textual references to existing and proposed changes in parish boundaries.)

Rocque, J. (1747), *A Plan of the Cities of London and Westminster and Borough of Southwark ...* (Facsimile edition, R. Hyde, *The A to Z of Georgian London*, London Topographical Society Publication 126, 1982).

Rosser, G., and Thurley, S. (1990), 'Whitehall Palace and King Street Westminster', *London Topographical Record*, **26**: 57–77.

Stone, J. M. (1913), 'Greenwich: its origins and early history', *Transactions of the Greenwich Antiquarian Society*, **4**: 175–85.

Strype, J. (ed.) (1720), *A Survey of the Cities of London and Westminster by John Stowe*, 2 vols, London: printed for A. Churchill. (Includes various parish maps and textual descriptions of parochial boundaries).

Webster, A. D. (1902), *Greenwich Park its History and Associations*, Greenwich: Henry Richardson. (Includes unattributed map of Greenwich dated 'about 1695'.)

Appendix III. Summary statistics

A. DATA FROM THE 1693–4 AID ASSESSMENTS

Taxation District	Area (ha)	Number of households	Household density (hh/ha)	Total rent value (£)	Land value (£/ha)	Rent range (£)	Mean household rent	Total stock value (£)	Stock range (£)	Mean stock value	Householders who owned stock (%)	Number of wealthy lodgers[2]
CITY OF LONDON:												
Aldersgate Ward Within	3.7	420	113.5	6,928	1,872	4 – 200	£15 18s.	13,958	25 – 1,333	£80 4s.	39.1	10
Aldersgate Ward Without	7.8	513	65.8	7,485	960	1 – 150	£14 14s.	18,158	25 – 683	£85 13s.	35.9	28
Aldgate Ward	13.4	1,050	78.4	18,893	1,410	1 – 200	£17 1s.	66,325	13 – 2,000	£123 10s.	46.0	52
Bassishaw Ward	2.4	141	58.8	4,188	1,745	5 – 150	£25 3s.	18,442	25 – 667	£163 4s.	61.0	25
Billingsgate Ward	5.3	392	74.0	14,800	2,793	5 – 840	£32 1s.	50,266	50 – 2,333	£184 3s.	58.7	39
Bishopsgate Ward Within	6.7	392	58.5	13,302	1,985	1 – 400	£31 13s.	38,062	17 – 600	£125 4s.	63.3	55
Bishopsgate Ward Without	18.0	1,612	89.6	15,545	864	1 – 185	£11 6s.	37,842	25 – 1,667	£119 0s.	17.1	43
Bread Street Ward	3.9	335	85.9	9,975	2,557	3 – 120	£29 5s.	38,042	17 – 1,333	£159 17s.	63.0	27
Bridge Ward Within	5.1	399	78.2	13,733	2,693	3 – 320	£32 16s.	42,000	33 – 800	£160 18s.	57.1	32
Broad Street Ward	11.5	805	70.0	25,545	2,221	2 – 1,458	£28 1s.	120,908	50 – 15,000	£236 3s.	49.2	115
Candlewick Ward	2.5	270	108.0	8,148	3,259	4 – 110	£29 16s.	39,408	25 – 1,667	£163 10s.	73.7	42
Castle Baynard Ward	10.9	755	69.3	17,083	1,567	2 – 900	£19 17s.	35,833	25 – 1,000	£90 14s.	45.4	52
Cheap Ward	5.3	369	69.6	16,693	3,150	5 – 200	£44 10s.	60,000	25 – 1,500	£143 4s.	81.8	116
Coleman Street Ward	12.4	574	46.3	11,425	921	2 – 120	£19 13s.	37,667	13 – 1,000	£111 15s.	46.9	68
Cordwainer Ward	4.3	358	83.3	8,738	2,032	2 – 112	£24 6s.	44,391	25 – 1,167	£142 6s.	71.5	56
Cornhill Ward	2.4	222	92.5	13,266	5,528	3 – 180	£51 7s.	20,142	25 – 1,250	£178 5s.	44.1	15
Cripplegate Ward Within	7.7	743	96.5	16,722	2,172	2 – 200	£21 14s.	58,050	25 – 2,000	£146 4s.	47.2	44
Cripplegate Ward Without	17.9	1,711	95.6	13,752	768	1 – 120	£8 9s.	16,983	25 – 2,667	£75 10s.	12.5	12
Dowgate Ward	6.0	385	64.2	8,503	1,417	1 – 200	£20 13s.	18,742	25 – 1,000	£167 7s.	26.8	6
Farringdon Ward Within	14.5	1,360	93.8	32,049	2,210	3 – 420	£22 8s.	94,141	25 – 3,500	£111 19s.	54.6	95
Farringdon Ward Without	50.1	4,145	82.7	77,983	1,557	1 – 400	£18 16s.	176,353	25 – 10,000	£100 4s.	36.1	257
Langbourne Ward	6.4	571	89.2	23,202	3,625	3 – 350	£40 5s.	65,700	25 – 1,200	£154 12s.	61.0	75
Lime Street Ward	3.1	201	64.8	6,603	2,130	1 – 631	£27 17s.	15,192	25 – 600	£104 15s.	57.2	29
Portsoken Ward	16.1	1,395	86.7	15,300	950	1 – 300	£11 6s.	28,858	25 – 1,100	£75 7s.	24.4	42
Queenhithe Ward	5.7	470	82.5	8,087	1,419	2 – 228	£17 0s.	17,017	25 – 300	£89 2s.	38.7	5
Tower Ward	11.6	805	69.4	26,853	2,315	2 – 1,200	£15 3s.	85,408	25 – 6,333	£139 11s.	65.5	77
Vintry Ward	4.5	403	89.6	7,653	1,701	3 – 140	£18 6s.	22,250	25 – 2,000	£119 0s.	41.9	81
Walbrook Ward	3.9	299	76.7	10,340	2,651	6 – 400	£32 17s.	41,533	25 – 1,500	£144 14s.	69.2	80
Total[1]	263.1	21,095	80.1	452,794	1,721	1 – 1,485	£19 18s.	1,321,671	13 – 15,000	£127 2s.	41.6	1,515

[1] Rounding of figures has in some instances introduced a degree of variation from totals given in tables in the main text.
[2] For the definition of 'wealthy lodgers', see above, p. 99.

A. DATA FROM THE 1693–4 AID ASSESSMENTS (CONTINUED)

Taxation District	Area (ha)	Number of households	Household density (hh/ha)	Total rent value (£)	Land value (£/ha)	Rent range (£)	Mean household rent	Total stock value (£)	Stock range (£)	Mean stock value	Householders who owned stock (%)	Number of wealthy lodgers
MIDDLESEX:												
St Andrew Holborn	58.0	2,628	45.3	39,607	683	1 – 150	£15 6s.	140,666	25 – 10,000	£210 5s.	18.7	180
St Botolph Aldgate	13.7	1,094	79.9	7,424	542	2 – 140	£10 14s.	26,065	13 – 3,200	£100 0s.	22.3	17
St Dunstan Stepney:[1]												
Bethnal Green	305.7	663	2.2	6,781	22	2 – 100	£12 2s.	17,775	25 – 3,000	£246 18s.	8.0	19
Limehouse	100.5	314	3.1	4,290	43	1 – 150	£13 18s.	12,233	50 – 400	£137 9s.	20.1	25
Mile End Old Town	274.1	288	1.1	4,418	16	1 – 200	£16 6s.	17,850	50 – 1,500	£278 18s.	17.4	13
Poplar and Blackwall	468.8	207	0.4	4,419	9	1 – 600	£11 3s.	8,350	25 – 1,000	£132 11s.	17.4	26
Ratcliff	45.3	846	18.7	7,532	166	1 – 200	£10 13s.	26,867	25 – 1,400	£137 2s.	20.1	23
Spitalfields	29.6	1,782	60.2	12,083	408	1 – 100	£6 17s.	32,342	25 – 1,000	£117 12s.	14.4	18
Wapping	100.4	2,195	21.9	10,542	105	1 – 150	£6 5s.	23,850	50 – 800	£148 3s.	6.5	17
St Giles Cripplegate[2]	97.4	785	8.1	9,912	102	1 – 96	£12 5s.	22,900	25 – 2,000	£118 1s.	20.0	34
St Giles in the Fields	100.2	2,825	28.9	51,906	518	1 – 462	£18 10s.	200,991	25 – 5,000	£198 12s.	29.4	181
St James Clerkenwell	128.2	810	6.3	9,794	76	1 – 342	£12 10s.	60,508	25 – 20,000	£220 17s.	26.8	56
St John at Hackney	1,335.6	565	0.4	9,981	8	1 – 350	£18 7s.	20,700	50 – 500	£172 10s.	14.2	40
St Katherine by the Tower	5.7	839	147.2	4,627	812	1 – 84	£5 10s.	10,850	25 – 600	£79 4s.	15.5	7
St Leonard Bromley by Bow	245.8	106	0.4	1,984	8	2 – 150	£17 8s.	4,200	100 – 500	£323 2s.	10.4	1
St Leonard Shoreditch	262.3	904	3.5	10,312	39	1 – 212	£12 13s.	27,258	25 – 1,000	£89 13s.	25.4	70
St Mary Islington	1,258.7	435	0.3	9,727	8	1 – 283	£10 0s.	31,167	25 – 2,167	£311 13s.	12.4	42
St Marylebone	609.7	27	<0.1	2,590	4	3 – 450	£92 16s.	4,400	25 – 1,000	£146 13s.	7.4	28
St Mary Whitechapel:	68.8	1,957	28.8	17,568	225	1 – 300	£9 19s.	53,866	25 – 2,000	£148 8s.	15.6	56
Wapping Whitechapel	16.6	1,536	92.5	10,229	616	1 – 150	£6 13s.	23,342	25 – 2,000	£91 11s.	15.9	11
St Pancras	1,081.8	235	0.2	7,175	7	1 – 240	£30 19s.	2,525	25 – 1,000	£631 5s.	0.4	3
St Paul Shadwell	27.5	1,204	43.8	9,512	346	1 – 120	£7 17s.	23,383	25 – 1,000	£85 1s.	20.8	24
St Sepulchre	7.9	264	33.4	5,981	757	3 – 140	£22 11s.	20,137	13 – 600	£72 19s.	64.8	105
Stratford, Bow and Old Ford	228.8	209	0.9	2,039	9	1 – 68	£9 17s.	3,350	50 – 1,000	£167 10s.	8.1	3
Total	6,871.1	22,718	3.3	260,433	38	1 – 600	£10 18s.	815,575	13 – 20,000	£156 15s.	18.5	999
INNS AND LIBERTIES:												
Barnard's Inn	0.2	–	–	–	–	–	–	1,200	25 – 300	£66 13s.	-	18
Gray's Inn	4.5	–	–	–	–	–	–	5,100	100 – 500	£182 3s.	-	28
Staple Inn	0.4	–	–	–	–	–	–	2,433	8 – 200	£101 8s.	-	24
Duchy Liberty (St Mary, Savoy)	12.5	801	64.1	26,449	2,116	2 – 200	£33 4s.	99,540	25 – 5,000	£185 15s.	47.1	159
Liberty of Norton Folgate	7.8	411	52.7	2,575	330	2 – 24	£6 5s.	6,425	25 – 500	£61 4s.	23.4	9
Liberty of the Rolls and Offices	4.5	265	58.9	6,149	1,366	4 – 160	£23 19s.	12,367	25 – 1,000	£105 14s.	37.0	19
Tower Liberty[3]	18.5	346	18.7	3,198	173	1 – 120	£9 17s.	9,412	13 – 600	£132 12s.	13.0	25
Total	48.4	1,823	37.7	38,371	793	1 – 200	£20 14s.	136,477	8 – 5,000	£153 14s.	33.2	282

[1] Data for Mile End New Town are not available. [2] Data for Golden Lane and Glasshouse Yard, and Old Street divisions of St Giles Cripplegate are not available. [3] Data for Artillery Ground division of Tower Liberty are not available.

A. DATA FROM THE 1693–4 AID ASSESSMENTS (CONTINUED)

Taxation District	Area (ha)	Number of households	Household density (hh/ha)	Total rent value (£)	Land value (£/ha)	Rent range (£)	Mean household rent	Total stock value (£)	Stock range (£)	Mean stock value	Householders who owned stock (%)	Number of wealthy lodgers
CITY OF WESTMINSTER:												
St Anne Soho	21.5	1,099	51.1	24,946	1,160	1 – 300	£22 16s.	112,379	13 – 5,000	£220 16s.	36.2	111
St Clement Danes	13.0	1,246	95.9	25,164	1,936	1 – 400	£21 14s.	62,266	25 – 1,000	£132 4s.	32.6	64
St James	64.0	2,304	36.0	48,766	762	1 – 320	£21 14s.	71,437	13 – 5,000	£163 2s.	16.3	60
St Margaret	174.4	3,143	18.2	37,634	216	1 – 300	£11 19s.	98,000	25 – 3,000	£150 2s.	16.0	144
St Martin in the Fields	568.0	3,363	5.9	89,006	157	1 – 500	£24 10s.	293,390	13 – 5,000	£164 11s.	37.8	492
St Paul Covent Garden	10.5	521	49.6	18,135	1,727	4 – 250	£34 8s.	123,366	50 – 4,500	£303 2s.	46.6	161
Total	851.4	11,676	13.7	243,651	286	1 – 500	£19 19s.	760,838	13 – 5,000	£179 18s.	27.4	1,032

B. HOUSEHOLD DATA FROM THE 1692 POLL TAX RETURNS

Ward	Number of households		Heads of household by gender/status					Number of children			Number of servants			Number of apprentices	Number of masters	Total recorded population[2]	Mean household size	Number of private coaches
	Principal	Lodger	Single[1]			Widows	Married men	m	f	?	m	f	?					
			m	f	?													
CITY OF LONDON:																		
Aldersgate Ward Within	396	283	167	90	20	15	387	56	66	331	151	196	0	93	66	1,971	2.90	3
Aldersgate Ward Without	445	142	90	93	5	46	353	116	161	89	45	227	2	162	115	1,775	3.02	6
Aldgate Ward	858	347	233	200	81	38	653	212	271	240	229	614	35	182	143	3,731	3.10	24
Bassishaw Ward	139	107	76	58	3	7	102	60	83	0	127	156	1	1	1	807	3.28	12
Billingsgate Ward	378	206	140	75	15	24	330	203	243	35	298	340	53	0	0	2,121	3.63	4
Bishopsgate Ward Within	385	182	126	74	12	42	313	15	30	393	157	356	3	184	142	2,059	3.63	11
Bishopsgate Ward Without	985	216	151	82	16	128	824	21	28	631	89	383	4	280	232	3,498	2.91	6
Bread Street Ward	317	169	142	62	4	34	244	4	0	362	347	309	5	0	0	1,785	3.67	3
Bridge Ward Within	364	113	121	36	3	22	295	15	12	439	310	333	99	0	0	2,024	4.24	4
Broad Street Ward	726	536	248	268	59	41	646	8	36	921	551	791	37	11	8	4,335	3.44	34
Candlewick Ward	260	173	124	47	8	35	219	4	8	265	256	257	2	0	0	1,464	3.38	4
Castle Baynard Ward	675	191	170	118	27	3	548	34	73	326	427	416	10	0	0	2,744	3.17	10
Cheap Ward	374	216	205	68	10	13	294	9	20	470	496	489	5	0	0	2,415	4.09	8
Coleman Street Ward	489	372	171	208	21	17	444	25	61	416	191	428	6	106	82	2,599	3.02	19
Cordwainer Ward	347	213	134	66	19	41	300	180	184	21	81	301	15	162	121	1,834	3.28	9
Cornhill Ward	181	87	73	16	15	22	142	6	3	225	287	230	2	12	8	1,189	4.44	6
Cripplegate Ward Within	726	382	213	153	26	88	628	270	302	211	421	551	8	175	118	3,750	3.38	4
Cripplegate Ward Without	961	169	158	171	9	41	751	40	59	272	56	298	4	277	216	2,918	2.58	0
Dowgate Ward	309	105	80	33	10	37	254	13	17	215	13	19	430	0	0	1,415	3.42	5
Farringdon Ward Within	1,253	1,004	469	296	71	144	1,277	62	74	1,025	475	884	105	372	255	6,657	2.95	6
Farringdon Ward Without	3,734	1,689	830	803	307	278	3,203	317	507	1,795	568	1,562	992	865	659	15,458	2.85	13
Langbourne Ward	509	325	246	88	43	55	402	14	30	661	535	540	166	8	7	3,240	3.88	23
Lime Street Ward	201	79	59	39	4	10	168	69	108	12	130	170	5	8	6	970	3.46	5
Portsoken Ward	740	83	170	70	19	47	517	0	5	507	36	255	7	274	218	2,443	2.97	1
Queenhithe Ward	402	103	79	27	4	30	365	10	6	239	191	206	0	1	1	1,548	3.07	0
Tower Ward	740	351	217	122	24	52	676	26	71	699	433	573	13	20	18	3,660	3.35	19
Vintry Ward	385	275	83	64	14	65	434	4	15	220	155	209	19	26	18	1,758	2.66	6
Walbrook Ward	283	171	75	77	53	30	219	5	12	303	4	3	604	0	0	1,644	3.62	7
Total	17,562	8,289	5,050	3,504	902	1,405	14,988	1,798	2,485	11,323	7,059	11,096	2,632	3,219	2,434	81,812	3.16	252

[1] Does not include widows.
[2] Includes co-resident kin.

C. OCCUPATIONAL DATA FROM THE 1692 POLL TAX RETURNS

Ward	I. Building				II. Manufacturing										
	Brick and stone	Glass	Wood	Crafts	Food	Drink	Wood-workers	Leather-workers	Metal-workers	Fine-metal workers	Instrument makers	Machine makers	Textile processers	Apparel makers	Printers and bookbinders
CITY OF LONDON:															
Aldersgate Within	3	2	7	4	8	1	16	3	17	97	13	10	11	178	4
Aldersgate Without	3	4	14	10	10	3	10	5	14	20	2	7	8	31	11
Aldgate	8	6	21	12	22	3	32	3	15	11	5	2	23	88	–
Bassishaw	1	–	1	–	–	–	–	–	–	1	–	–	7	3	–
Billingsgate	–	1	–	1	6	8	9	–	1	–	–	–	–	2	–
Bishopsgate Within	3	3	3	5	8	1	10	11	11	6	3	1	4	14	–
Bishopsgate Without	14	6	40	14	41	12	34	9	27	19	17	27	169	68	2
Bread Street	1	4	7	3	7	1	17	–	1	3	3	2	12	13	1
Bridge	2	2	2	3	9	2	14	–	2	9	9	–	6	18	–
Broad Street	–	–	1	1	4	1	1	1	–	5	–	–	1	–	–
Candlewick	–	1	6	3	12	–	18	–	2	8	6	7	11	42	–
Castle Baynard	18	4	20	9	14	4	43	2	8	5	6	5	11	41	17
Cheap	1	5	1	2	6	3	9	–	4	2	3	1	3	17	–
Coleman Street	3	–	4	–	4	–	–	1	4	–	6	–	4	7	1
Cordwainer	4	3	8	13	8	4	18	–	5	3	4	3	34	35	1
Cornhill	–	–	1	1	2	–	5	1	1	5	6	–	2	9	–
Cripplegate Within	7	4	45	10	24	2	16	5	14	67	6	11	28	21	2
Cripplegate Without	8	7	36	17	40	18	31	12	41	37	16	25	48	53	2
Dowgate	4	2	6	6	13	9	28	1	5	1	–	1	30	9	–
Farringdon Within	13	10	45	21	46	4	32	4	19	62	26	11	30	216	22
Farringdon Without	25	7	65	31	70	26	76	17	60	36	37	37	36	117	18
Langbourne	4	6	2	1	14	1	13	–	5	13	9	2	11	37	3
Lime Street	1	1	1	–	7	–	2	1	1	–	–	–	2	1	–
Portsoken	6	5	25	4	41	14	21	4	24	11	7	46	12	14	–
Queenhithe	13	4	17	9	15	18	16	–	8	2	4	3	23	27	–
Tower	–	–	–	–	–	–	–	–	–	–	1	–	–	–	–
Vintry	–	–	–	–	–	–	–	–	–	–	–	–	–	2	–
Walbrook	–	4	1	6	4	2	12	–	1	4	–	1	4	14	–
Total	143	91	379	185	435	137	483	80	290	427	189	202	532	1,075	84

C. OCCUPATIONAL DATA FROM THE 1692 POLL TAX RETURNS (CONTINUED)

Ward	III. Tradesman	IV. Dealing												V. Gentry
		Raw materials	Overseas trade	Financial services	Textiles	Apparel	Household wares	Food	Victualling	Tobacco	Medicines	Books and stationery	Shopkeeper[?]	
CITY OF LONDON:														
Aldersgate Within	–	3	2	9	6	11	16	12	40	2	2	3	–	–
Aldersgate Without	–	–	3	5	7	26	8	20	41	2	11	14	–	9
Aldgate	1	1	98	13	18	11	10	22	33	9	6	3	1	32
Bassishaw	–	–	51	1	1	–	1	1	6	1	1	1	–	14
Billingsgate	33	–	33	1	–	5	2	9	30	–	1	1	6	19
Bishopsgate Within	–	–	44	1	12	28	17	40	41	4	9	2	–	21
Bishopsgate Without	–	6	24	16	40	40	27	71	112	2	10	2	–	10
Bread Street	–	5	5	4	44	39	9	60	25	22	6	4	–	5
Bridge	–	4	12	3	46	58	20	65	24	1	8	10	–	8
Broad Street	88	–	130	11	–	3	3	10	22	–	5	2	11	87
Candlewick	3	8	62	6	11	40	9	9	18	–	7	1	–	17
Castle Baynard	–	8	6	1	26	12	8	7	34	2	3	10	–	19
Cheap	–	2	74	1	55	52	10	25	44	6	24	7	–	43
Coleman Street	–	–	34	11	7	6	1	6	10	–	2	–	–	17
Cordwainer	–	–	52	3	36	15	17	13	25	2	19	2	–	21
Cornhill	–	–	9	3	45	45	8	4	32	–	2	9	–	7
Cripplegate Within	–	1	18	2	29	19	22	36	44	–	7	3	–	30
Cripplegate Without	–	5	6	16	3	25	16	41	98	5	4	1	–	7
Dowgate	–	8	32	1	4	–	6	22	22	1	3	–	–	6
Farringdon Within	–	5	7	28	121	77	26	67	117	5	19	32	–	27
Farringdon Without	–	29	3	32	24	81	56	67	205	7	16	25	–	250
Langbourne	–	3	103	58	41	42	21	36	54	6	19	4	–	36
Lime Street	–	1	11	–	7	4	1	11	9	1	2	1	–	11
Portsoken	–	2	6	15	9	51	25	23	53	1	7	4	–	4
Queenhithe	–	21	2	1	2	4	8	44	37	4	4	–	–	4
Tower	107	–	101	3	–	–	–	–	5	–	–	–	14	76
Vintry	–	–	13	–	–	–	–	–	–	–	–	–	–	7
Walbrook	–	2	73	14	20	10	3	18	21	3	18	1	–	13
Total	232	113	1014	259	614	704	350	739	1202	86	215	142	32	800

C. OCCUPATIONAL DATA FROM THE 1692 POLL TAX RETURNS (CONTINUED)

Ward	VI. Services									VII. Transport			
	Officials	Clergy	Law	Medicine	Education	Clerical	General services	Journey-men	Arts and entertainment	Water	Vehicles	Horses	Porters and messengers
CITY OF LONDON:													
Aldersgate Within	2	3	1	5	4	–	31	–	–	–	2	–	6
Aldersgate Without	–	–	4	5	5	3	6	–	3	–	14	11	4
Aldgate	15	4	5	12	6	14	10	9	1	4	6	6	6
Bassishaw	4	2	5	2	1	4	2	–	1	–	–	–	1
Billingsgate	1	4	4	2	–	1	2	–	1	5	–	–	–
Bishopsgate Within	6	2	5	16	2	3	3	–	1	1	3	8	3
Bishopsgate Without	15	7	5	7	9	2	15	1	1	–	27	7	15
Bread Street	1	3	5	4	8	–	11	–	–	–	–	–	11
Bridge	3	3	6	6	2	1	7	–	1	–	–	–	11
Broad Street	3	12	30	8	7	2	–	–	–	–	–	–	–
Candlewick	2	2	2	6	1	3	6	3	–	1	–	–	4
Castle Baynard	13	5	67	6	2	24	8	2	1	1	–	2	15
Cheap	6	3	33	4	1	6	16	–	–	1	–	–	–
Coleman Street	1	5	10	2	–	8	2	–	–	–	–	1	–
Cordwainer	7	5	15	12	4	10	14	5	4	–	–	–	7
Cornhill	2	1	7	–	2	3	8	–	1	–	–	–	–
Cripplegate Within	11	9	20	10	4	9	9	1	–	–	–	–	–
Cripplegate Without	15	6	2	4	4	4	11	–	1	–	2	6	12
Dowgate	4	1	–	1	9	7	5	14	–	–	6	8	9
Farringdon Within	16	8	14	14	39	7	30	18	2	4	–	4	18
Farringdon Without	5	9	59	23	37	31	51	3	2	2	2	–	11
Langbourne	13	3	22	12	5	11	19	5	3	1	22	31	26
Lime Street	1	2	1	6	–	–	3	–	–	1	–	1	2
Portsoken	3	-	2	4	1	–	5	–	–	–	4	–	2
Queenhithe	6	5	9	2	–	2	10	–	–	1	–	1	10
Tower	8	6	4	1	–	–	–	–	–	26	–	2	37
Vintry	–	1	8	–	–	–	–	–	–	–	–	–	–
Walbrook	3	–	6	4	–	6	4	–	–	–	–	–	1
Total	166	111	351	178	153	161	288	61	23	48	87	88	198

Appendix IV. Location of taxation districts

The numbering used on the map on page 185 relates to the taxation district location coding used in the 1693–4 Four Shillings in the Pound Aid database as deposited in the History Data Archive at the University of Essex <hds.essex.ac.uk>. The names and spelling of the districts are as given in the original assessments.

KEY TO MAP

CITY OF LONDON (WARDS)

1 Aldersgate Ward Within
2 Aldersgate Ward Without
3 Aldgate Ward
4 Bassishaw Ward
5 Billingsgate Ward
6 Bishopsgate Ward Within
7 Bishopsgate Ward Without
8 Bread Street Ward
9 Bridge Ward Within
10 Broad Street Ward and Excise Office
11 Candlewick Ward
12 Castle Baynard Ward
13 Cheap Ward
14 Coleman Street Ward
15 Cordwainer Ward
16 Cornhill Ward
17 Cripplegate Ward Within
18 Cripplegate Ward Without
19 Dowgate Ward
20 Farringdon Ward Within
21 Farringdon Ward Without
22 Langbourne Ward
23 Limestreet Ward
24 Portsoken Ward
25 Queenhithe Ward
26 Tower Ward and Custom House
27 Vintry Ward
28 Walbrooke Ward

CITY OF WESTMINSTER (PARISHES/SUB-PAROCHIAL WARDS)

29 St Anne Soho (Westminster)

30 St Clement Danes
   30/01 Hollywell Ward
   30/02 Temple Barr Ward
   30/03 Sheere Lane Ward
   30/04 Drury Lane Ward
   30/05 Savoy Ward

31 St James Westminster
   31/01 Pall Mall Ward
   31/02 Rupert Street Ward
   31/03 Portugal Street Ward
   31/04 Windmill Street Ward
   31/05 James Street Ward
   31/06 St James Market Precinct

32 St Margaret Westminster
   32/01 Burgess Jones Ward (Upper/Lower King Street Ward)
   32/02 Burgess Reads Ward (Upper/Lower King Street Ward)
   32/03 Burgess Aynsworths Ward/New Palace Ward
   32/04 Burgess Henmans [Heninan's] Ward/Long Ditch Ward
   32/05 Sanctuary and Deanery
   32/06 Burgess Nortons Ward/Tuttlehill Street North Division
   32/07 Peter Street Division
   32/08 Milbanke Division
   32/09 Petty France Division

33 St Martin in the Fields
   33/01 Strand Upper Ward
   33/02 Spurr Alley Ward
   33/03 Out Ward
   33/04 New Street Ward
   33/05 Charing Cross Ward
   33/06 Drury Lane Ward
   33/07 Exchange Ward
   33/08 Long Acre Ward
   33/09 Bedfordbury Ward
   33/10 Suffolk Street Ward

34 St Paul Covent Garden
   34/01 East Division
   34/02 West Division

35 Dutchy Liberty
   35/01 Royal Ward
   35/02 Church Ward
   35/03 Middle Ward
   35/04 Savoy Ward
   35/05 Somerset House

36 The Rolls Liberty

39 Gray's Inn

METROPOLITAN AREAS IN THE COUNTY OF MIDDLESEX (PARISHES/SUB-PAROCHIAL WARDS OR HAMLETS)

42 St Leonard Bromley

46 St Andrew Holborn
   46/00 Saffron Hill, Hatton Garden and Ely Rents
   46/01 Liberty Above the Bars — First Book
   46/02 Liberty Above the Bars — Second Book

47 St Botolph without Aldgate

48 St Dunstan Stepney
   48/01 Hamlet of Bethnal Green
   48/02 Hamlet of Limehouse
   48/03 Hamlet of Mile End Old Town
   48/04 Hamlet of Poplar and Blackwall
   48/05 Hamlet of Ratcliffe
   48/06 Hamlet of Spittlefields
   48/07 Hamlet of Wapping Stepney

49	St Giles in the Fields	E	Golden Lane and Glasshouse Yard Division, St Giles
	49/01 Holborne End		without Cripplegate
	49/02 Old Town	F	Old Street Division, St Giles without Cripplegate
	49/03 Drury Lane Liberty	G	Old Artillery Ground
	49/04 Cock and Pye Fields	H	Mile End New Town
		I	St Luke Chelsea
50	St Giles Cripplegate	J	St Mary Battersea
		K	St Mary Lambeth
51	St James Clerkenwell	L	Christ Church Surrey
		M	St Saviour Southwark
52	St John Hackney	N	St Thomas Southwark
		O	St Olave Southwark
53	St Katherine by the Tower	P	St George the Martyr
		Q	St Mary Newington
54	St Leonard Shoreditch	R	St Mary Magdalen Bermondsey
		S	St Giles Camberwell
55	St Mary Islington	T	St Mary Rotherhithe
		U	St Nicholas Deptford
56	St Marylebone	V	East Greenwich
		W	County of Essex
57	St Mary Whitechapel		
	57/00 Whitechapel		
	57/01 Wapping Whitechapel		

58   St Pancras, Kentish Town

59   St Paul Shadwell

60   St Sepulchre Middlesex

61   Stratford/Bow

62   Liberty of Norton Folgate

63   Tower Liberty
    63/01   Tower Intra
    63/02   Tower Extra
    63/03   Well Close
    63/04   Trinity Minories

AREAS EITHER BEYOND THE LIMITS OF THE STUDY AREA OR
HAVING NO EXTANT FOUR SHILLING AID SOURCES

A   Westminster Abbey Precinct
B   Lincoln's Inn
C   The Temple
D   Charterhouse

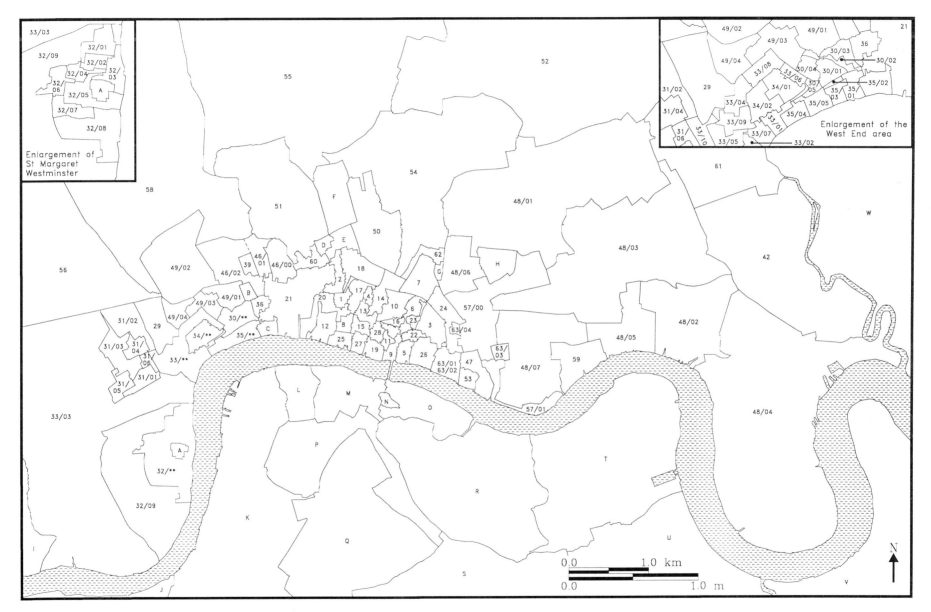

33/03

32/09
32/01
32/02
32/04
32/03
32/06
32/05
A
32/07
32/08

Enlargement of
St Margaret
Westminster

49/02
49/01
21
49/03
30/03
36
30/02
49/04
33/08
33/06
30/01
30/07
35/02
31/02
29
34/01
05
35/03
35/01
31/04
33/04
34/02
35/05
35/04
31/06
33/10
33/09
33/01
33/02
33/05
33/07
33/02

Enlargement of the
West End area

52

55

58

51

F

54

48/01

61

W

56

49/02

46/02

D
60
E
46/01
46/00

50

62
48/06
H
18
G
42

49/03
49/01
B
36
21
20
1
17
4
14
10
6
24
57/00
48/03
2
7
13
8
15
16
23
3
63/04
48/02
31/02
29
49/04
30/**
12
27
28
22
48/05
31/03
31/04
34/**
C
35/**
25
19
9
5
26
63/01
63/03
59
48/07
31/06
33/**
63/02
47
53
31/05
31/01

33/03

L
M
N
O
57/01

A
P
32/**

K
R
T
48/04

32/09
Q
U

I
S
V

0.0   1.0 km

0.0   1.0 m

N

Map showing taxation districts (for key see pp. 183–4)
Source: 1693–4 Aid database.

Bibliography

MANUSCRIPT SOURCES
(For Quarterly Poll Tax Returns and Four Shillings in the Pound Aid assessments, see Appendix I)

BL (British Library), Ms Sloane 3928.

CLRO (Corporation of London Records Office), Assessment Box 27.C, 'The Book of Entry for Specifications and Appeals, 1697'.

CLRO, Assessment Box 29.15, 'Assessment for the 1693 four shillings in the pound aid made upon the East India Company'.

CLRO, Assessment Box 35.B, 'A Collection for the poor taken upon the King's Letter, 1694'.

CLRO, Assessment Boxes 40 and 42 (1693–4 aid assessments for the parishes of rural Middlesex).

CLRO, Assessment Box 81.13, 'Instructions to Approved and Appointed Assessors'.

CLRO, Assessment Box 81.13, 'Warrant to Constables to arrest Collectors in St Bartholomew the Less'.

CLRO, Assessment Box 111.9, 'Commissioners' Clerk: Receipt for poundage'.

CLRO, Chamber Accounts Ms. 40/61.

CLRO, Chamber Accounts Ms. 40/62, 'Chamberlain's Posting Book'.

CLRO, Chamber Accounts Ms. 40/113, 'Book of Estreats on the second 4s. Aid'.

CLRO, Chamber Accounts Ms. 40/207.

PRINTED WORKS

Statutes:

1 William & Mary Session 1 c.1, *An Act for granting to Their Majesties an Aid of Foure Shillings in the Pound for One yeare for carrying on a vigorous War against France* (1688–9).

1 William & Mary Session 1 c.3, *An Act for the granting a present aid to their Majesties* (1688–9).

1 William & Mary Session 1 c.8, *An Act for abrogating the oaths of Supremacy and Allegiance and appointing other oaths* (1688–9).

1 William & Mary Session 1 c.13, *An Act for raising money by a poll, and otherwise, towards the reduction of Ireland* (1688–9).

1 William & Mary Session 1 c.18, *An Act for Exempting their Majesties Protestant Subjects dissenting from the Church of England from the Penalties of certain Laws* (1688–9).

1 William & Mary Session 1 c.20, *An Act for a grant to their Majesties of an aid of twelve pence in the pound for one year, for the necessary defence of their realms* (1688–9).

1 William & Mary Session 1 c.24, *An Act for an additional duty of excise upon beer, ale and other liquors* (1688–9).

1 William & Mary Session 1 c.31, *An Additional Act for the Appointing Commissioners for executing an Act of the present Parliament Entituled An Act for a Grant to their Majesties of an Ayde of Twelve Pence in the Pound for the Defence of their Realmes* (1688–89).

1 William & Mary Session 2 c.1, *An Act for a grant to their Majesties of an Aid of two shillings in the Pound for one yeare* (1689).

1 William & Mary Session 2 c.5, *An Act for a grant to their Majesties of an additional Aid of twelve pence in the Pound for one year* (1689).

1 William & Mary Session 2 c. 7, *An Act for review of the late Poll granted to their Majesties, and for an additional poll, towards the reduction of Ireland* (1689).

3 William & Mary c.5, *An Act for granting an aid to their Majesties of the sum of sixteen hundred and fifty one thousand seven hundred and two pounds eighteen shillings, towards the carrying on a vigorous war against France* (1692).

3 & 4 William & Mary c.6, *An Act for raising money by a poll payable quarterly for one year, for the carrying on a vigorous war against France* (1692–3).

4 William & Mary c 1, *An Act for granting to their Majesties an aid of four shillings in the pound for one year, for the carrying on a vigorous war against France* (1693).

5 William & Mary c.1, *An Act for granting to their Majesties an aid of four shillings in the pound for one year, for the carrying on a vigorous war against France* (1694).

5 & 6 William & Mary c.1, *An Act for granting to their Majesties an aid of four shillings in the pound, for the carrying on a vigorous war against France* (1694).

5 & 6 William & Mary c.14, *An Act for raising money by a poll payable quarterly for one year for carrying on a vigorous Warr against France* (1694).

5 & 6 William & Mary c.22, *An Act for the lycensing and regulateing Hackney-Coaches and Stage-Coaches* (1694).

5 & 6 William & Mary c.24, *An Act for building good and defensible ships* (1694)

6 William III c.3, *An Act for granting to his Majesty an aid of four shillings in the pound for one year; ...for the carrying on a vigours war against France* (1697).

7 William III c.5, *An Act for granting to his Majesty an aid of four shillings in the pound for one year, for the carrying on a vigours war against France* (1698).

9 William III c.38, *An Act for granting to his Majesty an aid, by a quarterly poll, for one year* (1700).

A true list of the Lords Spiritual and Temporal, together with the Citizens and Burgesses of the Parliament at *Westminster* on the 22th (*sic*) of this instant *November* 1695; as they have been Returned into the *Crown Office* in *Chancery* British Library 1865. c.16 (8).

Albert, W. (1972), *The Turnpike Road System in England 1663–1840*, Cambridge: Cambridge University Press.

Alexander, J. (1989a), 'The economic and social structure of the City of London, *c.*1700', unpublished Ph.D. thesis, University of London.

Alexander, J. (1989b), 'The economic structure of the City of London at the end of the seventeenth century', *Urban History Yearbook*: 47–62.

Alexander, J. (1992), 'The City revealed: an analysis of the 1692 Poll Tax and the 1693 4s. Aid in London', in Schurer and Arkell (1992), pp. 181–200.

Arkell, T. (1992), 'An examination of the Poll taxes of the later seventeenth century, the Marriage Duty Act and Gregory King', in Schurer and Arkell (1992), pp. 142–80.

Arlidge, A. (1694), *A Survey of Hatton Garden, 1694* (Facsimile edition, London Topographical Society Publication 128, 1983).

Baddeley, J.J. (1921), *Cripplegate, One of the Twenty-Six Wards in the City of London*, London: Hodder & Stoughton.

Baillie, G.H., Clutton, C., and Ilbert, C.A. (1956), *Old Clocks and Watches and their Makers*, London: E. & F.N. Spon.

Ball, M. (1977), *The Worshipful Company of Brewers: A Short History*, London: Hutchinson.

Barbon, N. (1689), *An Apology for the Builder, or A Discourse Shewing the Cause and Effects of the Increase of Building*, London.

Beckett, J.V. (1990), 'Taxation and economic growth in eighteenth-century England', *Economic History Review*, 2nd series, **43**: 377–403.

Beier, A.L. (1986), 'Engine of Manufacture: the trades of London', in Beier and Finlay (1986), pp. 141–67.

Beier, A.L., and Finlay, R. (eds) (1986), *London 1500–1700, The Making of the Metropolis*, London: Longman.

Bennell, J. (1989), 'Shop and office in medieval and Tudor London', *London and Middlesex Archaeological Society Transactions*, **40**: 189–206.

Bennett, E. (1952), *The Worshipful Company of Carmen of London, A Short History*, London: The Company.

Best, R.H. (1981), *Land Use and Living Space*, London: Methuen.

Betts, D.C., and Lawrence, I.B. (1962), 'Crossing the Thames: watermen and the new bridge', *History Today*, **12**: 799–806.

Blagden, C. (1960), *The Stationers Company: A History, 1403–1959*, London: Allen & Unwin.

Bocchi, F., and Denley, P. (eds) (1994), *Storia & Multimedia: Proceedings of the Seventh International Congress of the Association for History and Computing*, Bologna: Grafis Edizioni.

Booth, P.A. (1980), 'Speculative housing and the land market in London, 1660–1730: four case studies', *Town Planning Review*, **51**: 379–97.

Borsay, P. (1989), *The English Urban Renaissance: Culture and Society in the Provincial Town 1660–1770*, Oxford: Clarendon Press.

Boulton, J. (1987a), *Neighbourhood and Society: A London Suburb in the Seventeenth Century*, Cambridge: Cambridge University Press.

Boulton, J. (1987b), 'Neighbourhood migration in early modern London', in Clark and Souden (1987), pp. 107–49.

Bowen, E. (1720), *Britannia Depicta or Ogilby Improved...*, ed. J.B. Harley, 1970.

Bowler, C., and Brimblecombe, P. (1990), *Comparative Pollution History of the City of Westminster and Damage to Buildings of Cultural Importance*, Norwich: University of East Anglia School of Environmental Sciences (typescript held by Institute of Historical Research).

Brett-James, N.G. (1935), *The Growth of Stuart London*, London: Allen & Unwin.

Brimblecombe, P. (1987), *The Big Smoke: A History of Air Pollution in London Since Medieval Times*, London: Methuen.

Bromley, J.S., and Kossmann, E.H. (eds) (1971), *Metropolis, Dominion and Province: Papers Delivered to the Fourth Anglo-Dutch Historical Conference*, Britain and the Netherlands, vol. 4, The Hague: Nijhoff.

Brooks, C. (1974), 'Public finance and political stability: the administration of the Land Tax, 1688–1720', *Historical Journal*, **17**: 281–300.

Browning, A. (ed) (1953), *English Historical Documents, 1660–1714*, vol. 8, London: Eyre & Spottiswoode.

Bull, G.B.G. (1975–6), 'Introduction', in *Thomas Milne's Land Use Map of London and Environs in 1800*, London Topographical Society Publication 118 and 119.

Burridge, R. (1722), *A New Review of London. Being an Exact Survey...of Every Street, Lane, Court...and all Places...Within the Cities...or Suburbs of London, Westminster, and the Borough of Southwark...*, London: J. Roberts.

Bynum, W.F., and Porter, R. (eds) (1991), *Living and Dying in London*, Medical History supplement No. 11, London: Wellcome Institute for the History of Medicine.

Champion, J.A.I. (1995), *London's Dreaded Visitation: The Social Geography of the Great Plague in 1665*, Historical Geography Research Series 31, London: Historical Geography Research Group.

Chandaman, C.D. (1975), *The English Public Revenue, 1660–1688*, Oxford: Clarendon Press.

Chartres, J.A. (1977a), 'The capital's provincial eyes: London inns in the early eighteenth century', *London Journal*, **3**: 24–39.

Chartres, J.A. (1977b), *Internal Trade in England 1500–1700*, London: Macmillan.

Chartres, J.A. (1977c), 'Road carrying in England in the seventeenth century', *Economic History Review*, 2nd series, **30**: 73–94.

Chartres, J.A. (1980), 'Trade and shipping in the Port of London: Wiggins Key in the later seventeenth century', *Journal of Transactions in History*, 3rd series, **1**: 29–48.

Chartres, J.A. (1986), 'Food consumption and internal trade', in Beier and Finlay (1986), pp. 168–196.

Chaudhuri, K.N. (1978), *The Trading World of Asia and the English East India Company, 1660–1760*, Cambridge: Cambridge University Press.

Childs, J.C.R. (1987), *The British Army of William III, 1698–1702*, Manchester: Manchester University Press.

Childs, J.C.R. (1991), *The Nine Years' War and the British Army, 1688–97*, Manchester: Manchester University Press.

Clark, A. (ed.) (1898), *Aubrey's Brief Lives*, 2 vols., Oxford: Clarendon Press.

Clark, P. (1987), 'Migration in England during the late seventeenth and early eighteenth centuries', in Clark and Souden (1987), pp. 213–252.

Clark, P., and Slack, P. (eds) (1972), *Crisis and Order in English Towns, 1500–1700: Essays in Urban History*, London: Routledge.

Clark, P., and Souden, D. (eds) (1987), *Migration and Society in Early Modern England*, Totowa, New Jersey: Barnes & Noble.

Clay, C. (1978), *Public Finance and Private Wealth: The Career of Sir Stephen Fox, 1627–1716*, Oxford: Clarendon Press.

Clay, C. (1984), *Economic Expansion and Social Change: England 1500–1700, Volume 2, Industry, Trade and Government*, Cambridge: Cambridge University Press.

Clout, H. (ed) (1978), *Changing London*, Slough: University Tutorial Press.

Coleman, D.C. (1977), *The Economy of England, 1450–1750*, London: Oxford University Press.

Coleman, D.C., and John, A.H. (1976), *Trade, Government and Economy of Pre-Industrial England: Essays presented to F.J. Fisher*, London: Weidenfeld & Nicolson.

Collyer, J. (1761), *The Parents' and Guardians' Directory, and the Youth's Guide, in the Choice of a Profession or Trade, etc.*, London: R. Griffiths.

Colvin, H. (ed) (1976), *The History of the King's Works 1660–1782*, vol. 5, London: HMSO.

Corfield, P.J. (1982), *The Impact of English Towns, 1700–1800*, Oxford: Oxford University Press.

Corfield, P.J. (1987), 'Class by name and number in eighteenth-century Britain', *History*, **72**: 38–61.

Corfield, P.J. (1990), 'Defining urban work', in Corfield, and Keene (1990), pp. 207–30.

Corfield, P.J., and Keene, D. (eds) (1990), *Work in Towns, 850–1850*, Leicester: Leicester University Press.

Cox, A. (1989), 'Bricks to build a capital', in Hobhouse and Saunders (1989), pp. 3–17.

Crawford, A. (1977), *A History of the Vintners' Company*, London: Constable.

Crinò, A.M. (ed) (1968), *Un Principe di Toscana in Inghilterra e in Irlanda nel 1669*, Rome.

Dale, T.C. (ed) (1931), *The Inhabitants of London in 1638 : edited from Ms.272 in the Lambeth Palace Library*, London: Society of Genealogists.

Davenant, C. (1695), *An Essay upon Ways and Means of Supplying the War*, London: printed for Jacob Tonson.

Davies, K.G. (1957), *The Royal African Company*, London: Longmans, Green.

Davison, L., Hitchcock, T., Keirn T., and Shoemaker, R.B. (eds.), *Stilling the Grumbling Hive: The Response to Social and Economic Problems in England 1689–1750*, Stroud: Alan Sutton.

De Castro, J.P. (1921), 'London coaching and carriers inns in 1732', *Notes and Queries*, 12th series, **8**: 61–62, 84–86, 102–104.

De Laune, T. (1690), *Angliae Metropolis: or, the Present State of London*, London: G.L. for John Harris and Thomas Howkins.

Defoe, D. (1724–6), *A Tour thro' the Whole Island of Great Britain*, ed. P. Rogers, 1971, Harmondsworth: Penguin.

Dickinson, H.W. (1954), *Water Supply of Greater London*, Leamington Spa: Newcomen Society.

Dietz, B. (1986), 'Overseas trade and metropolitan growth', in Beier and Finlay (1986), pp. 115–40.

Dingwall, H.M. (1994), *Late Seventeenth-Century Edinburgh: a Demographic Study*, Aldershot: Scolar Press.

Diprose, J. (1868), *Some Account of the Parish of St Clement's Danes*, London: Diprose and Bateman.

DNB, Dictionary of National Biography, Oxford: Oxford University Press.

Dyos, H.J., and Aldcroft, D.H. (1969), *British Transport: An Economic Survey from the Seventeenth Century to the Twentieth Century*, Leicester: Leicester University Press.

Earle, P. (1989a), *The Making of the English Middle Class: Business, Society and Family Life in London 1660–1730*, London: Methuen.

Earle, P. (1989b), 'The female labour force in late seventeenth and early eighteenth century London', *Economic History Review*, 2nd series, **42**: 328–53.

Earle, P. (1994), *A City Full of People: Men and Women of London 1650–1750*, London: Methuen.

Emmison, F., and Stephens, R. (eds.) (1976), *Tribute to an Antiquary*, London: Leopard's Head Press.

Evelyn, J. (1661), *Fumifugium, or, The Inconvenience of the Aer and Smoak of London Dissipated Together with some Remedies Humbly Proposed*, London: W. Godbid for Gabriel Bedel and Thomas Collins.

Evelyn, J. (1666), *London Redivivum or London Restored*, ed. E.S. de Beer, 1938, Oxford: Clarendon Press.

Falkus, M.E. (1976), 'Lights in the dark ages of English economic history: town streets before the Industrial Revolution', in Coleman and John (1976), pp. 248–73.

Finlay, R.A.P., and Shearer, B.R. (1986), 'Population growth and suburban expansion', in Beier and Finlay (1986), pp. 37–59.

Fisher, F.J. (ed.) (1961), *Essays in the Economic and Social History of Tudor and Stuart England in Honour of R.H. Tawney*, Cambridge: Cambridge University Press.

Fisher, F.J. (1971), 'London as an "Engine of Economic Growth"', in Bromley and Kossmann (1971), pp. 3–16.

Forbes, T.R. (1971), *Chronicle from Aldgate: Life and Death in Shakespeare's London*, New Haven: Yale University Press.

Forbes, T.R. (1980), 'Weaver and Cordwainer: occupations in the parish of St Giles without Cripplegate, London, in 1654–93 and 1729–43', *Guildhall Studies in London History*, **4**: 119–32.

French, C.J. (1992), '"Crowded with traders and great commerce": London's domination of English overseas trade, 1700–1775', *London Journal*, **17**: 27–35.

Freshfield, E. (ed) (1895), *The Account Books of the Parish of St Bartholomew Exchange in the City of London, 1596–1698*, London: Rixon & Arnold.

Gadbury, J. (1691), *Nauticum Astrologicum: ... Unto which is Added a Diary of the Weather for XXI Years Together, Exactly Observed in London, with Sundry Observations Thereon*, London: printed for Matthew Street.

Gage, J. (1986), 'Bloomsbury Market: a unit in the Earl of Southampton's pioneer town planning', *Camden History Review*, **14**: 20–23.

Galinou, M. (ed) (1990), *London's Pride: the Glorious History of the Capital's Gardens*. London: Anaya Publishers.

Galloway, J.A., and Murphy, M. (1991), 'Feeding the City: medieval London and its agrarian hinterland', *London Journal*, **16**: 3–14.

GEC, G.E. Cokayne, *The Complete Peerage*, 2nd edn., London: St Catherine Press 1910–59.

George, M.D. (1966), *London Life in the Eighteenth Century*, Harmondsworth: Penguin Books.

Gerhold, D. (1988), 'The growth of the London carrying trade, 1681–1838', *Economic History Review*, 2nd series, **41**: 392–410.

Gibbard, P.L. (1985), *The Pleistocene History of the Middle Thames Valley*, Cambridge: Cambridge University Press.

Giuseppi, M.S. (1908), 'The River Wandle in 1610', *Surrey Archaeological Collections*, **21**: 170–91.

Glanville, P. (1980), 'The topography of seventeenth century London: a review of maps', *Urban History Yearbook 1980*: 79–83.

Glass, D.V. (1965), 'Two papers on Gregory King', in Glass and Eversley (1965), pp. 159–220.

Glass, D.V. (1966), *London Inhabitants Within the Walls, 1695*, London: London Record Society Publication 2.

Glass, D.V. (1969), 'Socio-economic status and occupations in the City of London at the end of the seventeenth century', in Hollaender and Kellaway (1969), pp. 373–389.

Glass, D.V., and Eversley, D.E.C. (eds) (1965), *Population in History: Essays in Historical Demography*, London: Edward Arnold.

Glennie, P. (1990), *'Distinguishing Men's Trades': Occupational Sources and Debates for Pre-census England*, Historical Geography Research Series 25, Bristol: Historical Geography Research Group.

Goose, N. (1980), 'Household size and structure in early-Stuart Cambridge', *Social History*, **5**: 347–85.

Graunt, J. (1662), *Natural and Political Observations made Upon the Bills of Mortality*, London: printed by Tho. Roycroft, for John Martin, James Allestry, and Tho. Dicas.

Green, E.M. (1990), 'The taxonomy of occupations in late eighteenth century Westminster', in Corfield and Keene (1990), pp. 164–181.

Hanson, J. (1989), 'Order and structure in urban design: the plans for the rebuilding of London after the Great Fire of 1666', *Ekistics*, **334–35**: 22–42.

Harding, V. (1990a), 'Gardens and open space in Tudor and early Stuart London', in Galinou (1990), pp. 44–55.

Harding, V. (1990b), 'The population of early modern London: a review of the published evidence', *London Journal*, **15**: 111–28.

Harris, J. (1990), 'A tour of London's gardens with John Rocque', in Galinou (1990), pp. 102–121.

Hatcher, J. (1993), *The History of the British Coal Industry, Volume 1, Before 1700: Towards the Age of Coal*, Oxford: Clarendon Press.

Hatcher, J., and Barker, T.C. (1974), *A History of British Pewter*, London: Longman.

Hatton, E. (1708), *A New View of London, etc.*, London: R. Chiswell.

Highfill, P.H., Burnim, K.A., and Langhans, E.A. (1973), *A Biographical Dictionary of Actors, Actresses, Musicians, Dancers, and other Stage Personnel in London 1660–1800*, vol. 2, Carbonell: Southern Illinois University Press.

Hitchcock, T. (1992), 'Paupers and preachers: The SPCK and the parochial workhouse movement', in Davison *et al* (1992), pp. 145–66.

Hobhouse, H., and Saunders, A. (1989), *Good and Proper Materials: The Fabric of London Since the Great Fire*, London Topographical Society Publication 140, London: Royal Commission on Historical Monuments England.

Holleander, A.E.J. and Kellaway, W. (1969), *Studies in London History Presented to Philip Edmund Jones*, London: Hodder & Stoughton.

Hollis, T. (1978), 'Water for London', in Clout (1978), pp. 118–27.

Holmes, G. (1969), *Britain after the Glorious Revolution*, London: Macmillan.

Holmes, G. (1982), *Augustan England: Professions, State and Society, 1680–1730*, London: Allen & Unwin.

Holmes, G. (1993), *The Making of a Great Power: Late Stuart and Early Georgian Britain, 1660–1722*, London: Longman.

Homer, R.F. (1989), 'The Pewterers of London', in Hornsby, Weinstein, and Homer (1989), pp. 10–14.

Hornsby, P.R.G., Weinstein, R., and Homer, R.F. (1989), *Pewter, A Celebration of the Craft: 1200–1700*, London: Museum of London.

Hoskins, W.G. (1968), 'Harvest fluctuations and English economic history, 1620–1759', *Agricultural History Review*, **16**, pp. 15–31.

Howe, E. (1950), *A List of London Bookbinders, 1648–1815*, London: Bibliographical Society.

Howell, J. (1657), *Londinopolis: An Historical Discourse or Perlustration of the City of London, the Imperial Chamber, and Chief Emporium of Great Britain*, London: J. Streater for H. Twiford.

Howgego, J.L. (1978), *Printed Maps of London circa 1553–1850*, 2nd edition, Folkestone: Dawson.

Humpherus, H. (1887), *History of the Origin and Progress of the Company of Watermen and Lightermen of the River Thames*, vols. 1 and 2, London: Prentice.

Imray, J. (1991), *The Mercers' Hall*, London Topographical Society Publication 143, London: The Mercers' Company.

Jones, C. (1993), 'A London Directory of Peers and Bishops for 1708–9', *London Journal*, **18**: 23–30.

Jones, D.W. (1988), *War and Economy in the Age of William III and Marlborough*, Oxford: Basil Blackwell.

Jones, E. (1980), 'London in the seventeenth century: an ecological approach', *London Journal*, **6**: 123–33.

Jones, E.L., Porter, S. and Turner, M. (1984), *A Gazetteer of English Urban Fire Disasters, 1500–1900*, Historical Geography Research Series 13, Norwich: Historical Geography Research Group.

Jones, P.E., and Judges, A.V. (1935–6), 'London population in the late seventeenth century', *Economic History Review*, **6**: 45–63.

Keay, J. (1991), *The Honourable Company: a History of the English East India Company*, London: Harper Collins.

Keene, D. (1990), 'Continuity and development in urban trades: problems of concepts and the evidence', in Corfield and Keene (1990), pp. 1–16.

King, G. (1696), *Natural and Political Observations and Conclusions upon the State and Condition of England*, printed in G. Chalmers, *Comparative State of Britain*, London: John Stockdale, 1804.

Kitch, M.J. (1986), 'Capital and kingdom: migration to later Stuart London', in Beier and Finlay (1986), pp. 224–51.

Langton, J. (1975), 'Residential patterns in pre-industrial cities: some case studies from seventeenth-century Britain', *Transactions of the Institute of British Geographers*, **65**: 1–27.

Laslett, P. (1992), 'Natural and political observations on the population of late seventeenth-century England: reflections

on the work of Gregory King and John Graunt', in Schurer and Arkell (1992), pp. 6–30.

Law, F.W. (1978), *The Worshipful Company of Spectacle Makers: a History*, London: The Company.

Lawson, P. (1993), *The East India Company: a History*, London: Longman.

Levin, J. (1969), *The Charter Controversy in the City of London, 1660–1688, and its Consequences*, London: Athlone Press.

Lloyd-Jones, H., Pearl, V., and Worden, B. (eds) (1981), *History and Imagination, Essays in Honour of H.R. Trevor-Roper*, London: Duckworth.

Lobel, M. (1976), 'Some reflections on the topographic development of the pre-industrial town in England', in Emmison and Stephens (1976), pp. 141–163.

Lobel, M. (ed) (1989), *The City of London from Prehistoric Times to c.1520*, The British Atlas of Historic Towns, vol. 3, Oxford: Oxford University Press.

Louw, H.J. (1981), 'Anglo-Netherlandish architectural exchange c.1600–c.1660', *Architectural History*, 24: 1–23.

Luttrell, N. (1691–3), *The Parliamentary Diary of Narcissus Luttrell, 1691–1693*, ed. H. Horwitz, 1972, Oxford: Clarendon Press.

Maitland, W. (1756), *The History and Survey of London: from its Foundation to the Present Time*, London.

Malament, B.C. (1980), *After the Reformation: Essays in Honor of J.H. Hexter*, Philadelphia: University of Pennsylvania Press.

Malcolm, L.W.G. (1934), 'Early history of streets and paving of London', *Newcomen Society Transactions*, **14**: 83–94.

Masters, B. (1974), *The Public Markets of the City of London Surveyed by William Leybourn in 1677*, London Topographical Society Publication 117.

Mathias, P. (1959), *The Brewing Industry in England, 1700–1830*, Cambridge: Cambridge University Press.

Milne, T. (1800), *Milne's Plan of the Cities of London and Westminster, circumjacent towns and parishes...* (Facsimile edition, *Thomas Milne's Land Use Map of London and Environs in 1800*, London Topographical Society Publication 118–119, 1975–6).

Mitchell, D. (ed) (1995), *Goldsmiths, Silversmiths and Bankers: Innovation and the Transfer of Skill, 1550 to 1750*, Stroud: Alan Sutton Publishing and Centre for Metropolitan History.

Morgan, W. (1682), *London &c. Actually Survey'd...* (Facsimile edition, Harry Margary in association with Guildhall Library, 1977).

Murdoch, T. (ed) (1985), *The Quiet Conquest: The Huguenots 1685 to 1985*, London: Museum of London.

Myers, R. (1990), *The Stationers' Company Archive: an Account of the Records 1554–1984*, Winchester: St Paul's Bibliographies.

Mylne, R.W. (1856), *Map of the Geology and Contours of London and its Environs* (Facsimile edition, London Topographical Society Publication 146, 1993).

Newman, P.C. (1985), *Company of Adventurers,* vol.1, Ontario: Viking Penguin.

O'Brien, P. (1988), 'The political economy of British taxation, 1660–1815', *Economic History Review*, 2nd series, **41**: 1–32.

Ogilby, J. (1675), *Brittania, volume the first, or an Illustration of the Kingdom of England*, ed. A. Duckham, 1939.

Ogilby, J. and Morgan, W. (1676), *A New and Accurate Map of the City of London, Distinct from Westminster and Southwark...* (Facsimile edition, ed. R. Hyde, *The A to Z of Restoration London*, London Topographical Society Publication 145, 1992).

Olsen, D.J. (1982), *Town planning in London: the Eighteenth and Nineteenth Centuries*, 2nd edition, New Haven: Yale University Press.

Ormsby, H.R. (1924), *London on the Thames: A Study of the Natural Conditions that Influenced the Birth and Growth of a Great City*, London: Sifton, Praed.

Parish Clerks (1693–4), *London Bills of Mortality*, London: The Company.

Parish Clerks (1732), *New Remarks of London: or, a Survey of the Cities of London and Westminster, of Southwark, and Part of Middlesex and Surrey, Within the...Bills of Mortality...*, London: E. Midwinter.

Patten, J. (1977), 'Urban occupations in pre-industrial England', *Transactions of the Institute of British Geographers*, new series, **2**: 296–313.

Pawson, E. (1977), *Transport and Economy: The Turnpike Roads of Eighteenth Century Britain*, London: Academic Press.

Pearl, V. (1981), 'Social policy in early modern London', in Lloyd-Jones, Pearl and Worden (1981), pp. 115–31.

Pepys, S. (1660–9), *The Diary of Samuel Pepys*, eds. R. Latham and W. Mathews, 11 vols., 1970–83, London: Bell.

Petty, W. (1662), *A Treatise of Taxes and Contributions*, in C.H. Hull (ed.), *The Economic Writings of Sir William Petty*, vol. I, 1899, Cambridge: Cambridge University Press.

Pevsner, N. (1973), *The Buildings of England, London, Volume I, The Cities of London and Westminster*, 3rd edition, Harmondsworth: Penguin.

Plomer, H.R. (1907), *A Dictionary of the Printers and Booksellers who were at work in England, Scotland and Ireland from 1641–1667*, London: Bibliographical Society.

Plomer, H.R. (1922), *A Dictionary of the Printers and Booksellers who were at work in England, Scotland and Ireland from 1668–1725*, London: Bibliographical Society.

Power, M.J. (1972), 'East London housing in the seventeenth century', in Clark and Slack (1972), pp. 237–62.

Power, M.J. (1978a), 'Shadwell: the development of a London suburban community in the seventeenth century', *London Journal*, **4**: 29–46.

Power, M.J. (1978b), 'The east and west in early-modern London', in E.W. Ives (ed), *Wealth and Power in Tudor England*, London: Athlone Press, 1978, pp. 167–85.

Power, M.J. (1986), 'The social topography of Restoration London', in Beier and Finlay (1986), pp. 199–223.

Power, M.J. (1990), 'The east London working community in the seventeenth century', in Corfield and Keene (1990), pp. 103–20.

Powicke, F.M., and Fryde, E.B. (eds) (1961), *Handbook of British Chronology*, 2nd edition, London: Royal Historical Society.

Prince, H. (1989), 'The situation of London', in Lobel (1989), pp. 1–5.

Ray, I. (1965), 'The sources of London's bricks', unpublished dissertation, Morley College, London.

Reddaway, T.F. (1940), *The Rebuilding of London After the Great Fire*, London: Edward Arnold.

Rivington, C.R. (1883), *The Records of the Worshipful Company of Stationers*, London: Nichols & Sons.

Robertson, A.B. (1959), 'The suburban food markets of eighteenth century London', *East London Papers*, **2**: 21–26.

Rocque, J. (1747), *A Plan of the Cities of London and Westminster and Borough of Southwark....* (Facsimile edition, R. Hyde, *The A to Z of Georgian London*, London Topographical Society Publication 126, 1982).

Roseveare, H. (1987), *Markets and Merchants in the Late Seventeenth Century: The Marescoe-David Letters 1668–*

1680, Records of Social and Economic History, new series 12, Oxford: Oxford University Press for The British Academy.

Roseveare, H. (1991), *The Financial Revolution 1660-1760*, London: Longman.

Rothstein, N.K.A. (1961), 'The silk industry in London, 1702–66', unpublished M.A. thesis, University of London.

Rudden, B. (1985), *The New River: A Legal History*, Oxford: Clarendon Press.

Sainty, J.C. (1972), *Office-Holders in Modern Britain, I, Treasury Officials, 1660–1870*, London: Athlone Press.

Sainty, J.C. (1975), *Office-Holders in Modern Britain, IV, Admiralty Officials, 1660–1870*, London: Athlone Press.

Schurer, K., and Arkell, T. (eds) (1992), *Surveying the People: The Interpretation and Use of Documentary Sources for the Study of Population in the later Seventeenth Century*, Oxford: Leopard's Head Press.

Schwarz, L.D. (1992), *London in the Age of Industrialisation: Entrepreneurs, Labour Force and Living Conditions, 1700–1850*, Cambridge: Cambridge University Press.

Scott, W.R. (1951), *The Constitution and Finance of English, Scottish and Irish Joint-Stock Companies, to 1720*, vols. 1–3, Cambridge: Cambridge University Press.

Scouloudi, I. (ed) (1985), *Huguenots in Britain and their French Background, 1550–1800*, Basingstoke: Macmillan.

Shesgreen, S. (1990), *The Criers and Hawkers of London: Engravings and Drawings by Marcellus Laroon*, Aldershot: Scolar.

Slack, P. (1985), *The Impact of the Plague in Tudor and Stuart England*, London: Routledge & Kegan Paul.

Slack, P. (1990) *The English Poor Law, 1531–1782*, Basingstoke: Macmillan.

Spence, C. (1994), 'Mapping London in the 1690s', in Bocchi and Denley (1994), pp. 746–56.

Spence, C. (1996), '"Accidentally killed by a cart": workplace, hazard and risk in late seventeenth century London', *European Review of History*, **3**: 9–26.

Statt, D. (1990), 'The City of London and the controversy over immigration, 1660–1722', *Historical Journal*, **33**: 45–61.

Steele, R.R. (1910), *Tudor and Stuart Proclamations, Volume 1, England and Wales*, Oxford: Clarendon Press.

Stern, W.M. (1960), *The Porters of London*, London: Longman.

Stern, W.M. (1981), 'The Company of Watermen and Lightermen of the City of London', *Guildhall Studies in London History*, **5**: 36–41.

Stone, L. (1980), 'The residential development of the West End of London in the seventeenth century', in Malament (1980), pp. 167–212.

Stow, J. (1603), *A Survey of London*, ed. C.L. Kingsford, 2 vols., 1908, Oxford: Clarendon Press.

Strype, J. (ed) (1720), *A Survey of the Cities of London and Westminster*, by John Stow, 2 vols., London: printed for A. Churchill.

Summerson, J. (1978), *Georgian London*, London: Penguin Books.

Survey of London (1957), *Spitalfields and Mile End New Town*, vol. 27, London: London County Council.

Survey of London (1960), *The Parish of St James Westminster, Part 1: South of Piccadilly*, vol. 29, London: London County Council.

Survey of London (1966), *The Parish of St Anne Soho*, vol. 33, London: Greater London Council.

Survey of London (1994), *Poplar, Blackwall and the Isle of Dogs: The Parish of All Saints*, vol. 43, London: Athlone Press/Royal Commission on Historical Monuments (England).

Swift, J. (1710), *A Description of a City Shower*, in P. Rogers (ed), *Jonathan Swift: the Complete Poems*, 1983, Harmondsworth: Penguin, pp. 113–14.

Sykes, C.S. (1985) *Private Palaces: Life in the Great London Houses*, London: Chatto & Windus.

Symonds, R.W. (1951), *Thomas Tompion, his Life and Work*, London: Batsford.

Thirsk, J., and Cooper, J.P. (eds) (1972), *Seventeenth-Century Economic Documents*, Oxford: Clarendon Press.

Turner, M., and Mills, D. (eds) (1986), *Land and Property: The English Land Tax 1692–1832*, Gloucester: Alan Sutton.

Unwin, D.J. (1981), *Introductory Spatial Analysis*, London: Methuen.

Vries, J. de (1984), *European Urbanisation, 1500–1800*, London: Methuen.

Walsh, C. (1995), 'The design of London goldsmiths' shops in the early eighteenth century', in Mitchell (1995), pp. 96–111.

Ward, W.R. (1953), *English Land Tax in the Eighteenth Century*, London: Oxford University Press.

Water Resources Board (1972), *The Hydrogeology of the London Basin*, Reading: Water Resources Board.

Weatherill, L.M. (1988), *Consumer Behaviour and Material Culture in Britain, 1660–1760*, London: Methuen.

Weinstein, R. (1990), 'London's market gardens in the early modern period', in Galinou (1990), pp. 80–101.

Weinstein, R. (1991), 'New urban demands in early modern London', in Bynum and Porter (1991), pp. 29–40.

Williamson, F. (1936), 'George Sorocold, of Derby: a pioneer of water supply', *Journal of the Derbyshire Archaeological and Natural History Society*, **57**: 43–93.

Wilmott, T. (1982), 'Excavations at Queen Street, City of London, 1953 and 1960, and Roman timber-lined wells in London', *Transactions of the London and Middlesex Archaeological Society*, **33**: 1–78.

Woodhead, J.R. (1965), *The Rulers of London 1660–1689: A Biographical Record of the Aldermen and Common Councilmen of the City of London,* London: London and Middlesex Archaeological Society.

Wrigley, E.A. (ed) (1966), *An Introduction to English Historical Demography From the Sixteenth to the Nineteenth Century*, London: Weidenfeld and Nicolson.

Wrigley, E.A. (1967), 'A simple model of London's importance in changing English society and economy, 1650–1750', *Past and Present*, **37**: 44–70.

Wrigley, E.A., and Schofield, R.S. (1981), *The Population History of England, 1541–1871: A Reconstruction*, London: Edward Arnold.

Index